365 DAILY DEVOTIONS TO CHANGE YOUR WORLD

A ONE MINUTE BIBLE FOR STUDENTS

iSTAND

THE POWER OF COURAGEOUS CHOICES

HOLMAN BIBLE PUBLISHERS

NASHVILLE, TENNESSEE

iStand: One Minute Bible™

Nashville, TN

ISBN 13: 978-0-8054-4793-4

Produced with the assistance of The Livingstone Corporation
(www.livingstonecorp.com)
Project staff includes: Dana Niesluchowski, Dave Veerman,
Linda Washington, Elizabeth Hubbard, Rachael Mitchell,
Mark Nesbitt, Gene Smiley, Jessica Kneller, Michael Leali.
Interior Design by: Mark Wainwright, Larry Taylor. Composition by: Joel Bartlett.
Cover Design by: Greg Pope

Dewey Decimal Classification: 242.2
Subject Heading: DEVOTIONAL LITERATURE \ CHRISTIAN LIFE \ BIBLE--STUDY

Printed in Canada
1 2 3 4 5 12 11 10 09 08
T

CONTENTS

THE POWER OF COURAGEOUS CHOICES

Life is all about making choices. Daily we choose when to get up, what to wear, what to eat, and where to go. And in all of those mundane, everyday choices, we confront a host of other, far more critical ones—choices to obey or disobey what we know God wants us to do, to speak up for what we know is right or remain silent, to take a stand for the truth and against evil or stay seated and merely wait for the world to change. Certainly, then, we need to know what choices to make and how to make them—positive, moral, ethical, and God-honoring choices. The Bible provides that needed insight and direction, guiding us and telling us how to respond in difficult situations, when to take a stand and how to make the tough choices.

Welcome to the *iSTAND: The Power of Courageous Choices* 365-day devotional. Sometimes taking a stand may be easy, especially when the choice is clear and our friends and family support us in the decision. At times, however, we may have to stand alone against formidable foes. That's when we'll know we're in a battle.

In Ephesians 6, Paul describes the struggle and challenges believers to stand strong: "Finally, be strengthened by the Lord and by His vast strength. Put on the full armor of God so that you can stand against the tactics of the Devil. For our battle is not against flesh and blood, but against the rulers, against the authorities, against the world powers of this darkness, against the spiritual forces of evil in the heavens. This is why you must take up the full armor of God, so that you may be able to resist in the evil day, and having prepared everything, to take your stand" (verses 10-13). To win this battle, to effectively and courageously stand for God and His truth, we will need the "the sword of the Spirit . . . . God's Word" (verse 17).

This book has been written to empower and embolden you to use your "sword," to discover the timeless truths from God's Word and apply them to your life—in the neighborhood, at school, in your family, and on the job.

As you work your way through these devotionals and Scripture selections, you will find stories of people (biblical and contemporary) doing just that—taking a positive, God-honoring stand. You will also find practical answers to tough questions along with biblical teachings about making courageous choices.

The book has been organized by months, weeks, and days, and it follows the Bible canonically (Genesis through Revelation), except in the Gospels, where we move through Jesus' life chronologically. As you read, you can begin almost anywhere—don't assume that you have to begin on today's date. You may want to start at the beginning, regardless of what day it is, and work your way through. Or you may want to begin in a specific section of Scripture (for example, the Gospels) and go from there.

On each day, you'll see a highlighted section of the Bible, a selected Bible reading, and the devotional for that day. During a typical week of devotional challenges you will find the following features (one per day):

ANCHOR POINTS

These short teachings on the foundational truths of Scripture provide insight and underscore life-related biblical principles.

NO BRAINER

Each of these lessons highlights an action-related command from God and challenges you to make the right choice.

TOUGH CHOICE

These real-life case studies show what making tough choices looks like in real life. Each story highlights a real moral dilemma.

TOUGH QUESTIONS

As the title implies, these notes present difficult questions about how to make God-honoring choices. The answers are also included.

JUST LIKE ME

It's easy to dismiss the people in Bible stories as out of touch because they lived so long ago. In these character profiles you'll see that you and they have much in common. And you'll learn valuable lessons from their examples.

DEPOSIT

On this day, you have a key verse to memorize. Depositing God's Word in your heart and mind will strengthen you to make courageous choices.

YOUR TURN

This day provides the opportunity and space for recording your thoughts and reflections on the week. You'll find a provocative question to help get you started.

The world needs men and women who will choose well, standing *against* what is wrong and standing *for* what is true, right, moral, ethical, and glorifying to God. Where do you stand?

JANEIRO
ENERO
JANVIER

JANUARY

GENNAIO
JANUAR
JANUARI

THE BIG PICTURE

GN 1:1–2:3

JANUARY 1

DAY 1

SNAPSHOT

GENESIS 1:1–5

In the beginning God created the heavens and the earth. Now the earth was formless and empty, darkness covered the surface of the watery depths, and the Spirit of God was hovering over the surface of the waters. Then God said, "Let there be light," and there was light. God saw that the light was good, and God separated the light from the darkness. God called the light "day," and He called the darkness "night." Evening came, and then morning: the first day.

GENESIS 1:26–27

Then God said, "Let Us make man in Our image, according to Our likeness. They will rule the fish of the sea, the birds of the sky, the livestock, all the earth, and the creatures that crawl on the earth." So God created man in His own image; He created him in the image of God; He created them male and female.

GENESIS 2:1–3

So the heavens and the earth and everything in them were completed. By the seventh day, God completed His work that He had done, and He rested on the seventh day from all His work that He had done. God blessed the seventh day and declared it holy, for on it He rested from His work of creation.

ANCHOR POINT

BEGINNINGS MATTER

Lots of people today think it makes sense to start with nothing; we start with God. No matter how many billions of years we want to imagine passing, nothing is still nothing. God can do a lot with a few billion years—or even a few seconds.

Human beings can come up with some elaborate ways to explain how things could come into being without God, but in doing so, they simply take for themselves the role of Creator. But creating an explanation isn't quite the same as creating a universe that strains our imaginations at the macroscopic as well as the microscopic levels.

Wise people have always known that if we start with the mystery of God whom we can't explain, everything else begins to make sense. If we start with nothing, then nothing makes sense.

People have a hard time explaining their longing for dignity, meaning, purpose, and value when they start by leaving God out of their view of life.

YOUR CHOICE

How does your life and the decisions you make reflect your awareness of God?

DAY 2

SNAPSHOT

GENESIS 4:1–4

Adam knew his wife Eve intimately, and she conceived and gave birth to Cain. She said, "I have had a male child with the LORD's help." Then she also gave birth to his brother Abel.

Now Abel became a shepherd of a flock, but Cain cultivated the land. In the course of time Cain presented some of the land's produce as an offering to the LORD. And Abel also presented an offering—some of the firstborn of his flock and their fat portions. The LORD had regard for Abel and his offering.

YOUR CHOICE

In what areas do you struggle to obey God?

TOUGH QUESTION

WHAT DOES GOD REALLY EXPECT FROM ME? DO I HAVE TO BE PERFECT IN ORDER TO PLEASE HIM?

When you look at Abel's life (Gn 4), do you ever think that you have to be perfect in order to please God?

Some people view God as an impossible taskmaster with impossibly high expectations. Ever think that way?

Here's the deal: like any loving parent, God expects His kids to act a certain way. (Think of your parents' expectations for you.) Some Christians may tell you about God's expectations based on where they are in their walk with Him. An abundance of advice often contributes to the belief that God expects way too much. If you are feeling overwhelmed, you might be listening to others' expectations rather than God's.

So, how can you please God? The story of Cain and Abel gives us part of the answer. Both of them brought something to God; yet only Abel's sacrifice pleased God. One reason was because Cain's heart was not really in his offering. He tried to please God out of obligation instead of love.

The first step in pleasing God is to examine our motivation for doing so. Do we really want to please Him, or are we going through the motions because someone told us we should?

Obedience is the second step to pleasing God. It means loving Him enough to listen to what He says, then following through on what we know He tells us to do.

Through the Holy Spirit, God speaks to us as we come to Him with willing hearts. He gently shows us areas in our lives that we need to examine and change according to His timetable, not someone else's.

THE BIG PICTURE

GN 4:1–16

JANUARY 3

DAY 3

SNAPSHOT

GENESIS 4:3–8

In the course of time Cain presented some of the land's produce as an offering to the LORD. And Abel also presented an offering—some of the firstborn of his flock and their fat portions. The LORD had regard for Abel and his offering, but He did not have regard for Cain and his offering. Cain was furious, and he was downcast.

Then the LORD said to Cain, "Why are you furious? And why are you downcast? If you do right, won't you be accepted? But if you do not do right, sin is crouching at the door. Its desire is for you, but you must master it."

Cain said to his brother Abel, "Let's go out to the field." And while they were in the field, Cain attacked his brother Abel and killed him.

JUST LIKE ME

CAIN: WHEN ANGER GOES TOO FAR

Anger is part of the human package. Anger motivates action. The kind of action that anger motivates has a lot to do with the kind of person we are. Way back at the beginning, and throughout the Bible, God doesn't tell people not to be angry. He Himself gets angry sometimes. What God is concerned about is what we do when we get angry.

God talked to Cain when he was angry. God didn't ask Cain "Why are you furious?" because He didn't know. God wanted Cain to realize why he was angry. He was angry at his brother who had done nothing to him. He should have been angry at God. But his brother was an easier target. Instead of getting angry at himself for taking a casual and thoughtless approach to worship, Cain got upset with his brother.

Even at this point God gave Cain a chance to straighten things out. He could redirect his anger toward something productive, like his own attitude. Instead, Cain let his anger go too far.

Can you see yourself in this situation? Feelings are real, but they can't fly on autopilot! They don't steer themselves well. Feelings are not meant to be in control. They can inform a decision, but they shouldn't be the sole factors in decisions. Cain reminds us that we're responsible for where we let our feelings take us.

YOUR CHOICE

What will determine the limits of your expressions of anger?

JANUARY 4

DAY 4

THE BIG PICTURE

GN 6:9–13

SNAPSHOT

GENESIS 6:11–13

Now the earth was corrupt in God's sight, and the earth was filled with violence. God saw how corrupt the earth was, for all flesh had corrupted its way on the earth. Then God said to Noah, "I have decided to put an end to all flesh, for the earth is filled with violence because of them; therefore I am going to destroy them along with the earth."

TOUGH CHOICE

DRINKING

A shout "Hey, Becca!" drifted across the school parking lot.

"Hey, Tara!" The cold November air tingled my cheeks as I waited for my tall, gangly best friend, Tara, to board the cross-country bus. We were headed to the regional cross-country meet.

"Saturday mornings come way too early," Tara grunted, hoisting her track bag above her ponytail, stepping over rows of underclassmen. We made our way to the back of the bus and settled in with a few of the other seniors.

"What did you all end up doing after the movie last night?" I asked, double-checking that my racing spikes were in my bag.

"Nothing really," she hesitated. "A few of us just went over to Robin's . . ." she trailed off. I could have finished her sentence: ". . . went over to Robin's to drink." Since the beginning of senior year summer, a lot of my friends had begun drinking. At first it came as a shock, but with the increasing regularity of their drinking, the less it shook me.

I had decided early on that I would not drink. I believed that the Lord's commandments to obey our authorities and to take care of our bodies translated into obeying the law and in taking into account our influence on those for whom alcohol will become addictive.

"It wasn't that much fun, really. Be glad that you weren't there," she said, shaking her head.

I wanted to tell her how much it hurt—how much it hurt not to be invited to hang out with the group any more. How much it hurt to know that my friends weren't entirely honest with me. How much it hurt to watch my friends make dangerous decisions.

I took a deep breath, smiled, and looked over at Tara. "Well, hey. Why don't you come over to my house tonight, and we'll rent a movie and make S'mores or something . . . something fun!"

She smiled back. "You're a good friend, Becca."

Much like Noah, the Lord has commanded us to stand apart—boldly. Noah set himself up to face ridicule when he began constructing the ark. Choosing not to drink in today's society may mean playing the outcast or facing scrutiny, too. But this is also a chance to accept a challenge from the Lord, and to face this challenge with Him fighting by our side.

Tara continued to drink through college, but after much turmoil and loneliness, she realized that drinking wasn't filling a void in her life. She came to me, knowing that I would speak truth to her and that I had "something" that fulfilled my life. I was able to share my faith with her and to see my best friend come to know the Lord.

YOUR CHOICE

With whom do you need to be a good friend by telling him or her the truth?

THE BIG PICTURE

GN 7:1–24

JANUARY 5

DAY 5

SNAPSHOT

GENESIS 7:1–10

Then the LORD said to Noah, "Enter the ark, you and all your household, for I have seen that you alone are righteous before Me in this generation. You are to take with you seven pairs, a male and its female, of all the clean animals, and two of the animals that are not clean, a male and its female, and seven pairs, male and female, of the birds of the sky—in order to keep offspring alive on the face of the whole earth. Seven days from now I will make it rain on the earth 40 days and 40 nights, and I will wipe off the face of the earth every living thing I have made."

And Noah did everything that the LORD commanded him. Noah was 600 years old when the deluge came and water covered the earth. So Noah, his sons, his wife, and his sons' wives entered the ark because of the waters of the deluge. From the clean animals, unclean animals, birds, and every creature that crawls on the ground, two of each, male and female, entered the ark with Noah, just as God had commanded him. Seven days later the waters of the deluge came on the earth.

YOUR CHOICE

To what degree will you practice wholehearted obedience to God?

NO BRAINER

THE FIRST DEADLINE

Some time after he was 500 years old, Noah was told by God to build the ark. It was ready when he was 600 years old. He must have labored on it with his sons for decades. The ship was built on dry land, far from water. The possibility of a flood seemed remote to the rapidly expanding human population.

The project took so long to complete that even the jokers and mockers must have run out of fresh material. There's something discouraging about working on a task without encouragement *or* resistance. When you are making tough choices, confirmation sometimes comes from the negative reactions of others. But continuing to do right when no one seems to care? That may be the ultimate tough choice. That's the choice Noah made.

Noah got notice of the deadline seven days in advance. He probably had other clues that the time was getting short. There's no indication that he had to round up the animals. They began to show up. But the spectacle of hundreds of animals filing into the ark, followed by Noah and his family, must have given those watching some cause for concern. Noah was about to be immortalized as one of history's greatest fools or one of the few survivors of the first extended chapter of human history. No one apparently changed their minds about joining Noah's folly. Once all were on board and the hatch was sealed, Noah faced the last in a long line of choices—he had to wait. We don't know when the loading process was completed, but God kept His schedule. On the seventh day all heaven broke loose with rains, floods, and judgment.

A key to understanding tough choices is a statement made several times about Noah that he "did everything that the LORD commanded him" (Gn 6:22; 7:5). Depending on our situation and personal make-up, the specifics of God's commands may come to us hard or easy. What makes a choice tough is often whether or not we have decided without reservations to do everything that the Lord commands us!

DAY 6

THE BIG PICTURE

GN 8:1–22

SNAPSHOT

GENESIS 8:14–22

By the twenty-seventh day of the second month, the earth was dry. Then God spoke to Noah, "Come out of the ark, you, your wife, your sons, and your sons' wives with you. Bring out every living thing of all flesh that is with you—birds, livestock, creatures that crawl on the ground—and they will spread over the earth and be fruitful and multiply on the earth."

So Noah, along with his sons, his wife, and his sons' wives, came out. All wildlife, all livestock, every bird, and every creature that crawls on the earth came out of the ark by their groups. Then Noah built an altar to the LORD. He took some of every kind of clean animal and every kind of clean bird and offered burnt offerings on the altar.

When the LORD smelled the pleasing aroma, He said to Himself, "I will never again curse the ground because of man, even though man's inclination is evil from his youth. And I will never again strike down every living thing as I have done. As long as the earth endures, seed-time and harvest, cold and heat, summer and winter, and day and night will not cease."

DEPOSIT

WORDS FROM GOD'S WORD TO STORE IN YOUR MIND AND HEART

"As long as the earth endures, seedtime and harvest, cold and heat, summer and winter, and day and night will not cease."—God

SNAPSHOT

GENESIS 9:8–17

Then God said to Noah and his sons with him, "Understand that I am confirming My covenant with you and your descendants after you, and with every living creature that is with you—birds, livestock, and all wildlife of the earth that are with you—all the animals of the earth that came out of the ark. I confirm My covenant with you that never again will all flesh be wiped out by the waters of a deluge; there will never again be a deluge to destroy the earth."

And God said, "This is the sign of the covenant I am making between Me and you and every living creature with you, a covenant for all future generations: I have placed My bow in the clouds, and it will be a sign of the covenant between Me and the earth. Whenever I form clouds over the earth and the bow appears in the clouds, I will remember My covenant between me and you and every living creature of all flesh: water will never again become a deluge to destroy all flesh. The bow will be in the clouds, and I will look at it and remember the everlasting covenant between God and every living creature of all flesh on earth."

God said to Noah, "This is the sign of the covenant that I have confirmed between Me and all flesh on the earth."

YOUR TURN

THE RAINBOW CONNECTION

As you read the account of God's promise to Noah (and all of us), think about your experiences that demonstrated God's faithfulness. Take a few minutes to jot down those examples that God brings to mind:

DAY 8

THE BIG PICTURE

GN 11:1–9

NO BRAINER

WHO WANTS TO BE BIGGER THAN GOD?

When Noah and his family came out of the ark, God told them to spread out all over the earth and fill it up with their descendants. After the geological catastrophe we call the flood was over, God restored and rebuilt and replenished the earth. He made it the beautiful, varied kaleidoscope of landscapes that we see today on Discovery Channel or—if you're lucky enough to have lots of money—perhaps on vacations! Earth really is an amazing planet that God has given human beings to inhabit.

So He nudged our ancestors out of the ark and toward the horizon. "Go! Explore! Find the particular part of the earth that I have made for *you* and make it yours," God seemed to say to Noah's descendants. But they were afraid, and didn't want to go far from one another.

It's not that hard to understand. The flood had erased virtually every family from the earth. We can empathize with those poor, shivering, fearful survivors wanting to stick together. "Let's build a city," they said to one another, "and live in it together, and make sure we don't get spread 'way out over the horizons to distant lands', like God is talking about. In fact, let's build a tower that reaches toward the heavens (remember how deep that water was last time!), and from great distances people will be able to look toward our tower and see who we are."

But God shook His head. "No, that's not what I intend for you. Not everybody in one place, making a name for yourselves, but everybody spread out in many places, fruitfully exploiting this variety of climates and topography, of seashores and mountains, wide meadows and narrow valleys, roaring cataracts and still lakes, this multicolored bright blue planet I have given you for a home."

And since they could no longer understand one another when they talked, they gave up trying to communicate and cooperate. They wandered off in every direction—just as God had intended for them to do all along.

SNAPSHOT

GENESIS 11:3–7

They said to each other, "Come, let us make oven-fired bricks." They had brick for stone and asphalt for mortar. And they said, "Come, let us build ourselves a city and a tower with its top in the sky. Let us make a name for ourselves; otherwise, we will be scattered over the face of the whole earth."

Then the Lord came down to look over the city and the tower that the men were building. The Lord said, "If, as one people all having the same language, they have begun to do this, then nothing they plan to do will be impossible for them. Come, let Us go down there and confuse their language so that they will not understand one another's speech."

YOUR CHOICE

Will you take His way or the highway?

THE BIG PICTURE

GN 12:1–9; 17:1–8

JANUARY 9

DAY 9

SNAPSHOT

GENESIS 12:1–4

The LORD said to Abram: Go out from your land, your relatives, and your father's house to the land that I will show you.

I will make you into a great nation, I will bless you, I will make your name great, and you will be a blessing.

I will bless those who bless you, I will curse those who treat you with contempt, and all the peoples on earth will be blessed through you.

So Abram went, as the LORD had told him, and Lot went with him. Abram was 75 years old when he left Haran.

JUST LIKE ME

ABRAM: GOING GOD'S WAY

What determines the choices you make? Your gut reaction? What your friends say? Information you found through Google?

When God told Abram to uproot his family and keep going until He gave the word to settle, Abram didn't argue or call for a focus group to get some feedback. His absolute trust in God's character provided enough impetus for him to move out. Although Abram did not know the how or when of God's promises ("I will make you into a great nation"—Gn 12:2), he made his choice and acted in obedience. Such obedience took incredible courage. Many years later, when God repeated His promise of blessing to Abram and even changed his name ("Your name will no longer be Abram, but your name will be Abraham, for I will make you the father of many nations"—Gn 17:5), Abraham obeyed once again.

Abraham went decades without seeing the results of God's promise to give him a son. Yet he continued to trust *God's* choices, even when he didn't know how the story would end, even at the risk of looking foolish to others. Sometimes he messed up (see the Hagar and Ishmael story). But for the most part, Abraham went God's way. Do you have the guts to do the same?

YOUR CHOICE

How will you respond when you sense that God is leading you to take a step of faith?

JANUARY 10

DAY 10

THE BIG PICTURE

GN 18:1–32

SNAPSHOT **GENESIS 18:1–4**

Then the LORD appeared to Abraham at the oaks of Mamre while he was sitting in the entrance of his tent during the heat of the day. He looked up, and he saw three men standing near him. When he saw them, he ran from the entrance of the tent to meet them and bowed to the ground. Then he said, "My lord, if I have found favor in your sight, please do not go on past your servant. Let a little water be brought, that you may wash your feet and rest yourselves under the tree."

TOUGH CHOICE

STRANGERS

I pulled my glasses off and rubbed my eyes with my fists. The numbers and symbols dotting the pages of my Calculus book were beginning to run together. "Maybe I'll just finish up tomorrow morning before class . . ." It was the first week of classes, and already my college professors were doling out homework like cheap candy on Halloween.

"Tap, tap, tap," a soft knock came from my door, and a mousy-looking girl stuck her head inside. "Hi, um . . . Rachel, right? I'm Christina. Two doors down across the hall."

"Oh, yeah, Hi."

She looked down at her feet, seeming a bit hesitant. "Do you want to come in?" I asked, not quite sure what to do with her, and not quite sure that I wanted company, with all the work I still had to do. I cleared a stack of clothes off my bed and motioned her to sit down. My small dormitory wasn't much bigger than a closet.

"Sorry to barge in so late. I saw that your light was on, and well . . ." she hesitated again, "I just needed to talk to somebody." She shrugged, but managed a hopeful smile.

Great. I do not *have time for this. I knew I should have closed my door all the way. Who comes barging into people's rooms at such ungodly hours of the night?*

"You see, I overheard you listening to some praise music the other morning, and I thought you would be a good person to talk to—a Christian."

It was as though the wind had been knocked out of me. "Oh, yes. Yes, I am a Christian." I hoped that my foul attitude and impatience hadn't shown through too much. I was embarrassed by my selfishness. "What did you need to talk about?"

And so began a conversation with Christina that lasted well into the night. She wanted to know about me, my faith, why I believed so diligently in a God that (to her) seemed removed. She wanted to vent about her family, the pressures there, and how to join a church. Our talk that night led to friendship. We both went our own direction as the years passed, but we remained friends, nonetheless.

Toward the end of my senior year, Christina and I ran across each other in the student center. After a brief catching-up, timid Christina looked down at her feet for a moment.

"You know, I'll regret not telling you this—that conversation we had at the beginning of freshman year, it changed my life. I just remember praying, calling out to God as I walked back toward the dorm that night, that He would give me someone to talk to. A friend. Someone that would speak truth to me. You were the only one awake on the entire floor. You really did save my life that night."

She smiled and shrugged, then turned to walk toward her next class. I watched her disappear into the sea of students. *Thank you, Lord, for Christina. Thank you for using me, despite myself, to reach out to the lost. And thank you for finding me when I too am lost.*

YOUR CHOICE **Who do you know, like Christina, who needs a friend like you?**

SNAPSHOT

GENESIS 19:12–17

Then the angels said to Lot, "Do you have anyone else here: a son-in-law, your sons and daughters, or anyone else in the city who belongs to you? Get them out of this place, for we are about to destroy this place because the outcry against its people is great before the LORD, and the LORD has sent us to destroy it."

So Lot went out and spoke to his sons-in-law, who were going to marry his daughters. "Get up," he said. "Get out of this place, for the LORD is about to destroy the city!" But his sons-in-law thought he was joking.

At the crack of dawn the angels urged Lot on: "Get up! Take your wife and your two daughters who are here, or you will be swept away in the punishment of the city." But he hesitated, so because of the LORD's compassion for him, the men grabbed his hand, his wife's hand, and the hands of his two daughters. And they brought him out and left him outside the city.

As soon as the angels got them outside, one of them said, "Run for your lives! Don't look back and don't stop anywhere on the plain! Run to the mountains, or you will be swept away!"

ANCHOR POINT

HONORING GOD

Talk about a challenging passage! How do we make sense of a story full of depraved mobs, extremely questionable parenting, and seemingly over-zealous punishment—one quick look back and you're dead? Today's news may seem bad, but this is over the top, off the charts!

A bigger issue is at play here, however: more important than the motivations of the crowd, deeper than Lot's issues, and more fundamental than Lot's wife's inability to follow a simple instruction. The bottom line is that God does not tolerate sin. These days He may not destroy the sin-filled cities around the world, but do not mistake His grace for tolerance. His hand may be held back at the present, but that is no reason for complacency.

God calls us, His people, to live lives that honor Him. We are to love Him, love others, and obey God's commands. Just because God has chosen to show us grace, don't for a minute believe that He does this because we are living such exemplary lives. Instead of comparing yourself with others and worrying about what they are doing, focus on living in a way that pleases God.

YOUR CHOICE

What questions would you not want God to ask you right now? What choices or changes do you need to make?

DAY 12

THE BIG PICTURE
GN 21:8–21

SNAPSHOT

GENESIS 21:8–14

The child grew and was weaned, and Abraham held a great feast on the day Isaac was weaned. But Sarah saw the son mocking—the one Hagar the Egyptian had borne to Abraham. So she said to Abraham, "Drive out this slave with her son, for the son of this slave will not be a co-heir with my son Isaac!"

Now this was a very difficult thing for Abraham because of his son. But God said to Abraham, "Do not be concerned about the boy and your slave. Whatever Sarah says to you, listen to her, because your offspring will be traced through Isaac. But I will also make a nation of the slave's son because he is your offspring."

Early in the morning Abraham got up, took bread and a waterskin, put them on Hagar's shoulders, and sent her and the boy away.

JUST LIKE ME

HAGAR AND ISHMAEL: WHEN LIFE IS UNFAIR

"I didn't ask for this. It's not fair." Ever say that? When life hands you a big pile of unfairness, advice like "when life hands you lemons, make lemonade" just doesn't cut it.

Hagar was the woman in the middle between Abraham and his wife, Sarah. This was the result of Abraham's following his wife's plan of using her slave to gain a son (a poor choice) instead of waiting for God (see Gn 16:1–5). Having provided a son for Abraham, a once-triumphant Hagar later found herself kicked to the curb at Sarah's command.

Perhaps Hagar thought that not just Abraham, but even *God* had abandoned her when God told Abraham to listen to Sarah on the matter and send her and Ishmael away. But an angel of God met her in the desert with a promise for her son to show that God still cared.

How do you usually respond to an unfair situation? Do you give in to bitterness or self-pity? Push the panic button? Instead of panicking or grousing, you can make another choice: you can take up the matter with God. Unfair situations provide a unique opportunity for you to experience God's help in a way you wouldn't otherwise.

YOUR CHOICE

What will you choose to believe about God when life is unfair?

SNAPSHOT

GENESIS 22:6–12

Abraham took the wood for the burnt offering and laid it on his son Isaac. In his hand he took the fire and the sacrificial knife, and the two of them walked on together.

Then Isaac spoke to his father Abraham and said, "My father."

And he replied, "Here I am, my son."

Isaac said, "The fire and the wood are here, but where is the lamb for the burnt offering?"

Abraham answered, "God Himself will provide the lamb for the burnt offering, my son." Then the two of them walked on together.

When they arrived at the place that God had told him about, Abraham built the altar there and arranged the wood. He bound his son Isaac and placed him on the altar, on top of the wood. Then Abraham reached out and took the knife to slaughter his son.

But the Angel of the LORD called to him from heaven and said, "Abraham, Abraham!"

He replied, "Here I am."

Then He said, "Do not lay a hand on the boy or do anything to him. For now I know that you fear God, since you have not withheld your only son from Me."

DEPOSIT

WORDS FROM GOD'S WORD TO STORE IN YOUR MIND AND HEART

Abraham answered, "God Himself will provide the lamb for the burnt offering, my son." Then the two of them walked on together (Gn 22:8).

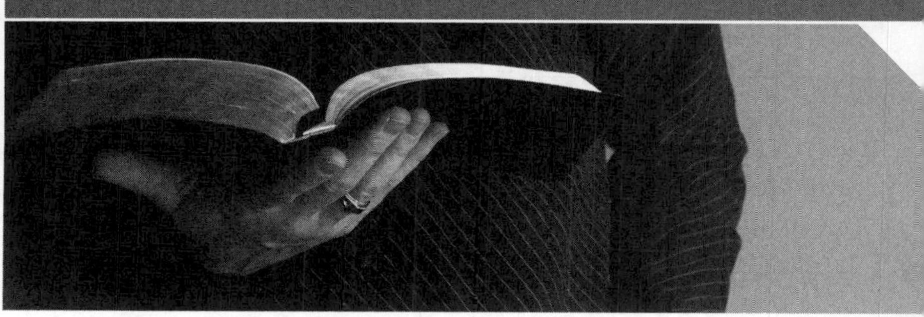

DAY 14

SNAPSHOT

GENESIS 24:10–21

The servant took 10 of his master's camels and departed with all kinds of his master's goods in hand. Then he set out for the town of Nahor, Aram-naharaim. He made the camels kneel beside a well of water outside the town at evening. This was the time when the women went out to draw water.

"LORD, God of my master Abraham," he prayed, "grant me success today, and show kindness to my master Abraham. I am standing here at the spring where the daughters of the men of the town are coming out to draw water. Let the girl to whom I say, 'Please lower your water jug so that I may drink,' and who responds, 'Drink, and I'll water your camels also'—let her be the one You have appointed for Your servant Isaac. By this I will know that You have shown kindness to my master."

Before he had finished speaking, there was Rebekah—daughter of Bethuel son of Milcah, the wife of Abraham's brother Nahor—coming with a jug on her shoulder. Now the girl was very beautiful, a young woman who had not known a man intimately. She went down to the spring, filled her jug, and came up. Then the servant ran to meet her and said, "Please let me have a little water from your jug."

She replied, "Drink, my lord." She quickly lowered her jug to her hand and gave him a drink. When she had finished giving him a drink, she said, "I'll also draw water for your camels until they have had enough to drink." She quickly emptied her jug into the trough and hurried to the well again to draw water. She drew water for all his camels while the man silently watched her to see whether or not the LORD had made his journey a success.

YOUR TURN

PLANNING WORK AND WORKING PLANS

How do you choose to approach difficult tasks? What difficult task are you facing right now and how will you respond to it?

THE BIG PICTURE

GN 24:28–67

JANUARY 15

DAY 15

SNAPSHOT

GENESIS 24:50–61

Laban and Bethuel answered, "This is from the LORD; we have no choice in the matter. Rebekah is here in front of you. Take her and go, and let her be a wife for your master's son, just as the LORD has spoken."

When Abraham's servant heard their words, he bowed to the ground before the LORD. Then he brought out objects of silver and gold, and garments, and gave [them] to Rebekah. He also gave precious gifts to her brother and her mother...

...They called Rebekah and said to her, "Will you go with this man?" She replied, "I will go." So they sent away their sister Rebekah and her nurse, and Abraham's servant and his men.

They blessed Rebekah, saying to her: "Our sister, may you become thousands upon ten thousands. May your offspring possess the gates of their enemies."

Then Rebekah and her young women got up, mounted the camels, and followed the man. So the servant took Rebekah and left.

JUST LIKE ME

ISAAC AND REBEKAH: ACCEPTING GOD'S GIFT

What's your idea of romance? Is it like in the movies where two cute people meet, are instantly attracted to each other, and star in a montage of scenes with the soundtrack going at full blast?

Isaac and Rebekah's relationship wasn't about attraction or finding the right person on eHarmony. In fact, theirs was an arrangement made by a faithful servant of Isaac's father, Abraham. But it began with a request by the servant for God to "grant me success today, and show kindness to my master Abraham" (Gn 24:12). God would make certain that Abraham's servant would recognize the right woman. The fact that Rebekah was attractive (see Gn 24:16) was a bonus.

Choosing to go with the servant was an act of faith on Rebekah's part, despite the rich gifts he offered. Sure, they benefited the family she would leave behind in order to marry Isaac. And sure, they showed that she would be well taken care of in her new household. But beyond that, her decision to go showed her belief in God's desire to give good gifts to His people (see Mt 7:11).

In a time when many people believe the worst about God—that He abandons people or loves to take the joy out of life—you can choose to believe that a good God gives good gifts.

YOUR CHOICE

What circumstances help you believe that God has your best interests at heart? What will you choose to believe about God's love for you?

DAY 16

GN 25:19–34

SNAPSHOT

GENESIS 25:27–34

When the boys grew up, Esau became an expert hunter, an outdoorsman, but Jacob was a quiet man who stayed at home. Isaac loved Esau because he had a taste for wild game, but Rebekah loved Jacob.

Once when Jacob was cooking a stew, Esau came in from the field, exhausted. He said to Jacob, "Let me eat some of that red stuff, because I'm exhausted." That is why he was also named Edom.

Jacob replied, "First sell me your birthright."

"Look," said Esau, "I'm about to die, so what good is a birthright to me?"

Jacob said, "Swear to me first." So he swore to Jacob and sold his birthright to him. Then Jacob gave bread and lentil stew to Esau; he ate, drank, got up, and went away. So Esau despised his birthright

YOUR CHOICE

What can you do today to honor your parents?

TOUGH QUESTION

HOW CAN I OBEY GOD WHEN MY PARENTS BELIEVE ONE THING AND I BELIEVE ANOTHER, YET I STILL LIVE IN THEIR HOME?

The biblical command to honor our parents can be hard enough, but living under their roof and honoring them when they don't believe in or live by biblical standards can make the relationships even more challenging. No matter the condition of our relationship with our parents or their beliefs, we have to obey Christ first and people second. This can be difficult to do at home because of the close nature of family relationships.

The key to getting through to others, especially at home, is humility. Christ displayed humility daily toward people He could have dismissed or condemned in an instant. Even while being ridiculed, questioned, and doubted, Jesus humbly walked down the path to an impending death.

Humility means preferring others above self. True humility is rare and can have a huge impact, especially in family relationships. No matter the condition of our relationship with our parents, they know us better than anyone else. So they can detect hypocrisy immediately, along with pride and selfishness. And, regardless of their spiritual state, they know that those aren't Christian traits.

It's easy to become defensive of our beliefs or knowledge of the Bible and our spiritual growth, taking every question or comment personally. But pride will push people away from us and the Lord. So, when a family member makes a snide comment about your faith, instead of reacting emotionally and firing back with a snappy put-down, you choose to hold your tongue and remain silent. Then wait for a better time to explain or answer. Remember, "A gentle answer turns away anger" (Pr 15:1).

Through honoring your parents, perhaps they will see Christ in you and want to follow Him too.

SNAPSHOT

GENESIS 27:18–24

When he came to his father, he said, "My father." And he answered, "Here I am. Who are you, my son?"

Jacob replied to his father, "I am Esau, your firstborn. I have done as you told me. Please sit up and eat some of my game so that you may bless me."

But Isaac said to his son, "How did you ever find it so quickly, my son?" He replied, "Because the Lord your God worked it out for me."

Then Isaac said to Jacob, "Please come closer so I can touch you, my son. Are you really my son Esau, or not?"

So Jacob came closer to his father Isaac. When he touched him, he said, "The voice is the voice of Jacob, but the hands are the hands of Esau." He did not recognize him, because his hands were hairy like those of his brother Esau; so he blessed him. Again he asked, "Are you really my son Esau?"

And he replied, "I am."

JUST LIKE ME

JACOB: THE HIGH COST OF A LIE

Ever lie to or trick a parent in some way and get away with it? At one time or another, everyone tries to buck the system with his or her parents, especially when something considered important is at stake (more freedom or responsibility, for example). We want it so badly that we'll do whatever it takes to get it—even lie to others.

Jacob tried to buck the system by tricking his father Isaac into giving him the birthright blessing that belonged to his twin brother, Esau, who had been born first. This blessing would entitle Jacob to a double portion of the inheritance. His plan would not have succeeded, however, without the collusion of his mother, Rebekah. Jacob was her favorite after all. Jacob made a bad, self-centered choice. And because of Jacob's deception, the family was torn apart for decades.

Family dynamics change as we grow older. We want our parents to see us as mature, responsible adults. One of the best ways to foster that is to behave with integrity toward them. Part of God's command to honor parents—a command that would come later in Israel's history (Ex 20:12) is a call to integrity. Have you answered the call?

YOUR CHOICE

How will you demonstrate responsibility in your relationship with your parents?

DAY 18

THE BIG PICTURE

GN 28:10–22

NO BRAINER

GOD'S ROLE IN HELPING US STAND

Most of us think that life is hard, other people are tough, and that if we're going to make it in life, we've got to be tough and shrewd ourselves, calculating and if necessary cutting a few corners to make sure we get what's rightfully ours. Jacob was the all-time poster boy for that way of thinking. He tricked and deceived, lied and manipulated, always trying to create an advantage for himself.

One time, however, he went too far. When Jacob stole what rightfully belonged to his brother, the father's blessing on his firstborn son, Esau had enough of Jacob's wily scams and determined to kill him. Their mother intervened and sent Jacob away to live with his uncle for a while, until brother Esau's rage cooled down. So this night he was en route to that getaway place, and he lay down to sleep on the ground, with a rock for a pillow.

What happened next was something Jacob never expected. God appeared to him, telling him he and his descendents would cover the earth, and that God would always stand as his protector.

Jacob heard from God's very voice that the Almighty was going to watch out for him. He need never trick or cheat anyone again. But even now he negotiated, letting God know that "*if* You do all these things—protect me, keep me fed and clothed, bring me back to my father's house safely, then You will be my God, and I will tithe to You from the riches You give me." In other words, "Well, we'll see."

Some of us are so stuck on thinking we have to "watch out for ourselves" that we don't even recognize God's abundant goodness when it is generously offered to us.

SNAPSHOT

GENESIS 28:11–15

He reached a certain place and spent the night there because the sun had set. He took one of the stones from the place, put it there at his head, and lay down in that place. And he dreamed: A stairway was set on the ground with its top reaching heaven, and God's angels were going up and down on it. The LORD was standing there beside him, saying, "I am the LORD, the God of your father Abraham and the God of Isaac. I will give you and your offspring the land that you are now sleeping on. Your offspring will be like the dust of the earth, and you will spread out toward the west, the east, the north, and the south. All the peoples on earth will be blessed through you and your offspring. Look, I am with you and will watch over you wherever you go. I will bring you back to this land, for I will not leave you until I have done what I have promised you."

YOUR CHOICE

Will you trust God to protect your best interests?

GENESIS 29:21–30

SNAPSHOT

Then Jacob said to Laban, "Give me my wife, for my time is completed. I want to sleep with her."...

...When morning came, there was Leah! So he said to Laban, "What is this you have done to me? Wasn't it for Rachel that I worked for you? Why have you deceived me?"

Laban answered, "It is not the custom in this place to give the younger daughter in marriage before the firstborn. Complete this week of wedding celebration, and we will also give you this younger one in return for working yet another seven years for me."

And Jacob did just that. He finished the week of celebration, and Laban gave him his daughter Rachel as his wife. And Laban gave his slave Bilhah to his daughter Rachel as her slave. Jacob slept with Rachel also, and indeed, he loved Rachel more than Leah. And he worked for Laban another seven years.

ANCHOR POINT

STANDING UP IN COMPLICATED RELATIONSHIPS

Jacob is hard to figure out. One minute he is receiving God's blessing; the next he is deceiving his father. He seems to run the gamut between following God and giving in to the base desires of his nature.

In this passage, he again reveals his complexity. In the beginning of the story he is impatient, urging the shepherd to water their flocks as they wait for the other flocks to arrive. Then, when his cousin shows up, he impulsively breaks with tradition and opens the well for her. Yet one month later, while working for his uncle, he strikes a deal that will cause him to work seven years in order to be able to marry Rachel. Seven years, just to get married—that's quite a wait! Would you be willing to work seven years for the right to marry your significant other? If he or she is standing next to you right now, you probably would answer yes, but really? In fact, can you imagine waiting and working that long and that hard for *anything*? Shepherding was not an easy gig.

Then imagine not getting what you waited and worked for and agreeing to work seven more years. Look past the whole crazy "Surprise! You married her sister!" and think for a moment about Jacob's patience.

YOUR CHOICE

When are you impatient with God? Choose His timing, even if it means waiting a while.

DAY 20

THE BIG PICTURE

GN 32:1–33:20

SNAPSHOT

GENESIS 32:17–23

And he told the first one: "When my brother Esau meets you and asks, 'Who do you belong to? Where are you going? And whose animals are these ahead of you?' then tell him, 'They belong to your servant Jacob. They are a gift sent to my lord Esau. And look, he is behind us.' "

He also told the second one, the third, and everyone who was walking behind the animals, "Say the same thing to Esau when you find him. You are to also say, 'Look, your servant Jacob is right behind us.' " For he thought, "I want to appease Esau with the gift that is going ahead of me. After that, I can face him, and perhaps he will forgive me."

So the gift was sent on ahead of him while he remained in the camp that night. During the night Jacob got up and took his two wives, his two female slaves, and his 11 sons, and crossed the ford of Jabbok. He took them and brought them across the stream, along with all his possessions.

DEPOSIT

WORDS FROM GOD'S WORD TO STORE IN YOUR MIND AND HEART

Then He said to Jacob, "Let Me go, for it is daybreak." But Jacob said, "I will not let You go unless You bless me" (Gn 32:26).

SNAPSHOT

GENESIS 37:12–24

His brothers had gone to pasture their father's flocks at Shechem. Israel said to Joseph, "Your brothers, you know, are pasturing the flocks at Shechem. Get ready. I'm sending you to them." "I'm ready," Joseph replied.

Then Israel said to him, "Go and see how your brothers and the flocks are doing, and bring word back to me." So he sent him from the valley of Hebron, and he went to Shechem.

A man found him there, wandering in the field, and asked him, "What are you looking for?"

"I'm looking for my brothers," Joseph said. "Can you tell me where they are pasturing their flocks?"

"They've moved on from here," the man said. "I heard them say, 'Let's go to Dothan.' " So Joseph set out after his brothers and found them at Dothan.

They saw him in the distance, and before he had reached them, they plotted to kill him. They said to one another, "Here comes that dreamer. Come on, let's kill him and throw him into one of the pits. We can say that a vicious animal ate him. Then we'll see what becomes of his dreams!"

When Reuben heard this, he tried to save him from them. He said, "Let's not take his life." Reuben also said to them, "Don't shed blood. Throw him into this pit in the wilderness, but don't lay a hand on him"—intending to rescue him from their hands and return him to his father.

When Joseph came to his brothers, they stripped off his robe, the robe of many colors that he had on. Then they took him and threw him into the pit. The pit was empty; there was no water in it.

YOUR TURN

FAMILY DYNAMICS

How are disagreements settled in your family?

JANUARY 22

DAY 22

THE BIG PICTURE

GN 39:1–23

SNAPSHOT

GENESIS 39:7–9

After some time his master's wife looked longingly at Joseph and said, "Sleep with me."

But he refused and said to his master's wife, ". . . He has withheld nothing from me except you, because you are his wife. So how could I do such a great evil and sin against God?"

TOUGH CHOICE

VOLLEYBALL

When I made the high school volleyball team, my parents had one stipulation: I could play and travel to tournaments, but church always came first.

"Okay, girls—gather around, gather around!" Coach Spade studied her clipboard as the team jogged toward the sideline. "Great practice today! You all are going to be unstoppable against North this weekend if you keep playing like that. Starters are going to be Ross, Oaks, Reagan, Li, Garret, and Mathis."

Yes! My first start. I can't wait to . . .

Cutting short my celebration, Coach Spade started to speak again. "Now, one other important note . . . listen up! The game is going to be on *Sunday*. It's no longer on Saturday due to a scheduling conflict in North's gym. Same time—9:00 a.m.—but *Sunday*."

My heart settled somewhere near my knees. *No! Surely not. I've worked so hard . . . my first week as a starter . . .*

The rest of the team headed toward the locker room, as I stood rooted in my spot. "Mathis, great practices this week! Really proud of the work you put in."

"Thanks, Coach," I mumbled, picking up a ball and turning it over in my hands, as I walked toward Coach Spade.

"Not nervous are you? Really, you keep focused and keep hustling, and you'll be . . ."

"Coach," I interrupted, "Coach, I don't think I'll be able to play on Sunday." I tossed the ball into the ball basket. "I *want* to play, but I *can't* play."

"What do you mean you 'can't' play?" she asked, a look of confusion locked between her forehead and eyebrows.

"Well, errr . . ." I fumbled, hesitant to give the real reason. "You see, I have church on Sunday mornings."

"I'm sorry to hear that," Coach Spade said, picking up the end of the net again. "When you joined this team, volleyball became your first priority. If you miss the game this weekend, you'll be penalized just as you would be for skipping a game or practice. You'll be required to sit out the subsequent game—next Thursday's."

"I understand, Coach," I said quietly. My face burned. I could feel tears welling up from the back of my eyes. "I'm sorry to let you down."

Coach Spade didn't say anything. She heaved the folded net over her shoulder and glanced back at me, disappointed.

Missing the game that weekend was not easy, nor being benched Thursday. I knew, however, that I had made the correct decision by making Christ my priority. Teammates questioned, even doubted, my decision. But some were curious, especially as I continued to work hard with a positive attitude in practice. It was this curiosity that provided me the chance to share my faith and Christ's love and grace!

YOUR CHOICE

In what situations do you need to remember to put God first—over a relationship, activity, or another interest?

TOUGH QUESTION

I'VE BEEN TRYING TO MAKE THE RIGHT CHOICES, BUT I'VE BEEN GETTING NOTHING BUT GRIEF. HOW DO I KEEP STANDING UP FOR WHAT I KNOW IS RIGHT?

When reading about great heroes of the faith (like Joseph), we can be amazed and encouraged by God's faithfulness toward them. Yet when we face hardship, discouragement, and trials, God's presence can seem far away. Sometimes the most frustrating "trials" are social, as we endure a steady stream of mocks, jeers, and criticism, simply because we are choosing to stand for Christ. They can wear us down.

To keep standing when all we've been getting is "grief," we first need to understand that enduring trials and maintaining strong beliefs in the face of adversity is impossible in our own strength. Instead, we must rely on God, completely, allowing Him to work in us and through us. This begins by yielding each situation to Him. You may find that posted Bible verses will be effective reminders—God's promises to be *for* you and *with* you.

Second, we should enlist others on our support team—we shouldn't try to do this alone. God tells us to "carry one another's burdens" (Gl 6:2), and fellow believers can do this through prayers, encouraging words, and insightful counsel.

Third, we should stop focusing only on ourselves. Others are struggling too. Selflessly reaching out can refresh your soul and encourage others, while giving you strength to face your own trials.

Finally, we need to realize that God promises to never give us more than we can handle and will give us a "way of escape" (1 Co 10:13). So we should keep our eyes and ears open to the next step, the "way" that He wants us to take. The Father knows you intimately, loves you unconditionally, and can give you the strength to endure and continue standing for what you know is right, for Him.

istand

SNAPSHOT

GENESIS 40:1–8

After this, the king of Egypt's cupbearer and his baker offended their master, the king of Egypt. Pharaoh was angry with his two officers, the chief cupbearer and the chief baker, and put them in custody in the house of the captain of the guard, in the prison where Joseph was confined. The captain of the guard assigned Joseph to them, and he became their personal attendant. And they were in custody for some time.

The cupbearer and the baker of the king of Egypt, who were confined in the prison, each had a dream. Both had a dream on the same night, and each dream had its own meaning. When Joseph came to them in the morning, he saw that they looked distraught. So he asked Pharaoh's officers who were in custody with him in his master's house, "Why are your faces sad today?"

"We had dreams," they said to him, "but there is no one to interpret them."

Then Joseph said to them, "Don't interpretations belong to God? Tell me your dreams."

YOUR CHOICE

In tough situations, what can you do to remind yourself of God's love, power, and presence?

DAY 24

THE BIG PICTURE
GN 41:1–36

SNAPSHOT

GENESIS 41:8–16

When morning came, he was troubled, so he summoned all the magicians of Egypt and all its wise men. Pharaoh told them his dreams, but no one could interpret them for him.

Then the chief cupbearer said to Pharaoh, "...Pharaoh had been angry with his servants, and he put me and the chief baker in the custody of the captain of the guard. He and I had dreams on the same night; each dream had its own meaning. Now a young Hebrew, a slave of the captain of the guards, was with us there. We told him our dreams, he interpreted our dreams for us, and each had its own interpretation. It turned out just the way he interpreted them..."

Then Pharaoh sent for Joseph, and they quickly brought him from the dungeon...

...Pharaoh said to Joseph, "I have had a dream, and no one can interpret it. But I have heard it said about you that you can hear a dream and interpret it."

"I am not able to," Joseph answered Pharaoh. "It is God who will give Pharaoh a favorable answer."

ANCHOR POINT

THE SHOW

What is striking about this passage, apart from the amazing dreams that Joseph is able to correctly interpret, is the fact that Joseph interpreted them at all. When the king's cupbearer remembered Joseph and his ability to interpret dreams, Joseph had been in prison for more than two years, this after years of living as a slave in a foreign land. If Joseph were a little upset with his situation, it would be hard to blame him. Sold into slavery, falsely accused, and sitting in prison, his life had not quite turned out as it was supposed to. He had dreamed of being a great leader. And the stars in the heavens had bowed to him. That probably felt like a very long time ago.

Yet when he was called to figure out what was going to happen, Joseph did just that; he didn't fall into petty revenge or demand freedom or compensation or even an apology for the way he had been treated. Joseph simply chose to follow God's leading, and he interpreted the dream. Joseph's interpretation allowed Egypt and the lands around it to avoid a terrible famine. His wise counsel convinced them to create stores of food to be used in the future. Because of his ability to see beyond himself and not think only of his own needs and desires, Joseph blessed an entire region.

YOUR CHOICE

How can you be sure you are not caught up in yourself and your problems? How can you choose to look, instead, to God and others?

SNAPSHOT

GENESIS 41:37–45

The proposal pleased Pharaoh and all his servants. Then Pharaoh said to his servants, "Can we find anyone like this, a man who has the spirit of God in him?" So Pharaoh said to Joseph, "Since God has made all this known to you, there is no one as intelligent and wise as you. You will be over my house, and all my people will obey your commands. Only with regard to the throne will I be greater than you." Pharaoh also said to Joseph, "See, I am placing you over all the land of Egypt." Pharaoh removed his signet ring from his hand and put it on Joseph's hand, clothed him with fine linen garments, and placed a gold chain around his neck. He had Joseph ride in his second chariot, and servants called out before him, "Abrek!" So he placed him over all the land of Egypt. Pharaoh said to Joseph, "I am Pharaoh, but without your permission no one will be able to raise his hand or foot in all the land of Egypt." Pharaoh gave Joseph the name Zaphenath-paneah and gave him a wife, Asenath daughter of Potiphera, priest at On. And Joseph went throughout the land of Egypt.

JUST LIKE ME

JOSEPH: JUST AS I AM

We all want to be known and appreciated for who we are. That's why being misunderstood is so painful. Joseph understood that pain. Because of his status as the favored son of Jacob (now Israel), Joseph made enemies of his brothers, especially after telling them about his dreams.

But Joseph's life didn't end after he was sold as a slave and later left in prison for many years. In fact, his ability as an interpreter of dreams was his ticket out of prison. What had been least appreciated by his brothers was now highly valued by the pharaoh of Egypt. So valued was it that Joseph soon found himself the second most important person in Egypt—the man with the plan to save lives during the coming drought. Talk about a huge responsibility!

Joseph could have played it safe by downplaying his ability to interpret dreams. After all, his family didn't want to hear what he had to say. And what if he blew it by giving the wrong interpretation to Pharaoh or messed up administratively? So many lives depended on him. But Joseph's dependence on God gave him the courage to be himself and to speak the truth.

Sometimes, being yourself is the greatest challenge you'll face. Do you have the courage?

YOUR CHOICE

What aspects of your personality make you uniquely qualified to help others? Who can you help today?

DAY 26

THE BIG PICTURE
GN 42:1–38

NO BRAINER

WHAT'S BETTER THAN GETTING EVEN?

Most of us have hassles with our siblings, even if we love them very much. But few ever experience the hatred and jealously that Joseph's 10 brothers felt for him. The favorite of his—and their—father, Joseph enjoyed privileges that the rest of the brothers did not, and they didn't like it. So upset were they with Joseph's pretensions of grandeur that they sold him into Egypt as a slave.

The strange thing about Joseph was that wherever he went he seemed to come out smelling like a rose. In slavery he became the household's chief butler. In prison, he became the foreman in charge of all the other prisoners. Then, the really big promotion: he became second only to Pharaoh himself in authority over the entire nation of Egypt. When Joseph brilliantly devised a scheme to put aside grain during a time of plenty—as a protection against years of famine that God had shown him were coming directly after—the whole nation was indebted to him.

The news that food was available for sale in Egypt reached Joseph's own brothers in Canaan, and they came to buy. They didn't recognize the dazzling young ruler who met them and sold them grain, though he knew very well who *they* were. Probably we would have instinctively wanted to get even with these nasty siblings that had caused him so much trouble, but Joseph had a better plan. He actually hid their money with which they'd paid for the food, so that when they got home, there in the bags was not only the rations that would save their lives, but cash with which they could come back a second time and purchase food again!

Joseph must have chuckled at his big trick. He poured out gracious generosity on these conniving brothers of his, without them even detecting it at first. And what an amazing reunion ensued. It's actually fun to return so much good for so much evil.

SNAPSHOT

GENESIS 42:6–8,25–26

Joseph was in charge of the country; he sold grain to all its people. His brothers came and bowed down before him with their faces to the ground. When Joseph saw his brothers, he recognized them, but he treated them like strangers and spoke harshly to them.

"Where do you come from?" he asked.

"From the land of Canaan to buy food," they replied.

Although Joseph recognized his brothers, they did not recognize him.

Joseph then gave orders to fill their containers with grain, return each man's money to his sack, and give them provisions for their journey. This order was carried out. They loaded the grain on their donkeys and left there.

YOUR CHOICE

What can you do to "bless" those who irritate, pester, or even bully you instead of getting even?

SNAPSHOT

GENESIS 43:26–30,34

When Joseph came home, they brought him the gift they had carried into the house, and they bowed to the ground before him.

He asked if they were well, and he said, "How is your elderly father that you told me about? Is he still alive?"

They answered, "Your servant our father is well. He is still alive." And they bowed down to honor him.

When he looked up and saw his brother Benjamin, his mother's son, he asked, "Is this your youngest brother that you told me about?" Then he said, "May God be gracious to you, my son." Joseph hurried out because he was overcome with emotion for his brother, and he was about to weep. He went into an inner room to weep. Then he washed his face and came out. Regaining his composure, he said, "Serve the meal."

Portions were served to them from Joseph's table, and Benjamin's portion was five times larger than any of theirs. They drank, and they got drunk with Joseph.

DEPOSIT

WORDS FROM GOD'S WORD TO STORE IN YOUR MIND AND HEART

"You planned evil against me; God planned it for good to bring about the present result—the survival of many people" (Gn 50:20).

DAY 28

THE BIG PICTURE

GN 44:1–34

SNAPSHOT

GENESIS 44:14–16

When Judah and his brothers reached Joseph's house, he was still there. They fell to the ground before him. "What is this you have done?" Joseph said to them. "Didn't you know that a man like me could uncover the truth by divination?"

"What can we say to my lord?" Judah replied. "How can we plead? How can we justify ourselves? God has exposed your servants' iniquity. We are now my lord's slaves—both we and the one in whose possession the cup was found."

YOUR TURN

UNDESERVING FORGIVENESS

How do you choose to react when someone points out a mistake you've made?

TOUGH QUESTION

WHAT KIND OF COURAGEOUS CHOICE MIGHT GOD WANT ME TO MAKE FOR MY FUTURE?

Being open to God's plan can be thrilling and terrifying at the same time. Although only God knows the future, He allows us to make important choices that affect our lives. Part of His plan is for us to choose to obey Him, no matter what. So consider these possible courageous choices.

- At school, you may need to choose to say no to peer pressure at the risk of being labeled a nerd and losing some friends.
- In your career, you may have to choose to work hard when the boss isn't around and everyone else is goofing off and you won't be rewarded for your extra effort anyway.
- With a love interest, you may have to choose to refuse to give in to the desire for sex (before marriage).
- With your parents, you may have to choose to act in a way that honors them, even though they aren't believers and are making poor choices themselves.
- In the community, you may have to take a stand for life, for the poor and homeless, and for others who are neglected or scorned by society.

Followers of Christ need to be prepared to face tough situations and decisions regularly. We can imagine choices that we hope God does not call us to make because they would be too difficult or too painful. But that's where we need to remember God's love and, then, trust Him for the outcome. God loves us too much to allow us to stay where we are, and He may direct us to a place where we have to make a bold decision—though a hard one—to follow Him. God will give us the strength to do what is right. But even if we fail to act or we make the wrong choice, He stands ready to forgive us.

SNAPSHOT

GENESIS 45:9–11

Return quickly to my father and say to him, "This is what your son Joseph says: 'God has made me lord of all Egypt. Come down to me without delay. You can settle in the land of Goshen and be near me—you, your children, and grandchildren, your sheep, cattle, and all you have. There I will sustain you, for there will be five more years of famine. Otherwise, you, your household, and everything you have will become destitute.' "

YOUR CHOICE

In which of those areas mentioned above do you anticipate having to make a difficult, but God-honoring, choice?

DAY 30

THE BIG PICTURE

GN 49:1–33

SNAPSHOT

GENESIS 49:22–26

Joseph is a fruitful vine, a fruitful vine beside a spring; its branches climb over the wall.

The archers attacked him, shot at him, and were hostile toward him.

Yet his bow remained steady, and his strong arms were made agile by the hands of the Mighty One of Jacob, by the name of the Shepherd, the Rock of Israel,

by the God of your father who helps you, and by the Almighty who blesses you with blessings of the heavens above, blessings of the deep that lies below, and blessings of the breasts and the womb.

The blessings of your father excel the blessings of my ancestors and the bounty of the eternal hills. May they rest on the head of Joseph, on the crown of the prince of his brothers.

ANCHOR POINT

A STRONG IMPRESSION

What would your father or mother say about you when they are older? What will be the defining characteristic of your life? Will you be known for your compassion? Will you be marked by your passion for Christ? Or will you be seen as the angry one or the proud one?

As Jacob spoke to each of his sons, many of them probably were a little uncomfortable with what he was saying. Jacob called Ruben unruly, like the sea. He labeled Simeon and Levi men of violence and said their descendants would be scattered. He called Dan a "poisonous snake." These certainly weren't the ringing endorsements and blessings that the brothers were hoping for. Others fared much better, however. Jacob described Judah as a "lion," Naphtali as a "deer," and Joseph as a "fruitful tree." They were blessed.

Where would you fall? Considering your character and actions, would you be characterized as a "poisonous snake" or a "fruitful tree" or something in between? Now is the time to consider the matter. Take time to reflect on your life patterns. Do you need to take another path; it is possible. You can make that choice; you can change. And if you are heading in the right direction, be sure to make the right choices to keep you there—good friends, mentors, practices that will keep you close to the heart of God.

YOUR CHOICE

What one aspect of your life right now do you hope will change in the next five years? What is one thing that you hope will remain and grow? What choices do you need to make to be sure that both happen?

THE BIG PICTURE
EX 1:8–2:10

JANUARY 31

DAY 31

SNAPSHOT

EXODUS 2:1–6b

Now a man from the family of Levi married a Levite woman. The woman became pregnant and gave birth to a son; when she saw that he was beautiful, she hid him for three months. But when she could no longer hide him, she got a papyrus basket for him and coated it with asphalt and pitch. She placed the child in it and set it among the reeds by the bank of the Nile. Then his sister stood at a distance in order to see what would happen to him.

Pharaoh's daughter went down to bathe at the Nile while her servant girls walked along the riverbank. Seeing the basket among the reeds, she sent her slave girl to get it. When she opened it, she saw the child—a little boy, crying.

JUST LIKE ME

THE MIDWIVES AND MOSES' MOTHER: TAKING A STAND TO PRESERVE LIFE

The struggle to preserve the lives of children isn't confined to picketing an abortion clinic. Even as far back as the time of Moses, people took a courageous stand so that unborn children could live.

Moses had a number of women to thank for preserving his life. First, there were the Egyptian midwives, Shiphrah and Puah, who refused to kill the male Hebrew babies they were charged with bringing into the world. Second, there was his mother, who kept her son hidden for months. For them, preserving Moses' life meant risking their own.

Ultimately, God was the main reason why Moses remained alive. He put the right people in place: Miriam to watch her tiny brother as he floated down the Nile and the daughter of Pharaoh who could not resist the infant. And Moses' mother had the reward of caring for her own son when Pharaoh's daughter needed someone to nurse him.

Perhaps their experiences seem far removed from your life. But you might be called upon one day to talk to a friend or a coworker who is trying to decide whether or not to abort a child. What will you say?

YOUR CHOICE

How can you take a stand to preserve life?

FEBRUARI
FEVRIER
FEBRUAR

FEBRUARY

FEBBRAIO
FEVEREIRO
FEBRERO

EXODUS 2:13–14 SNAPSHOT

The next day he went out and saw two Hebrews fighting. He asked the one in the wrong, "Why are you attacking your neighbor?"

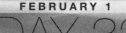

"Who made you a leader and judge over us?" the man replied. "Are you planning to kill me as you killed the Egyptian?"

Then Moses became afraid and thought: What I did is certainly known.

THE BIG PICTURE

EX 2:11–25

TOUGH CHOICE

RUNNING FROM GOD

I pulled out my daily planner and reviewed the next day's schedule—another jam-packed Wednesday, filled with studying, classes, and meetings. I flipped through the heavily marked pages of my planner. Booking my time seemed the only way to get my mind off graduation, finding a job, leaving my friends, "growing up" . . .

"Knock, knock, knock."

"Yep! Come in!" I shouted from my desk, writing "Leadership Meeting" on the following page.

"Hey, you busy?" Emily, one of my housemates walked in and nestled up into my reading chair. "We missed you at dinner tonight." Every Tuesday night during senior year, my six best friends, with whom I lived, and I would eat dinner together. It gave us a time to fellowship and catch up.

"Oh yeah, I had to finish my British Lit paper . . . sorry." For the third week in a row, I had skipped our dinner to study.

"You know, we've really missed you, in general, lately." I could feel the concern in her stare, as she tilted her head, inviting me to respond. Emily was one of my closest friends, but we'd had several confrontations that fall, mostly over how I'd been so distant and not myself. I knew the "accusations" were valid, but I didn't know what to do. The harder I tried to cling to control—control of my future, friendships, grades, relationships—the more out of control I felt. To protect myself from change-related grief, I was pushing away the people I loved.

"Emily . . ." I was embarrassed and angry. Not at her—at myself. "I don't know what's wrong with me. I know I've been distant . . ." I trailed off.

"What can I do, Jane? How can I be a friend to you? I want the old Jane back."

I looked down at my planner, fiddling with the page corners. "Me too," I murmured quietly. "Just have patience with me."

As I lay restless in bed that night, I ran over the conversation I'd had with Emily. *Why do I keep pushing away? I'm so tired of running . . . running . . . running.*

I turned on my bedside lamp. *Maybe reading will help me sleep.* I shuffled through a stack of books. At the bottom my Bible rested, closed. *I haven't touched this in a while.* I flipped it open and began to read: "The LORD is the One who will go before you. He will be with you; he will not leave you or forsake you. Do not be afraid or discouraged" (Dt 31:8).

Lord, please forgive me for running from You and for trusting in myself. I'm failing. I'm pushing my friends, family, and You away. I'm out of control. I slid out of bed and walked to my desk. I opened my planner, staring at the chaos. *Take this, Lord. Teach me to replace the clutter in my life with You. Teach me to trust You when I am afraid.*

Dealing with change is not easy. People cope in different ways, but pushing away from fellowship and running from the Lord will never result in security.

YOUR CHOICE

What changes do you need to make in your schedule to keep your priorities straight?

DAY 33

THE BIG PICTURE
EX 3:1–22

NO BRAINER

GOD'S BURNING BUSH

Many teenagers and young adults believe that where they live is the most boring place on earth, that the excitement and glamour of life must be "somewhere else." But few of us have lives so bland and monotonous as that of old Moses—he followed sheep and goats around as they ceaselessly sought for something to chew on in the sandy wastelands of the Sinai wilderness. Forty years on the backside of the desert, stillness and silence his closest companions, Moses' life had been, for a long, long time, uneventful.

Then one day that suddenly changed. Appearing before him was Almighty God, the maker of heaven and earth, the One known to Moses' ancestors—He who had promised to watch over the sons of Israel forever. And what an appearance! A blazing fire in a small shrub that wouldn't burn up, a ringing voice that demanded reverence, and a commission for Moses to accomplish. Right there is where the story catches us by surprise, for we naturally think that, like us, Moses would jump at the opportunity to escape his mundane existence and go be Somebody. But he didn't. Moses began a long argument with God, basically begging off the assignment. "Who am I to appear before Pharaoh?" was one of his excuses.

God's answer: "You're missing the point, Moses. It isn't a matter of who *you* are. What counts is *Who am I?* I'm sending you; I'm equipping you; I'm going to make every word you say to Pharaoh come true. All you have to do is simply do whatever I tell you to do." But Moses continued to beg off.

How would you respond? Would you be as stupidly stubborn as Moses and drag your feet if God were to offer you an exciting and perhaps difficult assignment? Or would you gladly leap to your feet and say, "Yes! Finally. Something *worth doing*. It's what God wants me to do. I'll do it!"

SNAPSHOT

EXODUS 3:2–6

Then the Angel of the Lord appeared to him in a flame of fire within a bush. As Moses looked, he saw that the bush was on fire but was not consumed. So Moses thought: I must go over and look at this remarkable sight. Why isn't the bush burning up?

When the Lord saw that he had gone over to look, God called out to him from the bush, "Moses, Moses!"

"Here I am," he answered.

"Do not come closer," He said. "Take your sandals off your feet, for the place where you are standing is holy ground." Then He continued, "I am the God of your father, the God of Abraham, the God of Isaac, and the God of Jacob." Moses hid his face because he was afraid to look at God.

YOUR CHOICE

What has God told you to do (you're sure about it—no ambiguity)? What's your first choice, your first step in doing what He wants?

SNAPSHOT

EXODUS 4:1–5

Then Moses answered, "What if they won't believe me and will not obey me but say, 'The Lord did not appear to you'?"

The Lord asked him, "What is that in your hand?"

"A staff," he replied.

Then He said, "Throw it on the ground." He threw it on the ground, and it became a snake. Moses ran from it, but the Lord told him, "Stretch out your hand and grab it by the tail." So he stretched out his hand and caught it, and it became a staff in his hand. "This will take place," He continued, "so they will believe that the Lord, the God of their fathers, the God of Abraham, the God of Isaac, and the God of Jacob, has appeared to you."

DEPOSIT

WORDS FROM GOD'S WORD TO STORE IN YOUR MIND AND HEART

"Now go! I will help you speak and I will teach you what to say" (Ex 4:12).

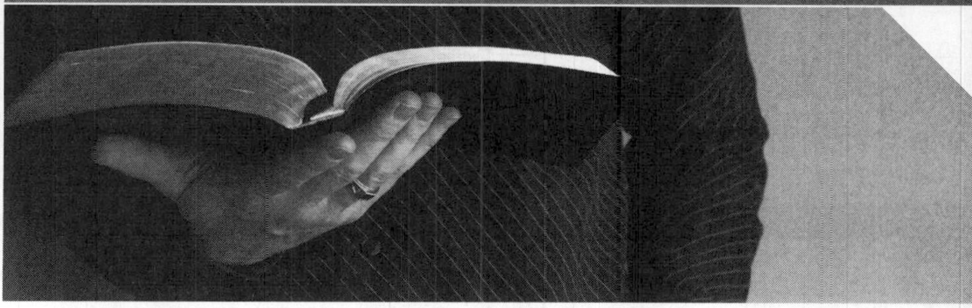

SNAPSHOT

EXODUS 5:1–5

Later, Moses and Aaron went in and said to Pharaoh, "This is what the LORD, the God of Israel, says: Let My people go, so that they may hold a festival for Me in the wilderness."

But Pharaoh responded, "Who is the LORD that I should obey Him by letting Israel go? I do not know the LORD, and what's more, I will not let Israel go."

Then they answered, "The God of the Hebrews has met with us. Please let us go on a three-day trip into the wilderness so that we may sacrifice to the LORD our God, or else He may strike us with plague or sword."

The king of Egypt said to them, "Moses and Aaron, why are you causing the people to neglect their work? Get to your labors!"

Pharaoh also said, "Look, the people of the land are so numerous, and you would stop them from working."

YOUR TURN

RESISTANCE

What have people said when you've tried to obey God?

EXODUS 6:12

But Moses said in the LORD's presence: "If the Israelites will not listen to me, then how will Pharaoh listen to me, since I am such a poor speaker?"

SNAPSHOT

FEBRUARY 5

DAY 36

THE BIG PICTURE

EX 6:1–13

TOUGH CHOICE

REJECTION

We sat in rows, alphabetically, across the sorority chapter room floor. It was the middle of Rush Week, and we had just finished the day's last round; that put us somewhere around midnight.

"Hurry up, girls!" Holly, our recruitment chair, shouted from the front of the room. "The faster we get this over with, the faster we can go." Muttering and shuffling filled the cramped and stuffy room.

I crossed my legs, trying to get comfortable on the hardwood floor. No use. "Okay, listen up," Holly waited for silence. "Remember, start with a good comment, then any negative comments, and end on a positive comment." My stomach churned. *Please be kind . . . even just tactful tonight.*

"Abbott, Carrie!" announced Holly, looking around the room for raised hands. "Yes, Sarah," she said pointing at a girl two rows behind me.

"Positive: Carrie was really excited to be here, and she is really sweet."

Holly pointed to another raised hand. "Negative: Whenever I see her out on the weekends she's tanked. And she sleeps around."

"Oh my gosh!" squealed the girl sitting next to her, "It's so true. She cheated with my roommate's boyfriend." The volume in the room rose quickly.

"Girls, GIRLS! Shut up!" shouted Holly. "You have to go positive, negative, positive. We can't have two negatives in a row." I felt sick to my stomach. *This is so mean,* I thought. "Okay, we need another positive," stated Holly.

"Well, she's really . . . sociable?" commented another girl in front of me, sarcasm in her voice.

"Okay, great!" said Holly making notes in her binder. "Next we have . . ." I couldn't sit through this any more. It wasn't right. I raised my hand. "What, Leah?"

I didn't know what I was going to say. "This is . . . this is wrong." I could feel heads turning toward me. "We're supposed to be a sorority with integrity and character. We're supposed to be finding girls who would fit well into our house and thrive here. We're just tearing girls apart . . ."

"Leah," Holly interrupted me, glaring down from the stage, "this is part of the process. We have to make cuts somehow, and this is the way we do it." I looked around the room, hoping that someone would speak up and agree with me. Silence.

I picked up my water bottle and binder and stood up. "I'm not going to be a part of this," I said quietly. "It's destructive, and it's just wrong."

"If you leave, you'll be fined . . . the whole amount!" Holly threatened.

"I know. I don't care. I'd rather pay $500 and have a clean conscience." I could hear snickers and whispering as I left, but I knew I was doing what the Lord wanted me to do.

Several days later at lunch, one of my sorority sisters approached me. "Thanks for standing up during Rush the other night. Katie and I left after the same thing happened on the next girl. You really showed courage. Thanks!"

Dear Lord, thank you for giving me the courage to face rejection. Provide these opportunities so that others may also seek to reflect You!

YOUR CHOICE **How do you respond when your stand is rejected?**

SNAPSHOT

EXODUS 7:2–5

"You must say whatever I command you; then Aaron your brother must declare it to Pharaoh so that he will let the Israelites go from his land. But I will harden Pharaoh's heart and multiply My signs and wonders in the land of Egypt. Pharaoh will not listen to you, but I will put My hand on Egypt and bring out the ranks of My people the Israelites, out of the land of Egypt by great acts of judgment. The Egyptians will know that I am the LORD when I stretch out My hand against Egypt, and bring out the Israelites from among them."

JUST LIKE ME

PHARAOH: STALLED BY STUBBORNNESS

What happens when a car stalls? If the car has a mechanical problem, it won't go anywhere unless it's towed to a garage to be fixed. A stubborn person is like a stalled car—someone who insists on his or her way and refuses to move from his or her position. Stubbornness became a way of life for the pharaoh of Moses' day.

Pharaoh dug in his heels about the Hebrew people. Having reaped the benefits of their enslavement, he didn't want to hear Moses and Aaron's plea on behalf of God to release their people. And when the Egyptian magicians were able to perform the same trick of turning their staffs into serpents, Pharaoh grew even more stubborn. Ten plagues later, the land was devastated and many people were dead—all because of one stubborn man.

What causes you to dig in your heels? Pride? Wanting to be right? While stubbornness doesn't always cost lives, it can involve other costs: relationships, damage to your integrity, and so on.

Taking a stand about what's right is one thing. Stubbornly clinging to unhealthy beliefs or one's own agenda is another. We need to be sure we're taking a stand for what's right rather than standing up for our pride.

YOUR CHOICE

How can you be sure that you're standing for what's right instead of being stubborn?

TOUGH QUESTION

HOW CAN I TAKE THE RIGHT STANDS AT SCHOOL AND WITH MY FRIENDS WITHOUT BEING LABELED AS WEIRD OR WACKO?

When Jesus walked the earth people reacted to Him in two ways: They either loved Him or hated Him. Today, people seem to react to Christians and the gospel message the same way: either with interest and respect or with disgust. Taking a bold stand for Christ always comes with risk, and those who align with Christ always put their social reputations on the line. So don't be surprised that some people don't understand.

Just because you identify yourself with Christ and choose to live according to Scripture doesn't mean that you have to act weird or wacko. The Bible says we are aliens on earth (1 Pt 2:11), but we don't have to behave like visitors from outer space by withdrawing from culture or people. God doesn't expect us to walk around holding a sign or wearing a shirt that proclaims, "I'm a Christian!" And we certainly don't have to approach people at school or work aggressively, trying to shove the gospel down their throats. Instead, we need to humbly, respectfully, and quietly preach a bold message to those around us, through how we live and then through our words.

So, let people around you know you are a Christian by how you love them (1 Jn 3:18)—let your Christ-like actions do the talking. Build relationships with people with the goal of friendship, not conversion. Be interested in other people and their stories before you share yours. God can use your quiet and loving actions to draw people to Himself. And if along the way some label you as weird, see it as a price for doing what God wants you to do. And thank Him for His promise to be with you in every situation.

SNAPSHOT

EXODUS 8:25–29

Then Pharaoh summoned Moses and Aaron and said, "Go sacrifice to your God within the country."

But Moses said, "It would not be right to do that, because what we will sacrifice to the LORD our God is detestable to the Egyptians. If we sacrifice what the Egyptians detest in front of them, won't they stone us? We must go a distance of three days into the wilderness and sacrifice to the LORD our God as He instructs us."

Pharaoh responded, "I will let you go and sacrifice to the LORD your God in the wilderness, but don't go very far. Make an appeal for me."

"As soon as I leave you," Moses said, "I will appeal to the LORD, and tomorrow the swarms of flies will depart from Pharaoh, his officials, and his people. But Pharaoh must not act deceptively again by refusing to let the people go and sacrifice to the LORD."

YOUR CHOICE

How will you respond the next time someone labels you as weird because of your beliefs?

DAY 39

EX 9:8–10:29

NO BRAINER

PAY ATTENTION

What does God have to do to get through to you? Break your teeth? In Egypt, after Moses and Pharaoh's sorcerers had gone a few rounds, each demonstrating their powers to manipulate the material world, the gloves suddenly came off, and God began to really pummel Egypt. He hit them with one devastating plague after another, trying to convince them to make the right choice (release the Israelites), each plague experienced by the Egyptians as if "it couldn't get any worse than this." But then when Pharaoh would harden his heart and refuse to acknowledge God and obey Him, Moses would return with another plague, this one worse that those that had preceded it.

He threw soot from a kiln into the air, and the fine black dust caused painful red sores to break out on every Egyptian, from the sorcerers themselves to the rest of the citizens. He called for hail, and huge balls of ice came crashing out of a thundering fiery sky, knocking people silly, killing animals, and crushing green plants to mush. Then a cloud of locusts so thick and so wide that it obscured the sun settled on the land, devouring every last bite of anything green that was left after the hail. By this time Pharaoh's sorcerers and advisors were practically screaming at him, "Don't you see what is happening? You are ruining this country! What is the matter with you? Acknowledge God before we're all wiped out!"

But Pharoah refused, and thick, almost palpable darkness fell over Egypt. For three days no one could see anything or anyone else. It was maddening and frightening. The Egyptians whimpered in their pain and agony, aghast that their king would not back off and let God's people go out to worship Him as they requested.

You have to wonder: What does it take for someone to recognize that God is God? Isn't it obvious that doing what He says is the right—the only safe—thing to do?

SNAPSHOT

EXODUS 9:23–28

So Moses stretched out his staff toward heaven, and the LORD sent thunder and hail. Lightning struck the earth, and the LORD rained hail on the land of Egypt. The hail, with lightning flashing through it, was so severe that nothing like it had occurred in the land of Egypt since it had become a nation. Throughout the land of Egypt, the hail struck down everything in the field, both man and beast. The hail beat down every plant of the field and shattered every tree in the field. The only place it didn't hail was in the land of Goshen where the Israelites were.

Pharaoh sent for Moses and Aaron. "I have sinned this time," he said to them. "The LORD is the Righteous One, and I and my people are the guilty ones. Make an appeal to the LORD. There has been enough of God's thunder and hail. I will let you go; you don't need to stay any longer."

YOUR CHOICE

Do you need to wait for catastrophes to hit before you will obey?

THE BIG PICTURE

EX 11:1–10; 12:29–36

FEBRUARY 9

DAY 40

SNAPSHOT

EXODUS 12:30–33

During the night Pharaoh got up, he along with all his officials and all the Egyptians, and there was a loud wailing throughout Egypt because there wasn't a house without someone dead. He summoned Moses and Aaron during the night and said, "Get up, leave my people, both you and the Israelites, and go, worship the LORD as you have asked. Take even your flocks and your herds as you asked, and leave, and this will also be a blessing to me."

Now the Egyptians pressured the people in order to send them quickly out of the country, for they said, "We're all going to die!"

ANCHOR POINT

FEARING GOD

Are you described as "strong-willed" or "stubborn"? These can be seen as desirable traits because you won't be a pushover or someone easily taken in. Yet stubbornness can get us into trouble, especially when we refuse to listen to God. We may know that He wants us to act a certain way, but, like a young child with his fingers in his ears, we refuse to listen and then stubbornly keep doing what God doesn't want.

In this passage, God told Pharaoh that the years of free labor were over, that the Israelites were being released, whether he liked it or not. Pharaoh was less than receptive to the idea. God wasn't using a typical method to get through to him, either; these were not gentle promptings or subtle hints. Instead, to make His points, God rained down plagues on Egypt. Yet Pharaoh refused to listen to God and resisted. He did not want to give up something that was making his life easier. And he lived to regret his choice.

What is God telling you? What is He trying to remove from your life? What is He trying to insert? Who are you supposed to befriend that you aren't? Who do you need to forgive or ask forgiveness from?

Pharaoh waited until it was too late, and he paid a terrible price for his stubbornness. Don't act like him.

YOUR CHOICE

When, lately, have you stubbornly refused to obey God? Write down the first couple of things that pop into your mind. Choose to give in to Him.

THE BIG PICTURE

EX 13:17–14:31

SNAPSHOT

EXODUS 14:19–22

Then the Angel of God, who was going in front of the Israelite forces, moved and went behind them. The pillar of cloud moved from in front of them and stood behind them. It came between the Egyptian and Israelite forces. The cloud was there in the darkness, yet it lit up the night. So neither group came near the other all night long.

Then Moses stretched out his hand over the sea. The LORD drove the sea back with a powerful east wind all that night and turned the sea into dry land. So the waters were divided, and the Israelites went through the sea on dry ground, with the waters like a wall to them on their right and their left.

DEPOSIT

WORDS FROM GOD'S WORD TO STORE IN YOUR MIND AND HEART

"The LORD will fight for you; you must be quiet" (Ex 14:14).

THE BIG PICTURE

EX 15:22–27; 17:1–7

FEBRUARY 11

DAY 42

SNAPSHOT

EXODUS 17:2–5

So the people complained to Moses: "Give us water to drink."

"Why are you complaining to me?" Moses replied to them. "Why are you testing the LORD?"

But the people thirsted there for water, and grumbled against Moses. They said, "Why did you ever bring us out of Egypt to kill us and our children and our livestock with thirst?"

Then Moses cried out to the LORD, "What should I do with these people? In a little while they will stone me!"

The LORD answered Moses, "Go on ahead of the people and take some of the elders of Israel with you. Take the rod you struck the Nile with in your hand and go."

YOUR TURN

NOT FAIR!

What do you complain to God about?

FEBRUARY 12

DAY 43

THE BIG PICTURE

EX 16:1–36

SNAPSHOT **EXODUS 16:11–12** The LORD spoke to Moses, "I have heard the complaints of the Israelites. Tell them: At twilight you will eat meat, and in the morning you will eat bread until you are full. Then you will know that I am the LORD your God."

TOUGH CHOICE

NO COMPLAINTS

"Adios, Carlita!" I waved from the doorway of the mission in Chalco, Mexico, as a little girl with long, dark hair skipped down the dusty street and into the fiery sunset, waving back at me over her shoulder.

Our mission team from the suburbs of Chicago had spent the week in her village, two hours outside of Mexico City. We had helped paint the mission walls, led Bible studies for the adults in the community, held Vacation Bible School for the children, evangelized in the community, and made our fair share of balloon animals in the plaza.

I walked back into the mission's courtyard and sat down at a table where several other team members were resting. "Phew! I'm exhausted," I said, collapsing into a metal folding chair. "Carlita and two of her friends taught me how to play *Numeros*—it's this clapping game that all the girls love." I rubbed my sore hands. It had been a good but long day, with cleaning in the morning, cooking in the hot kitchen during lunch time, and a spectacular game of street soccer in the afternoon.

Mark, who was sitting across the table, leaned back in his chair. "I could use a good meal and a shower right about now," he said, closing his eyes and resting his hands behind his head. Everyone around the tabled hummed in agreement.

The sound of metal clanking against metal broke the momentary silence. Brian, our team leader, emerged from inside the mission carrying a toolbox. He wiped sweat from his brow; his shirt was soaked and covered in dirt. "Hey guys, the water line is out again. No showers tonight." A unanimous groan rose from the group. "Sorry. We're trying our best to fix it." For five of our seven days in Chalco, we had been having water problems.

"This is ridiculous."

"I'm filthy."

"How hard is it to get a shower around here?" Nobody at the table was pleased. Brian looked weary and discouraged. I laid my head down on the table. *Lord, this is miserable. Please help the water to get fixed. But in the meantime, give us all patience and Christlike attitudes. We're here to serve you and further your kingdom.*

I raised my head back up, looking around at the frustrated faces. Not quite sure what to say or do, I suggested, "Let's play cards," purely on a whim. Nobody said anything at first, but then Mark offered, "Well, maybe that's not such a bad idea."

That night, the whole team sat under the stars in the courtyard teaching our Spanish brothers and sisters how to play different card games. The dirt, the language barrier, the exhaustion—were all forgotten as we built community and had fellowship with other believers.

Choosing not to complain is not easy, nor is it possible when we depend on our own will power. Going to the Lord in these moments, however, will open doors that lead to witnessing opportunities, friendships, and a strengthened relationship with Christ.

YOUR CHOICE **When do you need to stop complaining and start praising?**

TOUGH QUESTION

I WANT TO MAKE "COURAGEOUS CHOICES," BUT I'M AFRAID OF WHAT THEY MIGHT COST. WHAT SHOULD I DO?

You are right to assume that making a courageous choice for Christ will cost you something. Taking a moral stand might cost you a friendship, money and time, or even a job. But doing what God wants you to do is *priceless*. You can expect to pay a price for following Christ—but it's worth it.

Jesus told His disciples not to worry about what tomorrow might bring (Mt 6:34). Worrying about what your courageous choices might cost is out of your control. Just remember that God promises to meet all of our needs (Php 4:19), and He will provide strength and courage for every situation. It's all about Him, not us.

At this point, we may need a motive check. So here's an important question: Why do you want to live a courageous life, anyway? If it's for recognition or accolades, your motivation is fueled by pride. But if you sincerely want to obey God and live for Him, even in difficult circumstances, then God will give you the power and grace to make the brave decisions and endure the hardships.

Being afraid of a negative reaction or consequence can cripple you with fear. So if you are feeling afraid of what a stand for Christ might cost, consider what lies behind that feeling. Fear gets in the way of courage. God commanded Joshua many times to be strong and courageous (see Jos 1), but God also promised to be with him wherever he went. That promise never changes, and we need to choose to believe that God is who He says He is and that He can and will do what He says He can do. So do what you know God wants you to do, and trust Him for the outcome.

SNAPSHOT

EXODUS 18:14,17–19,21

When Moses' father-in-law saw everything he was doing for them he asked, "What is this thing you're doing for the people? Why are you alone sitting as judge, while all the people stand around you from morning until evening?"

"What you're doing is not good," Moses' father-in-law said to him. "You will certainly wear out both yourself and these people who are with you, because the task is too heavy for you. You can't do it alone. Now listen to me; I will give you some advice, and God be with you. You be the one to represent the people before God and bring their cases to Him. . . . But you should select from all the people able men, God-fearing, trustworthy, and hating bribes. Place them over the people as officials of thousands, hundreds, fifties, and tens."

YOUR CHOICE

What choice or stand are you hesitant to make because of the possible cost? What can you do to gather the courage to do what is right, regardless of the cost?

DAY 45

THE BIG PICTURE

EX 19:1–25

NO BRAINER

GOD'S HOLINESS

If you had a chance to meet God face-to-face, how would you prepare? When God called His people, Israel, to meet with Him, He let them know they shouldn't be casual about the occasion. And He gave them three days to purify themselves for the encounter. Even then He warned them that it would be dangerous.

Almost as soon as they set up camp at the base of Mount Sinai, the fireworks and earthquakes started going off. An ever-increasing spectacle of bright, flashing lights, heavy black smoke, trembling earthquakes, and loud blasts overwhelmed the people of Israel. God Himself, who had rescued them from the hands of the Egyptians by devastating those people and their land, was now making Himself known to His chosen people. The noises kept getting louder and the message from God relayed by Moses more frightening: God warned the people not to touch the sacred mountain, lest they die.

At first there was no problem—no one *wanted* to come near this terrifying holy place.

But as the trumpets blared louder and the mountain shook more and more, the people were almost mesmerized. God saw that they were in danger of losing their composure in a wild frenzy and breaking through the barriers and rushing forward into His holy presence. He hurriedly sent Moses back down to warn them again, "Don't even think about trying to push through into My holy presence and gaze upon Me. If you do you will die instantly."

God's holiness means just that—His separation from all that is mundane and worldly and unclean. It makes no sense for sinful humans to press themselves into His presence. But often we take God for granted and stroll into His presence, totally unprepared, without thinking. We're fortunate to still be alive!

SNAPSHOT

EXODUS 19:21–22

The LORD directed Moses, "Go down and warn the people not to break through to see the LORD; otherwise many of them will die. Even the priests who come near the LORD must purify themselves or the LORD will break out in anger against them."

YOUR CHOICE

How do you prepare for worship? For Bible study and prayer? What can you do to be ready to meet God face-to-face?

THE BIG PICTURE

EX 20:1–22

FEBRUARY 15

DAY 46

SNAPSHOT

EXODUS 20:3–4,7–8,12–17

Do not have other gods besides Me.

Do not make an idol for yourself...

Do not misuse the name of the LORD your God...

Remember to dedicate the Sabbath day.

Honor your father and your mother...

Do not murder.

Do not commit adultery.

Do not steal.

Do not give false testimony against your neighbor.

Do not covet ...

ANCHOR POINT

GOD'S STANDARDS

Here, in Exodus 20, we find the Ten Commandments. One commandment that people often find confusing occurs in verses 8–11—keeping the Sabbath, the day of rest.

In the New Testament (see Mt 12), Jesus seemed to disrespect the Sabbath. He healed on the seventh day, and His disciples "harvested" grain on that day. But Jesus wasn't pushing aside the day of rest. Instead, He was making the point that this one day in seven, the Sabbath, was instituted by God for our benefit, not the other way around. The religious leaders of the day had made Sabbath-keeping so burdensome that it was not a restful experience at all. Today, the opposite is true. Most Sabbath or Sunday restrictions have been thrown off, and people pretty much do what they want on this day. This extreme is not a good approach either.

The Sabbath is God's gift. We need at least one day in seven to rest from our labors, to reflect on life and its meaning, and to reconnect with God. Don't throw it away. Choose to embrace it, engage it, and enjoy it. Don't be a slave to the Sabbath, legalistically restricting all activity and condemning those who "break" it according to your standards, but don't belittle it either.

How would your life change if you established a few Sabbath guidelines? If you gave yourself time to rest, time to be with God, to listen? Carving out that time will be challenging because work, studies, sports, and other activities all clamor for attention. Stopping the flow, changing direction can be tough. Yet this one habit—putting aside a day to meet with God and rest in His presence—can have a life-long and positive impact.

YOUR CHOICE

How can you establish a Sabbath in your life? What would you have to limit? To what would you have to say no?

DAY 47

THE BIG PICTURE

EX 32:1–29

SNAPSHOT

EXODUS 32:1–4

When the people saw that Moses delayed in coming down from the mountain, they gathered around Aaron and said to him, "Come, make us a god who will go before us because this Moses, the man who brought us up from the land of Egypt—we don't know what has happened to him!"

Then Aaron replied to them, "Take off the gold rings that are on the ears of your wives, your sons, and your daughters and bring them to me." So all the people took off the gold rings that were on their ears and brought them to Aaron. He took the gold from their hands, fashioned it with an engraving tool, and made it into an image of a calf.

Then they said, "Israel, this is your God, who brought you up from the land of Egypt!"

JUST LIKE ME

AARON: GIVING IN TO PEER PRESSURE

Sometimes temptation waits until you get that big promotion or some other pat on the back. This was true of Moses' brother, Aaron. Aaron had been named the high priest of Israel. Having this position meant that he was the man in the gap—the one who offered the animal sacrifices for the sins of Israel before a holy God. But now, instead of offering a sacrifice for sin, the people of Israel wanted Aaron to make a golden calf for them to worship.

They were well aware of God's commandment against idolatry (Ex 20:3). After all, Moses had told them what God had said. And the people had ratified the agreement: "We will do everything that the Lord has commanded" (Ex 24:3). But just like us, they had the "out of sight, out of mind" mind-set. After all, Moses disappeared for 40 days. He might be dead, for all they knew. They needed *something* to worship—a god they could see.

Instead of taking a stand against idol worship, Aaron gave in and later tried to rationalize his actions. Was it *his* fault that the people wanted to sin? And didn't he try to remind them that they were making a big mistake? (see Ex 32:5). But the sad fact remains that he was part of the problem rather than part of the solution.

Sooner or later you might be faced with a decision like Aaron's—to take a stand for what's right or to give in to the wants of others. Will you stand or will you cave?

YOUR CHOICE

When are you most tempted to give in to the pressure of those around you?

THE BIG PICTURE

EX 40:1–38

FEBRUARY 17

DAY 48

SNAPSHOT

EXODUS 40:34–38

The cloud covered the tent of meeting, and the glory of the LORD filled the tabernacle. Moses was unable to enter the tent of meeting because the cloud rested on it, and the glory of the LORD filled the tabernacle.

The Israelites set out whenever the cloud was taken up from the tabernacle throughout all the stages of their journey. If the cloud was not taken up, they did not set out until the day it was taken up. For the cloud of the LORD was over the tabernacle by day, and there was a fire inside the cloud by night, visible to the entire house of Israel throughout all the stages of their journey.

DEPOSIT

WORDS FROM GOD'S WORD TO STORE IN YOUR MIND AND HEART

The cloud covered the tent of meeting, and the glory of the LORD filled the tabernacle (Ex 40:34).

FEBRUARY 18

DAY 49

THE BIG PICTURE

NM 12:1–16

SNAPSHOT

NUMBERS 12:2,9–11

They said, "Does the LORD speak only through Moses? Does He not also speak through us?" And the LORD heard it.

The LORD's anger burned against them, and He left.

As the cloud moved away from the tent, Miriam's skin suddenly became diseased, as white as snow. When Aaron turned toward her, he saw that she was diseased and said to Moses, "My lord, please don't hold against us this sin we have so foolishly committed."

YOUR TURN

JEALOUSY

What do you do when you find yourself feeling jealous of someone?

NM 13:1–14:4

DAY 50

SNAPSHOT

NUMBERS 13:30–31

Then Caleb quieted the people in the presence of Moses and said, "We must go up and take possession of the land because we can certainly conquer it!"

But the men who had gone up with him responded, "We can't go up against the people because they are stronger than we are!"

YOUR CHOICE

Will you believe the corroborating word of those who've seen God prove Himself true, or will you follow those who doubt and then give up?

NO BRAINER

DUE DILIGENCE

Twelve men, twelve points of view. Ten saw Canaan as a terrifying place, full of walled cities and giants. "We saw ourselves as grasshoppers next to them," they exclaimed to the listening crowds, "and what's even scarier, that's how they saw us too!" Ooh! the listening people moaned in unison. We'll never be able to take this land for ourselves!"

But two of the reconnaissance team presented a contrary, minority report. They had seen the same land, the same cities, and the same giants, even—yet they saw it all differently. They saw Canaan from the perspective of God's promise.

"Let's go up and take this place!" they shouted joyfully. "We can do this." And they really believed it because, well, simply because God had said they would do it. God never makes small talk or idle chatter. If God says He will do something, we can build our lives on that promise.

In this case, God had repeatedly told His people that He would bring them to a wonderful land of abundance. Not that long ago, He had freed them from the pharaoh of Egypt and his powerful army. Now, under the Lord's guidance, they would take the next step. The spies had seen the land and had confirmed the fertility of the land. "It is indeed, just as God said, a land 'flowing with milk and honey'," they affirmed. Yet they fearfully advised against going forward.

So, what will the people choose: to believe God's promise and the testimony of the two faithful witnesses, or to believe the ten naysayers who lacked courage or faith? Sadly, they chose against God's way and, subsequently, wandered in the wilderness for decades.

We face similar choices almost daily. We have God's promises in Scripture and the testimony of millions who have gone before. Why wouldn't we obey?

FEBRUARY 20

DAY 51

THE BIG PICTURE

NM 14:5–45

SNAPSHOT **NUMBERS 14:6–8** Joshua son of Nun and Caleb son of Jephunneh, who were among those who scouted out the land, tore their clothes and said to the entire Israelite community: "The land we passed through and explored is an extremely good land. If the Lord is pleased with us, He will bring us into this land, a land flowing with milk and honey, and give it to us."

TOUGH CHOICE

PEER PRESSURE

Economics notes, English book and binder, Spanish flashcards . . . I stuffed study materials into my backpack, checking off everything I would need in order to study for next week's exams.

"Come on, Einstein, we're going to be late for practice." Greg, one of my classmates and teammates, walked up beside me, lugging his track bag. I scanned the books in my locker one more time. "Ah, math book." I grabbed the thick textbook, slammed the locker door, and turned down the hallway toward the gym.

"Why are you bothering with the calc book?" he asked, jogging to keep up.

I looked over at Greg incredulously, but the look on his face was matter-of-fact. Are you kidding me?" I scoffed, "Greg, our final exam is on Monday. I'm spending half the weekend on this exam alone!"

"Why? It's going to be a breeze."

Totally perplexed, I asked, "Greg, what are you talking about? Dr. Sanders said that this is going to be the hardest test we've had yet, and you're not studying for it?"

"Why would I when we've got a copy of the exam?"

I stopped dead in my tracks. "What?"

"We've got a copy of the test. Max saw it lying in Sanders's printer and swiped it between classes. Hello 'A' on the calc final!" Greg looked like a kid in a candy store.

I felt sick, like I'd just eaten too *much* candy. "You mean, you're going to use the test . . . cheat?"

Greg lowered his voice, "Jake, the whole class knows that Max has the exam. Sanders has pounded us all year with his tests, and we all need good grades on this exam so that colleges aren't seeing Ds and Fs on our transcripts right before acceptance letters go out." He hesitated and then looked back at me, "So yes, I am going to look at the test, and so is everybody else. If you want to pass, you probably ought to as well."

I had trouble focusing during practice. All I could think about was what Greg had told me in the hallway, *"Everybody's going to use it; we need good grades for college."* It was *true;* I did need to pull off a miracle grade on the final to keep above a C. I also had three other exams to study for that weekend.

Back in the locker room, I sat down on the bench as people began to leave for the weekend. Bowing my head in my hands I prayed, *Lord, I know what my classmates are doing is wrong. I need to do well on this test, though. Help me to do what's right, what's pleasing to you. Amen.*

When I looked up, Greg was standing at the end of the row. "Listen, Jake, call me when you want to go over the exam. It's going to make life a lot easier!" He turned to go.

"Greg!" I shouted. He turned back around, "I won't be using the exam. That won't make life easier . . . not for me, at least. But feel free to come over and study this weekend if you decide to change your mind."

He laughed, walking away shaking his head. "I just don't get you sometimes, Jake."

YOUR CHOICE **What are you feeling pressured to do that you know you shouldn't?**

THE BIG PICTURE

NM 21:4–9

FEBRUARY 21

DAY 52

SNAPSHOT

NUMBERS 21:5–6

The people spoke against God and Moses: "Why have you led us up from Egypt to die in the wilderness? There is no bread or water, and we detest this wretched food!" Then the LORD sent poisonous snakes among the people, and they bit them so that many Israelites died.

The people then came to Moses and said, "We have sinned by speaking against the LORD and against you. Intercede with the LORD so that He will take the snakes away from us."

And Moses interceded for the people. Then the LORD said to Moses, "Make a snake image and mount it on a pole. When anyone who is bitten looks at it, he will recover." So Moses made a bronze snake and mounted it on a pole. Whenever someone was bitten, and he looked at the bronze snake, he recovered.

ANCHOR POINT

A NOT-SO-FINE WINE

This passage contains many profound truths: the healing power of faith as evidenced by those who simply looked at the bronze snake (Christ alluded to this story in predicting His death on the cross); Moses interceding for the people; the powerful judgment of God as well as His willingness to forgive and save. But here's an important one we could easily overlook: stop complaining.

Actually, like the Israelites, we are pretty good at complaining. This fine whine may come from immaturity or inexperience. But, perhaps it results from a feeling of entitlement; that is, we feel we *deserve* better. Most of our complaints highlight self-centeredness—it's all about us.

Whatever the cause, we have taken complaining to another level. We complain creatively and call it satire. We complain loudly and call it protest. We complain with our friends and call it sarcasm. We complain to companies and call it feedback.

Certainly satire, protest, and feedback have a place but not to so great an extent. Do we really need to focus so intently on what bothers us? What if we were able to release more of those perceived slights and minor irritations? What if we focused on what we *have* and the joys of life rather than what is lacking or causing us distress? This passage highlights what God thinks about it. Imagine the scene if poisonous snakes were to show up whenever someone complained. That would be a good time to start an exterminating business.

YOUR CHOICE

Listen to yourself today. What do you complain about? Why? What does it benefit you? How would your view of life change if you chose to complain less?

DAY 53

SNAPSHOT

NUMBERS 22:34–35

Balaam said to the Angel of the LORD, "I have sinned, for I did not know that You were standing in the path to confront me. And now, if it is evil in Your sight, I will go back."

Then the Angel of the LORD said to Balaam, "Go with the men, but you are to say only what I tell you." So Balaam went with Balak's officials.

YOUR CHOICE

How will you make sure that you control the music you listen to and not the other way around?

TOUGH QUESTION

SOME OF THE MUSIC I LISTEN TO HAVE LYRICS I KNOW GOD (OR MY PARENTS) WOULD NOT APPROVE OF. HOW DOES MY CHOICE OF MUSIC AFFECT ME? WHAT'S SO IMPORTANT ABOUT IT?

In some ways, this question has an obvious answer: Don't listen to those songs. It's that simple—we should never consciously choose to do something that we know God doesn't approve.

But behind your question lies the real issue—what your friends might think of you. We've already discussed the fact that obeying God *may* cost us popularity or friendship, but doing what God wants is much more important than being accepted by a certain person or group.

So if you know that the lyrics to the music you are listening to wouldn't gain the approval of God or your parents, move on and away from the music. Find another beat. So much music is available that you'll be able to find songs you like with better lyrics.

Music is an important aspect of culture that carries with it countless messages. And the messages that we hear and see filter into the mind and heart and affect how we think, believe, feel, and act. Advertisers know this, so they spend tons on broadcasting commercial jingles and on projecting certain images. Music can be a subtle force with strong influences and consequences.

Performers themselves can also influence culture and individuals. Fans of certain artists emulate their lifestyles, which often are in direct opposition to Christian living. "Shock" is another tactic to sell artists and their music. Their actions (dress, lifestyle, statements, etc.) may be shocking at first, but slowly they can be accepted as normal and even funny or cool. What was seen as outrageous a few years ago is seen as normal behavior today.

Music can be a positive or negative force in your life, but you have the control over how much it will influence you. Using godly wisdom, make the right choice.

THE BIG PICTURE

DT 29:1–29

FEBRUARY 23

DAY 54

SNAPSHOT

DEUTERONOMY 29:2–3

Moses summoned all Israel and said to them, "You have seen with your own eyes everything the LORD did in Egypt to Pharaoh, to all his officials, and to his entire land. You saw with your own eyes the great trials and those great signs and wonders."

JUST LIKE ME

MOSES: REVIEWING GOD'S GOODNESS

Coaches often gather their players together to assess the finesse or foibles of their plays. These review sessions serve as a reminder of how far the team has come and also what the team needs to do to stay on their A-game. These coaches want their teams to finish the season well.

While Moses wasn't exactly a coach, he had similar goals in mind for Israel. The best way for them to stay on their A-game was to keep their covenant with God. So he reminded them of where they had come from (Egypt) and what they were about to gain—the promised land of Canaan. They had God to thank for their arrival at this juncture.

Moses' retrospective came toward the end of his life, after 40 years of leading the Israelites. In his role as the deliverer of his people, Moses tried his best and made mistakes—one of which caused God to penalize him (see Nm 20:12). Although Moses would not enter the promised land, he still cared enough about the "team" to make sure they finished well.

Many times, we look forward rather than back. Sometimes a look back can be too painful as we contemplate the mistakes we've made. But we don't have to dwell on the wrongs we've done. Instead, we can recall God's mercy and grace and determine to stay on our A-game.

YOUR CHOICE

How do you keep track of what God has done for you?

FEBRUARY 24

DAY 55

THE BIG PICTURE

DT 30:1–20

SNAPSHOT

DEUTERONOMY 30:1–4

"When all these things happen to you—the blessings and curses I have set before you—and you come to your senses while you are in all the nations where the LORD your God has driven you, and you and your children return to the LORD your God and obey Him with all your heart and all your soul by doing everything I am giving you today, then He will restore your fortunes, have compassion on you, and gather you again from all the peoples where the LORD your God has scattered you. Even if your exiles are at the ends of the earth, He will gather you and bring you back from there."

DEPOSIT

WORDS FROM GOD'S WORD TO STORE IN YOUR MIND AND HEART

"I call heaven and earth as witnesses against you today that I have set before you life and death, blessing and curse. Choose life so that you and your descendants may live, love the LORD your God, obey Him, and remain faithful to Him. For He is your life, and He will prolong your life in the land the LORD swore to give to your fathers Abraham, Isaac, and Jacob" (Dt 30:19–20).

THE BIG PICTURE

DT 31:1–8

FEBRUARY 25

DAY 56

SNAPSHOT

DEUTERONOMY 31:7–8

Moses then summoned Joshua and said to him in the sight of all Israel, "Be strong and courageous, for you will go with this people into the land the LORD swore to give to their fathers. You will enable them to take possession of it. The LORD is the One who will go before you. He will be with you; He will not leave you or forsake you. Do not be afraid or discouraged."

YOUR TURN

STRONG MENTOR

Who is a "Moses" in your life?

FEBRUARY 26

DAY 57

THE BIG PICTURE

DT 34:1–12

NO BRAINER

FINISHING WELL

In Moses' long lifetime he had many opportunities to spectacularly succeed or spectacularly fail. On some of those occasions, it looked as though failure would be the result. Yet somehow, as he leaned hard on God, Moses would see the insurmountable difficulties gradually dwindle or—on other, more dramatic occasions—see his opposition disappear in a thunderous clap of sea water or watch the earth swallow a whole family clan of his adversaries.

Moses had been tempted to give up; the people under his care wearied him with their immaturity and continuous complaining and rebellion. Yet he held steady for 40 years in the wilderness, wandering with his stubborn charges.

But the time had come for Moses to be "gathered to his fathers" as the old Hebrew euphemism for dying put it. He knew it was time because God had told him. He could have whined and complained, "Why can't I go over into the land too, Lord? I've brought them all the way here, to the very edge of the land, the border, but you tell me I'm not to go into the land, just get a look at it from the top of yonder mountain. It's not fair."

Instead, with the same steady, practiced faithfulness, Moses carried out God's final instructions. The first order of business was to appoint and anoint a successor. Relinquishing power to another isn't easy, if you've had it in your own hands for a long time. History is filled with grisly tales of old kings who murdered those who were about to replace them. But Moses brought Joshua out in front of the entire nation, anointed him as his successor, and told the people, "From now on, follow him as you have followed me."

Then, in humility, he obeyed God one last time. With everyone watching, he walked up the mountain. Obedience at the end of life follows, naturally, from a lifetime of obedience.

SNAPSHOT

DEUTERONOMY 34:10–12

No prophet has arisen again in Israel like Moses, whom the LORD knew face to face. He was unparalleled for all the signs and wonders the LORD sent him to do against the land of Egypt—to Pharaoh, to all his officials, and to all his land, and for all the mighty acts of power and terrifying deeds that Moses performed in the sight of all Israel.

YOUR CHOICE

What will you start practicing now, so that you may finish well?

istand

THE BIG PICTURE
JOS 1:1–18

FEBRUARY 27
DAY 58

SNAPSHOT

JOSHUA 1:5–9

"No one will be able to stand against you as long as you live. I will be with you, just as I was with Moses. I will not leave you or forsake you.

"Be strong and courageous, for you will distribute the land I swore to their fathers to give them as an inheritance. Above all, be strong and very courageous to carefully observe the whole instruction My servant Moses commanded you. Do not turn from it to the right or the left, so that you will have success wherever you go. This book of instruction must not depart from your mouth; you are to recite it day and night, so that you may carefully observe everything written in it. For then you will prosper and succeed in whatever you do. Haven't I commanded you: be strong and courageous? Do not be afraid or discouraged, for the LORD your God is with you wherever you go."

JUST LIKE ME

JOSHUA: CHOOSING TO FACE THE CHALLENGES

Newspaper or online want ads list the requirements needed for a particular job. "Must have at least a bachelor's degree; master's degree preferable"; "must have proficiency in all the software needed for the position." Many people might go for a job interview even if they aren't sure they're fully qualified.

God told Joshua about the requirements needed to fill the leadership position vacated by the death of Moses. These requirements can be boiled down to four words: "Be strong and courageous" (Jos 1:6). In other words, "Be willing to take a stand, Joshua, when courage is demanded." You have only to read the Book of Joshua to see how apt that advice was. But Joshua didn't have to stand alone. God promised to be with him. Joshua rose to the challenge, proving that he was the right person for the job.

Maybe your life won't involve conquering a city like Joshua had to do. But other challenges will call for the same characteristics—strength and courage—that God affirmed in Joshua. Or, it may call for the development of other characteristics. The thing is, are you willing to take the plunge like Joshua and do what God wants?

YOUR CHOICE

What challenge are you facing right now?
What courageous choice should you make?

DAY 59

SNAPSHOT

JOSHUA 2:1–7

Joshua son of Nun secretly sent two men as spies from Acacia Grove, saying, "Go and scout the land, especially Jericho." So they left, and they came to the house of a woman, a prostitute named Rahab, and stayed there.

. . . Then the king of Jericho sent word to Rahab and said, "Bring out the men who came to you and entered your house, for they came to investigate the entire land."

But the woman had taken the two men and hidden them. So she said, "Yes, the men did come to me, but I didn't know where they were from. At nightfall, when the gate was about to close, the men went out, and I don't know where they were going. Chase after them quickly, and you can catch up with them!" But she had taken them up to the roof and hidden them among the stalks of flax that she had arranged on the roof.

YOUR CHOICE

When might you feel pressured to treat immorality or false teachings as OK? How will you respond?

TOUGH QUESTION

MY SCHOOL IS REQUIRING US TO LEARN MORE ABOUT WHAT IS "POLITICALLY CORRECT." WHAT CHOICE DO I HAVE WHEN THOSE IN AUTHORITY ARE PRESSURING ME TO ACCEPT BEHAVIOR THAT I THINK IS IMMORAL?

If we look to Jesus and His example, we see Him living and loving people who were the outcasts of society and many in the depths of immorality. He accepted sinful people, loving them just as they were. But he didn't approve of their behavior. Jesus came to save the lost, and He reached out to them, repeatedly. Following Christ's example, we should reach out in love to those who are lost.

But this doesn't mean that we are to *tolerate* sin, in ourselves and others. Unfortunately, "tolerance" seems to have become the highest value in our society. And this word has come to mean "accept without judgment" and, even, "celebrate" the differences among people.

Certainly, in following Christ's example, we need to love all people and see each person as a valued creation of God—regardless of the person's lifestyle, moral code, ethical stance, or religious persuasion. But also following Christ's example, we know that this doesn't mean *approving* what everyone does or says. A person has a right to his or her opinions, for example, but that doesn't mean those opinions are *right* (true). People can be wrong, even sincerely wrong.

Following Jesus' example, you are to be a person of influence, not one influenced by immoral behaviors. You can set your own standards according to God's Word, but you can't hold others to God's standards when they don't have a relationship with Him. Jesus didn't instruct you to be the moral judge of others but of yourself.

Believers are often accused of being intolerant of other people's behavior and beliefs. Jesus spoke to this issue when He taught about loving your enemies and praying for those who persecute you. Imitating Jesus, and loving the people around us no matter their lifestyle, sexual preference, or religion, should shape how we live.

MAART
MARAS
MARZ
MARCH
MARZO
MARCO
MARCHA

JOSHUA 3:16b–17

SNAPSHOT

The water flowing downstream into the Sea of the Arabah (the Dead Sea) was completely cut off, and the people crossed opposite Jericho. The priests carrying the ark of the LORD's covenant stood firmly on dry ground in the middle of the Jordan, while all Israel crossed on dry ground until the entire nation had finished crossing the Jordan.

MARCH 1

DAY 60

THE BIG PICTURE

JOS 3:1–17

TOUGH CHOICE

GUIDANCE

I flipped my cell phone shut and stared at it. *Is this really happening?*

"Who was that?" Annie, my college girlfriend, walked into the room carrying two plates of cheesecake. We had just returned from a celebratory graduation dinner and had brought dessert back to my house.

"Phil Savage," I said in disbelief.

"Who?"

"The Cleveland Browns' general manager." I looked up from my phone at her. Her eyebrows peaked, as she set the plates down on the coffee table in front of me.

"Well," she began, sitting down next to me, "what did he want to talk to you about?"

I shook my head. "They want me to try out for the team." Saying the words aloud made them sound even more unbelievable. My coaches and family had urged me to try and play in the NFL, but I had put the thought of playing pro football behind me after the draft had passed without any calls.

"When are try-outs?" Annie asked quietly, her big eyes full of questions.

"They want me in Cleveland tomorrow morning," I said, no longer hungry for the uneaten cheesecake in front of me.

"That's fast," she said, pausing for a moment. "What are you thinking?"

"I mean, I'm really excited. It's the Browns . . . it's just so unexpected! What about grad school? If I make the team, I'll have to turn my acceptance down. And then there's Eddy's wedding this summer. I'm a groomsman. I might have to miss that. It's . . . it's just a lot. Fast." It was all so fantastic. This was a dream come true, but not at all under the circumstances I had anticipated.

"What are you going to do?" Annie's words reeled me back into the room. She was calm.

"I don't know," I said honestly. "What do you think I should do?"

She tilted her head and looked earnestly at me. I knew she couldn't be thrilled about the call. It would mean a seven-hour drive just to see each other. We had talked about the possibility before. "You have to try out," she said rather suddenly. "It looked like this door had been closed, but clearly the Lord has swung it wide open. I really think you need to go up to Cleveland." Her voice quivered a bit, and she swallowed hard.

"I always wanted this, but there are so many uncertainties." My thoughts wouldn't slow down.

"John," Annie grabbed my hand, "God has opened this door, and you need to have faith that He wants you to walk through it. He will provide you with answers in due time. As believers, we are called to take leaps of faith. This is one of those times!" She didn't take her eyes off me. She was right.

I nodded my head and closed my eyes. *Lord, this is an opportunity I've dreamed about all my life. It's so sudden and I thought that this chance had passed me by, but if it's Your will that I try out and make this team, please guide me as I take a step of faith. Help me to trust You and to glorify You around the other players. Thank You for always being present. Amen.*

YOUR CHOICE **How would you illustrate God's guidance in your life?**

DAY 61

SNAPSHOT

JOSHUA 6:15–20

Early on the seventh day, they started at dawn and marched around the city seven times in the same way. That was the only day they marched around the city seven times. After the seventh time, the priests blew the trumpets, and Joshua said to the people, "Shout! For the Lord has given you the city. But the city and everything in it are set apart to the Lord for destruction. Only Rahab the prostitute and everyone with her in the house will live, because she hid the men we sent. But keep yourselves from the things set apart, or you will be set apart for destruction. If you take any of those things, you will set apart the camp of Israel for destruction and bring disaster on it. For all the silver and gold, and the articles of bronze and iron, are dedicated to the Lord and must go into the Lord's treasury."

So the people shouted, and the trumpets sounded. When they heard the blast of the trumpet, the people gave a great shout, and the wall collapsed.

ANCHOR POINT

FOR GOD'S USE

At times, doing what God wants can look pretty foolish. Imagine, for example, what the people of Jericho thought as they looked out over their city walls to see thousands of Israelites marching around, day after day. "Is this the mighty army of God? What new war tactic is this, anyway—are they trying to bore us to death? Make us dizzy?" Imagine the mockery that God's people endured as they made their daily trek around the walls. No weapons, no point of attack, just walking, not even a word spoken all day long.

Many of the actions and attitudes that God want us to choose will seem foolish to those who don't know God and don't look at life from His point of view. Why wait until you are married? Why not get drunk? Why can't people choose alternative lifestyles? Who is to say they are wrong?

Defending a God-centered worldview can sometimes feel like marching silently around a city wall—utterly foolish (until the walls fall down). In fact, in 1 Corinthians 1:18, Paul states that the cross is *foolishness* to those who don't believe in Christ. We are called to stand for things that sometimes don't seem to make a lot of sense—"because God said so" doesn't cut it—but it's right. We need to faithfully do what God has asked us to do and let Him deal with the "walls."

YOUR CHOICE

When do you find it difficult to stand as a follower of Christ? How do you react when friends and others mock you for your "foolish" faith? Choose God's way and trust Him for the final outcome.

JOS 7:1–26

DAY 62

SNAPSHOT

JOSHUA 7:3–7,10–11

After returning to Joshua they reported to him, "Don't send all the people, but send about 2,000 or 3,000 men to attack Ai. Since the people of Ai are so few, don't wear out all our people there." So about 3,000 men went up there, but they fled from the men of Ai. The men of Ai struck down about 36 of them and chased them from outside the gate to the quarries, striking them down on the descent. As a result, the people's hearts melted and became like water.

Then Joshua tore his clothes and fell before the ark of the LORD with his face to the ground until evening, as did the elders of Israel; they all put dust on their heads. "Oh, Lord GOD," Joshua said, "why did You ever bring these people across the Jordan to hand us over to the Amorites for our destruction? If only we had been content to remain on the other side of the Jordan."

The LORD then said to Joshua, "Stand up! Why are you on the ground? Israel has sinned. They have violated My covenant that I appointed for them. They have taken some of what was set apart. They have stolen, deceived, and put [the things] with their own belongings."

DEPOSIT

WORDS FROM GOD'S WORD TO STORE IN YOUR MIND AND HEART

"This book of instruction must not depart from your mouth; you are to recite it day and night, so that you may carefully observe everything written in it. For then you will prosper and succeed in whatever you do" (Jos 1:8).

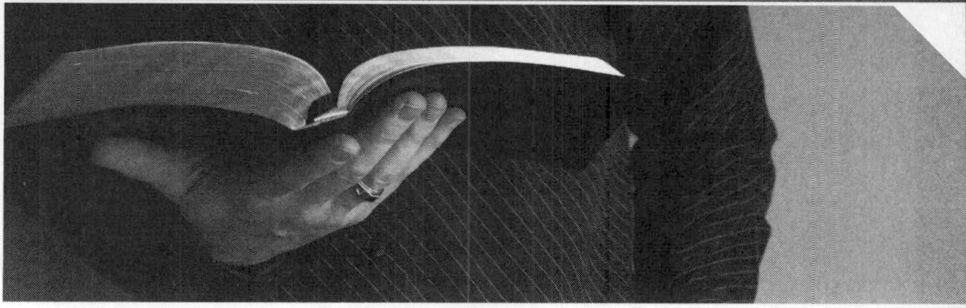

DAY 63

THE BIG PICTURE
JOS 10:1–15

SNAPSHOT

JOSHUA 10:12–14

On the day the LORD gave the Amorites over to the Israelites, Joshua spoke to the LORD in the presence of Israel:

"Sun, stand still over Gibeon,
and moon, over the valley of Aijalon."
And the sun stood still
and the moon stopped,
until the nation took vengeance on its enemies.
Isn't this written in the Book of Jashar?
So the sun stopped
in the middle of the sky
and delayed its setting
almost a full day.

There has been no day like it before or since, when the LORD listened to the voice of a man, because the LORD fought for Israel. Then Joshua and all Israel with him returned to the camp at Gilgal.

YOUR TURN

A MIGHTY GOD

How do you know God is powerful?

TOUGH QUESTION

I'M A NEW CHRISTIAN, AND MY PARENTS OFTEN RIDICULE MY FAITH. HOW SHOULD I CHOOSE TO RESPOND TO THEIR NEGATIVE AND HURTFUL COMMENTS?

Humility is the best and most Christlike response to any kind of ridicule or persecution. That's a difficult but necessary choice to make.

When we take a close look at Jesus in the pages of the New Testament, we find Him continuously responding gently and humbly to those who questioned, harassed, and eventually killed Him. The natural response to someone who makes fun of us would be defensiveness and anger. But that's not the Jesus way.

We can become discouraged when parents, siblings, or close friends and relatives don't accept our professions of faith or, worse yet, treat us poorly because of what we believe. So we need to keep our focus on God and what He thinks of us. And it helps to remember that Jesus suffered much worse at the hands of the Pharisees and the Romans.

Sometimes the best response is silence—simply saying nothing, no excuses, reasons, arguments, or snappy comebacks. Other times call for a measured, verbal answer; but, even then, it should be given with calm sincerity.

Let your actions be your best argument for the reality of your faith. Choose to live the right way—loving, serving, and honoring your parents. Remember to pray for them as well. Perhaps they will be drawn to Christ through the way you live.

SNAPSHOT

JOSHUA 23:6–8,12–13

"Be very strong, and continue obeying all that is written in the book of the law of Moses, so that you do not turn from it to the right or left and so that you do not associate with these nations remaining among you. Do not call on the names of their gods or make an oath to them; do not worship them or bow down to them. Instead, remain faithful to the LORD your God, as you have done to this day."

"For if you turn away and cling to the rest of these nations remaining among you, and if you intermarry or associate with them and they with you, know for certain that the LORD your God will not continue to drive these nations out before you. They will become a snare and a trap for you, a scourge for your sides and thorns in your eyes, until you disappear from this good land the LORD your God has given you."

YOUR CHOICE

What will you say or do when someone you love belittles your faith?

DAY 65

THE BIG PICTURE
JOS 24:1–31

NO BRAINER

HOPE TO HISTORY

Joshua had been taking stands throughout his entire life. He had been one of two spies who had given a good report about Canaan, he had trusted God to divide the Jordan River, and he had marched around Jericho. After a lifetime of courageous choices, why would his death be any different?

Instead of reviewing his own life, Joshua summarized what God had done throughout Israel's history. He began with Abraham, describing how God led him out of a polytheistic society and into something greater. Joshua reminded the people that God freed them from the Egyptians, protecting them even when they had their backs to the Red Sea. Countless times, the Israelites were victorious over their obstacles because of God's mighty works.

Joshua did not stop there. He challenged the people to put away their idols and serve the Lord wholeheartedly. Joshua took a stand, saying, "As for me and my family, we will worship the Lord" (Jos 24:15). He didn't wait for the people to respond first; he told them directly where he stood. His statement implied that no matter what the rest of the Israelites were going to do, he would always serve his God.

That's one aspect of making courageous decisions. You can't always wait to see how everyone else acts. At times, you will have to make the first decision and take a stand before anyone else does anything. People may follow your example, but some may not. We need to be willing to make the first move and set an example by taking a stand from the beginning.

Checking motives is an important part of taking a stand. We need to make sure that we are not making decisions just because we want to be admired for our courage or be recognized for our leadership. We should be taking stands because we want to remain obedient to God and to live according to His Word.

SNAPSHOT

JOSHUA 24:14–18

"Therefore, fear the Lord and worship Him in sincerity and truth. Get rid of the gods your ancestors worshiped beyond the Euphrates River and in Egypt, and worship the Lord. But if it doesn't please you to worship the Lord, choose for yourselves today the one you will worship: the gods your fathers worshiped beyond the Euphrates River, or the gods of the Amorites in whose land you are living. As for me and my family, we will worship the Lord."

The people replied, "We will certainly not abandon the Lord to worship other gods! For the Lord our God brought us and our fathers out of the land of Egypt, the place of slavery and performed these great signs before our eyes. He also protected us all along the way we went and among all the peoples whose lands we traveled through. The Lord drove out before us all the peoples, including the Amorites who lived in the land. We too will worship the Lord, because He is our God."

YOUR CHOICE

Who is watching you to see what you will do and then follow your example?

THE BIG PICTURE

JDG 4:4–24

MARCH 7

DAY 66

SNAPSHOT

JUDGES 4:8–9

Barak said to her, "If you will go with me, I will go. But if you will not go with me, I will not go."

"I will go with you," she said, "but you will receive no honor on the road you are about to take, because the LORD will sell Sisera into a woman's hand." So Deborah got up and went with Barak to Kedesh.

JUST LIKE ME

DEBORAH: WILLING TO GO

Some people go the extra mile to show their concern for others. The lives of Mother Teresa and Francis of Assisi are proof of that. But what about Deborah? She was a wife and mother as well as a prophet and judge of Israel. So she had tons of people to be concerned about. But beyond that, Deborah went the extra mile by going to war against the enemies of Israel simply because she was asked to do so.

After giving God's marching orders to Barak, the chosen commander of Israel's army, Deborah barely blinked when Barak made his counteroffer—"I will go, but only if you go with me" (Jdg 4:8). Despite the risks, Deborah said yes. So, when Barak and the army faced the army of the Canaanites, there was Deborah shouting encouragement. Her actions probably left Barak without a doubt that Deborah *actually* cared, rather than someone who simply talked about caring.

God may lead you out of your comfort zone in order to help a friend or a family member. How far would you go to help someone you cared about?

YOUR CHOICE

What will you do to show your concern for others?

SNAPSHOT

JUDGES 6:36–40

Then Gideon said to God, "If You will deliver Israel by my hand, as You said, I will put a fleece of wool here on the threshing floor. If dew is only on the fleece, and all the ground is dry, I will know that You will deliver Israel by my strength, as You said." And that is what happened. When he got up early in the morning, he squeezed the fleece and wrung dew out of it, filling a bowl with water.

Gideon then said to God, "Don't be angry with me; let me speak one more time. Please allow me to make one more test with the fleece. Let it remain dry, and the dew be all over the ground." That night God did as Gideon requested: only the fleece was dry, and dew was all over the ground.

OBEDIENCE

What altars have you built? For example, do you have an altar to the god of materialism? How do money and possessions consume your attention and time? In what ways do you "worship" at this altar?

Or, perhaps, you have an altar to popularity. How does that god affect your life each day? What decisions do you make based on what others will think of you?

Or you may be tempted to have personal achievement at your life's center. If so, what have you sacrificed on that altar?

Whatever your false gods and altars, God wants you to destroy them. This may involve, as it did for Gideon, a very public element. Destroying the altar to the god of materialism may involve giving up certain activities (like shopping, for example) or giving away possessions. In turning from other gods, you may have to stop hanging around certain people or scale back on certain activities. Your friends will wonder what's up with you when you make these changes.

When that happens, make another choice: Instead of making lame excuses, simply state that God wants you to do things differently? Will you have the guts to say He asked you to tear down an altar to a false god?

YOUR CHOICE

What altars in your life need to be torn down?
What step can you take today to begin the process?

THE BIG PICTURE

JDG 7:1–25

MARCH 9

DAY 68

SNAPSHOT

JUDGES 7:9–15

That night the LORD said to him, "Get up and go into the camp, for I have given it into your hand. But if you are afraid to go to the camp, go with Purah your servant. Listen to what they say, and then you will be strengthened to go to the camp." So he went with Purah his servant to the outpost of the troops who were in the camp.

Now the Midianites, Amalekites, and all the Qedemites had settled down in the valley like a swarm of locusts, and their camels were as innumerable as the sand on the seashore. When Gideon arrived, there was a man telling his friend about a dream. He said, "Listen, I had a dream: a loaf of barley bread came tumbling into the Midianite camp, struck a tent, and it fell. The loaf turned the tent upside down so that it collapsed."

His friend answered: "This is nothing less than the sword of Gideon son of Joash, the Israelite. God has handed the entire Midianite camp over to him."

When Gideon heard the account of the dream and its interpretation, he bowed in worship. He returned to Israel's camp and said, "Get up, for the LORD has handed the Midianite camp over to you."

JUST LIKE ME

GIDEON: TRUSTING GOD'S CHOICES

How much do you trust God? Eventually Gideon thought he trusted God enough to lead the people against their enemies—the Midianites. Getting to that point of trust took a long conversation with the angel of the Lord and a miracle of God.

Obviously believing he had safety in numbers, Gideon amassed an impressive army of 32,000 men. But God crunched the numbers and came up with 300 that He wanted to use. Seeing as how the Midianites "were as innumerable as the sand on the seashore"—too many to count (Jdg 7:12), defeating them would seem a challenge indeed. But God had a point to make in proposing such a small fighting force—He wanted everyone to know that Israel would be victorious because of Him. And God later provided assurance of victory during a night-time reconnaissance.

Gideon could have pouted or put on an air of martyrdom when told that he would face a seemingly invincible army with just 300 guys. Instead, he trusted God to make up the deficit.

What are your "deficits"? You know the ones—the situations in which you're tempted to feel inadequate. Are you willing to trust God's choices for you, even when you're not sure of the outcome?

YOUR CHOICE

In what area of your life do you need to trust God more?

MARCH 10

DAY 69

THE BIG PICTURE

JDG 13:1–25

SNAPSHOT

JUDGES 13:2–5

There was a certain man from Zorah, from the family of Dan, whose name was Manoah; his wife was barren and had no children. The Angel of the Lord appeared to the woman and said to her, "It is true that you are barren and have no children, but you will conceive and give birth to a son. Now please be careful not to drink wine or other alcoholic beverages, or to eat anything unclean; for indeed, you will conceive and give birth to a son. You must never cut his hair, because the boy will be a Nazirite to God from birth, and he will begin to save Israel from the power of the Philistines."

DEPOSIT

WORDS FROM GOD'S WORD TO STORE IN YOUR MIND AND HEART.

"But if it doesn't please you to worship the Lord, choose for yourselves today the one you will worship: the gods your fathers worshiped beyond the Euphrates River, or the gods of the Amorites in whose land you are living. As for me and my family, we will worship the Lord" (Jos 24:15).

istand

THE BIG PICTURE

JDG 14:1–20

MARCH 11

DAY 70

SNAPSHOT

JUDGES 14:1–3

Samson went down to Timnah and saw a young Philistine woman there. He went back and told his father and his mother: "I have seen a young Philistine woman in Timnah. Now get her for me as a wife."

But his father and mother said to him, "Can't you find a young woman among your relatives or among any of our people? Must you go to the uncircumcised Philistines for a wife?"

But Samson told his father, "Get her for me, because I want her."

YOUR TURN

SAMSON'S RIDDLE

Earlier this week, you read about Joshua. You can contrast his life with Samson. One knew how to take a stand; the other wandered through life. How carefully do you consider the wisdom of your parents?

MARCH 12

DAY 71

THE BIG PICTURE

JDG 15:1–20

SNAPSHOT

JUDGES 15:12–15

They said to him, "We've come to arrest you and hand you over to the Philistines." Then Samson told them, "Swear to me that you yourselves won't kill me."

"No," they said, "we won't kill you, but we will tie you up securely and hand you over to them." So they tied him up with two new ropes and led him away from the rock.

When he came to Lehi, the Philistines came to meet him shouting. The Spirit of the LORD took control of him, and the ropes that were on his arms became like burnt flax and his bonds fell off his wrists. He found a fresh jawbone of a donkey, reached out his hand, took it, and killed 1,000 men with it.

YOUR CHOICE

Who will you ask to mentor you in your Christian walk?

TOUGH QUESTION

WHAT PROOF DO YOU HAVE THAT MISTAKES USUALLY DON'T CORRECT THEMSELVES?

Making a major change and heading in a new direction after living a self-centered life can be difficult. It will take discipline, determination, and strength, but you can do it with Christ working in you (Php 4:13). Live for Christ one day, one step, at a time. The big choice here is to spend time daily reading the Bible and talking with God about your needs. You don't need to make a big announcement about your new life; people will see the changes and, like you, be amazed at God's work in you.

A mentor will also help in this life transition. This should be a more mature Christian who can encourage you and hold you accountable. People will know you as a certain kind of person, and you may find it difficult to outlive your reputation. And be careful—it's easy to fall back into old habits. That's why a mentor can be such a great help for keeping you on track as he or she asks you the tough questions and provides support.

Friends are a huge influence, so your choice of friends can determine the direction your life takes. If your friends push you to party, you probably will need to find a new group of friends. That can be tough, and may mean losing popularity and walking a lonely road for a while. But your life will be headed in the right direction. Continue to pray for those old friends; God may give you a future opportunity to influence them for Him.

DAY 72

THE BIG PICTURE

JDG 16:1–21

SNAPSHOT

JUDGES 16:16–17

Because she nagged him day after day and pled with him until she wore him out, he told her the whole truth and said to her, "My hair has never been cut, because I am a Nazirite to God from birth. If I am shaved, my strength will leave me, and I will become weak and be like any other man."

TOUGH CHOICE

POPULAR

I was convinced that Jeremy would be able to hear my heart pounding, as I pressed my ear to the phone. As fast as my heart was beating, though, my mind was racing even faster.

What do I say? What do I say? The question ricocheted through my mind. Jeremy was captain of the soccer team and one of the most well-liked and popular guys in the senior class. He was smart, funny. He even had a regular attendance record at youth group. Our friendship had started in trigonometry class earlier that year. The small talk that had begun during class had led to some really great phone conversations and lunch-time discussions.

"Uh . . . Rachel? Are you still there?" *Even his voice is attractive.*

"Yeah, I'm still here," I said a bit hesitantly.

My excitement was dampened by the rest of Jeremy's reputation, though. He was the guy that everyone wanted at their parties, mainly because he was sure to be *wildly* entertaining. He had dated a long list of girls, none of whom had gleaming reputations. And his behavior on the soccer field was colorful at times, to say the least.

"So what's it going to be, Rachel? Will you come to J.D.'s party with me this Saturday night?"

My palms were sweaty and my throat was dry. "Oh, Jeremy, I don't know. I know it would be a ton of fun . . ." *and bring me a bit of popularity,* ". . . but . . ." *I also know that starting a relationship with you could encourage me to compromise things that my faith is very clear about,* ". . . I'm not going to be able to go with you on Saturday night."

YOUR CHOICE

Where will you draw the line between having fun in the present and committing to God's purpose for your life?

THE BIG PICTURE
JDG 16:22–31

SNAPSHOT

JUDGES 16:27–30

The temple was full of men and women; all the leaders of the Philistines were there, and about 3,000 men and women were on the roof watching Samson entertain them. He called out to the LORD: "Lord GOD, please remember me. Strengthen me, God, just once more. With one act of vengeance, let me pay back the Philistines for my two eyes." Samson took hold of the two middle pillars supporting the temple and leaned against them, one on his right hand and the other on his left. Samson said, "Let me die with the Philistines." He pushed with all his might, and the temple fell on the leaders and all the people in it. And the dead he killed at his death were more than those he had killed in his life.

ANCHOR POINT

GOD'S PATIENCE

Regardless of what you have done, or even what you will do, God still can use you as long as you return to Him and submit to His leadership and guidance. Samson had squandered his gift of strength. He had married against God's plan and had paid a terrible price. Yet blind and enslaved, he cried out to God and was heard. Samson had been called to a very specific task—to free God's people from their enemies, and, in this situation, to kill his captors, the Philistines. Samson was able to do what he was called to do because he wholeheartedly gave himself to God.

You may feel as though God is distant. You may have wandered down a path that has led to pain and suffering for yourself and those around you. You may even feel blinded or enslaved to your current circumstances. So right now you may feel useless to God. But nothing could be further from the truth.

Certainly your calling is quite different from Samson's (no Philistines in sight these days), but God has a purpose for your life, a vital role for you to play in His plan. If you have chosen a different, a wrong, path or if you believe you have failed God, don't despair or give up. Turn back to God and ask Him to forgive you. He will! Choose to turn your life around with His help.

YOUR CHOICE

What from your past still haunts you?
How can you release it to God?

SNAPSHOT

RUTH 1:11–17

But Naomi replied, "Return home, my daughters. Why do you want to go with me? Am I able to have any more sons who could become your husbands? Return home, my daughters. Go on, for I am too old to have another husband…"

…But Ruth replied:

Do not persuade me to leave you or go back and not follow you.

For wherever you go, I will go, and wherever you live, I will live;

your people will be my people, and your God will be my God.

Where you die, I will die, and there I will be buried.

May the LORD do this to me, and even more,

if anything but death separates you and me.

YOUR CHOICE

What decision are you hesitant to make because of the possible cost?

NO BRAINER

RIGHT FRIENDS AND LASTING RELATIONSHIPS

Naomi's life had fallen apart. She had lost her husband, her sons, and was living in a foreign country. The only thing she had left were two widowed daughters-in-law, Orpah and Ruth. The news that Judah had been blessed with a good harvest was a source of hope for the three women, so they decided to travel to Naomi's hometown.

On the way, Naomi told Orpah and Ruth to go back to their homes in Moab so they could find husbands for themselves there. Naomi made the courageous decision to be selfless. She could have easily remained silent and kept her companions, but she chose to put Ruth and Orpah's needs before her own. Naomi knew that she did not have anything to offer them, so she made the sacrificial choice of letting them go.

After finally being convinced that heading home would be the best option, Orpah kissed her mother-in-law goodbye and left. Ruth, however, refused to leave Naomi's side. She chose to travel to Judah, saying that she would go wherever Naomi went and would live where Naomi lived. She gave up her right to return home and find a new husband among her own people in order to remain with her mother-in-law.

Sometimes, taking a stand means giving things up. Just like Naomi gave up one of her companions and Ruth gave up her homeland and the hope of a new husband, you may have to sacrifice something as a result of taking a stand. You may have to give up a certain activity that is wrong, a relationship that is unhealthy, or you may lose friends when you take a stand for something. Don't think that making courageous decisions will be easy. Remember that taking a stand may cost you, but it is well worth it.

MARCH 16

DAY 75

THE BIG PICTURE

RU 2:1–23

SNAPSHOT

RUTH 2:10–14

She bowed with her face to the ground and said to him, "Why are you so kind to notice me, although I am a foreigner?"

Boaz answered her, "Everything you have done for your mother-in-law since your husband's death has been fully reported to me: how you left your father and mother, and the land of your birth, and how you came to a people you didn't previously know. May the LORD reward you for what you have done, and may you receive a full reward from the LORD God of Israel, under whose wings you have come for refuge."

"My lord," she said, "you have been so kind to me, for you have comforted and encouraged your slave, although I am not like one of your female servants."

At mealtime Boaz told her, "Come over here and have some bread and dip it in the vinegar sauce." So she sat beside the harvesters, and he offered her roasted grain. She ate and was satisfied and had some left over.

JUST LIKE ME

RUTH AND NAOMI: SEEKING GOD'S BEST

"I've heard about you." When have you heard someone say that about you? How did that person look when he or she made that statement?

Boaz, a relative of the widow Naomi, had similar words for Ruth, the Moabite widow. Ruth did not have to do her own PR. Her sterling reputation as a hard worker and a loyal daughter-in-law had preceded her. In fact, everyone knew that she was a woman of quality.

Because of Ruth's love and loyalty, which had been proven during her move from Moab to Bethlehem, Naomi sought the best husband for her. And the best candidate was Boaz, the kindly landowner and Naomi's close relative. Boaz already had proven his compassion and character by providing for Ruth as she gleaned grain. Consequently, Naomi recognized God working behind the scenes to bring about this blessing for Ruth.

An impressed Boaz acknowledged that given the choice, Ruth could have pursued a younger man. But instead Ruth followed her mother-in-law's advice by seeking God's best.

Seeking God's best does not mean you're on an ego trip. It simply means you acknowledge that God knows what's best for you. Ruth was willing to trust her entire life to God's leading. Are you?

YOUR CHOICE

Where do you sense God is leading you these days?

RU 3:1–18

MARCH 17

DAY 76

SNAPSHOT

RUTH 3:7–13

After Boaz ate, drank, and was in good spirits, he went to lie down at the end of the pile of barley. Then she went in secretly, uncovered his feet, and lay down.

At midnight, Boaz was startled, turned over, and there lying at his feet was a woman! So he asked, "Who are you?"

"I am Ruth, your slave," she replied. "Spread your cloak over me, for you are a family redeemer."

Then he said, "May the Lord bless you, my daughter. You have shown more kindness now than before, because you have not pursued younger men, whether rich or poor. Now don't be afraid, my daughter. I will do for you whatever you say, since all the people in my town know that you are a woman of noble character. Yes, it is true that I am a family redeemer, but there is a redeemer closer than I am. Stay here tonight, and in the morning, if he wants to redeem you, that's good. Let him redeem you. But if he doesn't want to redeem you, as the Lord lives, I will. Now, lie down until morning."

DEPOSIT

WORDS FROM GOD'S WORD TO STORE IN YOUR MIND AND HEART

But Ruth replied: "Do not persuade me to leave you or go back and not follow you. For wherever you go, I will go, and wherever you live, I will live; your people will be my people, and your God will by my God.Where you die, I will die, and there I will be buried. May the Lord do this to me, and even more, if anything but death separates you and me" (Ru 1:16–17).

MARCH 18

DAY 77

THE BIG PICTURE

RU 4:1–22

SNAPSHOT

RUTH 4:13–17

Boaz took Ruth and she became his wife. When he was intimate with her, the LORD enabled her to conceive, and she gave birth to a son. Then the women said to Naomi, "Praise the LORD, who has not left you without a family redeemer today. May his name be famous in Israel. He will renew your life and sustain you in your old age. Indeed, your daughter-in-law, who loves you and is better to you than seven sons, has given birth to him." Naomi took the child, placed him on her lap, and took care of him. The neighbor women said, "A son has been born to Naomi," and they named him Obed. He was the father of Jesse, the father of David.

YOUR TURN

A HAPPY ENDING

What future reasons could there be for obeying God today?

SNAPSHOT

1 SAMUEL 1:11, 24–28

Making a vow, she pleaded, "Lord of Hosts, if You will take notice of Your servant's affliction, remember and not forget me, and give Your servant a son, I will give him to the Lord all the days of his life, and his hair will never be cut."

When she had weaned him, she took him with her to Shiloh, as well as a three-year-old bull, two and one-half gallons of flour, and a jar of wine. Though the boy was still young, she took him to the Lord's house at Shiloh. Then they slaughtered the bull and brought the boy to Eli.

"Please, my lord," she said, "as sure as you live, my lord, I am the woman who stood here beside you praying to the Lord. I prayed for this boy, and since the Lord gave me what I asked Him for, I now give the boy to the Lord. For as long as he lives, he is given to the Lord."

JUST LIKE ME

HANNAH: DESPERATE AND DETERMINED

In a time when a woman took her identity from the family she produced, Hannah knew the stigma of infertility. Being reminded of this fact by her rival each day made it even worse. But Hannah didn't float in a pool of pity. Instead she took her desperation for a son to the Lord. She didn't downplay it, even at the risk of looking ridiculous in front of Eli, the priest.

Hannah took a calculated risk by making a vow to the Lord to dedicate her firstborn son to His service. This meant the child would be in her care for only a short time. But having a son was worth the eventual loss of his presence.

Although Eli misunderstood Hannah at first, God never did. Hannah's desperation and lack of pride gained God's full attention as well as His *yes*. He gave her not just one child, but *several*.

And Hannah kept her vow to the Lord before the other children came into the picture—she gave her firstborn son, Samuel, to Eli. Samuel later became Israel's great, and last, judge.

Sometimes we try to hang on to our pride when it comes to prayer. We might pray once or twice and then drop it or get angry with God when we think He's not listening. Hannah's desperation drove her to pray more, rather than less, and to honor God.

If you're feeling the ragged edge of desperation, how can you determine to honor God even in this situation?

YOUR CHOICE

What drives you to pray more? Less?

MARCH 20

DAY 79

THE BIG PICTURE

1 SM 3:1–21

SNAPSHOT

1 SAMUEL 3:10–14

The LORD came, stood there, and called as before, "Samuel, Samuel!"

Samuel responded, "Speak, for Your servant is listening."

The LORD said to Samuel, "I am about to do something in Israel that everyone who hears about it will shudder. On that day I will carry out against Eli everything I said about his family, from beginning to end. I told him that I am going to judge his family forever because of the iniquity he knows about: his sons are defiling the sanctuary, and he has not stopped them. Therefore, I have sworn to Eli's family: The iniquity of Eli's family will never be wiped out by either sacrifice or offering."

TOUGH CHOICE

MISSIONARY

It was the last week of high school, which also meant it was the last week of Mrs. West's European history class. The course had been grueling all year, but somehow I had managed two "A" semesters. History had never been a particular interest of mine, so studying for tests meant hours of painful memorization.

Victory music trumpeted in my head as I laid my final exam booklet on Mrs. West's desk and then sank back into my chair in the corner. *Done at last!*

"Hey, George!" Alex whispered behind me. "What are you studying in college, again? Are you going to have to take any more of these Euro classes? Jared says he's going to have to."

"I don't think I'll have to," I whispered back. "I'm planning on being a missionary."

"You're going to be a missionary?" Jared had clearly been eavesdropping, as usual. "You can't make money doing that. One of the guys at my uncle's law firm makes ninety thousand bucks a year! That's why I'm working toward law school."

I shrugged; I had gotten used to this kind of reaction:

You want to be a missionary? Like in Africa?

Yes. I don't know where for sure, though.

Oh . . . right.

"Sometimes, I wish I could be more sure about the details of my future—my career and the cars and houses I would buy with my salary," I said to Jared and Alex, "but I know that I was called to be a missionary. I just don't know where God wants me to serve." This was the most difficult part.

The bell rang, signaling the end of the day—the last day of senior year. As I stuffed my pencil into my backpack, Mrs. West walked in my direction.

"George," she said. "I read your last essay on the effects of the Enlightenment on the current spiritual decline in Europe and, knowing your intentions of being a missionary, I can't help but ask if you've ever considered a European country as a mission field . . ."

YOUR CHOICE

What attitude will you choose when you have to wait for God's specific directions?

TOUGH QUESTION

SO MANY OF MY FRIENDS ARE DYEING THEIR HAIR AND GETTING NOSE RINGS OR EVEN TATTOOS. I DON'T WANT TO LOOK LIKE A GEEK, BUT I ALSO DON'T WANT TO JUST FOLLOW THE CROWD. WHAT SHOULD I DO?

Wild hair, nose rings, and tattoos are cosmetic features that have no moral value in themselves. They may not be the wisest fashion statements, but they're not sinful in themselves. The problem comes, as you have already figured out, when you make choices based on being accepted by a certain group. That reveals a deeper issue of insecurity and a poor self-concept. Needing to be like everyone else seems to imply that you don't like the way you are. You can be in fashion (not geek-like) without going to extremes.

You can still be friends with people who dye their hair and get nose rings and tattoos, but you should decide for yourself if you truly want any of those. If you choose not to change your looks to fit in, your friends should understand your choice and respect you for it.

Fashions, especially extreme ones, quickly fade. Something that is considered hot today will be forgotten in a few months (see Pr 31:30). Concentrate, instead, on what lasts, something that does not change: God and His love. Check out Psalm 139, an amazing statement on your God-given uniqueness. God created you to be one-of-a-kind, on purpose and for a reason. He wants to have a relationship with you, fill you up, and satisfy your soul, so you don't have to find security and satisfaction in things that don't last (see Mt 6:19). God's plan is for you to be satisfied with who He has created you to be. Being secure and walking closely with the Lord is an attractive quality and will intrigue those around you. You will be an attractive person without needing any kind of fashion fad.

SNAPSHOT

1 SAMUEL 8:1–5

When Samuel grew old, he appointed his sons as judges over Israel. His firstborn son's name was Joel and his second was Abijah. They were judges in Beer-sheba. However, his sons did not walk in his ways—they turned toward dishonest gain, took bribes, and perverted justice.

So all the elders of Israel gathered together and went to Samuel at Ramah. They said to him, "Look, you are old, and your sons do not follow your example. Therefore, appoint a king to judge us the same as all the other nations have."

YOUR CHOICE

How important are outward appearances to you and your friends? What can you do or wear to reflect the real you?

MARCH 22

DAY 81

THE BIG PICTURE

1 SM 8:6–22

SNAPSHOT

1 SAMUEL 8:6–7

When they said, "Give us a king to judge us," Samuel considered their demand sinful, so he prayed to the LORD. But the LORD told him, "Listen to the people and everything they say to you. They have not rejected you; they have rejected Me as their king."

TOUGH CHOICE

SISTERS

A fire danced in the fireplace as Christmas music hummed in the background. I smiled as I turned the pages of a family photo album, reminiscing about past years. I stopped on one of my favorite photos: a picture of my older sister, Claire, and me. It was taken on Christmas day when I was only three and Claire was seven. Fifteen years later, Christmas day looked drastically different.

This year, my mom, dad, and I were celebrating Christmas without Claire for the second year in a row. Ever since Claire was nineteen, she had been living in an apartment with her boyfriend, Cole. As I stared at the seven-year-old in the picture, I thought about how much it had hurt my parents to see their daughter making unwise decisions: *Claire, the Bible clearly states that marriage has been set aside for living with your significant other. We wish you saw this, too. But we will always love you.*

They had told Claire that they could not support her choice, but they had no way of stopping her if that's what she wanted.

Family gatherings during the holidays had become tense; Christmas ended in a huge argument the first year after Claire moved in with Cole. My parents and Claire started meeting just for dinner from time to time, and eventually they never got together at all. Claire wanted to live her life her own way, without input from Mom and Dad.

I closed the photo album, staring at the family Christmas tree. So many memories of hanging ornaments, singing carols, reading the Christmas story together . . . *I don't resist my parents' advice just because it hinders my plans, do I? I would feel horrible if I hurt them the way Claire has hurt the family.*

I let my eyes climb the tree, focusing on the twinkling ornaments. My gaze settled on Gabriel, who hovered at the top of the tree. *I think I'd listen to my parents . . . I hope I would. I wish Claire would so that we could be a family again. God placed my parents above me to provide wisdom and counsel. I can't reject them so defiantly—I'd be rejecting God.*

YOUR CHOICE

What will you do when wise counsel (even from your parents) conflicts with your plans?

1 SM 9:1–21

SNAPSHOT

1 SAMUEL 9:14–19

Saul and his attendant were entering the city when they saw Samuel coming toward them on his way to the high place. Now the day before Saul's arrival, the LORD had informed Samuel, "At this time tomorrow I will send you a man from the land of Benjamin. Anoint him ruler over My people Israel. He will save them from the hand of the Philistines because I have seen the affliction of My people, for their cry has come to Me." When Samuel saw Saul, the LORD told him, "Here is the man I told you about; he will rule over My people."

Saul approached Samuel in the gate area and asked, "Would you please tell me where the seer's house is?"

"I am the seer," Samuel answered. "Go up ahead of me to the high place and eat with me today. When I send you off in the morning, I'll tell you everything that's in your heart."

YOUR CHOICE

When have you disqualified yourself from being used by God? How will your attitude change?

NO BRAINER

LOST DONKEYS

Saul was wandering around Zuph with a servant, spending hours trying to find some escaped donkeys. What an incredibly average job for the future king of Israel! His father had sent him after the wandering livestock, but Saul could not find them anywhere. Both he and the servant were growing tired. They knew they should return home soon, so they stopped to think about what they should do. When the servant had the bright idea of finding the well-known prophet who lived in the area, Saul agreed. The two set off to find the "seer" who was, in fact, Samuel. They hurried to ask him where their donkeys were.

Little did they know that God had already spoken to Samuel. God had told Samuel the previous day that He would send him the man who was to become Israel's first king. The three of them met, and Samuel knew immediately that Saul was the one. When Samuel told Saul that he was the hope of Israel, Saul responded by saying that he was from the smallest tribe and the most insignificant family within that tribe.

A person doesn't have to be famous or powerful to be used by God. He can and does use virtually anyone, even someone like Saul—and someone like us! (Of course, how we respond to God's opportunities and meet those challenges is important, too—but that's another story.)

So don't forget that God can and wants to use you, regardless of your background, personal history, or limitations. When you take a stand for Him, you (yes you) can make a difference.

Another important lesson in this story is that God can use any kind of situation to accomplish His purpose. Saul was chasing after donkeys when he was chosen as king. So always be on the lookout for how God might want to use you right where you are—you don't have to wait to be king.

DAY 83

THE BIG PICTURE

1 SM 10:1–27

SNAPSHOT

1 SAMUEL 10:24–27

Samuel said to all the people, "Do you see the one the Lord has chosen? There is no one like him among the entire population."

And all the people shouted, "Long live the king!"

Samuel proclaimed to the people the rights of kingship. He wrote them on a scroll, which he placed in the presence of the Lord. Then, Samuel sent all the people away, each to his home.

Saul also went to his home in Gibeah, and brave men whose hearts God had touched went with him. But some wicked men said, "How can this guy save us?" They despised him and did not bring him a gift, but Saul said nothing.

DEPOSIT

WORDS FROM GOD'S WORD TO STORE IN YOUR MIND AND HEART

But the Lord told him, "Listen to the people and everything they say to you. They have not rejected you; they have rejected Me as their king" (1 Sm 8:7).

SNAPSHOT

1 SAMUEL 14:6–14

Jonathan said to the attendant who carried his weapons, "Come on, let's cross over to the garrison of these uncircumcised men. Perhaps the LORD will help us. Nothing can keep the LORD from saving, whether by many or by few."

His armor-bearer responded, "Do what is in your heart. You choose. I'm right here with you whatever you decide."

"All right," Jonathan replied, "we'll cross over to the men and then let them see us. If they say, 'Wait until we reach you,' then we will stay where we are and not go up to them. But if they say, 'Come on up,' then we'll go up, because the LORD has handed them over to us—that will be our sign."

They let themselves be seen by the Philistine garrison, and the Philistines said, "Look, the Hebrews are coming out of the holes where they've been hiding!" The men of the garrison called to Jonathan and his armor-bearer. "Come on up, and we'll teach you a lesson!" they said.

"Follow me," Jonathan told his armor-bearer, "for the LORD has handed them over to Israel." Jonathan went up using his hands and feet, with his armor-bearer behind him. Jonathan cut them down, and his armor-bearer followed and finished them off. In that first assault Jonathan and his armor-bearer struck down about 20 men in a half-acre field.

YOUR TURN

A SON TO MAKE A FATHER PROUD

What would it mean to have a friend like Jonathan?

DAY 85

THE BIG PICTURE

1 SM 16:1–13

NO BRAINER

APPEARANCES

The Lord had just given Samuel a command to anoint Israel's next king. Yet the old king was still alive! Samuel knew that if he obeyed God, King Saul might kill him. In order to obey God, he would have to go against Saul.

Taking a stand sometimes requires us to contradict or oppose people of prominence or position. Many celebrities and leaders do not encourage godly behavior. Thus, making a courageous decision to do what God wants will often mean doing the opposite of what the majority of the world selects. Taking a stand for God may mean doing something unappealing, even risky.

Samuel knew that obeying God was a far better choice than pleasing Saul, so he packed up his bags, grabbed the olive oil, and headed to Bethlehem. Then, when he met with Jesse and his sons, Samuel relied on God to tell him which son to anoint. When Samuel saw Jesse's eldest, probably tall and handsome with a confident air, he thought that he was looking at the next king of Israel. But God said no and told him to keep looking, with the understanding that while people usually judge by outward appearance, God looks at the heart. Eventually, Samuel anointed the youngest son, David, who had been out in the field, tending sheep and hadn't even been called to the family gathering.

Samuel's choice to obey God and to follow Him led him directly to God's person, the next—and great—king of Israel, David, a very unlikely choice. So remember that God sees behind the personal facades and into the heart. Imagine what might have happened if Samuel hadn't listened to God and had gone with his first instinct and anointed Eliab!

SNAPSHOT

1 SAMUEL 16:6–7,11–13

When they arrived, Samuel saw Eliab and said, "Certainly the LORD's anointed one is here before Him."

But the LORD said to Samuel, "Do not look at his appearance or his stature, because I have rejected him. Man does not see what the LORD sees, for man sees what is visible, but the LORD sees the heart."

Samuel asked him, "Are these all the sons you have?"

"There is still the youngest," he answered, "but right now he's tending the sheep." Samuel told Jesse, "Send for him. We won't sit down to eat until he gets here." So Jesse sent for him. He had beautiful eyes and a healthy, handsome appearance.

Then the LORD said, "Anoint him, for he is the one." So Samuel took the horn of oil, anointed him in the presence of his brothers, and the Spirit of the LORD took control of David from that day forward. Then Samuel set out and went to Ramah.

YOUR CHOICE

What is God asking you to do that doesn't seem reasonable or logical?

1 SAMUEL 17:4–7 SNAPSHOT

Then a champion named Goliath, from Gath, came out from the Philistine camp. He was nine feet, nine inches tall and wore a bronze helmet and bronze scale armor that weighed 125 pounds. There was bronze armor on his shins, and a bronze sword was slung between his shoulders. His spear shaft was like a weaver's beam, and the iron point of his spear weighed 15 pounds. In addition, a shield-bearer was walking in front of him.

DAY 86

THE BIG PICTURE

1 SM 17:1–31

TOUGH CHOICE

EVOLUTION

"All right class, settle down. Remember that tomorrow we are having the debate on intelligent design versus evolution. Finish up your research and come prepared to defend your views." Mr. Graham began erasing the chalkboard as he spoke. "If you don't have a strong opinion on the subject, just go with whichever one you think you can best argue."

I began to gather my books and notes for the next day's debate. I knew that arguing creationism would be a challenge against a group of peers who were adamant that evolution was completely accurate, but the creationist side in class would also be a lot smaller than the evolutionist side.

My friend, Josh, would be part of the creationist side. We had attended the same church and knew that the earth had been created by God, not merely a "big bang."

"Hey, Josh! Are you ready for this debate tomorrow?"

Josh looked up; his head had been buried in his hands. "We're toast, Caroline," he lamented. "They've got Paul on their team."

Paul was the best debater in the class and a science fanatic. "Speaking of Paul, he's walking this direction now," I said, seeing Paul moving toward us, wearing his typical smirk.

"So, I can't wait to hear your lack of an argument tomorrow," he gloated. "It's okay, not all of us can understand logic."

"Paul, would you knock it off?" Josh remained seated, staring at his desk.

"Paul, there are scientific facts that both disprove evolution and prove intelligent design," I added. "We're looking forward to debating tomorrow."

"Right," muttered Paul, scornfully.

As Paul walked away, the importance and significance of the debate weighed on me. If we failed, some people in the class might begin to doubt the existence of God.

"Come on, Josh. Let's start organizing our notes. But first, let's pray that the Lord uses our words to reach those needing to hear about His glory!"

YOUR CHOICE

What will you do when you are forced to rely on your confidence in God to deal with those who mock you and your faith?

DAY 87

THE BIG PICTURE
1 SM 17:32–58

SNAPSHOT

1 SAMUEL 17:45–50

David said to the Philistine, "You come against me with a dagger, spear, and sword, but I come against you in the name of the LORD of Hosts, the God of Israel's armies—you have defied Him. Today, the LORD will hand you over to me. Today, I'll strike you down, cut your head off, and give the corpses of the Philistine camp to the birds of the sky and the creatures of the earth. Then all the world will know that Israel has a God, and this whole assembly will know that it is not by sword or by spear that the LORD saves, for the battle is the LORD's. He will hand you over to us."

When the Philistine started forward to attack him, David ran quickly to the battle line to meet the Philistine. David put his hand in the bag, took out a stone, slung it, and hit the Philistine on his forehead. The stone sank into his forehead, and he fell on his face to the ground. David defeated the Philistine with a sling and a stone. Even though David had no sword, he struck down the Philistine and killed him.

ANCHOR POINT

DEFEATING OUR GIANTS

Some life issues are huge and seem insurmountable: the death of a sibling, parent, or friend, health problems, financial downturns, a relational loss, or another challenge. Each of these can seem like an unwinnable battle—just too hard. Time to give up and go home.

At those times, we can feel totally on our own, abandoned. That's when we must remember that God has not sent us into battle alone and unprotected. We fight on the side of the Lord Almighty, the all powerful One, and He is with us at every step. God has promised to stand with us, just as He stood with David. We can ask Him for help and claim His strength as our own. Claiming that promise, David chose to stand for God and His people. And we can join David in crying out, "I come to you in the name of the Lord Almighty—the God of the armies of Israel!"

What "giants" or obstacles block your path and seem invincible, insurmountable? No matter what you are facing today, remember that the Mighty One is on your side.

YOUR CHOICE

How can you better rely on the strength of the Lord Almighty? What strong stand do you need to take for God, His work, and His people, despite the odds against you?

TOUGH QUESTION

HOW CAN I TAKE A STAND IN CLASS WITHOUT MAKING MY TEACHER MAD AND TURNING EVERYONE OFF?

Christians can boldly share their faith and take a stand for Christ without turning people off to Him. Although Jesus did, in fact, offend certain people, the people he offended the most were the religious leaders of the day. But they were offended by Jesus' message, not by how He delivered it.

In Mark 2:16–17 we read about Jesus telling the Pharisees that He is eating with the "sinners" because it's not "those who are well" who need a doctor, "but the sick." The Pharisees were offended that Jesus would spend time with such low-lifes and didn't recognize their own sickness in the form of pride.

Jesus didn't come wielding a verbal sword, correcting and attacking left and right. Instead, He came with a gentle word and a loving touch for hurting people, to save them, and give them hope. We should take the same approach. We can easily feel attacked for our faith (and sometimes the attacks will be vicious), but displaying a defensive and hostile attitude doesn't display Christ's love. Jesus loved those who were hostile to Him, and we should do the same.

At times our faith will be directly challenged, with certain subjects, outrageous statements, and lines of discussion that are contrary to the Bible. So we need to ask God for wisdom to know when to speak up and when to remain silent. And then, when we speak out, we need to display a Christlike attitude of humility and gentleness, our words sprinkled with grace.

So allow God's message, the Bible, to offend the hearer, but not your words or tone of voice. Be firm, but pleasant, knowing that you are imitating Christ's actions and attitude. In Matthew 5, Jesus says, "Blessed are the peacemakers, because they will be called sons of God" (v. 9). Even when being attacked for your views, you can be a gift of peace.

SNAPSHOT

1 SAMUEL 18:10–14

The next day an evil spirit from God took control of Saul, and he began to rave inside the palace. David was playing [the harp] as usual, but Saul was holding a spear, and he threw it, thinking, "I'll pin David to the wall." But David got away from him twice.

Saul was afraid of David, because the LORD was with David but had left from Saul. Therefore, Saul reassigned David and made him commander over 1,000 men. David led the troops and continued to be successful in all his activities because the LORD was with him.

YOUR CHOICE

When do you think you might find it necessary to stand up for your faith in class? How can you do that in a humble and peace-making way?

SNAPSHOT

1 SAMUEL 20:27–34

However, the day after the New Moon, the second day, David's place was still empty, and Saul asked his son Jonathan, "Why didn't Jesse's son come to the meal either yesterday or today?"

Jonathan answered, "David asked for my permission to go to Bethlehem. He said, 'Please let me go because our clan is holding a sacrifice in the town, and my brother has told me to be there. So now, if you are pleased with me, let me go so I can see my brothers.' That's why he didn't come to the king's table."

Then Saul became angry with Jonathan. . .

Jonathan answered his father back: "Why is he to be killed? What has he done?"

Then Saul threw his spear at Jonathan to kill him, so he knew that his father was determined to kill David. He got up from the table in fierce anger and did not eat any food that second day of the New Moon, for he was grieved because of his father's shameful behavior toward David.

JUST LIKE ME

JONATHAN: WALKING THE TIGHTROPE

Due to the ongoing busyness of life we get pretty adept at juggling relationships. But seldom are we expected to choose between a friend and a parent the way Jonathan was.

Jonathan walked a tightrope between his father Saul and his best friend David. How do you avoid betraying your best friend when your father wants him dead? As the king, Saul's word was law, and David was now public enemy number one, thanks to Saul's insane jealousy. But Jonathan chose to honor both without betraying the other and nearly lost his life in the process. Although Jonathan didn't shy away from confronting his father about the wrong done to David, he did so in a respectful way. Also, he honored his friend above his own wishes. Jonathan was the crown prince—the one who would have ascended to the throne after Saul. But God had chosen David to be the next king, a plan with which Jonathan chose not to interfere—contrary to his father's wishes.

We often say we're committed to friends or family. But have we truly counted the cost of these commitments? Being committed may involve confronting a wrong or breaking the status quo in some way. It might also involve walking a tightrope between relationships. What does this tightrope look like in your life?

YOUR CHOICE **How can you be faithful to God and to your friends at the same time?**

THE BIG PICTURE

1 SM 24:1–22

MARCH 31

DAY 90

SNAPSHOT

1 SAMUEL 24:3–7

When Saul came to the sheep pens along the road, a cave was there, and he went in to relieve himself. David and his men were staying in the back of the cave, so they said to him, "Look, this is the day the LORD told you about: 'I will hand your enemy over to you so you can do to him whatever you desire.' " Then David got up and secretly cut off the corner of Saul's robe.

Afterwards, David's conscience bothered him because he had cut off the corner of Saul's robe. He said to his men, "I swear before the LORD: I would never do such a thing to my lord, the LORD's anointed. I will never lift my hand against him, since he is the LORD's anointed." With these words David persuaded his men, and he did not let them rise up against Saul.

Then Saul left the cave and went on his way.

DEPOSIT

TO STORE IN YOUR MIND AND HEART

But the LORD said to Samuel, "Do not look at his appearance or his stature, because I have rejected him. Man does not see what the Lord sees, for man sees what is visible, but the LORD sees the heart" (1 Sm 16:7).

APRIL
AVRIL
APRIL
APRIL
APRILE
ABRIL
ABRIL

1 SM 25:1–42

APRIL 1

DAY 91

SNAPSHOT

1 SAMUEL 25:23–28

When Abigail saw David, she quickly got off the donkey and fell with her face to the ground in front of David. She fell at his feet and said, "The guilt is mine, my lord, but please let your servant speak to you directly. Listen to the words of your servant. My lord should pay no attention to this worthless man Nabal, for he lives up to his name: His name is Nabal, and stupidity is all he knows. I, your servant, didn't see my lord's young men whom you sent. Now my lord, as surely as the LORD lives and as you yourself live, it is the LORD who kept you from participating in bloodshed and avenging yourself by your own hand. May your enemies and those who want trouble for my lord be like Nabal. Accept this gift your servant has brought to my lord, and let it be given to the young men who follow my lord. Please forgive your servant's offense, for the LORD is certain to make a lasting dynasty for my lord because he fights the LORD's battles. Throughout your life, may evil not be found in you."

YOUR TURN

UNDESERVING FORGIVENESS

How does God keep you from making big mistakes?

DAY 92

THE BIG PICTURE

1 SM 28:1–25

NO BRAINER

OCCULT PRACTICES

Saul had decreed that all mediums and psychics were banned from their practices (so no more Ouija boards in Israel). He had outlawed occult practices. But when the Philistines were preparing to attack, he needed a fast answer. So he turned to his advisors, who told him exactly where to find a medium (a person who claims to be able to talk to the dead).

Saul was reversing his field, backing away from his commitment. Although he had outlawed all occult practices, he was seeking a medium to tell him what to do. Saul's original stand had been right, but he was caving in under pressure.

Saul's advisors certainly were no help. Instead of reminding him of his ban and encouraging him to do what was right and obey God, they pushed him in the wrong direction.

This strange incident (read the whole story for the dramatic and tragic conclusion) provides many lessons. Actually, Saul shows us how *not* to act, and his actions here reveal his true character. No wonder he wasn't fit to be king.

So here are the lessons: First, when we know an action is wrong, especially something condemned in God's Word, we should stick to our convictions and avoid it at all costs. Second, we should beware of advisors—friends, associates, coworkers—who try to lead us astray. Taking a stand begins much earlier than when we're suddenly faced with a crisis.

SNAPSHOT

1 SAMUEL 28:15–17

"Why have you disturbed me by bringing me up?" Samuel asked Saul. "I'm in serious trouble," replied Saul. "The Philistines are fighting against me and God has turned away from me. He doesn't answer me any more, either through the prophets or in dreams. So I've called on you to tell me what I should do."

Samuel answered, "Since the LORD has turned away from you and has become your enemy, why are you asking me? The LORD has done exactly what He said through me: The LORD has torn the kingship out of your hand and given it to your neighbor David."

YOUR CHOICE

What friends and associates tend to urge you to make the wrong choices?

THE BIG PICTURE

2 SM 5:1–12

APRIL 3

DAY 93

SNAPSHOT

2 SAMUEL 5:1–2

All the tribes of Israel came to David at Hebron and said, "Here we are, your own flesh and blood. Even while Saul was king over us, you were the one who led us out to battle and brought us back. The LORD also said to you, 'You will shepherd My people Israel and be ruler over Israel.' "

ANCHOR POINT

PLEASING TO GOD

Don't be discouraged if you aren't acknowledged right away for your accomplishments. You may have to wait. Consider David who as a young man had been anointed as Israel's next king. But he had to wait several years, for God's timing, before assuming the throne. Patience can be difficult to learn, but it is invaluable and will serve you well for a lifetime. Often, however, learning patience takes patience.

At times God's appointed path seems to have too many twists and turns—detours. Moving slowly from point to point, we can wonder if we'll ever reach the goal. Sometimes we may even feel as though the journey has been a waste of time. But God's way is always best, even though we wonder where it is leading.

Don't be overly concerned if your good works are not recognized or rewarded (or if someone else gets the credit that you deserve). God knows you—your heart and your actions. And He's the only One who really matters.

YOUR CHOICE

What goals have you set for your life? How do you think you might react if life took an unexpected turn? How can you better align yourself with what God wants for you?

APRIL 4

DAY 94

THE BIG PICTURE

2 SM 9:1–13

SNAPSHOT **2 SAMUEL 9:6–7**

Mephibosheth son of Jonathan son of Saul came to David, bowed down to the ground and paid homage. David said, "Mephibosheth!"

"I am your servant," he replied.

"Don't be afraid," David said to him, "since I intend to show you kindness because of your father Jonathan. I will restore to you all your grandfather Saul's fields, and you will always eat meals at my table."

TOUGH CHOICE

MOCKING

The third period bell rang, signaling the beginning of English class and the end of my life. It was speech day. My stomach churned. I disliked public speaking, but I hated public speaking when Alan was in the audience.

It seemed that no matter what I did, Alan always had a wise crack comment. If I answered a question incorrectly in class, Alan was sure to make a snide remark. If I made an error during baseball practice, Alan was sure to remind me (and the rest of the team) in the dugout. Even when I did something right, Alan managed to make me feel dumber than a rock.

I was the third person in class to give my speech, which was on early American literature. I managed to hit all the key points, finish within the time constraints, and remember the names of all the different works we had studied. Alan was the last person scheduled to give his speech that day. He strode to the front of the class with his typical air of cocky confidence and began: "Many people consider the mid- to late 1600s as the birth of early American literature. If you consider the myths and legends passed down orally by the Native Americans, though . . ." Alan looked up at the ceiling, fidgeting a bit. He began again:

" . . . If you consider the myths and legends passed down by the Native Americans . . ." He looked back up at the ceiling, closing his eyes and rocking on his feet. Again:

" . . . Passed down by the Native Americans . . ."

People in the class began to whisper and snicker as Alan stammered through his speech, or at least what he could remember of it. As he mumbled his closing, the class erupted into full-blown laughter. Only the end-of-class bell put an end to the humiliation, as everyone filed out into the halls.

"Wh-wh-where are we sitting for lunch today?" My friend, Luke, asked me. I could see Alan out of the corner of my eye. He was still a bright shade of red.

"Um . . . um . . . I . . . um," Luke continued to taunt Alan.

Here was my opportunity; I could finally turn the tables on Alan. It would feel so good to exact some revenge. *Or would it?*

The look on Alan's face seemed to be begging for mercy.

"Hey, man, come on," I said. "Give Alan a little slack. The topic was hard, and besides, our speeches weren't all that fascinating either."
I surprised myself. I had dreamed about the chance to give Alan a dose of his own medicine. The look on his face, though, reminded me of my own after a usual Alan-encounter. *I'd want people to give me a break. Christ would . . .*

YOUR CHOICE **How will you respond when given the opportunity to get even with someone?**

THE BIG PICTURE

2 SM 11:1–27

APRIL 5

DAY 95

SNAPSHOT

2 SAMUEL 11:5–9,16–17

The woman conceived and sent word to inform David: "I am pregnant."

David sent orders to Joab: "Send me Uriah the Hittite." So Joab sent Uriah to David. When Uriah came to him, David asked how Joab and the troops were doing and how the war was going. Then he said to Uriah, "Go down to your house and wash your feet." So Uriah left the palace, and a gift from the king followed him. But Uriah slept at the door of the palace with all his master's servants; he did not go down to his house.

When Joab was besieging the city, he put Uriah in the place where he knew the best enemy soldiers were. Then the men of the city came out and attacked Joab, and some of the men from David's soldiers fell in battle; Uriah the Hittite also died.

JUST LIKE ME

DAVID: DISTRACTED TO DEATH

We often hear of individuals who try to cover up one crime by committing another: The murderer who uses arson to cover up a murder; the drug addict who steals to keep up his or her habit.

David, the anointed king and a man after God's own heart (see 1 Sm 13:14), doesn't usually fit the profile of the desperate criminal. But after being distracted by the sight of Bathsheba, all he could think about was how he could get what he wanted. But problem after problem resulted when adultery became the means to an end. To cover up the sin, which resulted in a pregnancy, Bathsheba's husband had to be dealt with. Soon David was guilty of murder as well.

David's cover-up led to drastic consequences. The son from his liaison with Bathsheba died. Nathan, the prophet, confronted David with his sin and reminded David of the God who saw all. This same God promised that trouble would always plague David's family.

Tempted to cover up instead of confess? Consider what happens when you ignore a boil: The infection continues to build up under the surface until the boil is lanced. And God, who is never distracted, is in the lancing business. Better deal with the wrong now. You may not be able to afford the consequences.

YOUR CHOICE

What sinful distraction is pulling you the wrong way? What can you do to make the *right*, God-honoring choice?

DAY 96

SNAPSHOT

2 SAMUEL 12:5–10

David was infuriated with the man and said to Nathan: "As surely as the LORD lives, the man who did this deserves to die! Because he has done this thing and shown no pity, he must pay four lambs for that lamb."

Nathan replied to David, "You are the man! This is what the LORD God of Israel says: 'I anointed you king over Israel, and I delivered you from the hand of Saul. I gave your master's house to you and your master's wives into your arms, and I gave you the house of Israel and Judah, and if that was not enough, I would have given you even more. Why then have you despised the command of the LORD by doing what I consider evil? You struck down Uriah the Hittite with the sword and took his wife as your own wife—you murdered him with the Ammonite's sword. Now therefore, the sword will never leave your house because you despised Me and took the wife of Uriah the Hittite to be your own wife.'"

YOUR CHOICE

What friend do you need to lovingly and humbly confront about sinful choices? What can you do to help this person move in God's direction?

TOUGH QUESTION

MY FRIEND, ALSO A CHRISTIAN, IS MAKING SOME BAD CHOICES. WHAT CAN I DO TO HELP HER?

Seeing a Christian friend struggle can be frustrating. And we're not sure what to say when this friend is making bad choices and heading down the wrong path. We know that confrontation could cost the friendship. On the other hand, the consequences of the friend's bad choices could be disastrous. So what do we do?

The first step is to evaluate the choice the friend is making: Is it sinful or just a somewhat foolish action? A sin should be confronted, but in love. For example, "As your friend, I need to say that I believe that would be wrong—God's Word is very clear about it." With a foolish choice, the most helpful response would be advice or counsel. You could say something like, "Are you sure you want to do that? I think a better way would be to . . ."

If your friend's choice would endanger him or her or someone else (for example, your friend is talking about suicide or violence, or something similar), you should share the information with an adult who can help.

The sad fact is that confronting a friend about a bad choice may cost the friendship. People don't like being told that what they are doing is wrong and may react defensively or in anger. But we owe the truth to them, even if it hurts to give it.

Remember, however, that the responsibility for your friend's choices and actions rests on him or her, not on you. And you can't force your friend to change; that's another choice your friend must make for himself or herself.

The most important action you can take is *prayer*, asking God to give you insight to know how to respond and the courage to do it (see Eph 6:18). Trust that the Lord will deal with your friend's behavior.

2 SM 13:1–19

SNAPSHOT

2 SAMUEL 13:7–14

David sent word to Tamar at the palace: "Please go to your brother Amnon's house and prepare a meal for him."

Then Tamar went to his house while Amnon was lying down. She took dough, kneaded it, made cakes in his presence, and baked them. She brought the pan and set it down in front of him, but he refused to eat. Amnon said, "Everyone leave me!" And everyone left him. "Bring the meal to the bedroom," Amnon told Tamar, "so I can eat from your hand." Tamar took the cakes she had made and went to her brother Amnon's bedroom. When she brought them to him to eat, he grabbed her and said, "Come sleep with me, my sister!"

"Don't, my brother!" she cried. "Don't humiliate me, for such a thing should never be done in Israel. Don't do this horrible thing! Where could I ever go with my disgrace? And you—you would be like one of the immoral men in Israel! Please, speak to the king, for he won't keep me from you." But he refused to listen to her, and because he was stronger than she was, he raped her.

DEPOSIT

WORDS FROM GOD'S WORD TO STORE IN YOUR MIND AND HEART

David responded to Nathan, "I have sinned against the Lord." Then Nathan replied to David, "The Lord has taken away your sin; you will not die" (2 Sm 12:13).

THE BIG PICTURE
2 SM 13:20–39

SNAPSHOT

2 SAMUEL 13:22–29

Absalom didn't say anything to Amnon, either good or bad, because he hated Amnon since he disgraced his sister Tamar.

Two years later, Absalom's sheepshearers were at Baal-hazor near Ephraim, and Absalom invited all the king's sons. Then he went to the king and said, "Your servant has just hired sheepshearers. Will the king and his servants please come with your servant?"

The king replied to Absalom, "No, my son, we should not all go, or we would be a burden to you." Although Absalom urged him, he wasn't willing to go, though he did bless him.

"If not," Absalom said, "please let my brother Amnon go with us." The king asked him, "Why should he go with you?" But Absalom urged him, so he sent Amnon and all the king's sons.

Now Absalom commanded his young men, "Watch Amnon until he is in a good mood from the wine. When I order you to strike Amnon, then kill him. Don't be afraid. Am I not the one who has commanded you? Be strong and courageous!" So Absalom's young men did to Amnon just as Absalom had commanded. Then all the rest of the king's sons got up, and each fled on his mule.

YOUR TURN

FAMILY DYSFUNCTIONS

Are you more likely to have committed David's sin or Amnon's or Absalom's?

istand

2 SAMUEL 15:21–22

SNAPSHOT

But in response, Ittai vowed to the king, "As surely as the LORD lives and as my lord the king lives, wherever my lord the king is, whether it means life or death, your servant will be there!"

"March on," David replied to Ittai. So Ittai the Gittite marched past with all his men and the children who were with him.

APRIL 9

DAY 99

THE BIG PICTURE

2 SM 15:1–37

TOUGH CHOICE

LEAVING THE PARTY

Awkward silence crept through the room as Alyssa pulled on her coat. Just minutes before, the laughter and conversation could have drowned out an express rail locomotive. Everyone had turned to watch my friend. I wasn't sure what to do.

Alyssa and I had come to the party earlier that evening, expecting to have fun with some of our friends from high school. The party had started off well; everyone was sitting in one room, playing games, and enjoying themselves. I had met a few new people and was talking to one of them when Alyssa came and tugged on my sleeve. She was clearly upset.

"Carly, Joy's parents aren't here," she said, dragging me into the kitchen.

"Oh. I didn't know," I began. I knew that my parents wouldn't be thrilled with the new set of circumstances, but nobody was jumping from the balconies or breaking furniture.

"I don't think it's that big of a deal Alyssa . . ."

"And three guys just showed up with six-packs and a keg," she whispered, loudly.

"Oh," I said quietly. This did change things. I stared from the kitchen into the party room. I had really been having fun. I liked these people.

"Carly? Carly!"

"What, Alyssa?" I snapped.

"Let's go. Come on. Let's get our coats." She walked back through the family room, grabbing her coat off the couch. I lingered a moment, then slowly moved toward the edge of the family room.

"Alyssa! Where are you going?" shouted Joy. "The fun's just starting!"

"Home," said Alyssa boldly. "Your parents aren't home and people are drinking."

People began to turn and look.

"Don't be a prude," shouted Joy. "Stay!"

"No way! I'm not hanging around," Alyssa said, unabashed.

"Fine, you can leave then," a guy near the stereo said. "You're going to miss out on the fun, though."

Alyssa grabbed her purse. She didn't respond. I hadn't moved from my spot when Alyssa turned toward me. "Are you coming?" she asked pointedly.

I took a deep breath and said, "Yeah, I'm coming with you . . ."

YOUR CHOICE

When your friend takes a stand, are you willing to stand next to her or him?

DAY 100

2 SM 18:1–18

SNAPSHOT

2 SAMUEL 18:9–13

Absalom was riding on his mule when he happened to meet David's soldiers. When the mule went under the tangled branches of a large oak tree, Absalom's head was caught fast in the tree. The mule under him kept going, so he was suspended in midair. One of the men saw him and informed Joab. He said, "I just saw Absalom hanging in an oak tree!"

"You just saw him!" Joab exclaimed. "Why didn't you strike him to the ground right there? I would have given you 10 silver pieces and a belt!"

The man replied to Joab, "Even if I had the weight of 1,000 pieces of silver in my hand, I would not raise my hand against the king's son. For we heard the king command you, Abishai, and Ittai, 'Protect the young man Absalom for me.' If I had jeopardized my own life—and nothing is hidden from the king—you would have abandoned me."

YOUR CHOICE

Today, what can you do to honor your parents or stepparents?

TOUGH QUESTION

I'VE HAD A LOT OF DISAGREEMENTS WITH MY STEPPARENT. THE BIBLE SAYS I SHOULD HONOR MY FATHER AND MOTHER, BUT HOW DO I DO IT?

These days, families can become very complicated, with birth parents, foster parents, adoptive parents, stepparents—some children have a combination. But the biblical principle is clear: God has put children into families for their protection and nurture, and He has given the adults in charge of those families the responsibility to care for their children.

Sometimes a stepparent can be the most difficult to honor, especially after a divorce, because the person has taken the place of the child's mom or dad. But the command still applies.

The Bible also tells children to "obey" their parents (Col 3:20). And this command applies for as long as children are under their parents' authority. The only exception is if a parent tells a child to do something that God forbids (for example, to commit a crime, to turn away from Christ, etc.).

Even as adults, the command to "honor" never ends. We don't have to agree with them and pretend to be happy with their own poor choices, but we should treat them with respect and pray for them.

People who live together will often disagree and come into conflict. No one's perfect, and we can't always be in a good mood. So don't expect your home to be conflict-free. Here's a suggestion: Closely evaluate the disagreements you are experiencing with your stepparent. What are they usually about? Who starts them? Are the issues and conflicts ever resolved? Then think about how you can choose a Christlike attitude and action in that situation.

Displaying humility to a stepparent and confessing one's faults no matter how great or small is a sign of maturity and obedience. Asking forgiveness will not only diffuse the disagreement but it will reconcile and build the relationship between you and your stepparent. Expressing humility and forgiveness are ways to honor others.

SNAPSHOT

1 KINGS 1:24–27

"My lord king," Nathan said, "did you say, 'Adonijah is to become king after me, and he is the one who is to sit on my throne?' For today he went down and lavishly sacrificed oxen, fattened cattle, and sheep. He invited all the sons of the king, the commanders of the army, and Abiathar the priest. And look! They're eating and drinking in his presence, and they're saying, 'Long live King Adonijah!' But he did not invite me—me, your servant—or Zadok the priest or Benaiah son of Jehoiada or your servant Solomon. I'm certain my lord the king would not have let this happen without letting your servant know who will sit on my lord the king's throne after him."

YOUR CHOICE

With whom do you need to communicate directly about a conflict or other issue?

NO BRAINER

GOOD DECISIONS

Adonijah had been a spoiled child who wanted to rule the world. Now that he was older, he wanted to rule Israel even though he wasn't next in line. He took his father's horses and got a bunch of his friends to run in front of him, to make him look important, even royal. Then, to elevate the hype even further, Adonijah threw a huge celebration but didn't invite those who were still loyal to David. The uninvited included the intended next king, Solomon, Zadok (a priest), and Nathan (a prophet).

When Solomon's mother, Bathsheba, heard about this, she was concerned that her son was not going to be king as promised. So she went to David and reminded him of his promise and respectfully asked why Adonijah would be king instead of her son.

Bathsheba showed concern for her boy and a desire for justice—and talking to the king took courage. Bathsheba also made a courageous decision by directly consulting David instead of stirring up trouble behind the scenes, trying to get a posse started for Solomon or tearing Adonijah down with rumors.

When a choice or action involves someone else, we should talk to the affected person directly. Talking behind someone's back or trying to solve a problem or conflict in a sneaky, backhanded way dishonors God. Instead of taking His way, for Him, we will be taking a stand for sin.

APRIL 12

DAY 102

THE BIG PICTURE

1 KG 1:28–53

SNAPSHOT

1 KINGS 1:49–53

Then all of Adonijah's guests got up trembling and went their separate ways. Adonijah was afraid of Solomon, so he got up and went to take hold of the horns of the altar.

It was reported to Solomon: "Look, Adonijah fears King Solomon, and he has taken hold of the horns of the altar, saying, 'Let King Solomon first swear to me that he will not kill his servant with the sword.' "

Then Solomon said, "If he is a man of character, then not a single hair of his will fall to the ground, but if evil is found in him, then he dies." So King Solomon sent for him, and they took him down from the altar. He came and paid homage to King Solomon, and Solomon said to him, "Go to your home."

ANCHOR POINT

CONFUSING WORLD

What do your reactions tell you about the condition of your heart? Are you running from things you should be embracing? Do you have a bad attitude toward someone? Have you become cynical about church? What is it that sends you running from the table, like Adonijah and his friends? Is your conscience bothering you?

Talk is cheap, and we can mouth pious platitudes while harboring sin in our hearts. Our actions reveal what we're like on the inside, our true nature. When we are pushed or find ourselves in a tight spot, our responses may surprise us. Bad habits that we thought we had under control suddenly re-appear. Nasty thoughts we never would consider when fully in control fill our minds. Caustic words we put behind us are suddenly on our lips. How can this happen?

When we trusted Christ as Savior, we became "new," but we still have our old sin nature. Yet because sin has been defeated, we now have the freedom to choose to *not* act on those sinful impulses, but to obey God and live for Him. This gives us hope for the future and allows us to let go of past failures. We are not called to perfection here on earth—just to walk God's way, one step, one choice, at a time.

YOUR CHOICE

To what have you reacted poorly recently? What does that reveal about the condition of your heart? What do you need to do to make it right?

THE BIG PICTURE

1 KG 3:1–15

APRIL 13

DAY 103

SNAPSHOT

1 KINGS 3:9–13

"So give Your servant an obedient heart to judge Your people and to discern between good and evil. For who is able to judge this great people of Yours?"

Now it pleased the Lord that Solomon had requested this. So God said to him, "Because you have requested this and did not ask for long life or riches for yourself, or the death of your enemies, but you asked discernment for yourself to understand justice, I will therefore do what you have asked. I will give you a wise and understanding heart, so that there has never been anyone like you before and never will be again."

JUST LIKE ME

SOLOMON: WHEN WISDOM ISN'T ENOUGH

What's the biggest request you've ever made? What do you think you'd ask for if you knew your request would be granted?

Solomon's biggest, and best, request was asking God for wisdom as he began his reign as king of Israel. Solomon's humility before God earned him not only wisdom but great wealth too. Thus, Solomon's reign began with a powerful, godly choice. And he amazed everyone when he used his wisdom to make other godly decisions. One famous example involved two women who were arguing over a baby (1 Kg 3:16–28). Soon Solomon's fame reached the queen of Sheba, who couldn't resist visiting to see for herself. So far so good.

But even the man known the world over for his wisdom could still make mistakes. And Solomon made many bad choices. A major one involved his harem of 700 wives—many of foreign birth. What's wrong with that? First, having a harem violated one of God's commands: "He must not acquire many wives for himself, so that his heart won't go astray" from the Lord (Dt 17:17). And that's exactly what happened to Solomon. His wives encouraged him to worship "other gods" (1 Kg 11:4), and soon he was choosing their gods over the one true God. Because of this idolatry, God promised to take part of the kingdom away from Solomon. But even in that judgment God had mercy on Solomon, because of his father, David. Solomon's son, Rehoboam, would retain one tribe—Judah.

Having wisdom is not a guarantee that you'll always do what is right. But regular consultations with the source of wisdom—God—and the owner's manual—His Word—will help.

YOUR CHOICE

What are you doing to help you make wise, God-honoring decisions?

DAY 104

1 KG 3:16–28

SNAPSHOT

1 KINGS 3:23–28

The king replied, "This woman says, 'This is my son who is alive, and your son is dead,' but that woman says, 'No, your son is dead, and my son is alive.' " The king continued, "Bring me a sword." So they brought the sword to the king. Solomon said, "Cut the living boy in two and give half to one and half to the other."

The woman whose son was alive spoke to the king because she felt great compassion for her son. "My lord, give her the living baby," she said, "but please don't have him killed!" But the other one said, "He will not be mine or yours. Cut him in two!"

The king responded, "Give the living baby to the first woman, and don't kill him. She is his mother." All Israel heard about the judgment the king had given, and they stood in awe of the king because they saw that God's wisdom was in him to carry out justice.

DEPOSIT

WORDS FROM GOD'S WORD TO STORE IN YOUR MIND AND HEART

So God said to him, "Because you have requested this and did not ask for long life or riches for yourself, or the death of your enemies, but you asked discernment for yourself to understand justice, I will therefore do what you have asked. I will give you a wise and understanding heart, so that there has never been anyone like you before and never will be again" (1 Kg 3:11–12).

1 KG 6:1–38

DAY 105

SNAPSHOT

1 KINGS 6:37–38

The foundation of the LORD's temple was laid in Solomon's fourth year in the month of Ziv. In his eleventh year in the eighth month, in the month of Bul, the temple was completed in every detail and according to every specification. So he built it in seven years.

YOUR TURN

FOLLOWING DIRECTIONS

What can you learn from Solomon about making and carrying out plans?

THE BIG PICTURE

1 KG 10:1–13

SNAPSHOT

1 KINGS 10:6–10

She said to the king, "The report I heard in my own country about your words and about your wisdom is true. But I didn't believe the reports until I came and saw with my own eyes. Indeed, I was not even told half. Your wisdom and prosperity far exceed the report I heard. How happy are your men. How happy are these servants of yours, who always stand in your presence hearing your wisdom. May the LORD your God be praised! He delighted in you and put you on the throne of Israel, because of the LORD's eternal love for Israel. He has made you king to carry out justice and righteousness."

Then she gave the king four and a half tons of gold, a great quantity of spices, and precious stones. Never again did such a quantity of spices arrive as those the queen of Sheba gave to King Solomon.

YOUR CHOICE

Today, in what "small" areas do you have the opportunity to obey God?

TOUGH QUESTION

MY FRIENDS SEND ME GAMES AND MP3 FILES THAT I KNOW THEY DOWNLOADED ILLEGALLY. EVERYBODY IS DOING IT . . . I WISH I HAD THE COURAGE TO SAY NO. WHAT SHOULD I DO?

If you know that the games and MP3 files are illegal, you need to say no. To disobey the law is to disobey God. Obeying God is the most important lifelong lesson you can learn, and many Bible characters provide great examples of obedience in tough situations. God told Joshua to walk around the outer walls of Jericho for six days in a row, for example. Then, on the seventh day Joshua was to have the Israelites walk around the city seven times blowing trumpets, and at the final lap everyone was to yell. This was not the typical way to conquer a city. But God had asked Joshua to do it, so Joshua did what God told him to do.

Esther is another great example of obedience, and you can read her story in the book titled with her name.

In contrast, the passage for today tells of King Solomon, who had a great start in his reign, but ended poorly as a result of his disobedience. Infatuated with women, he took numerous wives and lovers, along with their gods, and led the nation into immorality and idolatry.

In each situation, these biblical characters were faced with crucial choices—to obey or not obey. Our situations may not be as dramatic (conquered any cities lately?), but we face similar choices, which your question illustrates.

Disobeying God often is the easier way—after all, floating with the current takes no effort (even a dead fish can do that). Going against the flow takes strength and courage. But every time we make that courageous choice, we grow stronger and better prepared to meet the next challenge. So the next time someone offers a pirated game or MP3 file, politely refuse. And if they ask why, calmly and respectfully explain your allegiance to God.

THE BIG PICTURE

1 KG 12:1–24

APRIL 17

DAY 107

SNAPSHOT

1 KINGS 12:6–9

Then King Rehoboam consulted with the elders who had served his father Solomon when he was alive, asking, "How do you advise me to respond to these people?"

They replied, "Today if you will be a servant to these people and serve them, and if you respond to them by speaking kind words to them, they will be your servants forever."

But he rejected the advice of the elders who had advised him and consulted with the young men who had grown up with him and served him. He asked them, "What message do you advise that we send back to these people who said to me, 'Lighten the yoke your father put on us'?"

YOUR CHOICE

What godly, wise, and trusted counselors can you ask for advice in making important decisions?

NO BRAINER

WISE COUNSEL

King Rehoboam made a foolish choice. After succeeding his father, Solomon, to the throne, he made the wise decision to ask what he should do, how he should rule. A group of intelligent and experienced advisors suggested that the new king lighten the people's burdens. Next, Rehoboam asked his friends for their advice. Asking them wasn't wrong. The problem was that Rehoboam chose the self-centered, short-sighted advice of his young friends over the wise, older counselors.

Rehoboam could have ignored the counsel of his peers, of course, but losing their respect and friendship meant more to him than doing what he knew was right. So he blew it and divided the kingdom.

The lesson is clear: we need to ask for advice from godly, competent, and trustworthy counselors, and then take it. A choice like that may cost some friends, but it could save the family or church or team or community.

APRIL 18

DAY 108

THE BIG PICTURE

1 KG 17:1–24

SNAPSHOT

1 KINGS 17:8–11

Then the word of the LORD came to him: "Get up, go to Zarephath that belongs to Sidon, and stay there. Look, I have commanded a woman who is a widow to provide for you there." So Elijah got up and went to Zarephath. When he arrived at the city gate, there was a widow woman gathering wood. Elijah called to her and said, "Please bring me a little water in a cup and let me drink." As she went to get it, he called to her and said, "Please bring me a piece of bread in your hand."

TOUGH CHOICE

OBEDIENCE

"I don't know what to do, Tim. The resources and manpower just aren't available." I guided the phone cord around my metal desk and walked toward the open window. Sweat continued to pour down my brow, but at least the hot Ecuadorian breeze provided circulation.

Tim, one of my old college roommates, sighed thoughtfully on the other end of the phone. He had always been sensible, and I trusted his wisdom. "What do you *want* to do, Randy?"

I watched several kids playing catch in front of the project house, using the balls and mitts our service group had brought down to the village over a year ago. "I *want* to stay. I *want* to build a school. I *want* to set up a scholarship program." I paused, overwhelmed by my own vision. "I want a lot for this village. But we're out of funds, and our team of fifteen is down to eight. I need people who are going to see this vision out."

"Randy, I wish I had half your passion. What a blessing. You do risk bigger let-downs when you've invested yourself so deeply, but you also stand to experience overwhelming joy."

"I'm just tired of wanting something so badly and not seeing returns. Why isn't the Lord providing? I've been praying." I sat down on the windowsill, leaning against the side.

"Randy, I believe that the Lord is going to honor your work—but it will be on His timetable. Perhaps He needed you to put the vision in motion, and others will carry it to fruition. Perhaps you're so tangled up in the details of making *your* plan succeed, the Lord's trying to recapture your focus. He provides in mysterious ways. But if you feel called to stay in Ecuador, obey!"

I let his words sink in and simmer. They stung because they were true.

I continued to work in the village with my team. I prayed for an obedient heart and that my own master vision wouldn't detract from what the Lord was already accomplishing. Then, several months later, a call came through:

"Randy Smitson? This is Jim Charles, calling on behalf of the university's Board of Grants..."

He offered resources to build a schoolhouse, support to buy school supplies, and funding to set up a scholarship program.

"I don't know what to say, Mr. Charles. God is so good. How can I ever thank you?"

"Keep following the Lord, for starters. He's doing mighty work through you. You can also agree to host groups of university students each semester. We'd like to build upon the work you've already begun, allowing students to practice communication, study economics, and establish ties with other nations. What do you say?"

"Yes. Definitely yes!"

Tears poured down my face as I hung up the phone—to think that I had nearly given up. "I will obey, Lord. I will continue to obey because I trust you. This is *Your* will and vision."

YOUR CHOICE **What are you convinced God wants you to do? What are your dreams for serving Him?**

SNAPSHOT

1 KINGS 18:30–39

Then Elijah said to all the people, "Come near me." So all the people approached him... He said, "Fill four water pots with water and pour it on the offering to be burned and on the wood." Then he said, "A second time!" and they did it a second time. And then he said, "A third time!" and they did it a third time. So the water ran all around the altar; he even filled the trench with water.

At the time for offering the [evening] sacrifice, Elijah the prophet approached [the altar] and said, "LORD God of Abraham, Isaac, and Israel, today let it be known that You are God in Israel and I am Your servant, and that at Your word I have done all these things. Answer me, LORD! Answer me so that this people will know that You, Yahweh, are God and that You have turned their hearts back."

Then Yahweh's fire fell and consumed the burnt offering, the wood, the stones, and the dust, and it licked up the water that was in the trench. When all the people saw it, they fell facedown and said, "Yahweh, He is God! Yahweh, He is God!"

ANCHOR POINT

ANSWERED PRAYERS

What do you do in times of need? Do you seek solace in a slice of cake? Does exercise help to quiet the nagging doubt? Does shopping gloss over the pain? We all have little gods we go to when we find life to be too much for us. We get busy, play video games, read, watch TV—anything to try to help us cope with the problems we face.

In today's passage, the Israelites were struggling with a terrible drought. In their desperation, they called out to Baal, whom they thought would answer.

Do your little gods ever answer you? They may provide some comfort—eating a half gallon of ice cream does have a soothing aspect to it. In the end, however, they will remain silent and, quite possibly, give you an upset stomach.

Only one God will answer your call—the God of Elijah, the one true God. Don't be discouraged if fire does not come down from heaven. He doesn't always answer that way. Just know that He cares and will answer. He will provide what you need, when you need it.

YOUR CHOICE

Remember a time when God clearly answered one of your prayers. How did God answer? Can you remain confident that He will answer in the future as well?

THE BIG PICTURE

1 KG 19:1–21

SNAPSHOT

1 KINGS 19:9b–13a

Then the word of the LORD came to him, and He said to him, "What are you doing here, Elijah?"

He replied, "I have been very zealous for the LORD God of Hosts, but the Israelites have abandoned Your covenant, torn down Your altars, and killed Your prophets with the sword. I alone am left, and they are looking for me to take my life."

Then He said, "Go out and stand on the mountain in the LORD's presence." At that moment, the LORD passed by. A great and mighty wind was tearing at the mountains and was shattering cliffs before the LORD, but the LORD was not in the wind. After the wind there was an earthquake, but the LORD was not in the earthquake. After the earthquake there was a fire, but the LORD was not in the fire. And after the fire there was a voice, a soft whisper. When Elijah heard it, he wrapped his face in his mantle and went out and stood at the entrance of the cave.

JUST LIKE ME

ELIJAH: WHEN DEPRESSION NARROWS THE VIEW

Ever find yourself feeling down? When you're depressed, even the slightest addition to your schedule can seem overwhelming.

The prophet Elijah was well acquainted with depression. After the spiritual high of Mount Carmel where this lone prophet of God triumphed over 850 prophets of Baal and Asherah (see 1 Kg 18), Elijah came down to earth quickly due to death threats from Queen Jezebel. All he could think about was running and hiding. He thought he was isolated and doomed—no way out.

In helping Elijah, God didn't provide pat answers or platitudes. First, He gave the weary prophet food and water to meet his physical needs. Then God revealed Himself, not through what we might expect—a spectacular, rock-shattering wind or earthquake—but in a gentle whisper. And later, He reminded Elijah of an important truth: Elijah was not alone. Other prophets still followed God. And one of those prophets—Elisha—would be Elijah's successor.

Depression has a way of telescoping life down to its narrowest point. It's difficult to see beyond the tunnel, no matter how many "lights" others proclaim are at the end. But as Elijah's experience indicates, God waits beyond the tunnel. Even if we can't sense His presence, He's there.

YOUR CHOICE

In what practical ways has God provided for you when you felt down?

THE BIG PICTURE
1 KG 21:1–29

APRIL 21
DAY 111

SNAPSHOT

1 KINGS 21:17–24

Then the word of the LORD came to Elijah the Tishbite: "Get up and go to meet Ahab king of Israel, who is in Samaria. You'll find him in Naboth's vineyard, where he has gone to take possession of it. Tell him, 'This is what the LORD says: Have you murdered and also taken possession?' Then tell him, 'This is what the LORD says: In the place where the dogs licked Naboth's blood, the dogs will also lick your blood!' "

Ahab said to Elijah, "So, you have caught me, my enemy."

He replied, "I have caught you because you devoted yourself to do what is evil in the LORD's sight. This is what the LORD says: 'I am about to bring disaster on you and will sweep away your descendants:

I will eliminate all of Ahab's males,

both slave and free, in Israel;

I will make your house like the house of Jeroboam son of Nebat and like the house of Baasha son of Ahijah, because you have provoked My anger and caused Israel to sin. The LORD also speaks of Jezebel: The dogs will eat Jezebel in the plot of land at Jezreel:

He who belongs to Ahab and dies in the city, the dogs will eat,

and he who dies in the field, the birds of the sky will eat.' "

DEPOSIT

WORDS FROM GOD'S WORD TO STORE IN YOUR MIND AND HEART

After the earthquake there was a fire, but the LORD was not in the fire. And after the fire there was a voice, a soft whisper. When Elijah heard it, he wrapped his face in his mantle and went out and stood at the entrance of the cave. Suddenly, a voice came to him and said, "What are you doing here, Elijah?" (1 Kg 19:12–13).

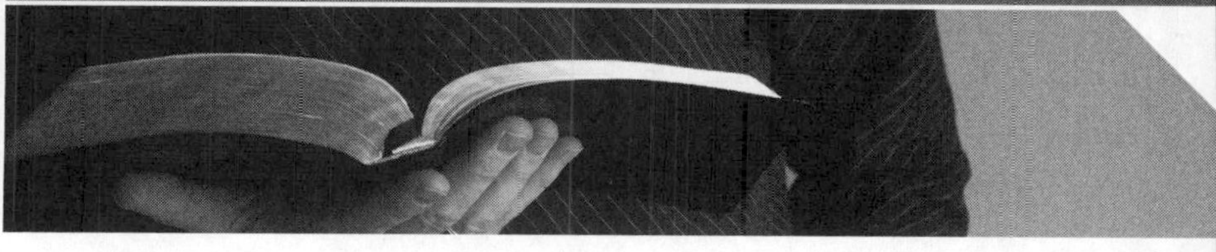

THE BIG PICTURE

1 KG 22:29–40

SNAPSHOT

1 KINGS 22:34–40

But a man drew his bow without taking special aim and struck the king of Israel through the joints of his armor. So he said to his charioteer, "Turn around and take me out of the battle, for I am badly wounded!" The battle raged throughout that day, and the king was propped up in his chariot facing the Arameans. He died that evening, and blood from his wound flowed into the bottom of the chariot. Then the cry rang out in the army as the sun set, declaring:

Each man to his own city,

and each man to his own land!

So the king died and was brought to Samaria. They buried the king in Samaria. Then someone washed the chariot at the pool of Samaria. The dogs licked up his blood, and the prostitutes bathed in it, according to the word of the LORD that He had spoken.

The rest of the events of Ahab's reign, along with all his accomplishments, the ivory palace he built, and all the cities he built, are written about in the Historical Record of Israel's Kings. Ahab rested with his fathers, and his son Ahaziah became king in his place.

YOUR TURN

THE DEATH OF KING AHAB

When are you tempted to think that you can hide from God?

SNAPSHOT

2 KINGS 2:9–12

After they had crossed over, Elijah said to Elisha, "Tell me what I can do for you before I am taken from you."

So Elisha answered, "Please, let there be a double portion of your spirit on me."

Elijah replied, "You have asked for something difficult. If you see me being taken from you, you will have it. If not, you won't."

As they continued walking and talking, a chariot of fire with horses of fire suddenly appeared and separated the two of them. Then Elijah went up into heaven in the whirlwind. As Elisha watched, he kept crying out, "My father, my father, the chariots and horsemen of Israel!" Then he never saw Elijah again. He took hold of his own clothes and tore them into two pieces.

ANCHOR POINT

ELIJAH'S CHARIOT

Elisha knew what he wanted. He wanted to succeed Elijah as prophet to Israel. He persisted, even as Elijah told him to wait, to stay. He kept going, even though he knew his mentor was to be taken from him. When the time came, and Elijah asked him what he wanted, Elisha was ready. He asked for a double portion of Elijah's spirit. In other words, Elisha wanted to be able to do the work Elijah was doing, but even more so.

What do you want very badly right now? A certain career that you are looking toward? A certain lifestyle that you hope to attain? Do you want to be famous or rich or otherwise successful? Having ambitions and aspirations is not bad, but remember that ultimately, those outcomes aren't up to you or anyone around you. God will grant you what He sees fit for you. Just like Elisha had to wait until Elijah's dramatic exit to find out if he would be granted the prophetic role, we often have to wait to see what God will do with our lives.

Striking a balance between working and building for the future and waiting for God to reveal His plan can be difficult. Answers don't come easily, and as in today's passage, life can be confusing at times. Remember, God has called you, has given you talents and abilities, and has a plan for you. Your job is to be ready for it.

YOUR CHOICE

Where do you see yourself in five years? Ten? What can you be doing right now to be ready for that? How would you respond if God were to completely change the direction of your life?

THE BIG PICTURE
2 KG 2:13–25

NO BRAINER

GOD'S DECISION

This story of Elijah and Elisha has many lessons. We can see, for example, the power of a mentor and the love and loyalty of a strong friendship. We can also see the power of God working through His chosen spokespersons. But something else is evident here, beneath the surface. Read the beginning of the chapter, and you'll find this phrase: "Yes, I know. Be quiet." In saying this, Elisha was responding to the question (and implied statement) by the sons of the prophets, "Do you know that today the Lord will take your master away from you?"

The Bible doesn't explain Elisha's answer. Perhaps he didn't want to be reminded of this painful truth because he was already dealing with his grief over losing his "master," his beloved friend and mentor. Maybe he didn't want to be drawn into a theological discussion about God's purposes in this coming event and what the future would hold. Or perhaps Elisha didn't want to allow even a slight opening for doubt about what he knew God wanted *him* to do.

Elisha *knew* that God would take Elijah from him. And Elisha *knew* that God wanted him to be Elijah's successor. Confident in that knowledge, he did what he knew God wanted.

These notes are called "no brainers" because they highlight obvious commands in Scripture that we are to obey. No excuses or rationalizations allowed. And no detours or sidetracks. When we know what God wants, we need to simply affirm, like Elisha, "Yes I know" and then shut out any voice that might try to influence us to make the wrong choice.

So here's the question: What do you know about God, for sure? What do you know He wants you to do?

SNAPSHOT

2 KINGS 2:13–16

Elisha picked up the mantle that had fallen off Elijah and went back and stood on the bank of the Jordan. Then he took the mantle Elijah had dropped and struck the waters. "Where is the LORD God of Elijah?" he asked. He struck the waters himself, and they parted to the right and the left, and Elisha crossed over.

When the sons of the prophets from Jericho, who were facing him, saw him, they said, "The spirit of Elijah rests on Elisha." They came to meet him and bowed down to the ground in front of him.

Then the sons of the prophets said to Elisha, "Since there are 50 strong men here with your servants, please let them go and search for your master. Maybe the Spirit of the LORD has carried him away and put him on one of the mountains or into one of the valleys."

He answered, "Don't send them."

YOUR CHOICE:

What voices often attempt to convince you to make the wrong choice? How will you answer them?

THE BIG PICTURE

2 KG 5:1–27

APRIL 25

DAY 115

SNAPSHOT

2 KINGS 5:11–14

But Naaman got angry and left, saying, "I was telling myself: He will surely come out, stand and call on the name of Yahweh his God, and will wave his hand over the spot and cure the skin disease. Aren't Abana and Pharpar, the rivers of Damascus, better than all the waters of Israel? Could I not wash in them and be clean?" So he turned and left in a rage.

But his servants approached and said to him, "My father, if the prophet had told you to do some great thing, would you not have done it? How much more should you do it when he tells you, 'Wash and be clean'?" So Naaman went down and dipped himself in the Jordan seven times, according to the command of the man of God. Then his skin was restored and became like the skin of a small boy, and he was clean.

JUST LIKE ME

NAAMAN: PUTTING ASIDE PRIDE

When we're sick, we want immediate relief, especially when we're hurting. Pain or illness has a way of humbling us. But Naaman, a proud commander of the army of Aram, wanted to be healed of leprosy on his own terms. His pride desired the pomp and circumstances of a fawning Elisha and an instant miracle. And he had the cash to pay for high-quality service. Instead of offering some exotic cure, a messenger from Elisha told Naaman to wash in the muddy Jordan River.

Naaman was appalled. And if he had clung stubbornly to his pride and had rejected Elisha's advice, he would have missed God's miracle.

Psalm 138:6 shows God's view of pride: "Though the LORD is exalted, He takes note of the humble; but He knows the haughty from afar." Naaman experienced God from afar when he arrived in pride at Elisha's door. But once he came down off his high horse, he experienced God's incredible power and grace.

Have you ever tried to put your best face forward even when you're desperately in need of help? Desperation and pride can't coexist. Many times we're given a choice: seek help or hang on to pride.

YOUR CHOICE

Who do you usually go to when you're in need, desperate for help? Why?

APRIL 26

DAY 116

THE BIG PICTURE

2 KG 11:1–21

SNAPSHOT

2 KINGS 11:7–8

"Your two divisions that go off duty on the Sabbath are to provide protection for the LORD's temple. You must completely surround the king with weapons in hand. Anyone who approaches the ranks is to be put to death. You must be with the king in all his daily tasks."

TOUGH CHOICE

HERO

"Who can tell me what a 'hero' is?" Several little arms shot into the air, straining to grab my attention.

"Oh! Oh! Oh!" Henry, one of my first grade Sunday school students, waved his arm, clearly struggling to stay seated.

"Yes, Henry." I nodded at the freckle-faced boy, whose two front teeth were just starting to grow back in.

"A hero is someone you want to be like when you grow up. Like a really good soccer player or the president."

"Good, Henry!" Another hand shot up. "Yes, Margaret."

"My hero is Rocket Girl. She's a singer, and I want to be a singer just like her!" She buried her reddening cheeks in her hands, bashfully.

"Who is your hero, Miss Olivia?" The pig-tailed girl sitting in my lap looked up over her shoulder at me. "Who do you want to be like when you're all grown up?"

Ten little sets of eyes watched me, eyebrows peaked with interest.

"Well, gosh," I said, taken aback, "I don't really have an answer."

They'd stumped their college-age teacher. *Who is my hero?* When I was young, my heroes had been Olympic gymnasts and basketball stars. I still admired the talent demonstrated by professional athletes, but I didn't want to *be* them. The icons of my youth now showed up only to promote muscle-ache creams and pills for sore joints. *Surely there is somebody!*

"Come on, Miss Olivia! Who do you want to be like when you get older?"

The answer struck me suddenly. It was obvious, but I had never thought of her as a *hero*. "Miss Stacey is who I want to be like when I grow up," I said.

"Who's that," asked Henry pointedly, scrunching up his face.

"Miss Stacey is my mom's best friend. She and her husband Mr. Ken used to babysit my brother and me. She was so much fun! We'd make homemade pizzas together; she'd let us sleep on the floor in sleeping bags; she taught me to face my fear of dogs; she encouraged me to be confident and to always face tough decisions; and she loved Jesus very, very much!"

"But what famous thing did she do?" asked Henry, emphasizing the "famous."

"Well, nothing famous—not all heroes are famous, I suppose. But she was interested in me and cared about me, and she helped me through some really tough times. For that, she's my hero, and that's who I want to be like."

As we get older, the glitz and glamour of fame and stardom begin to lose their luster. Talent rusts, beauty ages, and new stars replace the old. In short, the things of this world that earn widespread glory are most often temporary. Heroes, however, do exist in this broken world. While these individuals are still human, they seek the Lord and demonstrate Christlike qualities. They exemplify servanthood, humility, grace, care, joy, and love. The "Miss Staceys" of this world may not be rich or famous, but they will always be heroes.

YOUR CHOICE **Who are you choosing as your role models, heroes?**

TOUGH QUESTION

SOME OF THE PEOPLE IN MY COMMUNITY ARE THE "CROSS ALL THE T'S AND DOT THE I'S" KIND OF PEOPLE. HOW CAN I TAKE A STAND FOR FREEDOM IN CHRIST WHEN I'M AROUND LEGALISTIC CHRISTIANS?

Jesus often confronted legalistic religious leaders (Pharisees). He constantly preached about heart attitudes as opposed to being careful to do all the right things. Many believed Jesus' message and began to follow Him. The Pharisees, however, were so caught up in following, and enforcing, their legal minutiae that they rejected what Jesus had to offer and killed Him for His message of freedom from their rules.

Rules aren't bad or wrong to follow—check out the Ten Commandments, for example. Remember, Jesus said that He did not come to abolish the law, but to fulfill it (Mt 5:17). But far more important that all the laws and rules is the Person—Christ. Someone can be the grand champion of religious rule-keeping and be far from God. He's much more interested in who we love than in what we do. In fact, check out these passages where God says He wants "mercy" and *sincere* obedience rather than "sacrifice" (1 Sm 15:22–23; Pss 40:6–8; 51:16–19; Jr 7:21–23; Hs 6:6; Am 5:21–24; Mc 6:6–8).

You can be a breath of fresh air to the legalistic Christians around you by living out a joyful relationship with Christ. The deeper you understand His relationship with you, the more filled up your heart will be and the more it will overflow to the people around you. Your joy will be contagious, and people will want the same relationship with Christ that you have. But be sensitive to those who believe differently and are weaker in this area. The Bible teaches clearly that we shouldn't abuse our freedom or cause a weaker believer to stumble or fall (see 1 Co 8). So unless these people want to force you to do something *contrary* to God's Word, don't make a big deal about *their* legalistic tendencies.

SNAPSHOT

2 KINGS 23:1–3

So the king sent messengers, and they gathered to him all the elders of Jerusalem and Judah. Then the king went to the LORD's temple with all the men of Judah and all the inhabitants of Jerusalem, as well as the priests and the prophets—all the people from the youngest to the oldest. As they listened, he read all the words of the book of the covenant that had been found in the LORD's temple. Next, the king stood by the pillar and made a covenant in the presence of the LORD to follow the LORD and to keep His commandments, His decrees, and His statutes with all his mind and with all his heart, and to carry out the words of this covenant that were written in this book; all the people agreed to the covenant.

YOUR CHOICE

How can you lovingly live your freedom in Christ?

DAY 118

THE BIG PICTURE

EZR 3:8–13

SNAPSHOT

EZRA 3:10–11

When the builders had laid the foundation of the LORD's temple, the priests, dressed in their robes and holding trumpets, and the Levites descended from Asaph, holding cymbals, took their positions to praise the LORD, as King David of Israel had instructed. They sang with praise and thanksgiving to the LORD: "For He is good; His faithful love to Israel endures forever." Then all the people gave a great shout of praise to the LORD because the foundation of the LORD's house had been laid.

DEPOSIT

WORDS FROM GOD'S WORD TO STORE IN YOUR MIND AND HEART

They sang with praise and thanksgiving to the LORD: "For He is good; His faithful love to Israel endures forever." Then all the people gave a great shout of praise to the LORD because the foundation of the LORD's house had been laid (Ezr 3:11).

THE BIG PICTURE

NEH 2:1–20

APRIL 29

DAY 119

SNAPSHOT

NEHEMIAH 2:4–6

Then the king asked me, "What is your request?"

So I prayed to the God of heaven and answered the king, "If it pleases the king, and if your servant has found favor with you, send me to Judah and to the city where my ancestors are buried, so that I may rebuild it."

The king, with the queen seated beside him, asked me, "How long will your journey take, and when will you return?" So I gave him a definite time, and it pleased the king to send me.

YOUR TURN

REBUILDING THE RUINS

What relationships in your past need to be rebuilt?

DAY 120

THE BIG PICTURE
NEH 5:1–19

SNAPSHOT

NEHEMIAH 5:6–11

I became extremely angry when I heard their outcry and these complaints. After seriously considering the matter, I accused the nobles and officials, saying to them, "Each of you is charging his countrymen interest." So I called a large assembly against them and said, "We have done our best to buy back our Jewish countrymen who were sold to foreigners, but now you sell your own countrymen, and we have to buy them back." They remained silent and could not say a word. Then I said, "What you are doing isn't right. Shouldn't you walk in the fear of our God and not invite the reproach of our foreign enemies? Even I, as well as my brothers and my servants, have been lending them money and grain. Please, let us stop charging this interest. Return their fields, vineyards, olive groves, and houses to them immediately, along with the percentage of the money, grain, new wine, and olive oil that you have been assessing them."

JUST LIKE ME

NEHEMIAH: ADVOCATE FOR THE POOR

What gets your blood boiling? Nehemiah was infuriated at the social injustice of his day, namely the way the poor in Jerusalem were being treated during a time of famine. Because of the taxes demanded by the king of Persia, lands were being mortgaged. Because of the exorbitant interest on the loans, sons and daughters were being sold into slavery to pay debts. Nehemiah was appalled that the people of Israel would take advantage of their own people. But beyond such feelings, Nehemiah took action by directly confronting those involved. He took a courageous stand. This wall-builder was not afraid to get his hands dirty.

The homeless. The poor. Kids trapped in abusive homes. Elderly people bilked by con artists. These are the scenes of social injustice in our day. Many times we fear getting involved due to time commitments or the thought of leaving our comfort zone. If scenes of social injustice deeply disturb you, are you prepared to go beyond your feelings and take a stand for right?

YOUR CHOICE

How will you take a stand against social injustice?

MEI
MAI
MAI
MAY
MAGGIO
MAIO
MAYO

THE BIG PICTURE

NEH 8:1–18

MAY 1

DAY 121

SNAPSHOT

NEHEMIAH 8:1–3

When the seventh month came and the Israelites had settled in their towns, all the people gathered together at the square in front of the Water Gate. They asked Ezra the scribe to bring the book of the law of Moses that the LORD had given Israel. On the first day of the seventh month, Ezra the priest brought the law before the assembly of men, women, and all who could listen with understanding. While he was facing the square in front of the Water Gate, he read out of it from daybreak until noon before the men, the women, and those who could understand. All the people listened attentively to the book of the law.

YOUR CHOICE

What can you do to improve your Bible-reading habits?

NO BRAINER

READING GOD'S WORD

The Israelites had so much joy and enthusiasm when it came to the Scriptures. When the scrolls were opened and read, the people gathered around to listen. They stood up in respect for God's Word and praised the Lord for everything He had done. Several days later, they gathered to study the law again, this time in greater depth. When they learned that they were supposed to live in shelters during the celebration they were having, they immediately went out and built them. They were filled with joy and eagerness to obey God.

We know the Bible is God's Word (in fact, that's probably why you have this book). And we say that it tells us what to believe and how to live. Yet we can easily put off reading and studying Scripture. And even more disturbing, we can neglect *applying* the biblical principles and direct commands—actually doing what we know God wants us to do.

In contrast, God's people in this passage received His Word with attention, honor, and joy. Then they made the life changes that they heard God speaking to them.

How often do you read the Bible: just "one minute" a day? Occasionally? When you *have* to? Remember, God's Word is "profitable for teaching, for rebuking, for correcting for training in righteousness" (2 Tm 3:16). So be a regular reader—and doer—of the Word (Jms 1:23).

MAY 2

DAY 122

THE BIG PICTURE

EST 1:1–22

SNAPSHOT

ESTHER 1:10–12

On the seventh day, when the king was feeling good from the wine, Ahasuerus commanded Mehuman, Biztha, Harbona, Bigtha, Abagtha, Zethar, and Carkas, the seven eunuchs who personally served him, to bring Queen Vashti before him with her royal crown. He wanted to show off her beauty to the people and the officials, because she was very beautiful. But Queen Vashti refused to come at the king's command that was delivered by his eunuchs. The king became furious and his anger burned within him.

TOUGH CHOICE

FOR GRANTED

Two rickety ceiling fans clicked above our heads on the restaurant patio. The sweltering sun made it a particularly hot June afternoon. Several tables covered with plastic tablecloths were pushed together to hold our large group that had just come from my grandmother's funeral. I sat between my mom, Judy's, two best friends: Mary Lou, her best childhood friend, and Tammy, her best adulthood friend.

"Do you remember the time Bootsie adopted that baby rabbit and fed it from a bottle until it got strong enough to live on its own?"

"She did have a heart for little stragglers."

"Reminds me of the time Bootsie told Principal Dean that if Mrs. Grommit didn't start treating Judy nicely, she'd personally visit Mrs. Grommit during class to set her straight."

"Now how did she get the name 'Bootsie'?"

"What all the kids in the neighborhood called her because of the slippers she wore around the house."

I leaned forward and rested my elbows on the table, my back damp with sweat. Members of my mom's side of the family were spread around the table, all of them boisterous and very southern. Intermixed were members of my dad's side of the family, clean-cut and mild-mannered. My grandmother's passing had brought both sides of my family together for the first time. How such starkly different groups of people could ever be related had always perplexed me.

My Aunt Wanda's booming twang pulled my attention to the end of the table: ". . . and then Bootsie said to Larry, 'Larry, you think the sun came up just to hear you crow!'" The whole table erupted in laughter as my aunt reminisced about another one of Granny Bootsie's choice expressions. I smiled, looking around the table at the faces of my family. Such . . . *joy.* The intimacy of the moment overwhelmed me. *Why have I always taken my family for granted?*

Miss Tammy rubbed my back and leaned over, close so I could hear above the talking. "Your Granny Bootsie was an amazing lady. I wish I could have known her better."

"She'd be so happy to have everyone together like this. I wish she was here . . ." I said, suddenly choked up, ". . . just so she could hear how much people really loved her, appreciated her."

Miss Tammy's kind and knowing eyes rested on my face. "She knows," she said quietly, "and I have a feeling your Granny Bootsie is seeing and hearing all of this."

I believed her. My grandmother loved the Lord, and I knew she was with God, happier and healthier than she had ever been on this earth. I closed my eyes. *Dear Lord, please tell Granny Bootsie I'm sorry for taking her for granted. Tell her that I love her and miss her. We all do.*

YOUR CHOICE **What can you do to not take loved ones for granted?**

TOUGH QUESTION

MY FRIENDS ARE GOING TO SEE THE NEWEST MOVIE, BUT IT'S RATED R FOR VIOLENCE AND NUDITY. WHAT SHOULD I DO?

Following the crowd is easy. We don't want to make waves, so we go places, say things, and act certain ways to avoid conflicts and save friendships. But if we have decided to stand for Christ, we will be confronted with choices where we must draw the line and say "no further," where we must step away from the crowd. This is one of those occasions.

Movies, like music and other cultural influences can subtly but powerfully affect us. We may sincerely think (or conveniently rationalize), "this movie has no effect on me—it's just a movie." In reality, we are greatly influenced by what we see and hear. That's why companies spend so much on commercials—they know the power of visual and audio advertising. When we are *not* thoughtful about what we are opening our minds to, we can become desensitized to violence, sex, foul language, and unbiblical worldviews and lifestyles.

So we should be very careful about our entertainment choices.

If you take a thoughtful and prayerful approach about the potential influences of media, you will say no quite often. Taking this stand will mean having to explain your choice to friends and family, but this will give you the opportunity to positively influence your friends and call them to a higher standard. Be prepared, however, for ridicule—that's just how some people will respond. But that's OK; better to do what God wants and take a little heat.

God calls His people to dwell on "whatever is true whatever is honorable, whatever is just, whatever is pure, whatever is lovely, whatever is commendable—if there is any moral excellence and if there is any praise" (Php 4:8). So use that verse as an entertainment guide.

iSTAND

SNAPSHOT

ESTHER 2:15–18

Esther was the daughter of Abihail, the uncle of Mordecai who had adopted her as his own daughter. When her turn came to go to the king, she did not ask for anything except what Hegai, the king's trusted official in charge of the harem, suggested. Esther won approval in the sight of everyone who saw her.

Esther was taken to King Ahasuerus in the royal palace in the tenth month, the month Tebeth, in the seventh year of his reign. The king loved Esther more than all the other women. She won more favor and approval from him than did any of the other virgins. He placed the royal crown on her head and made her queen in place of Vashti. The king held a great banquet for all his officials and staff. It was Esther's banquet. He freed his provinces from tax payments and gave gifts worthy of the king's bounty.

YOUR CHOICE

With what wrong entertainment choices are you being tempted?

MAY 4

DAY 124

THE BIG PICTURE

EST 3:1–15

SNAPSHOT

ESTHER 3:5–6

When Haman saw that Mordecai was not bowing down or paying him homage, he was filled with rage. And when he learned of Mordecai's ethnic identity, Haman decided not to do away with Mordecai alone. He set out to destroy all of Mordecai's people, the Jews, throughout Ahasuerus' kingdom.

ANCHOR POINT

DANGER AND COURAGE

Why didn't Mordecai just bow to Haman? Wouldn't you have? Why be so stubborn? Even if Mordecai didn't approve of Haman and did not respect his authority, all he would have had to do was bow a couple of times a day. Then the conflict would have been over, for him and for all of the Jews in the kingdom! Wasn't he being unreasonable? The other way certainly would have been easier.

How often do we do take the easy way out? How many little compromises do we make to allow life to be a little smoother? Just go with the flow—it will all be over soon, and it doesn't really matter. That movie isn't so bad. The lyrics might be questionable, but who listens to the lyrics?

Remember, doing what is right will not always be easy or popular. God never promises anyone an easy life. He never says that to follow Him will bring a person a ton of friends. He does promise unconditional love, protection, and grace. Mordecai chose those promises over taking the easy way out. Will you have the courage to do the same when you are called to make an unpopular choice?

YOUR CHOICE

What are you simply letting slide even though you know you should be taking action? What step can you take this week to move in the right direction?

THE BIG PICTURE
EST 4:1–17

MAY 5

DAY 125

SNAPSHOT

ESTHER 4:13–17

Mordecai told the messenger to reply to Esther, "Don't think that you will escape the fate of all the Jews because you are in the king's palace. If you keep silent at this time, liberation and deliverance will come to the Jewish people from another place, but you and your father's house will be destroyed. Who knows, perhaps you have come to the kingdom for such a time as this."

Esther sent this reply to Mordecai: "Go and assemble all the Jews who can be found in Susa and fast for me. Don't eat or drink for three days, night and day. I and my female servants will also fast in the same way. After that, I will go to the king even if it is against the law. If I perish, I perish." So Mordecai went and did everything Esther had ordered him.

DEPOSIT

WORDS FROM GOD'S WORD TO STORE IN YOUR MIND AND HEART

"If you keep silent at this time, liberation and deliverance will come to the Jewish people from another place, but you and your father's house will be destroyed. Who knows, perhaps you have come to the kingdom for such a time as this" (Est 4:14).

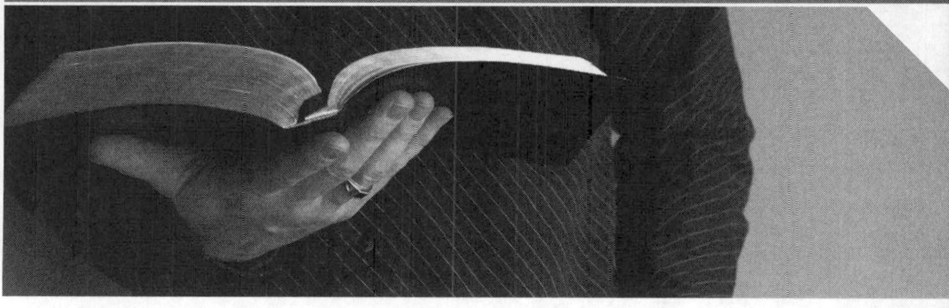

MAY 6

DAY 126

THE BIG PICTURE

EST 5:1–14

SNAPSHOT

ESTHER 5:1–2

On the third day, Esther dressed up in her royal clothing and stood in the inner courtyard of the palace facing it. The king was sitting on his royal throne in the royal courtroom, facing its entrance. As soon as the king saw Queen Esther standing in the courtyard, she won his approval. The king extended the golden scepter in his hand toward Esther, and she approached and touched the tip of the scepter.

YOUR TURN

RISKING IT ALL

When was the last time you did something scary to obey God?

SNAPSHOT

ESTHER 7:1–4

The king and Haman came to feast with Esther the queen. Once again, on the second day while drinking wine, the king asked Esther, "Queen Esther, whatever you ask will be given to you. Whatever you seek, even to half the kingdom, will be done."

Queen Esther answered, "If I have obtained your approval, my king, and if the king is pleased, spare my life—this is my request; and spare my people—this is my desire. For my people and I have been sold out to destruction, death, and extermination. If we had merely been sold as male and female slaves, I would have kept silent. Indeed, the trouble wouldn't be worth burdening the king."

ANCHOR POINT

GOD PROTECTS HIS PEOPLE

At times God surprises us—when He works through simple means as well as elaborate schemes. The book of Esther records one of those surprising occasions. Scholars have debated about whether this book should be included in the Bible. Nowhere in Esther is God mentioned. No prayers are recorded. The book seems to be a thoroughly secular tome, dealing with egotistical men and manipulative women. How does this show us anything about God?

We don't have to look too closely at today's passage to see God's fingerprints all over this story. It is amazing to see how it plays out. A king who has trouble sleeping. A queen who plans a banquet. A reward for past service. The elements fall into place swiftly, all aligning to bring about the salvation of a people.

Often our lives work that way. So many small happenings blur our vision of the big picture—until much later. We may have felt that God had abandoned us, that since He was not explicitly evident He must not have been there at all. But, as with Esther, He was there, orchestrating events and protecting His people. If we can trust God even when we cannot see His hand, we can certainly live in His peace.

YOUR CHOICE

In what situations do you doubt God's protection?
How has that changed your approach to life?
How can you better trust God to take care of you?

SNAPSHOT

JOB 1:1–5

There was a man in the country of Uz named Job. He was a man of perfect integrity, who feared God and turned away from evil. He had seven sons and three daughters. His estate included 7,000 sheep, 3,000 camels, 500 yoke of oxen, 500 female donkeys, and a very large number of servants. Job was the greatest man among all the people of the east.

His sons used to have banquets, each at his house in turn. They would send an invitation to their three sisters to eat and drink with them. Whenever a round of banqueting was over, Job would send for his children and purify them, rising early in the morning to offer burnt offerings for all of them. For Job thought: Perhaps my children have sinned, having cursed God in their hearts. This was Job's regular practice.

JUST LIKE ME

JOB: CHOOSING TO STAY CONNECTED EVEN WHILE SUFFERING

How do you respond when you're in pain or suffering in some way? Do you stoically bear it or do you want others to know just how much and to what degree you're suffering, especially if the suffering seems unfair? Some people rant at God, demanding to know why He put them through such agony. Others go into a depression of silence and despair. Job chose to praise.

Job stands as the archetype of suffering. Having lost all of his children, his wealth and health in just a day, Job could have complained or cursed, but he chose to praise instead, contrary to his wife's advice (see Jb 2:9). Job wasn't superhuman. In many of the dialogues throughout the book of Job, we see him struggling to come to terms with a horrendous chain of events. Although he questioned God, the lines of communication remained open between Job and his Creator. Job took a stand for truth when he proclaimed God's goodness at the lowest point in his life.

In suffering, we're reminded of our fragile state as humans—that "we are dust" (Ps 103:14). But Job's experience reminds us that we must remain connected to our Creator. As in Job's situation, God may not answer our demands for an explanation to our suffering. But He provides His presence and His peace.

YOUR CHOICE

In difficult times, how will people know that you trust in God?

THE BIG PICTURE

JB 2:1–13

MAY 9

DAY 129

SNAPSHOT

JOB 2:7–10

So Satan left the LORD's presence and infected Job with incurable boils from the sole of his foot to the top of his head. Then Job took a piece of broken pottery to scrape himself while he sat among the ashes.

His wife said to him, "Do you still retain your integrity? Curse God and die!"

"You speak as a foolish woman speaks," he told her. "Should we accept only good from God and not adversity?" Throughout all this Job did not sin in what he said.

NO BRAINER

WHEN BAD THINGS HAPPEN

If you ever think you have it bad, remember Job. He lost *everything*—literally—except for a bitter wife and insensitive friends. Home, livestock, workers—all gone. Even his children died. And then he lost his health. In a very short time, Job plunged from prosperity to poverty, from wealth to waste, from a mansion to a garbage heap. So put yourself in his sandals. How would you feel? What would you do? And, even more important, what would you think of God?

When tragedy strikes, many people react with anger toward God: "How could He do this to me?" Others find their faith sinking in a sea of doubt. And who can blame them, we may think—after what they've gone through. That's how Job's wife responded—remember, she lost everything, too. "Curse God and die!" she spat out to Job as he scratched his sores.

Yet Job stood strong in his faith. The Bible explains "Throughout all this Job did not sin in what he said" (Jb 2:10). Amazing. Now look at Job's reply to his wife's suggestion. He exclaimed, "Should we accept only good from God and not adversity?" (Jb 2:10). What a profound insight.

When life is good—that is, we're well fed, surrounded by loving friends and family, healthy, and secure, with spending money to spare—we think that's normal, the way life should be. And we take all those *blessings* for granted. Seldom does anyone question what he or she has done to deserve all those benefits. When something bad happens, however, even something as small as a sports injury or a fender-bender, we wonder, "Why me?" That's because we assume that pain and suffering are the exceptions in life and that we should be sheltered from problems and struggles. We think we deserve "good" and that "bad" events should happen to someone else.

Job got it right, and we should follow his example. Instead of focusing on our circumstances, we should keep our focus on God. We should trust Him, regardless of our situation. Later, Job would exclaim, "Even if He kills me, I will hope in Him" (Jb 13:15).

Remember: only God sees the big picture; God loves you and cares about what you're going through; God's way is best—it really is.

YOUR CHOICE

What has happened recently where you've been tempted to be angry with God?

DAY 130

THE BIG PICTURE
JB 38:1–41

SNAPSHOT

JOB 38:1–7

Then the Lord answered Job from the whirlwind. He said:

Who is this who obscures My
counsel
with ignorant words?
Get ready to answer Me like a man;
when I question you, you will
inform Me.
Where were you when I established
the earth?
Tell Me, if you have understanding.
Who fixed its dimensions? Certainly
you know!
Who stretched a measuring line
across it?
What supports its foundations?
Or who laid its cornerstone
while the morning stars sang together
and all the sons of God shouted
for joy?

YOUR CHOICE

What can you do to focus on God and His love for you instead of on your circumstances?

TOUGH QUESTION

I FEEL DEPRESSED A LOT. YET, I'M A CHRISTIAN AND AM SUPPOSED TO HAVE THE "JOY" OF THE LORD IN ME. HOW CAN I OVERCOME THE HARD TIMES AND CHOOSE TO BE HAPPY?

Depression has many causes, but sometimes we can feel depressed when we hear all the bad news in the world or when things aren't working out the way we thought they would in our lives. That's when we need a focus check so we can move our attention off our problems and onto God.

A common misconception is that Christians are supposed to be happy all the time. Happiness is an emotion, and it's impossible to continually wear a silly smile and feel giddy. Joy is a character trait, and you can have joy without feeling happy. Joy is present underneath the ups and downs of emotions and the unpredictable nature of circumstances. It is confidence that God is working in us and through us and for us (Rm 8:28).

God might put you in a tough situation where a positive attitude seems impossible, but you can have joy in any circumstance. James 1:2–3 commands believers to "consider it a great joy, my brothers, whenever you experience various trials, knowing that the testing of your faith produces endurance." God is the source of joy, and focusing on the truth about God can bring joy to your soul. God's character never changes, and He is good and will fulfill His promises.

The ultimate reason for joy, however, is the fact that Jesus died on the cross in your place, taking the penalty for your sins, and then He rose from the dead. He loves you that much (Jn 3:16). (That should make you want to shout!) And He gives you the great hope of one day living with Him in heaven. That hope brings joy because God never changes, His truth never changes, and His promises will be fulfilled.

So choose truth and you'll find joy!

JOB 42:7–8

After the LORD had finished speaking to Job, He said to Eliphaz the Temanite: "I am angry with you and your two friends, for you have not spoken the truth about Me, as My servant Job has. Now take seven bulls and seven rams, go to My servant Job, and offer a burnt offering for yourselves. Then My servant Job will pray for you. I will surely accept his prayer and not deal with you as your folly deserves. For you have not spoken the truth about Me, as My servant Job has."

SNAPSHOT

MAY 11

DAY 131

THE BIG PICTURE

JB 42:1–17

TOUGH CHOICE

MOUNTAIN TOP

Beef jerky had never tasted so good. The day's ten-mile hike into the southern Rockies with my Bible study group had left me famished and willing to eat just about anything. I took another bite of the smoky-tasting leather. *Not too bad.*

The setting sun and the clear sky promised a chilly night. I leaned back against a nearby rock, propping my left leg up on my backpack. My ACL surgery had been almost a year ago, but hiking all day had made my knee stiff and sore.

"Okay, guys. If you'll gather around and pull out your Bibles, we'll start tonight's devotional," said Clay, our youth leader. "We'll be in the book of Job."

I reached for my Bible and flipped it open as Clay began with a short prayer and started to read:

"Does Job fear God for nothing?" Satan replied. "Haven't You placed a hedge around him, his household, and everything he owns? You have blessed the work of his hands, and his possessions are spread out in the land. But stretch out your hand and strike everything he owns, and he will surely curse you to your face."

"Very well," the LORD told Satan, "everything he owns is in your power. However, you must not lay a hand on Job himself . . ."

As Clay depicted Job's continual faithfulness to the Lord, I stared into the smoldering embers of the campfire. *I am not faithful like Job. Nowhere close.*

"What difference does it make to know that God always has the final word in our lives?" Clay proposed to the group, looking up from his Bible. "Josh, your thoughts?"

I shifted my weight against the rock that was now jabbing into my back. "Well, I guess it's supposed to be reassuring…but why would the Lord allow such hardship for someone who loved Him?" I stared down at my swollen knee.

Clay didn't answer immediately. I knew he understood my question. I was supposed to go to college on a soccer scholarship, but it had all slipped away with one misplanted step—and *snap.*

"Josh, look out over the ridge. What do you see?"

I looked up. "More ridges," I said, skeptically.

"Yes! And while the ridges appear to get smaller, it doesn't mean we're on the highest ridge in the range. Our lives are a series of peaks and valleys that prepare us for a lifelong journey. During our time on earth, we'll never know what lies over the next ridge. But we do know that the Lord will travel alongside us, and we do know that heaven, alone, is the ultimate peak."

The message was difficult to stomach. "I know the Lord allowed my injury for a reason. It's just hard to understand why, when I can't see what the future holds."

Clay smiled, "And there, Josh, begins your journey with the Lord. Lean on Him. Let Him carry your pack. There is no better way to strengthen your faith, and there is nothing He wants more!"

YOUR CHOICE **What personal setbacks or life situations have caused you to lose perspective? What can you do to see life from God's point of view?**

DAY 132

SNAPSHOT

PSALM 1:1–3

How happy is the man
who does not follow the advice of the wicked,
or take the path of sinners,
or join a group of mockers!
Instead, his delight is in the LORD's instruction,
and he meditates on it day and night.
He is like a tree planted beside streams of water
that bears its fruit in season
and whose leaf does not wither.
Whatever he does prospers.

DEPOSIT

WORDS FROM GOD'S WORD TO STORE IN YOUR MIND AND HEART

How happy is the man who does not follow the advice of the wicked, or take the path of sinners, or join a group of mockers! Instead, his delight is in the LORD's instruction, and he meditates on it day and night (Ps 1:1–2).

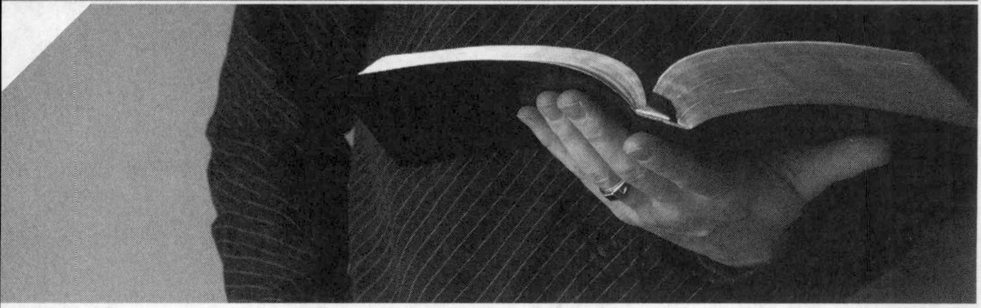

THE BIG PICTURE

PS 8:1–9

MAY 13

DAY 133

SNAPSHOT

PSALM 8:3–4

When I observe Your heavens,
the work of Your fingers,
the moon and the stars,
which You set in place,
what is man that You remember him,
the son of man that You look after him?

YOUR TURN

THE VALUE OF HUMANS

How do you know you have worth?

THE BIG PICTURE

PS 23:1–6

NO BRAINER

A SHEEP'S SONG

If "the LORD is my shepherd," what, exactly, does that mean? How should that truth affect how we live, how we take a stand for Christ?

First we must understand that we are, in fact, *sheep*—beings that need protection and guidance. Sheep are totally dependent on their shepherd for safety, shelter, and sustenance. An individual sheep who wanders off on its own will soon be in trouble—lost, hungry, and perhaps surrounded by wolves.

We also know that the ultimate well-being of a flock of sheep depends on the competence of the shepherd. Sheep being watched and led by a lazy, inept, or evil shepherd will be nearly as bad off as the individual sheep that goes astray. But God is the perfect Shepherd—all powerful, all knowing, and loving. He will guide us the *right* way.

It only makes sense, then, to stay close to our Shepherd.

When we take a stand, the Shepherd is standing with us. If we are not standing with the Shepherd, we are weak, vulnerable, and wandering lambs. But with our Shepherd, we can even face wolves with boldness.

And our Shepherd promises much more. He will renew our strength, allowing us to keep standing and not become exhausted. He will guide us in choosing when and where to stand. He will protect and comfort us when we face adversity.

Because the Lord is your Shepherd, you have everything you need.

SNAPSHOT

PSALM 23:1–3

The LORD is my shepherd;
there is nothing I lack.
He lets me lie down in green pastures;
He leads me beside quiet waters.
He renews my life;
He leads me along the right paths
for His name's sake.

YOUR CHOICE

How can you get closer to the Shepherd?

THE BIG PICTURE

PS 51:1–19

MAY 15

DAY 135

SNAPSHOT

PSALM 51:2–5

Wash away my guilt,
and cleanse me from my sin.
For I am conscious of my rebellion,
and my sin is always before me.
Against You—You alone—I have sinned
and done this evil in Your sight.
So You are right when You pass sentence;
You are blameless when You judge.
Indeed, I was guilty when I was born;
I was sinful when my mother conceived me.

JUST LIKE ME

DAVID: WHEN YOU'RE *REALLY* SORRY

"Sor-ree." Ever hear that from someone? Many young children say it when they're not really sorry (except to have been caught) but are forced to apologize under a parent's stern eye. But the criticized behavior rarely changes.

You won't find a "sor-ree" attitude in David's psalm. The prophet Nathan had confronted David about his adultery with Bathsheba and the murderous cover-up. And David had, then, exhibited the kind of sincere contrition that clearly pleased God and once again cemented his reputation as a man after God's heart (see 2 Sm 12:13). That's what this psalm is about. David owned up to the wrong and provided a textbook example of how to repent. He further came out of hiding by admitting that the sin was part of his makeup as a sinful person—not just a one-time deal or something he was "trapped" into. Most important of all, he acknowledged he had sinned against God.

Taking responsibility for our actions, for having hurt someone, can be difficult. And even when we do, we sometimes wallow in the embarrassment and shame and can't move on. But owning up and moving on are courageous choices we must make. David wrote this psalm so he *could* move on. It demonstrated his belief that the God of the universe would not hold his sin against him once David admitted it. We can have this same assurance when we approach God. In fact, because of Jesus, we're doubly assured!

YOUR CHOICE

What, if anything, do you need to release to God in order to move on?

DAY 136

THE BIG PICTURE

PS 103:1–22

SNAPSHOT

PSALM 103:8–11

The Lord is compassionate and
gracious,
slow to anger and full of faithful love.
He will not always accuse us
or be angry forever.
He has not dealt with us as our sins
deserve
or repaid us according to our offenses.
For as high as the heavens are above
the earth,
so great is His faithful love
toward those who fear Him.

TOUGH QUESTION

I WANT TO SHARE MY FAITH WITH KIDS AT SCHOOL. HOW CAN I RELATE TO THEM WHILE STILL STANDING FOR MY BELIEFS?

The challenge for a Christian is to be in the world but not of the world. In other words, God want us to be involved in the world, to love people, to stand for His truth, to serve, and to make a difference. He doesn't expect us to withdraw and live in a cave or just hang with other Christians. At the same time, we are to be different from the world in our values, thoughts, and actions (Rm 12:1–2).

The best way to relate to your friends is to be a good friend: caring, loyal, dependable, truthful, and so forth. Then, when you share your beliefs or take a stand for what you know is right, they will respect you and your stance. And they'll listen to you because you've earned the right to be heard.

Relating to your friends requires you to have a kind and nonjudgmental attitude. Sharing your faith is received well when it is not shared forcefully or with a prideful attitude.

Relating to your friends, but standing for your beliefs, requires you to engage in culture in order to let Christ's light shine through you. At times you will encounter attitudes, actions, and activities that go against your Christian commitment. If your friends go that direction, you should try to understand them without condemning them.

Standing up for your beliefs requires you to be well-read and knowledgeable about issues that might come up. Evolution, abortion, drinking, drugs—these are just a few possible topics. Sharing your faith can happen naturally when tough issues arise. It's important to be in the Word of God consistently so that you can recall key Bible verses. And here's a crucial biblical truth to remember: "A gentle answer turns away anger, but a harsh word stirs up wrath" (Pr 15:1).

YOUR CHOICE

Which of your friends would be most open to Christ's Good News? What can you do to share God's story with them?

THE BIG PICTURE

PS 139:1–24

MAY 17

DAY 137

SNAPSHOT

PSALM 139:1–5

LORD, You have searched me and known me.
You know when I sit down and when I stand up;
You understand my thoughts from far away.
You observe my travels and my rest;
You are aware of all my ways.
Before a word is on my tongue,
You know all about it, LORD.
You have encircled me;
You have placed Your hand on me.

ANCHOR POINT

HOW WELL GOD KNOWS US

This passage presents an amazing testament to the depth of God's knowledge. Consider how much you know about your friends and family. It's not anywhere near the level of understanding that is discussed in these verses. Yet this is the level to which God knows us, understand us, and loves us.

When faced with a passage like this, we have to wonder about our view of God. How real does this passage feel? Do you really believe that God knows everything about you? Did He write down all of your days before you were born? Is He big enough to actually know all of these facts about every person who has ever been born? Can God really know each person to that level?

Or is He a smaller god, one who fits better as an agent of our will?

Letting God be God can be a challenge. Often we would rather deal with a god that we can control somewhat. When faced with the breadth of God's knowledge, either we can embrace this truth about our incredible God and take comfort in the fact that He knows us thoroughly, or we can reject it and pass it off as a fairy tale. How will you respond?

YOUR CHOICE

Do you really believe that God knows you this well? If so, how does this truth affect how you live?

MAY 18

DAY 138

THE BIG PICTURE

PS 145:1–21

SNAPSHOT **PSALM 145:8–9**

The Lord is gracious and compassionate,
slow to anger and great in faithful love.
The Lord is good to everyone;
His compassion rests on all He has made.

TOUGH CHOICE

CREATIVITY

"Well, what do you think?" I asked, resting my guitar on the step in front of me. A steady ocean breeze swayed across the porch of the little bungalow that my two best friends and I had settled into for the weekend. One last getaway before graduation.

"Whitney, it's your best song yet. The lyrics are pure poetry!" said Emma, rocking on the porch swing.

"I just can't believe how far you've come on the guitar," said Julie from atop the porch railing. "Seriously, when are you going to get a demo recorded?"

I stood up, gazing across the sand and into the ocean. *So peaceful.*

"Really, Whit—you need to give this a shot. The Lord's clearly given you the gift of song and songwriting. You ought to at least give the music industry a try," said Emma.

I turned toward my two friends. They'd been my biggest encouragers and supporters over the last few years. "You guys are great, you know that?" I said, smiling at their eager expressions. "It's just not that easy with the wedding coming up this summer. Carter and I both agree that I need to find a steady job, so we can start saving up for seminary." I twisted the engagement ring around my finger. "Chasing these singing dreams just isn't practical."

Julie threw her head back. "But, Whit, this is what you were born to do! Forget practicality for once."

"Julie's right, Whit. If you really want this, you're going to have to let go of the practical decisions," said Emma, giving me the you-know-I'm-right look.

That night I walked along the beach, letting the tide ride up and wash over my ankles. Billions and billions of starts dotted the sky. *God placed each and every one of them.* The thought overwhelmed me.

"Oh, Lord. What should I do?" I asked aloud. "I love singing so much, but the timing just doesn't feel right for pursuing a career in this industry." I sat down in the sand. "I know you're the one who gave me this gift, this passion, but how do I use it?"

I listened to the waves wash in and out, the breeze rush through the palm branches. It was as though nature, itself, had written a song of praise.

All you have made will praise you, Lord. . . . The verse from Psalms 145 surfaced in my thoughts, as another wave pushed up the beach toward my feet. *Even these waves that do nothing more than wash in and right back out every day are praising you, Lord.*

"God, I don't know where to draw the line between being responsible and finding a steady job, and pursuing what I love, using the talents you've given me. All I know is that I love you, I love to sing, and I want to use my songs to bring glory to you."

I looked back up at the sky, just as a shooting star shot across the dazzling canvas. "Lord, thank you for instilling a bit of your creativity in me, and in doing so, providing a way in which I can praise you daily."

YOUR CHOICE

What talent should you be developing and using for God's glory?

THE BIG PICTURE

PR 4:1–27

MAY 19

DAY 139

SNAPSHOT

PROVERBS 4:10–14

Listen, my son. Accept my words,
and you will live many years.
I am teaching you the way of wisdom;
I am guiding you on straight paths.
When you walk, your steps will not be hindered;
when you run, you will not stumble.
Hold on to instruction; don't let go.
Guard it, for it is your life.
Don't set foot on the path of the wicked;
don't proceed in the way of evil ones.

DEPOSIT

WORDS FROM GOD'S WORD TO STORE IN YOUR MIND AND HEART

Trust in the LORD with all your heart,
and do not rely on your own understanding;
think about Him in all your ways, and He will
guide you on the right paths (Pr 3:5–6).

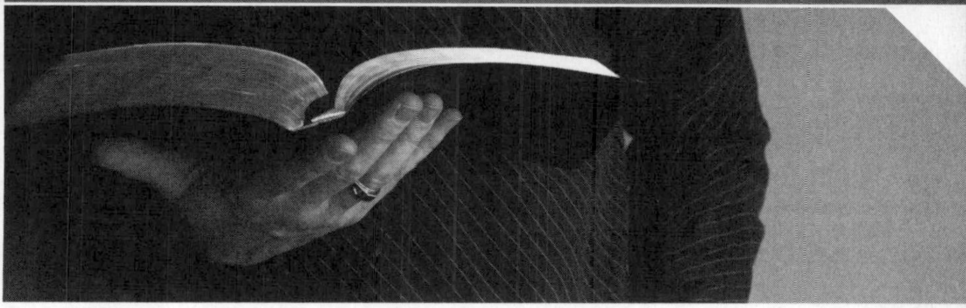

DAY 140

THE BIG PICTURE

PR 5:1–23

SNAPSHOT

PROVERBS 5:15–21

Drink water from your own cistern,
water flowing from your own well.
Should your springs flow in the streets,
streams of water in the public squares?
They should be for you alone
and not for you to share with strangers.
Let your fountain be blessed,
and take pleasure in the wife of your youth.
A loving doe, a graceful fawn—
let her breasts always satisfy you;
be lost in her love forever.
Why, my son, would you be infatuated
With a forbidden woman
or embrace the breast of a stranger?
For a man's ways are before the LORD's eyes,
and He considers all his paths.

YOUR TURN

WISE WORDS ABOUT SEX

How do these words match what you hear around you every day?

TOUGH QUESTION

I'M BEGINNING TO SEE THAT MY PARENTS ARE NOT PERFECT PEOPLE EITHER AND MAKE POOR CHOICES. WHAT SHOULD I DO WHEN I DISAPPROVE OF SOMETHING THEY ARE DOING?

Recognizing good choices and bad choices indicates a maturing faith and growth in your spiritual life. Seeing good or bad choices in a friend's life is one thing, but seeing it in the lives of your parents is another. God has set your parents to be the authority over you, and seeing them make poor decisions that you wouldn't even make for yourself can be painful.

In Matthew 18:15–17 Jesus teaches how to deal with a close relationship when that person sins. First, we should "go and rebuke the person in private." Of course, rebuking a close friend or one's parents will take tact and the correct attitude. The Bible tells us to "honor" our parents, and that command never expires. Thus, we should always speak to our parents with respect and humility—certainly not with pride, anger, or sarcasm. So we can explain to our parents that we disagree with their decision and why we do. This could provide a great opportunity for sharing our faith with them.

Depending on your relationship with your parents, they may receive your words well and stop making bad decisions. If they don't respond well to your rebuke, then know that you have said your peace, and let it go. They aren't forcing *you* to make bad decisions, so you should continue to follow Christ and His commands and trust that the Holy Spirit will convict your mom and dad. Only God can change a person's heart, and you can rest in the freedom that you are not responsible for your parents' bad decisions.

SNAPSHOT

ECCLESIASTES 12:1

So remember your Creator in the days of your youth:

Before the days of adversity come,
and the years approach when you will say,
"I have no delight in them."

YOUR CHOICE

In what way do your choices influence your parents and their choices?

MAY 22

DAY 142

THE BIG PICTURE

IS 6:1–13

SNAPSHOT

ISAIAH 6:8

Then I heard the voice of the Lord saying:
Who should I send?
Who will go for Us?
I said:
Here I am. Send me.

TOUGH CHOICE

DESPITE MYSELF

From my seat on the cabin's wooden floor, I could see millions of stars twinkling across the night sky and dipping into the lake. The windows were open, allowing a light, Ozark breeze to pacify the room.

Little bugs danced above the lantern that sat in the middle of our cabin's circle, made up of twelve 14-year-old campers and two college counselors. I was working my second summer as a counselor at the camp where I had been a camper so many years before. My legs ached from coaching four classes of cross-country each day. My arms felt like putty after hoisting a dozen girls over the challenge wall. My head pounded from lack of sleep. And my soul ached from depression. I missed my family and friends. I was anxious, not knowing what I wanted to do with my future after senior year. I felt lonely, despite being surrounded by hundreds of campers. And I felt distant from the Lord, discouraged by my lack of passion compared to the previous summer.

"No, wait! My very favorite part of camp was water skiing for the first time," Molly, one of my campers, exclaimed, pulling my attention back into our little cabin. It was the last night of the term, and each of the girls was sharing her favorite part of camp.

"Thanks, Molly. That's a good one," said my co-counselor Libby, moving the group along. "What about you, Allie?" Allie was the smallest of the bunch. She was quick to serve others, and she always asked thought-provoking questions. Eager and curious, she reminded me quite a bit of myself at that age.

"Well," she said softly, playing with the end of her braid, "I would have to say my runs with Heather." She looked over at me and smiled bashfully. "I just really loved getting to go on runs with her during free time. She and I had very good conversations, and she really encouraged me."

"Thanks, Allie," I said, nearly moved to tears. "Running with you was my favorite part of camp, too!" I had no idea that she appreciated our runs so much. She was a talented runner and needed to log miles each week during the summer for her school cross-country team. I invited her to run with me during my off period so she could get in the miles. Each run brought a new conversation topic: Witnessing to friends, dating, balancing priorities, the difference between perfectionism and using the talents with which we've been blessed. I had never thought much about the impact of these talks. I was just happy to have good company while I escaped the chaos of camp.

I leaned back into the shadows, bowing my head. *Lord, forgive me for my feelings of self-pity and for putting you in a box. It was your will that I come to camp this summer, and you have used me to reach campers, even when I was feeling useless and discouraged. Place my focus on you—not my own feeling of success when I've done my "Christian duties." Thank you for Allie and the impact she's had on me. Thank you for using me, despite myself.*

YOUR CHOICE **When are you tempted to feel sorry for yourself, to get tired of serving? How can you change your focus from self to God?**

THE BIG PICTURE
IS 53:1-12

MAY 23
DAY 143

SNAPSHOT

ISAIAH 53:3–5

He was despised and rejected by men,
a man of suffering who knew what sickness was.
He was like one people turned away from;
He was despised, and we didn't value Him.
Yet He Himself bore our sicknesses,
and He carried our pains;
but we in turn regarded Him stricken,
struck down by God, and afflicted.
But He was pierced because of our transgressions,
crushed because of our iniquities;
punishment for our peace was on Him,
and we are healed by His wounds.

ANCHOR POINT

THE SUFFERING SERVANT

The suffering Messiah portrayed in today's passage was nothing like what people were waiting for. They expected a conquering king who would defeat their enemies, set them free, and rule the world in power and glory. The people of Israel weren't interested in Isaiah's description. In fact, years later when Christ did come, even His disciples did not make the connection. They only understood years later, after His death and resurrection, that Jesus was the "Suffering Servant" who had been prophesied centuries before.

Do you find that at times you wish Jesus were different? For example, wouldn't you like Him to return and straighten out the various messes the church has made? Or have you ever thought: Why doesn't He tell us precisely how to worship? Why do we have so many denominations and arguments? Just show us the right way.

But God doesn't. Instead, He has given us the Bible, which contains timeless truths that we need to apply to our specific situations. He has also given us the perfect example to follow—His Son. Jesus was humble, and He was obedient, even to suffering and death. If we could live like Jesus did, perhaps we wouldn't need Him to come down and straighten us out.

YOUR CHOICE

How does the suffering Messiah affect your view of Christ? How should you live in light of this model?

DAY 144

SNAPSHOT

JEREMIAH 1:4–5

The word of the LORD came to me:

I chose you before I formed you in the womb;

I set you apart before you were born.

I appointed you a prophet to the nations.

JUST LIKE ME

JEREMIAH: CALLED TO A DIFFICULT TASK

If you've ever thought you had to be of a certain age in order to be useful to God, consider Jeremiah. Called to be a prophet as a youth, Jeremiah had an excuse at the ready: "Oh no, LORD GOD! Look, I don't know how to speak since I am only a youth" (Jr 1:6). But God didn't immediately respond, "You know, you're right! I'll wait till you're older." Instead, He refused to allow Jeremiah to coast on that excuse. Not only that, God equipped Jeremiah to speak His words.

Jeremiah had one of the most difficult ministries a prophet can have: proclaiming God's coming judgment on a people—His people—mired in rebellion. As God warned Jeremiah, the people would not listen to him and would instead fight against him (Jr 1:19), especially as he warned of the coming exile.

How quick would you be to say yes to such a task? Many people, if they are honest, would admit to feeling resentful, especially if we're given no opportunity to refuse. But Jeremiah did not refuse, even though the opposition to his ministry grew steadily worse over the years.

What stands in your way of giving your life totally into God's control? Your youth? Your plans? Do you think there is any excuse you can name that God can't overcome?

YOUR CHOICE

What can you do for God where you are right now?

SNAPSHOT

JEREMIAH 36:19–23

The officials said to Baruch, "You and Jeremiah must hide yourselves and tell no one where you are." Then they came to the king at the courtyard, having deposited the scroll in the chamber of Elishama the scribe, and reported everything in the hearing of the king. The king sent Jehudi to get the scroll, and he took it from the chamber of Elishama the scribe. Jehudi then read it in the hearing of the king and all the officials who were standing by the king. Since it was the ninth month, the king was sitting in his winter quarters with a fire burning in front of him. As soon as Jehudi would read three or four columns, Jehoiakim would cut the scroll with a scribe's knife and throw the columns into the blazing fire until the entire scroll was consumed by the fire in the brazier.

YOUR CHOICE

What can you do to make Bible reading and study a more regular part of your daily schedule?

NO BRAINER

THE BOOK BURNING

Here's the deal. Jeremiah was God's prophet. That means he had been chosen and appointed and gifted by God to declare His Word to the people, especially the leaders of Judah. In fact, the first couple of verses of chapter 36 explain, "In the fourth year of Jehoiakim son of Josiah, king of Judah, this word came to Jeremiah from the LORD: 'Take a scroll, and write on it all the words I have spoken to you concerning Israel, Judah, and all the nations from the time I first spoke to you during Josiah's reign until today.'"

So Jeremiah does just that—he dictates God's message to his secretary, Baruch, and delivers it to the king. But the king not only rejects the message; he shreds the scroll and burns it, showing utter contempt for Jeremiah and, by extension, for God.

We may wonder how anyone could treat God's Word so terribly, yet people still act that way today—sometimes, even those who profess to believe that the Bible is divinely inspired and inerrant. They may not cut it with a knife and burn it (although that happens in some cultures), but they rip it in other ways. God's Word is disrespected when we make fun of passages we don't understand; when we treat it casually, almost flippantly, as though it's simply another book; when we don't read and study it regularly; when we ignore its plain teachings or refuse to obey them.

So here's the big question: How do you treat the holy Scriptures? Despite what others may think about the Bible, choose to read, study, and apply it. Take your stand for discovering God's message to you in His Word.

DAY 146

THE BIG PICTURE

JR 38:1–13

SNAPSHOT

JEREMIAH 38:4–6

The officials then said to the king, "This man ought to die, because he is weakening the morale of the warriors who remain in this city and of all the people by speaking to them in this way. This man is not seeking the well-being of this people, but disaster."

King Zedekiah said, "Here he is; he's in your hands since the king can't do anything against you." So they took Jeremiah and dropped him into the cistern of Malchiah the king's son, which was in the guard's courtyard, lowering Jeremiah with ropes. There was no water in the cistern, only mud, and Jeremiah sank in the mud.

DEPOSIT

WORDS FROM GOD'S WORD TO STORE IN YOUR MIND AND HEART

"For I know the plans I have for you—this is the LORD's declaration—plans for your welfare, not for disaster, to give you a future and a hope" (Jr 29:11).

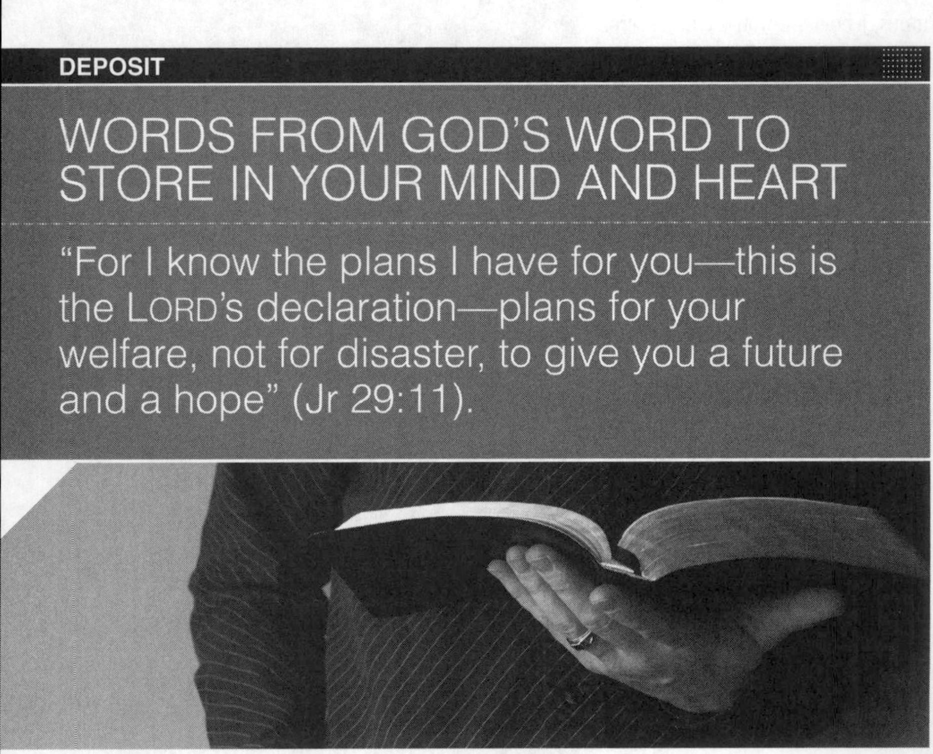

SNAPSHOT

EZEKIEL 37:1–6

The hand of the LORD was on me, and He brought me out by His Spirit and set me down in the middle of the valley; it was full of bones. He led me all around them. There were a great many of them on the surface of the valley, and they were very dry. Then He said to me, "Son of man, can these bones live?"

I replied, "Lord GOD, only You know."

He said to me, "Prophesy concerning these bones and say to them: Dry bones, hear the word of the LORD! This is what the Lord GOD says to these bones: I will cause breath to enter you, and you will live. I will put tendons on you, make flesh grow on you, and cover you with skin. I will put breath in you so that you come to life. Then you will know that I am the LORD."

YOUR TURN

A VALLEY OF DRY BONES

What can you do to better understand God's plan for the world?

MAY 28

DAY 148

THE BIG PICTURE

DN 1:1–21

SNAPSHOT

DANIEL 1:8–10

Daniel determined that he would not defile himself with the king's food or with the wine he drank. So he asked permission from the chief official not to defile himself. God had granted Daniel favor and compassion from the chief official, yet he said to Daniel, "My lord the king assigned your food and drink. I'm afraid of what would happen if he saw your faces looking thinner than those of the other young men your age. You would endanger my life with the king."

TOUGH CHOICE

FAITHFULNESS

I dropped onto my hotel bed in Rhein, Germany, staring up at the ceiling. My knee throbbed after a particularly hard hit during the game against the Berlin Thunder earlier that day. For the past three months my cramped hotel room had been a home of sorts while I trained and played football as an American in the European football league. My goal was to earn a spot on an NFL team after gaining a bit more experience overseas.

Sitting up, I pulled a book off my bedside table and began to read, trying to ignore the loud music in the adjoining room.

Knock, knock! "Luke, man, you coming? We're leaving for the bars." Viktor, one of my teammates from Sweden, walked into the room.

I set my book down and sat up. "Hey, Viktor. I don't . . ."

"Come on, man. We are celebrating the victory," he urged in a heavy accent. "Let loose. Drink. Bring home a girl!" A wide smile spread across his face as he clapped his hands together.

I chuckled a little, shaking my head at his cabin-fever-induced eagerness. "Thanks, but no thanks, Viktor. It's a night in for me."

"But the girls, Luke!" he dropped his hands and threw his head back, exasperated.

"Viktor, friend," I said leaning back against the pillows on my bed, "You know I already have a girlfriend back home in the States!"

"But this is Germany! She will never know. Come out and have fun!"

How do I explain this to him and not sound self-righteous? "Here's the thing," I began tentatively. "I don't want to hook up with girls at the bars. My girlfriend trusts me," I paused, but then added, "and even if I wasn't dating, the girls at the bars only care about fooling around, and I'm not interested in that."

Viktor stared at me, bewildered and perplexed. He started to say something, but stopped. Hesitantly, he asked, "This decision, is this something to do with your religion?"

"You could say that," I said, curious to see how he would respond to my answer. A lot of the guys had given up on inviting me out to the bars and clubs when they found out I was "religious."

"Hmm . . ." He appeared to be mulling the thought over in his head. "You are an interesting fellow, Luke. Maybe we'll talk some time about your religion." His words were thoughtful, earnest.

Voices from the hall announced the group's departure. Viktor glanced over his shoulder at the door. "I will see you tomorrow, then?"

"Sounds good, Viktor. Have fun tonight."

Viktor laughed, "Yes . . . but not *too much* fun." He turned and left to join the other guys from the team.

I started to read, but closed my book after a moment. *Thanks, Lord, for giving me the strength to resist temptation and not go along with the crowd. Help Viktor resist temptation tonight, and please provide another opportunity for me to share more about my faith. Amen.*

YOUR CHOICE **When have you been tempted to do something wrong, thinking, "No one will ever know"? What helped you make the right, God-honoring choice?**

SNAPSHOT

DANIEL 2:13–19a

The decree was issued that the wise men were to be executed, and they searched for Daniel and his friends, to execute them.

Then Daniel responded with tact and discretion to Arioch, the commander of the king's guard, who had gone out to execute the wise men of Babylon. He asked Arioch, the king's officer, "Why is the decree from the king so harsh?" Then Arioch explained the situation to Daniel. So Daniel went and asked the king to give him some time, so that he could give the king the interpretation.

Then Daniel went to his house and told his friends Hananiah, Mishael, and Azariah about the matter, [urging] them to ask the God of heaven for mercy concerning this mystery, so Daniel and his friends would not be killed with the rest of Babylon's wise men. The mystery was then revealed to Daniel in a vision at night.

YOUR CHOICE:

In what authority relationships, right now, do you need to add a dose of tact and discretion? For what "rulers" in your life do you need to be praying?

NO BRAINER

A KING'S DREAM

Daniel had a problem, a big problem. Nebuchadnezzar, the wacko king of Babylon, in a fit of anger after his impossible request hadn't been fulfilled, decreed that *all* the wise men in the land ("diviner-priests, mediums, sorcerers, and [other influential wise men]"—verse 2) should be rounded up and executed—killed, eliminated, wiped out. Daniel and his friends were included in that round-up even though they hadn't done anything to offend the king. Because they were "wise men," they were guilty by association.

So what did Daniel do? The Bible says, "Then Daniel responded with tact and discretion to Arioch." "Tact and discretion"—that would be the most unlikely response for most people. He could have made demands, angrily defended himself, and railed about the unfairness of it all. And if he had lost his cool, he would have lost the battle . . . and his life. But Daniel could choose to remain calm in this life-threatening situation because he trusted in God. Then, after buying some time, he and his friends prayed earnestly for divine mercy and guidance.

You probably won't be faced with the prospect of execution, but you may have to deal with other "decrees" from those in authority over you. The principal says your Christian club can't meet in a certain room. A teacher assigns a killer paper. An employer demands extra hours. A coach gives someone else your starting spot.

While the natural instinct might be to react with anger, bitterness, cynicism, or some other bad attitude, a response like Daniel's would be much better, and Christlike. Choose to answer with "tact and discretion" if you disagree with the ruling. Then make the situation a matter of prayer.

DAY 150

SNAPSHOT

DANIEL 2:31–36

"My king, as you were watching, a colossal statue appeared. That statue, tall and dazzling, was standing in front of you, and its appearance was terrifying. The head of the statue was pure gold, its chest and arms were silver, its stomach and thighs were bronze, its legs were iron, and its feet were partly iron and partly fired clay. As you were watching, a stone broke off without a hand touching it, struck the statue on its feet of iron and fired clay, and crushed them. Then the iron, the fired clay, the bronze, the silver, and the gold were shattered and became like chaff from the summer threshing floors. The wind carried them away, and not a trace of them could be found. But the stone that struck the statue became a great mountain and filled the whole earth.

"This was the dream; now we will tell the king its interpretation."

YOUR CHOICE

Where have you seen God at work recently?

TOUGH QUESTION

OUR WORLD TRIES TO EXPLAIN *EVERYTHING* AS A PRODUCT OF NATURAL PROCESSES. HOW CAN I TAKE A STAND FOR MY GOD WHO SPEAKS THROUGH DREAMS AND CAN EVEN TELL SOMEONE ELSE THE MEANING OF IT?

God created the heavens and the earth, and He established the cycles of day and night, seasons, birth and death—the natural order. But God is *supernatural* and isn't bound by His creation. We can't predict or foretell what His mighty hand will do.

Jesus promised to send another Counselor—the Holy Spirit (Jn 14:16). About this third Person in the Trinity, Jesus said, "The world is unable to receive Him because it doesn't see Him or know Him. But you do know Him, because He remains with you and will be in you" (Jn 14:17). So don't be surprised when people refuse to acknowledge a supernatural source or God-answer for anything. People who don't know Christ do not think supernaturally.

Regarding dreams, we see from today's passage that God has spoken through dreams in the past. He still can do so if He so chooses. On the other hand, we must be careful at ascribing every unusual event to God's intervention. The main way that God speaks to us today is through His Word, the Bible. Certainly He can, and does, use sermons, music, friends, art, circumstances, and, perhaps, even dreams, but the messages from those sources *must* be consistent with Scripture; otherwise they're not from God.

In John 16 we read about Jesus telling His disciples about what the Holy Spirit will do. "He will convict the world about sin, righteousness, and judgment: about sin, because they do not believe in Me; about righteousness, because I am going to the Father and you will no longer see Me; and about judgment, because the ruler of this world has been judged" (v. 8).

Jesus encourages us to not be discouraged if the world does not understand or rejects God's ways. Despite misunderstanding and opposition, we can stand firm in our faith by quietly allowing the Holy Spirit to do the convicting.

SNAPSHOT

DANIEL 3:13–18

Then in a furious rage Nebuchadnezzar gave orders to bring in Shadrach, Meshach, and Abednego. So these men were brought before the king. Nebuchadnezzar asked them, "Shadrach, Meshach, and Abednego, is it true that you don't serve my gods or worship the gold statue I have set up? Now if you're ready, when you hear the sound of the horn, flute, zither, lyre, harp, drum, and every kind of music, fall down and worship the statue I made. But if you don't worship it, you will immediately be thrown into a furnace of blazing fire—and who is the god who can rescue you from my power?"

Shadrach, Meshach, and Abednego replied to the king, "Nebuchadnezzar, we don't need to give you an answer to this question. If the God we serve exists, then He can rescue us from the furnace of blazing fire, and He can rescue us from the power of you, the king. But even if He does not rescue us, we want you as king to know that we will not serve your gods or worship the gold statue you set up."

JUST LIKE ME

SHADRACH, MESHACH, AND ABEDNEGO: HOLDING ON IN THE HEAT

"When the heat is on . . ." We all know this phrase. But seldom has it been so literal as it was with Shadrach, Meshach, and Abednego—three friends of Daniel, the Old Testament prophet. Having already taken a stand for integrity in their youth by refusing to partake of the rich diet of King Nebuchadnezzar's court, the three men further risked their lives by refusing to worship a statue of gold at the king's order. Death in a fiery furnace was the penalty for their refusal.

According to the text, Shadrach, Meshach, and Abednego left it up to God about whether or not a rescue would take place. Regardless of God's choice, they would remain faithful to Him. So God's rescue at the climax of their story vindicated their faith.

Heat can be a blessing and a hazard. It can help shape a diamond or completely destroy a house. But in the hands of a master craftsman like God heat can temper a life to a peak of usefulness. In what way are you feeling the heat today? Allow God to use the pressure you're under to shape you further.

YOUR CHOICE

What risks have you taken lately on behalf of God and His kingdom?

JUNI
JUIN
JUNI
JUNE
GIUGNO
JUNHO
JUNIO

THE BIG PICTURE

DN 5:1–30

JUNE 1

DAY 152

SNAPSHOT

DANIEL 5:1–8

King Belshazzar held a great feast for 1,000 of his nobles and drank wine in their presence. Under the influence of the wine, Belshazzar gave orders to bring in the gold and silver vessels that his predecessor Nebuchadnezzar had taken from the temple in Jerusalem, so that the king and his nobles, wives, and concubines could drink from them. . . .

At that moment the fingers of a man's hand appeared and began writing on the plaster of the king's palace wall next to the lampstand. As the king watched the hand that was writing, his face turned pale, and his thoughts so terrified him that his hip joints shook and his knees knocked together. The king called out to bring in the mediums, Chaldeans, and astrologers. He said to these wise men of Babylon, "Whoever reads this inscription and gives me its interpretation will be clothed in purple, have a gold chain around his neck, and have the third highest position in the kingdom." So all the king's wise men came in, but none could read the inscription or make known its interpretation to him.

ANCHOR POINT

THE WRITING ON THE WALL

You've probably heard the expression, "the handwriting is on the wall," meaning that a certain outcome is inevitable. Most people probably don't know the phrase's meaning. And virtually no one would have any idea of its source. But here's the answer—it comes right from today's passage.

When Belshazzar saw the handwriting, he didn't have a clue either: "numbered" . . . "weighed" . . . "divided." But when Daniel gave the explanation, Belshazzar learned what was going to happen and why. God had judged Belshazzar, and His punishment was coming, soon.

The inevitability of God's judgment can be a scary proposition. But it's sure, and we should be ready for it.

If you need to take care of something between you and God, do it *sooner* rather than later. Belshazzar should have learned from his predecessor, Nebuchadnezzar, who had been humbled by God and had repented. Instead, Belshazzar knowingly defiled the temple and paid dearly for it. God's judgment and punishment came upon him instantly.

This story should put the fear of God in us. His judgment can be swift. It can be severe. Just because God has shown mercy in the past, giving us time to change our ways, does not mean He will continue to do so.

YOUR CHOICE

What writing do you see on the walls of your life?
What is God telling you to do, to change?

THE BIG PICTURE

DN 6:1–28

SNAPSHOT

DANIEL 6:10–16

When Daniel learned that the document had been signed, he went into his house. The windows in its upper room opened toward Jerusalem, and three times a day he got down on his knees, prayed, and gave thanks to his God, just as he had done before. Then these men went as a group and found Daniel petitioning and imploring his God. So they approached the king and asked about his edict: "Didn't you sign an edict that for 30 days any man who petitions any god or man except you, the king, will be thrown into the lions' den?"

The king answered, "As a law of the Medes and Persians, the order stands and is irrevocable."

Then they replied to the king, "Daniel, one of the Judean exiles, has ignored you, the king, and the edict you signed, for he prays three times a day." As soon as the king heard this, he was very displeased; he set his mind on rescuing Daniel and made every effort until sundown to deliver him.

Then these men went to the king and said to him, "You as king know it is a law of the Medes and Persians that no edict or ordinance the king establishes can be changed."

So the king gave the order, and they brought Daniel and threw him into the lions' den. The king said to Daniel, "May your God, whom you serve continually, rescue you!"

DEPOSIT

WORDS FROM GOD'S WORD TO STORE IN YOUR MIND AND HEART

When Daniel learned that the document had been signed, he went into his house. The windows in its upper room opened toward Jerusalem, and three times a day he got down on his knees, prayed, and gave thanks to his God, just as he had done before (Dn 6:10).

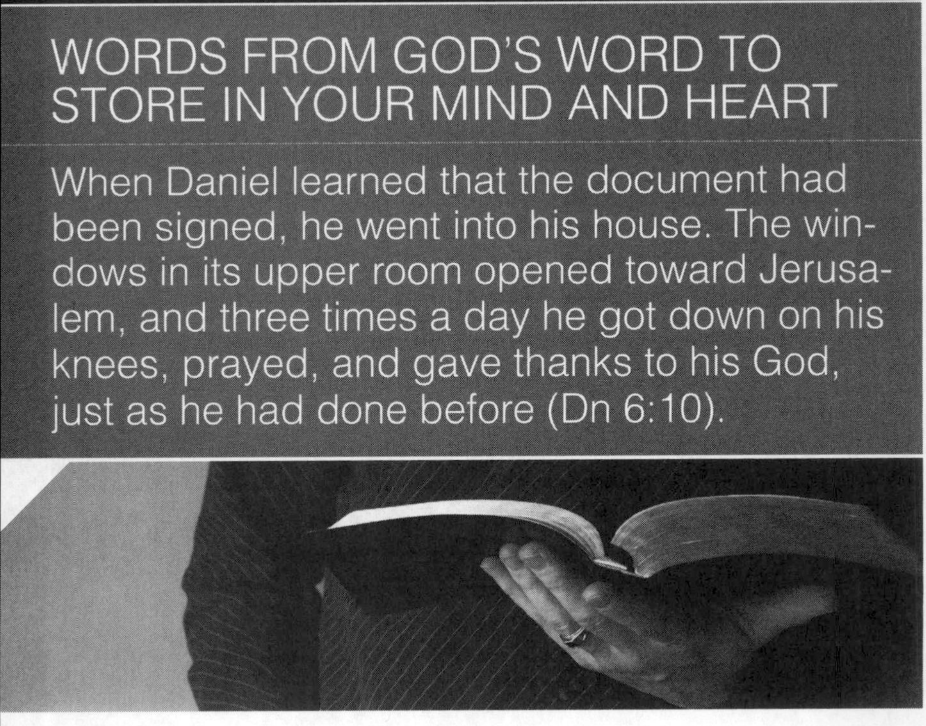

THE BIG PICTURE

JNH 1:1–2:10

JUNE 3

DAY 154

SNAPSHOT

JONAH 1:8–12

Then they said to him, "Tell us who is to blame for this trouble we're in. What is your business and where are you from? What is your country and what people are you from?"

He answered them, "I am a Hebrew. I worship Yahweh, the God of the heavens, who made the sea and the dry land."

Then the men were even more afraid and said to him, "What is this you've done?" For the men knew he was fleeing from the LORD's presence, because he had told them. So they said to him, "What should we do to you to calm this sea that's against us?" For the sea was getting worse and worse.

He answered them, "Pick me up and throw me into the sea so it may quiet down for you, for I know that I'm to blame for this violent storm that is against you."

YOUR TURN

BENDING GOD'S DIRECTIONS

When did you last try to avoid doing what you knew God wanted you to do?

THE BIG PICTURE
JNH 3:1–4:11

SNAPSHOT

JONAH 4:6–11

Then the LORD God appointed a plant, and it grew up to provide shade over Jonah's head to ease his discomfort. Jonah was greatly pleased with the plant. When dawn came the next day, God appointed a worm that attacked the plant, and it withered.

As the sun was rising, God appointed a scorching east wind. The sun beat down on Jonah's head so that he almost fainted, and he wanted to die. He said, "It's better for me to die than to live."

Then God asked Jonah, "Is it right for you to be angry about the plant?" "Yes," he replied. "It is right. I'm angry enough to die!"

So the LORD said, "You cared about the plant, which you did not labor over and did not grow. It appeared in a night and perished in a night. Should I not care about the great city of Nineveh, which has more than 120,000 people who cannot distinguish between their right and their left, as well as many animals?"

JUST LIKE ME

JONAH: UNIMPRESSED BY GRACE

When you're forced to do what you don't want to do, how do you respond? Jonah, having been thwarted in his travel arrangements, went to Nineveh and preached its destruction "according to the LORD's command" (Jnh 3:3). But Jonah's true attitude, his anger, was revealed in his response to the Lord's desire to show mercy to the people of Nineveh (see Jnh 3:10–4:3). How dare the Lord renege on His promise to destroy the city! And after dragging Jonah there too!

Jonah's prejudice toward the people of Nineveh came from knowledge of their cruelty, war mongering, and other aspects of "wickedness" (Jnh 1:2) that made them ripe for destruction. To Jonah's chagrin, the mercy of God truly extended to those who didn't deserve it! We call that *grace*.

We may be quicker to gloat when we read about the punishment of those we think are deserving of it, than we are to ask God for mercy on their behalf. Yet when *we* need mercy, we don't want God to skimp on it.

Tempted to react like Jonah—just along for the ride and secretly resentful—when God acts in a way that's contrary to your views? Consider the lesson that Jonah learned. God cannot behave in a way that is contrary to His nature, no matter how much we may desire Him to do so. Instead, we can recall the many times that He treated us far more graciously than we deserved.

YOUR CHOICE

When has God shown grace to you? With what results?

LK 1:1–4; JN 1:1–18

JUNE 5

DAY 156

SNAPSHOT

JOHN 1:1–5

In the beginning was the Word,
and the Word was with God,
and the Word was God.
He was with God in the beginning.
All things were created through Him,
and apart from Him not one thing was created
that has been created.
Life was in Him,
and that life was the light of men.
That light shines in the darkness,
yet the darkness did not overcome it.

ANCHOR POINT

BEGINNINGS

The incarnation of Christ is the central truth of the Christian faith. Without His birth, life, death, and resurrection, nothing else really matters. Therefore, the records of Jesus' time here on earth are of utmost importance. When Luke and John set out to chronicle that time, they both prefaced their works with descriptions of just how important this event was. Luke begins his Gospel with a personal note to his friend, Theophilus, describing what he is about to embark on. John starts with an overview of the life of Christ from the beginning of time until He becomes the Savior of the world. Incredible.

Yet, often when we come to the events of the gospel, we read quickly through them and move on. The stories are familiar; and because they are often repeated from book to book, the familiarity we feel can lessen the impact of the words. But they are records of the most important events in history. These events were recorded so that we may, as Luke points out, "know the certainty of the things about which you have been instructed" (Lk 1:4). Be sure you don't make too little of the Gospels, because based on what Luke and John said, it seems like it would be difficult to make too much of them.

YOUR CHOICE

Have the events of the Gospels lost some of their impact on your life? Has the repetition drained some of the meaning for you? How can you restore the power of the Gospels in your life?

JUNE 6

DAY 157

THE BIG PICTURE

LK 1:5–25

SNAPSHOT

LUKE 1:18–19

"How can I know this?" Zechariah asked the angel. "For I am an old man, and my wife is well along in years."

The angel answered him, "I am Gabriel, who stands in the presence of God, and I was sent to speak to you and tell you this good news."

TOUGH CHOICE

FOREST FIRE

Jamie's face was pallid. The camp director's wife stood on one of the mess hall benches, quickly scanning the room full of campers. "I need everyone to listen!" she announced firmly. The mealtime chatter dissolved at the urgency in her voice. "The forest fires have changed direction and are now moving rapidly toward camp. I need you to hurry back to your cabins, grab your sleeping bags and toothbrushes—nothing else—and line up with your cabin at the flag pole. We are evacuating camp." She paused, the authority in her countenance wavering. "Hurry . . . now."

Flames leapt over the western ridge and down into our camp's valley as we sped down the road through the Rockies. An hour later, our vans arrived at a church in town. From the parking lot we watched a mammoth stack of smoke rise from the valley on the horizon. It looked as though an H-bomb had been detonated.

"Gather around!" Andy, the camp director motioned for everybody to move in close. "All right. Praise Jesus, we're all safe," he began in his calming voice. "Here is what we know. Tonight, we will be staying at this church. We'll have some worship time and then get some sleep. We've been in touch with the fire chief, and nobody can get into the valley where camp is located. The roads have been blocked off; even fire crews have been evacuated. We don't know whether or not camp is standing anymore; but the Lord is in control, we're safe, and we have shelter tonight. Let's go inside and praise Him for these blessings."

The next morning the sun was shining outside, but streams of smoke lingered on the horizon. Shortly after a breakfast Andy ran out of the church. "I just received a call from the fire chief," he said, winded. "Camp is still standing! Everything around it—right up to the back of the cabins—burned. The chief said he'd never seen anything like it—an absolute miracle!"

I couldn't believe it! The Lord had literally put His thumb down on the camp, protecting it.

Leaving camp the next day was disappointing, but as I looked out the airplane window, down onto the fire-pocked mountains, I thought about Andy's parting words: Satan wanted camp destroyed. He wanted to deter this group of campers. Something about us threatened him. But Christ spared camp and campers. He too knew that there was something special about our group.

I closed my eyes and leaned back in my chair, clutching my sleeping bag and toothbrush. I hadn't showered in almost three days, and I reeked of smoke.

"So, where are you coming from?" the elderly lady in the seat next to mine asked.

"Durango," I said, sitting up. "I was at camp there, but we were evacuated because of the fires."

"Oh my!" she gasped, putting a hand to her mouth. "Was everyone okay?"

I didn't answer immediately. I smiled, contemplating the miracle through which I had just lived. I had been speechless as the events unfurled, but the door for witnessing was now standing wide.

I see, Lord. You are already providing opportunities to share about your might and goodness. Thank you for this story. Light a fire beneath me; let your light shine!

YOUR CHOICE **What miracles have you witnessed in your life? In what ways have those experiences changed the way you live?**

LK 1:26–56

SNAPSHOT

LUKE 1:34–38

Mary asked the angel, "How can this be, since I have not been intimate with a man?"

The angel replied to her:

"The Holy Spirit will come upon you,

and the power of the Most High will overshadow you.

Therefore the holy One to be born

will be called the Son of God.

And consider your relative Elizabeth—even she has conceived a son in her old age, and this is the sixth month for her who was called barren. For nothing will be impossible with God."

"I am the Lord's slave," said Mary. "May it be done to me according to your word." Then the angel left her.

YOUR CHOICE

How do you feel about serving God, doing His will?

NO BRAINER

READY TO SERVE

Everyone knows about the virgin Mary—even the Beetles mentioned her in a song way back when, and, supposedly, "Madonna" is named after her. And regardless of a person's religious background or persuasion, he or she knows that Mary gave birth to Jesus. After all, she's included in all those Christmas paintings and nativity sets.

But few realize that when the angel visited Mary and informed her that she would bear the Savior of the world, she was just a teenager, probably about 15. So there she was, a very young woman engaged to an older man, living under the rule of an occupying, foreign government, and without much in the way of status or income. And, boom, the grand entrance and announcement: "You will conceive and give birth to a son" (Lk 1:31). After collecting herself and asking a very important question about how this could possibly happen to her, a virgin, Mary responds. Notice her attitude, especially: "'I am the Lord's slave,' said Mary. 'May it be done to me according to your word.'" The news must have seemed outrageous, impossible; yet Mary humbly submitted to God and His plan for her life.

So here's the question: If God were to share with you a word about your future or ask you to do something, how would you respond?

He does speak to us. The Bible is jammed with direct commands and principles for living. And each one comes with a choice, often involving a course of action but always involving our attitude. So when we realize that God is the One who is addressing us and that He wants to use us, may we also respond, "May it be done to me according to your word."

JUNE 8

DAY 159

THE BIG PICTURE

LK 1:57–80

SNAPSHOT

LUKE 1:59–66

When they came to circumcise the child on the eighth day, they were going to name him Zechariah, after his father. But his mother responded, "No! He will be called John."

Then they said to her, "None of your relatives has that name." So they motioned to his father to find out what he wanted him to be called. He asked for a writing tablet and wrote:

HIS NAME IS JOHN

And they were all amazed. Immediately his mouth was opened and his tongue set free, and he began to speak, praising God. Fear came on all those who lived around them, and all these things were being talked about throughout the hill country of Judea. All who heard about him took it to heart, saying, "What then will this child become?" For, indeed, the Lord's hand was with him.

JUST LIKE ME

ZECHARIAH: LEARNING THROUGH SILENCE

Ever have to learn something the hard way? You're in good company. When a messenger angel was sent to the priest Zechariah to announce the upcoming birth of his son, John, Zechariah still expressed disbelief. After all, were not Zechariah and his wife, Elizabeth, too old to have a child? But Zechariah's desire for proof to back up the angel's message netted him a rebuke from the angel and God's disciplinary action. Zechariah was rendered mute until his son's circumcision.

But silence undoubtedly taught Zechariah a lesson or two, which came through in his Holy Spirit-fueled prophecy. Also, Zechariah stood up to family members who couldn't understand why he would give his son a name that no other family member had.

What lessons have you learned through consequences you've faced? Zechariah chose to praise God rather than to express resentment for nine months of silence. Sometimes learning the hard way is a lesson well learned.

YOUR CHOICE

What step of faith will you take this week?

THE BIG PICTURE

MT 1:1–25

JUNE 9

DAY 160

SNAPSHOT

MATTHEW 1:18–21

The birth of Jesus Christ came about this way: After His mother Mary had been engaged to Joseph, it was discovered before they came together that she was pregnant by the Holy Spirit. So her husband Joseph, being a righteous man, and not wanting to disgrace her publicly, decided to divorce her secretly.

But after he had considered these things, an angel of the Lord suddenly appeared to him in a dream, saying, "Joseph, son of David, don't be afraid to take Mary as your wife, because what has been conceived in her is by the Holy Spirit. She will give birth to a son, and you are to name Him Jesus, because He will save His people from their sins."

DEPOSIT

WORDS FROM GOD'S WORD TO STORE IN YOUR MIND AND HEART

The Word became flesh and took up residence among us. We observed His glory, the glory as the One and Only Son from the Father, full of grace and truth (Jn 1:14).

SNAPSHOT

LUKE 2:4–7

And Joseph also went up from the town of Nazareth in Galilee, to Judea, to the city of David, which is called Bethlehem, because he was of the house and family line of David, to be registered along with Mary, who was engaged to him and was pregnant. While they were there, the time came for her to give birth. Then she gave birth to her firstborn Son, and she wrapped Him snugly in cloth and laid Him in a feeding trough—because there was no room for them at the inn.

YOUR TURN

JESUS IS BORN!

What does Christmas mean to you?

LK 2:21–39

SNAPSHOT

LUKE 2:25–32

There was a man in Jerusalem whose name was Simeon. This man was righteous and devout, looking forward to Israel's consolation, and the Holy Spirit was on him. It had been revealed to him by the Holy Spirit that he would not see death before he saw the Lord's Messiah. Guided by the Spirit, he entered the temple complex. When the parents brought in the child Jesus to perform for Him what was customary under the law, Simeon took Him up in his arms, praised God, and said:

Now, Master,
You can dismiss Your slave in peace,
according to Your word.
For my eyes have seen Your salvation.
You have prepared it
in the presence of all peoples—
a light for revelation to the Gentiles
and glory to Your people Israel.

YOUR CHOICE

If you really believed that you could meet Jesus in church, how would that change your approach to attending services and worshiping?

NO BRAINER

JESUS' FIRST TRIP TO CHURCH

It's safe to say that Simeon had been to church (the temple) thousands of times during his long life. We don't know much about him except that he was "righteous and devout" and that he expected that before his death he would get to see the Messiah, in person. So at every temple visit, Simeon would look expectantly for the Savior. Imagine him thinking and wondering, again and again through the years: "Could this be the One?"

A case certainly can be made for Simeon being special, unique, since he had received personal communication from God, and a promise about his future. Yet, in many ways, Simeon is like us, and we can identify with Simeon and learn from his example.

Simeon was an old man, so just imagine how many temple visits had *not* produced an encounter with Christ. Yet when Jesus appeared, he was ready to meet Him. Over those years Simeon could have become bored with the routine—*another sacrifice, more prayers, no Messiah*. Or he could have harbored serious doubts about what God had told him—*Was that really God who spoke to me? Did I get the message right? Will this ever happen?*

Instead, from what we can tell from the text, Simeon faithfully attended and worshiped and anticipated that what God had promised would happen. He believed God and faithfully fulfilled his temple duties; thus he was "guided by the Spirit" (Lk 2:27).

So, here the question: How do we approach church and worship? Have our visits become routine, boring, and dull? Jesus has promised to be with us in our gatherings (Mt 18:20), and He will. Just imagine how worship would change if we fully expected to meet Him!

DAY 163

SNAPSHOT

MATTHEW 2:9–12

After hearing the king, they went on their way. And there it was—the star they had seen in the east! It led them until it came and stopped above the place where the child was. When they saw the star, they were overjoyed beyond measure. Entering the house, they saw the child with Mary His mother, and falling to their knees, they worshiped Him. Then they opened their treasures and presented Him with gifts: gold, frankincense, and myrrh. And being warned in a dream not to go back to Herod, they returned to their own country by another route.

YOUR CHOICE

What would a God-seeker learn about Christ from watching you?

TOUGH QUESTION

I'VE HEARD IT SAID, "THE WISE STILL SEEK HIM." WHAT DOES THAT SEEKING MEAN IN THE WORLD TODAY? WHEN SO MANY SEEM EAGER TO BOLDLY DECLARE HE ISN'T WORTH SEEKING, HOW DO I TAKE A STAND?

Seeking to know God is not a widespread practice these days. Usually those who believe in Christ and profess to know Him are labeled as rigid and narrow. The vast majority of people seem to be running away from Christ, not to Him.

But some people do sincerely seek God. You can tell sincere seekers by the kind of questions they ask and how they ask those questions—where they aren't nit-picking or sharpshooting but really want answers. And you can identify them by some of their comments.

Seekers often sense a lack in their lives, a "God-shaped vacuum," and so they look for meaning, purpose, and direction. Sometimes people will begin to seek the truth when they are confronted with tragedy or personal crisis. In some cases, the search begins as their minds are opened and they begin to wonder, "Is this all there is?" And some people are moved by the beauty of creation and want to know the Creator.

With these seekers, we must remember two very important points. First, God is the One who is doing His work in the person, drawing him or her to Himself. Our part in the process is to pray and to share the Good News—and, when the opportunity arises, to lead that person to Christ.

Second, the Bible promises that God "rewards those who seek Him" (Heb 11:6). The Bible is filled with examples of the most unlikely people being dramatically changed through the power of the Holy Spirit. Consider, for example, Matthew, the tax collector, and Paul, the persecutor of Christians. This truth should give us hope. Even the most virulent anti-Christian crusader can be turned around.

We need to keep praying and pointing people not to us, but to Christ.

MATTHEW 2:19–21 After Herod died, an angel of the Lord suddenly appeared in a dream to Joseph in Egypt, saying, "Get up! Take the child and His mother and go to the land of Israel, because those who sought the child's life are dead." So he got up, took the child and His mother, and entered the land of Israel.

SNAPSHOT

JUNE 13

DAY 164

THE BIG PICTURE

MT 2:13–23

TOUGH CHOICE

EXCITEMENT

When I began applying to colleges, I didn't submit applications to any schools within 500 miles of my home. I felt the Lord readying and preparing me to spread my wings. I was eager to escape the Midwest, live on my own, and have a fresh start. Four years later, I had achieved what I set out to accomplish. I had graduated from a university in the Southeast (700 miles from home), had established a network of friends in the area, and was looking for jobs in all the major surrounding cities.

"Thank you, Ms. Lazarus. I'm really looking forward to interning with your company this summer," I said into the phone, trying to control my excitement at the internship offer I had just received.

"Thank you, Carrie! We'll fax you some paperwork on Monday and will look forward to seeing you the following week in Atlanta."

"Wonderful. I'll see you then. Good-bye." I laid the phone on the desk and ran into the kitchen, where my parents were finishing lunch. I had returned home for a short visit—just until I confirmed my work plans.

"I got the internship!" I announced, grabbing an apple out of the fruit basket and taking a bite. "I start Monday after next!"

"Congratulations," they said in unison, clearly pleased.

"Oh! I need to call Amy to let her know the good news!" I turned to retrieve my phone from the study, but as I hurried down the hallway, my dog jumped up in front of me, ready to play. I leapt to the side, attempting to avoid stumbling over her, and landed awkwardly.

Crack. "Ow!" I crumpled to the floor, stunned by the sudden pain in my right foot. *Please, Lord, no.*

Six hours later, I was horizontal on our couch. I stared at my foot, propped up on pillows and encased in a knee-high hard cast. *You'll be on crutches for eight weeks . . . no weight on the foot . . . walking with the cast for two weeks or so after that . . . don't get the cast wet . . . and no driving until the cast is off.* The doctor's words replayed over and over in my head. *No driving until the cast is off.*

It meant I would have to turn down the internship in Atlanta. I wouldn't be able to drive from the city to the office on my own. *What are you doing, God? I was supposed to be in Atlanta, beginning my career. Now I'm stuck at home again, more dependent than I've been since I was 12. Why are you keeping me here?*

I wrestled the pillows under my foot, trying to get comfortable. "Agh!" I fell back on the couch; frustrated, foot throbbing, and discouraged.

Stop. Rest. The words were clear, as though someone else in the room had spoken.

Okay, Lord. Okay. I'm listening. What are you doing? Where are you taking me? I'm listening. I opened my eyes, staring down at my cast.

Stop. Rest.

I remained awake on the couch late into the night, just thinking. I had been so focused on escaping, I had forgotten to seek God's direction. Perhaps God was using my broken foot to literally slow me down and grab my attention.

I'm here, God. I'm back home. I don't understand why, but I know You want me here right now. Let this be a time of growth and healing—physically and spiritually.

YOUR CHOICE **How might God be using perceived setbacks and defeats to strengthen you for His future service?**

JUNE 14

DAY 165

THE BIG PICTURE

LK 2:41–52

SNAPSHOT

LUKE 2:41–46

Every year His parents traveled to Jerusalem for the Passover Festival. When He was 12 years old, they went up according to the custom of the festival. After those days were over, as they were returning, the boy Jesus stayed behind in Jerusalem, but His parents did not know it. Assuming He was in the traveling party, they went a day's journey. Then they began looking for Him among their relatives and friends. When they did not find Him, they returned to Jerusalem to search for Him. After three days, they found Him in the temple complex sitting among the teachers, listening to them and asking them questions.

JUST LIKE ME

JESUS: WISE BEYOND HIS YEARS

Many people judge breadth of knowledge or wisdom on the basis of age and experience. But how much knowledge, wisdom, or experience do we expect a 12-year-old to have? Yet Jesus was not the average 12-year-old, as He proved in His encounter with the teachers in the temple. How often do we hear that someone was "astounded" by the understanding of a preteen? Yet Jesus showed maturity in the way He listened to and asked questions of the teachers. Because Jesus was confident, rather than cocky, they didn't ignore Him or drive Him away. He earned their respect, even at a young age.

Does this behavior characterize your interactions with others? Sadly, we sometimes feel compelled to show off what we know, thinking that cockiness is the way to earn respect or get noticed like the proverbial squeaky wheel.

No matter how old we are, we can still learn a thing or two from 12-year-old Jesus' example. He approached the teachers with a listening attitude rather than a prideful one. And if the Son of God thought He had something to learn, how much more so do we?

YOUR CHOICE

How can you convey your knowledge, curiosity, or experience in a way that draws rather than repels others?

THE BIG PICTURE

MK 1:1–13

JUNE 15

DAY 166

SNAPSHOT

MARK 1:9–11

In those days Jesus came from Nazareth in Galilee and was baptized in the Jordan by John. As soon as He came up out of the water, He saw the heavens being torn open and the Spirit descending to Him like a dove. And a voice came from heaven:

You are My beloved Son;
I take delight in You!

ANCHOR POINT

JESUS' BAPTISM

Mark chose to open his gospel in a very succinct yet incredibly deep way, anchoring Christ's coming in Old Testament prophecy. He chronicles the fulfillment of that prophecy not only in Christ but also in John the Baptist preparing the way for the Lord. Mark lays out the preparation of Jesus for ministry, His baptism and confirmation from God, and His temptation in the desert.

Mark is revealing Christ's spiritual pedigree, His journey as the Savior of the world. This pedigree is confirmed by prophecy, by John the Baptist, and by God the Father. Jesus is ready to begin His public ministry.

You have a spiritual pedigree, a journey you have taken to where you now stand. You have been prepared for ministry, God has guided your path, and you are ready. You may not have prophecies written about you—and you certainly aren't the Savior—but you have been brought to this point in your life for a purpose. Christ's purpose was to express the Good News of the gospel to everyone He met and to reveal the love and grace of God. What has He prepared you to do?

YOUR CHOICE

Look back over your life; can you see how God has been preparing you to be His minister? What events have shaped you? Who has impacted you, encouraged you?

JUNE 16

DAY 167

THE BIG PICTURE

JN 1:19–34

SNAPSHOT

JOHN 1:29–34

The next day John saw Jesus coming toward him and said, "Here is the Lamb of God, who takes away the sin of the world! This is the One I told you about: 'After me comes a man who has surpassed me, because He existed before me.' I didn't know Him, but I came baptizing with water so He might be revealed to Israel."

And John testified, "I watched the Spirit descending from heaven like a dove, and He rested on Him. I didn't know Him, but He who sent me to baptize with water told me, 'The One you see the Spirit descending and resting on—He is the One who baptizes with the Holy Spirit.' I have seen and testified that He is the Son of God!"

DEPOSIT

WORDS FROM GOD'S WORD TO STORE IN YOUR MIND AND HEART

And Jesus increased in wisdom and stature, and in favor with God and with people (Lk 2:52).

istand

SNAPSHOT

JOHN 1:35–42

Again the next day, John was standing with two of his disciples. When he saw Jesus passing by, he said, "Look! The Lamb of God!"

The two disciples heard him say this and followed Jesus. When Jesus turned and noticed them following Him, He asked them, "What are you looking for?" They said to Him, "Rabbi" (which means "Teacher"), "where are You staying?"

"Come and you'll see," He replied. So they went and saw where He was staying, and they stayed with Him that day. It was about 10 in the morning.

Andrew, Simon Peter's brother, was one of the two who heard John and followed Him. He first found his own brother Simon and told him, "We have found the Messiah!" (which means "Anointed One"), and he brought Simon to Jesus.

When Jesus saw him, He said, "You are Simon, son of John. You will be called Cephas" (which means "Rock").

YOUR TURN

JESUS' FIRST DISCIPLES

How would someone know that you're a disciple of Jesus?

JUNE 18

DAY 169

THE BIG PICTURE

JN 2:1–25

SNAPSHOT

JOHN 2:13–16

The Jewish Passover was near, so Jesus went up to Jerusalem. In the temple complex He found people selling oxen, sheep, and doves, and He also found the money changers sitting there. After making a whip out of cords, He drove everyone out of the temple complex with their sheep and oxen. He also poured out the money changers' coins and overturned the tables. He told those who were selling doves, "Get these things out of here! Stop turning My Father's house into a marketplace!"

TOUGH CHOICE

SURPRISES

"And what are your plans now that you've graduated, Cathy?" Carmen's dad asked me at our graduation luncheon.

Honestly! If another person asks me what I'm doing with my life, I'm going to scream.

"I'm not quite sure yet, Mr. Bartelli," I said as politely and sweetly as possible. "Still interviewing and looking at my options!"

He shoveled a large bite of graduation cake into his mouth. "Well as an English and Psychology major, have you considered teaching?" He asked between bites, refusing to let me escape the same conversation I'd had with every other parent that day.

No! I don't want to be a teacher. I don't know what I want to do! "We'll see!" I smiled and turned, hurrying to the kitchen and slipping out the back door of the house that my roommates and I had lived in our senior year. I walked through the grass over to our hammock and sat down, kicking off my shoes. Patches of blue sky were visible through the large oak tree branches.

What's wrong with me, Lord? Why don't I have something that I'm passionate about like my roommates? Just tell me what to do, and I'll do it!

For the first time in my life, my future felt largely in my own hands. Nobody was telling me what came next. *Lord, I'm scared to make a decision. What if I move to the wrong city and can't find a job? What if I choose the wrong job and fail?*

"Hey, there you are!" My best friend Grace walked over from the house. "I've been looking for you." I sat up in the hammock, hanging my legs over the side so she could sit down. "What have you been doing out here?"

We pushed off the ground, rocking the hammock back and forth. "Just thinking," I said. "How did you know what you wanted to do after graduation?"

She thought for a moment. "I don't know. I heard about my internship at Bible study and just went after it." She looked over at me. "Don't worry, Cathy, you're going to figure out what to do. The Lord will open doors."

"I know," I sighed. "I just feel like He's been awfully quiet lately, and I'm feeling more and more pressure to figure out my future."

Grace put her hands behind her head, staring up through the oak leaves. "Maybe He is answering by being quiet. Maybe Christ wants you to take a step of faith—commit to a path that you truly enjoy, and just trust that He will take care of you."

I turned her words over in my head. *I've never chosen a path based on my own passions and interests. My ultimate goal has always been to excel and please everyone.*

Grace continued, "The Lord never fails to answer our prayers. Sometimes, the way in which He answers is unexpected and surprising, but I really believe that the Lord is preparing you for something, Cathy. He's forcing you out of your comfort zone."

Her words encouraged me. I knew she was right. "Thanks, Grace. I needed to hear that." *And thank You, Jesus, for sending me a reminder!*

YOUR CHOICE **What do you need to do to better listen to God?**

JOHN 3:1–8

There was a man from the Pharisees named Nicodemus, a ruler of the Jews. This man came to Him at night and said, "Rabbi, we know that You have come from God as a teacher, for no one could perform these signs You do unless God were with him."

Jesus replied, "I assure you: Unless someone is born again, he cannot see the kingdom of God."

"But how can anyone be born when he is old?" Nicodemus asked Him. "Can he enter his mother's womb a second time and be born?"

Jesus answered, "I assure you: Unless someone is born of water and the Spirit, he cannot enter the kingdom of God. Whatever is born of the flesh is flesh, and whatever is born of the Spirit is spirit. Do not be amazed that I told you that you must be born again. The wind blows where it pleases, and you hear its sound, but you don't know where it comes from or where it is going. So it is with everyone born of the Spirit."

JUST LIKE ME

NICODEMUS: MOVING FROM FEAR TO FAITH

Picture this: you're a teacher of the law—highly educated and respected among your people. As someone so highly respected, you would make sure you traveled among the best circles wouldn't you? After all, you have a reputation to maintain.

Such was the lot of Nicodemus. Yet even with such status, Nicodemus knew enough to know that he didn't know everything. Something was missing in his well-ordered life. And Jesus, the new teacher in town, who seemed to have come "from God" (Jn 3:2), had an amazing array of answers and incredible power. But fearing the comments of his colleagues, Nicodemus chose the veil of nighttime to talk with Jesus. That way, no one had to know, and his reputation would remain intact.

Although Nicodemus wasn't quite ready to come out of the closet as a follower of Jesus, he later did at the crucifixion. He was with Joseph of Arimathea when it came time to claim Jesus' body (see Jn 19:38–39).

Nicodemus was willing to bypass his fear and the pride of his status to connect with the One who set aside His glory as God to become human. What are you willing to set aside in order to connect with Him?

YOUR CHOICE

What, if anything, stands between you and a deeper connection with God?

DAY 171

THE BIG PICTURE

JN 3:22–36; LK 3:19–20

NO BRAINER

POINTING TO JESUS

John had achieved celebrity status, with large crowds assembling on the outskirts of town to hear him preach. He was wild and radical and a powerful preacher with a life-changing message. And John had gathered a faithful flock of "disciples," an inner circle of men who accepted his message, stood with him, and helped spread the word.

Then along came Jesus.

At their Jordan encounter, John had exclaimed, "Here is the Lamb of God, who takes away the sin of the world!" (Jn 1:29), and he had seen the Spirit descend and had heard God the Father proclaim, "You are My beloved Son. I take delight in You!" (Lk 3:22). John knew that the whole purpose of his ministry was to prepare the way for Jesus, the Christ.

But the warmth of the spotlight must have felt good. We know that some of John's disciples were enjoying the glow and notoriety and that they felt threatened by the rise in Jesus' popularity. We can hear them breathlessly and nervously exclaim to John, their leader, "Everyone is flocking to Him!" (Jn 3:26)—as if to say, "Who does Jesus think He is, anyway? This is *our* territory, *our* time, *our* crowd."

But John knew who he was, and he knew who Jesus was, and he humbly replied, "He must increase, but I must decrease." In other words: "It's all about Jesus, not me. My role is to point people to Him. He's the only One that matters."

We may not wear strange clothes, eat weird food, and preach in the wilderness like John the Baptist, but we have a similar role—to point people to Jesus. Sometimes those who are supposed to be "bearing witness to the Light" (see Jn 1:6–10) get confused and think *they* are "the light." But everything should be about Jesus and His message, not about us, the messengers.

Remember: it's not about you; it's about Him.

SNAPSHOT

JOHN 3:25–30

Then a dispute arose between John's disciples and a Jew about purification. So they came to John and told him, "Rabbi, the One you testified about, and who was with you across the Jordan, is baptizing—and everyone is flocking to Him."

John responded, "No one can receive a single thing unless it's given to him from heaven. You yourselves can testify that I said, 'I am not the Messiah, but I've been sent ahead of Him.' He who has the bride is the groom. But the groom's friend, who stands by and listens for him, rejoices greatly at the groom's voice. So this joy of mine is complete. He must increase, but I must decrease."

YOUR CHOICE

When you share God's Good News, how can you take the spotlight off yourself and put it on Christ?

THE BIG PICTURE

JN 4:1–42

JUNE 21

DAY 172

SNAPSHOT

JOHN 4:39–42

Now many Samaritans from that town believed in Him because of what the woman said when she testified, "He told me everything I ever did." Therefore, when the Samaritans came to Him, they asked Him to stay with them, and He stayed there two days. Many more believed because of what He said. And they told the woman, "We no longer believe because of what you said, for we have heard for ourselves and know that this really is the Savior of the world."

ANCHOR POINT

JESUS CHANGES A TOWN

This passage presents a great picture of Christ's compassion. He crossed racial and religious boundaries to talk with this woman. He did not judge her for her indiscretions, though He did not allow her to gloss over them either. Jesus balanced the truth about her lifestyle with the wonderful news of forgiveness. In the process He brought an entire town to salvation.

Today, one of our greatest challenges is knowing how to relate to others with compassion and love. Unfortunately, many Christians have a reputation for dealing poorly with people who hold different views or live different lifestyles. Our response has tended to land on the side of judgment rather than grace. Yet in the Gospels we find Jesus rarely condemning blatant sinners. He reserved His strongest words for the religious hypocrites.

If we are truly striving to be Christlike, we must show compassion and grace to everyone. With a simple conversation, Christ changed an entire town. Just think what we could do if we followed His example.

YOUR CHOICE

With what people would you be uncomfortable talking about spiritual things? How can you follow the example of Christ in reaching out to people who are different from you in some way?

DAY 173

THE BIG PICTURE

JN 4:43–54

SNAPSHOT

JOHN 4:46–50

Then He went again to Cana of Galilee, where He had turned the water into wine. There was a certain royal official whose son was ill at Capernaum. When this man heard that Jesus had come from Judea into Galilee, he went to Him and pleaded with Him to come down and heal his son, for he was about to die.

Jesus told him, "Unless you people see signs and wonders, you will not believe."

"Sir," the official said to Him, "come down before my boy dies!"

"Go," Jesus told him, "your son will live." The man believed what Jesus said to him and departed.

YOUR CHOICE

When have you been tempted to be "mismatched with unbelievers"?

TOUGH QUESTION

THIS PERSON I'M DATING IS NOT A CHRISTIAN, BUT WE'VE BEEN FRIENDS FOR A REALLY LONG TIME. WHAT SHOULD I DO?

There's good news and bad news. Which do you want to hear first?

The bad news is that you shouldn't be in a dating relationship with someone who doesn't share your commitment to Christ. In His Word, God says, "Do not be mismatched with unbelievers. For what partnership is there between righteousness and lawlessness? Or what fellowship does light have with darkness?" (2 Co 6:14). And the Bible has numerous sad stories of God's followers who, because of close relationships with nonbelievers, turned away from God (Solomon, for example). Many differences between two people can be worked around and compromised, but not faith—it's just too important.

Does this mean you should break up? Probably—but don't be mean or self-righteous about it. Simply explain that your faith means everything to you, that your values and life priorities differ, and that you are heading down a different road. This talk will be difficult if you care about this person, but don't let your emotions sway you from doing what you know God wants you to do.

The good news is that because you two have been long-time friends, you respect each other. Close friends can talk honestly, listening and affirming. Your close relationship will provide a communication bridge, and you'll be able to share your belief in Christ and your reasons for believing. Whether or not this person embraces the faith also, you at least, will have been faithful and will have moved along the process. Perhaps, in the future, someone else will be the one to lead your friend to Christ.

Breaking a relationship is painful. But God promises to "supply all your needs" in Christ Jesus (Php 4:19), and He will bring healing. This will be a tough choice, but the right one.

THE BIG PICTURE

LK 4:16–30

JUNE 23

DAY 174

SNAPSHOT

LUKE 4:24–30

He also said, "I assure you: No prophet is accepted in his hometown. But I say to you, there were certainly many widows in Israel in Elijah's days, when the sky was shut up for three years and six months while a great famine came over all the land. Yet Elijah was not sent to any of them—but to a widow at Zarephath in Sidon. And in the prophet Elisha's time, there were many in Israel who had serious skin diseases, yet not one of them was healed—only Naaman the Syrian."

When they heard this, everyone in the synagogue was enraged. They got up, drove Him out of town, and brought Him to the edge of the hill their town was built on, intending to hurl Him over the cliff. But He passed right through the crowd and went on His way.

DEPOSIT

WORDS FROM GOD'S WORD TO STORE IN YOUR MIND AND HEART

For God loved the world in this way: He gave His One and Only Son, so that everyone who believes in Him will not perish but have eternal life (Jn 3:16).

THE BIG PICTURE

MK 1:16–39

SNAPSHOT

MARK 1:16–20

As He was passing along by the Sea of Galilee, He saw Simon and Andrew, Simon's brother. They were casting a net into the sea, since they were fishermen.

"Follow Me," Jesus told them, "and I will make you fish for people!" Immediately they left their nets and followed Him. Going on a little farther, He saw James the son of Zebedee and his brother John. They were in their boat mending their nets. Immediately He called them, and they left their father Zebedee in the boat with the hired men and followed Him.

YOUR TURN

FOLLOWING JESUS

What specific things have you left behind to follow Christ?

THE BIG PICTURE

LK 5:1–39

JUNE 25

DAY 176

SNAPSHOT

LUKE 5:27–32

After this, Jesus went out and saw a tax collector named Levi sitting at the tax office, and He said to him, "Follow Me!" So, leaving everything behind, he got up and began to follow Him.

Then Levi hosted a grand banquet for Him at his house. Now there was a large crowd of tax collectors and others who were guests with them. But the Pharisees and their scribes were complaining to His disciples, "Why do you eat and drink with tax collectors and sinners?"

Jesus replied to them, "The healthy don't need a doctor, but the sick do. I have not come to call the righteous, but sinners to repentance."

JUST LIKE ME

MATTHEW: LEAVING IT ALL BEHIND

How much of your life do you expect to change as you grow deeper in or even develop a relationship with God? A little bit? A lot? For many people, depth in their relationship with God depends on how satisfied they feel in life.

After receiving a personal invitation from the Master Himself, Matthew, also known as Levi, immediately left his tax booth and became a follower of Jesus. Matthew didn't wait to see if he would receive a better offer, nor did he weigh the pros and cons. Instead he knew intrinsically that Jesus' offer was the best he would ever receive. He even began to influence his friends by hosting a dinner for Jesus and inviting them.

While we don't know how Matthew reacted when the Pharisees expressed disdain at Jesus' decision to eat with "tax collectors and sinners" (Lk 5:30), we know what Jesus had to say on the matter: "I didn't come to invite good people to turn to God. I came to invite sinners" (see Lk 5:31). Matthew had enough humility to know he was in the latter category.

Matthew knew that something was missing from his life—a soul satisfaction his money or status couldn't fix. This was proved by the way he quickly left everything behind—including his pride. Where do you see yourself? In the "satisfied" or "good" category" The "sinner" category? What aspects of your life reflect your choice?

YOUR CHOICE

What are you willing to leave behind in order to follow Jesus?

JUNE 26

DAY 177

THE BIG PICTURE

JN 5:1–47

SNAPSHOT

JOHN 5:19–23

Then Jesus replied, "I assure you: The Son is not able to do anything on His own, but only what He sees the Father doing. For whatever the Father does, the Son also does these things in the same way. For the Father loves the Son and shows Him everything He is doing, and He will show Him greater works than these so that you will be amazed. And just as the Father raises the dead and gives them life, so the Son also gives life to anyone He wants to. The Father, in fact, judges no one but has given all judgment to the Son, so that all people will honor the Son just as they honor the Father. Anyone who does not honor the Son does not honor the Father who sent Him."

ANCHOR POINT

JESUS DEMONSTRATES HE IS GOD'S SON

In this passage we find the first public declaration recorded in John by Jesus that He is indeed God's Son. Jesus pretty much lays it out—I am the Son and if you believe in Me you will have eternal life. Jesus was not just a great teacher. He did not come to simply instruct the world on how to live in peace and grace. He is the Son of God, the Messiah, the Promised One. His job was to do the Father's will by the power of the Father through the Spirit. That will included Jesus dying on a cross and being raised to life again, bringing salvation to all who believe.

The religious leaders of the time responded to Jesus' claim to be the Son of God by plotting to kill Him. They were enraged over His words and actions; He threatened their lofty place as leaders in the community. This claim, and its implications, still resonates today. Everyone must deal with this claim, whether they like it or not. It still threatens, and it is a call to change, to a totally different life.

YOUR CHOICE

What does Jesus' claim of being the Son of God threaten in your life? What have you given up to follow Him? What do you think you may have to give up in the future?

MK 2:23–3:19

SNAPSHOT

MARK 2:25–28

He said to them, "Have you never read what David and those who were with him did when he was in need and hungry—how he entered the house of God in the time of Abiathar the high priest and ate the sacred bread—which is not lawful for anyone to eat except the priests—and also gave some to his companions?" Then He told them, "The Sabbath was made for man and not man for the Sabbath. Therefore the Son of Man is Lord even of the Sabbath."

YOUR CHOICE

What can you do to be more grace-filled rather than legalistic?

NO BRAINER

RIGHTEOUS RULES

If you know anything about the Pharisees, you know they liked rules. And they had tons of them: regulations for every occasion. Originally, the rules came from a good source (God's Law, the first five books of the Bible) and from good motives (the desire to obey God, to do what He required). But through the years, these well-meaning and pious Jewish religious leaders had added their interpretations to God's laws, as well as sub-laws, sub-sub-laws, and tangent regulations. Eventually they had accumulated hundreds of them. In the process, they had become the experts, the only ones who could accurately interpret and enforce all those rules.

So these men were alarmed when they observed Jesus' disciples picking a few heads of grain (which the Pharisees considered "work") on the Sabbath (the day of rest). Jesus responded to their question by giving them a brief Bible lesson and then pointing out that "the Sabbath was made for man and not man for the Sabbath" (Mk 2:27).

Besides the great irony that these men were enforcing *God's* laws by questioning *God Himself* (Jesus) about breaking *His* laws, they missed the point entirely—the reason for the laws in the first place. And they were so focused on their rules that they missed the Savior.

We shouldn't be too hard on the Pharisees. Today we still overemphasize laws. Usually we feel good about ourselves (and think we gain God's approval) when we keep the rules, and we judge those who don't and feel spiritually superior to them. Playing the "holier-than-thou" game is easy. This is called "legalism," and it's our default position.

Instead, we need to remember who stands behind God's laws (God) and focus on Him. If we stand with Him, we'll take the right stand on His laws. Instead of condemning those who break God's laws (ourselves included), we'll point them to the Author and His mercy and grace.

JUNE 28

DAY 179

THE BIG PICTURE

MT 5:1–16

SNAPSHOT

MATTHEW 5:13–16

"You are the salt of the earth. But if the salt should lose its taste, how can it be made salty? It's no longer good for anything but to be thrown out and trampled on by men.

"You are the light of the world. A city situated on a hill cannot be hidden. No one lights a lamp and puts it under a basket, but rather on a lampstand, and it gives light for all who are in the house. In the same way, let your light shine before men, so that they may see your good works and give glory to your Father in heaven."

TOUGH CHOICE

SALT AND LIGHT

Morgan's feet pounded the dirt next to mine as we charged through the forest preserve and down another path. Every few strides I could catch a glimpse of Lake Radcliff on our left, through the dense leaves.

"It's just," Morgan panted between breaths, "Susan's the older one. I shouldn't have to take care of her. When we decided to live together this year, I figured we'd both matured enough to avoid the drama from when we were younger."

Morgan and her older sister, Susan, had moved in together since they were back in the same city, attending the same graduate school. The transition had not been smooth.

"I just want to live my own life! I want to go out without dragging Susan along. I don't want to feel guilty when I don't take her with me," she panted.

I turned my legs over faster to keep up. "Have you tried talking to Susan?"

Morgan's ponytail whipped to the side as she looked over at me. "Talk?" *Pant.* "To Susan?" *Pant.* "It would crush her. I avoid conflict at all costs so she'll stay happy."

"Dealing with conflict doesn't always require you to shove things under the carpet, or to get walked on like a rug," I said, leaning into the steep hill. "Susan's 25. She doesn't need you to coddle her. She needs you to be salt in her life, and this starts with honesty."

"Honesty? Bailey, honesty would kill Susan because it would mean confronting her insecurities and reminding her of the fact that she's 25, single, and miserable." Morgan stopped in her tracks, resting her hands on her knees. We had reached the top of the hill.

"Morgan, bottling up this frustration is not healthy. Salt on Susan's wounds will sting, but it will also open doors for both of you to live more fulfilling lives in which Christ is your source of joy."

"How do you suggest I confront my older sister? I'm the one who smoothes things over in the family. I don't throw salt on wounds. I just want everyone happy."

I sat down on a fallen tree, overlooking the lake. Sweat rolled off the sides of my knees. "The Lord never said, 'Blessed are the people-pleasers.' He said that we are to be the salt of this world—a light for Him."

Morgan sat down next to me. "I want us both to live full lives. I just don't want to hurt her." She stared out over the lake.

"I think Susan will appreciate knowing that she can count on you to speak truth to her. Your sister knows you love her, but you aren't helping her by enabling her negativity and insecure tendencies. Be a light for her."

Morgan picked up a rock and tossed it into the lake. "I hate how you're always right," she laughed, shaking her head. "But I love you for it, too."

YOUR CHOICE **How will you confront a friend with the truth?**

THE BIG PICTURE

MT 5:17–30

JUNE 29

DAY 180

TOUGH QUESTION

I'VE TRIED TO TAKE A STAND A FEW TIMES, BUT I HAVEN'T DONE VERY WELL. WHAT SHOULD I DO?

When you became a Christian, you were forgiven of all your sins: past, present, and future. Christ's death on the cross and His resurrection made this forgiveness available. This means that we don't have to make blood sacrifices periodically for our sins like the Jewish people had to do. But, because we are fallible and sinful human beings, we still choose to sin. We would love it if sin had been eradicated from our lives forever when we trusted Christ as Savior—life would be so much easier—but it doesn't work that way. We won't be totally free from sin until we are in heaven with Christ.

Our propensity to do what we know is wrong proves that we need Christ, our Savior. Yes, we have been saved the *penalty* for our sins—eternal separation from God. And we have been saved from the *power* of sin; that is, we can choose to do what is right through the power of the Holy Spirit in us. But our vulnerability to sin reminds us how much we need to rely on God daily.

Choosing to take the right stand takes time, and it is a result of our growth as followers of Christ. It requires us to be humble enough to ask God to reveal our sins and shortcomings and then confessing them to Him (see 1 Jn 1:9). Growth happens when we sin, are forgiven, and then, when faced with the same sin again, we choose not to sin. Slowly that spiritual growth allows us to take stands in places and for causes that we couldn't before.

So don't get discouraged when you mess up. Align your heart with the Lord's through genuine confession and press on. You will be tested, but with time your faith will grow. Then taking a stand will become a habit, a natural part of your life.

SNAPSHOT

MATTHEW 5:27–30

"You have heard that it was said, Do not commit adultery. But I tell you, everyone who looks at a woman to lust for her has already committed adultery with her in his heart. If your right eye causes you to sin, gouge it out and throw it away. For it is better that you lose one of the parts of your body than for your whole body to be thrown into hell. And if your right hand causes you to sin, cut it off and throw it away. For it is better that you lose one of the parts of your body than for your whole body to go into hell!"

YOUR CHOICE

When have you failed to take a stand for Christ recently, where you know you should have? What do you need to confess to God?

JUNE 30

DAY 181

THE BIG PICTURE

MT 5:31–48

SNAPSHOT

MATTHEW 5:43–45

"You have heard that it was said, Love your neighbor and hate your enemy. But I tell you, love your enemies and pray for those who persecute you, so that you may be sons of your Father in heaven. For He causes His sun to rise on the evil and the good, and sends rain on the righteous and the unrighteous."

DEPOSIT

WORDS FROM GOD'S WORD TO STORE IN YOUR MIND AND HEART

"In the same way, let your light shine before men, so that they may see your good works and give glory to your Father in heaven" (Mt 5:16).

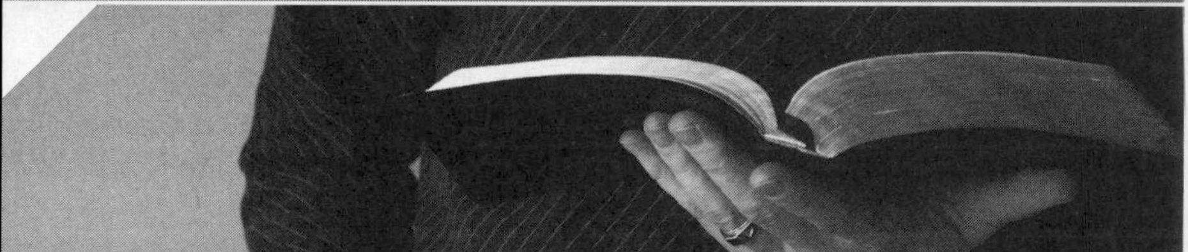

JULI
JULLIET
JULI
JULY
LUGLIO
JULHO
JULIO

THE BIG PICTURE

MT 6:1–18

JULY 1

DAY 182

SNAPSHOT

MATTHEW 6:1–4

"Be careful not to practice your righteousness in front of people, to be seen by them. Otherwise, you will have no reward from your Father in heaven. So whenever you give to the poor, don't sound a trumpet before you, as the hypocrites do in the synagogues and on the streets, to be applauded by people. I assure you: They've got their reward! But when you give to the poor, don't let your left hand know what your right hand is doing, so that your giving may be in secret. And your Father who sees in secret will reward you."

YOUR TURN

DOING GOOD THINGS

How do your public and private lives compare?

JULY 2

DAY 183

THE BIG PICTURE

MT 6:19–34

SNAPSHOT

MATTHEW 6:19–21

"Don't collect for yourselves treasures on earth, where moth and rust destroy and where thieves break in and steal. But collect for yourselves treasures in heaven, where neither moth nor rust destroys, and where thieves don't break in and steal. For where your treasure is, there your heart will be also."

TOUGH CHOICE

MONEY

The sky outside my window was first-day-of-spring blue. The grass was green. Slight breeze. And I was sitting at my desk, studying spreadsheets with my dad.

"Focus, Miley. What did I just say?"

"Oh, uh . . ." I let my daydream of going outside for a bike ride or run slip out the window. "You were saying that I should withhold three . . ."

"Five."

"Five percent of my paycheck to put in my, uh . . ."

"401 . . ."

"401-K plan."

"Come on, Miley. Now that you've graduated and accepted a job, you need to set up a budget. You're not five years old any more. You've got to take responsibility for your money."

I sighed, "I know. I want to be responsible; it's just my last weekend before 'real life' starts."

"Welcome to being an adult. Okay, five percent retirement, five percent insurance and medical, another seven for taxes, ten percent rent; eight percent food and utilities . . ."

My head was beginning to spin.

". . . I'd say twelve percent gas and travels, twenty percent for entertainment and leisure . . ."

"Seriously," I groaned, "aren't we already over one hundred percent?"

"No, and don't forget about ten percent for tithing."

I glared at him. Tithing, taxes, insurance: they were no big deal for my mom and him. A couple hundred dollars here and there was chump change to them.

"Why are you acting like this, Miley? This is not a big deal!"

"It is to me. It stresses me out. I can't afford to live on my own. How am I supposed to save anything?"

"Miley, you will be able to save some. That's why I'm helping you set up this budget—so that you will have a leg up and start investing and handling your money wisely."

"I know," I said, wringing my hands. "Money just makes me nervous. What if there isn't enough?"

He took off his reading glasses and laid them next to the keyboard. "Miley, I haven't seen this side of you before. You've never been in need. The Lord has always provided. He will continue to do so as long as you're responsible, tithing, and not letting money become an idol."

"I just hate how everyone's out to make a buck—or one hundred—off me."

He laughed. "Oh, Miley. That's part of the game. I know how easy it is to fall into the trap of finding security in money, but this is sinful and miserable. Being a good steward also means giving back to God—it is His, after all. It also means helping others. Think of all the friends you have in mission right now. They need funding. The fact that you'll be getting a weekly paycheck opens up so many doors to serve your friends while furthering Christ's kingdom. What do you say?"

I took a deep breath. "I say if I owed you a nickel for every time you had to knock sense into me, I'd be broke." I picked up my dad's glasses and handed them back to him. "Thanks, dad—I needed to hear that. Now, how about assigning five percent of that leisure money to Christ's kingdom? My friend Connie has started some great ministries as an intern on campus."

YOUR CHOICE **How is your commitment to Christ reflected in your saving and spending?**

THE BIG PICTURE

MT 7:1–12

JULY 3

DAY 184

SNAPSHOT

MATTHEW 7:1–5

"Do not judge, so that you won't be judged. For with the judgment you use, you will be judged, and with the measure you use, it will be measured to you. Why do you look at the speck in your brother's eye but don't notice the log in your own eye? Or how can you say to your brother, 'Let me take the speck out of your eye,' and look, there's a log in your eye? Hypocrite! First take the log out of your eye, and then you will see clearly to take the speck out of your brother's eye."

YOUR CHOICE

When, recently, have you been judgmental? What courageous choice do you need to make about your own attitudes and actions?

NO BRAINER

A CRITICAL EYE

Hypocrite! Now there's a nasty word. No one wants to wear that label.

A hypocrite is someone who professes to believe one thing but acts the opposite. An ice cream hypocrite, for example, would be a person who professes to hate the stuff (for a variety of reasons), and who publicly refuses even a spoon, yet is discovered to have a freezer filled with the frozen delights. Hypocrites abound in every life arena, in all occupations and walks of life: politicians, lawyers, teachers, sales reps, financial advisors, construction workers, police officers, even ministers (to name a few).

So why does Jesus call the person described in this passage a "hypocrite"? Pretty strong words—a very harsh indictment.

Jesus is saying that when we judge others, then we should be judged by those same standards. We can't make ourselves the exception to the rule. If a certain behavior is wrong for the other person, then it's wrong for us. In fact, the actions condemned in others are often a problem of the one who condemns. And some people are so concerned with how everyone else is acting that they overlook or rationalize their own faults, shortcomings, and sins. Jesus says, therefore, that a person who is quick to judge someone else while ignoring his or her own sins is a hypocrite.

In short, Jesus is saying that "iStand" begins with us—standing for the right attitudes and actions in us, our lives. That's the primary spiritual battlefield, the place where we must be absolutely brutal in making courageous choices.

DAY 185

THE BIG PICTURE
MT 7:13–29

SNAPSHOT

MATTHEW 7:24–27

"Therefore, everyone who hears these words of Mine and acts on them will be like a sensible man who built his house on the rock. The rain fell, the rivers rose, and the winds blew and pounded that house. Yet it didn't collapse, because its foundation was on the rock. But everyone who hears these words of Mine and doesn't act on them will be like a foolish man who built his house on the sand. The rain fell, the rivers rose, the winds blew and pounded that house, and it collapsed. And its collapse was great!"

ANCHOR POINT

THROUGH JESUS' EYES

You will know them by their fruit. The actions of people, not their words, reveal the contents of their heart. In this passage Christ warns believers that many will claim to be His followers who, in the end, are not. In fact, many people will come to the end of their lives and discover that they haven't done much for God at all.

Today many people vie for our attention and allegiance, promising wealth, health, power, and success. These individuals and groups may be involved in great causes—feeding the poor, healing the sick, and caring for the environment. They sound good and seem sincere. How do you know who to trust? How do you know who is following Christ and who is just using His name to bolster their fund-raising? Jesus laid out a system for determining the genuine article: Look at how that person lives: "You'll recognize them by their fruit" (Mt 7:16). Concerning this fruit, Galatians 5:22–23 says, "But the fruit of the Spirit is love, joy, peace, patience, kindness, goodness, faith, gentleness, self-control. Against such things there is no law." A good person will yield good fruit.

YOUR CHOICE

On which side of this equation do you find yourself? How about your friends? What about the people you are reading, watching on TV? What life-fruits are they bearing?

LK 7:1–17

DAY 186

TOUGH QUESTION

WHAT DOES IT MEAN TO TAKE A STAND FOR CHRIST AT WORK? I MEAN, I DON'T WANT TO LOSE MY JOB.

Taking a stand for Christ on the job begins with your lifestyle. You should work at setting a positive example for your employer and fellow employees about what a follower of Christ looks like. This includes being honest, working hard and well (see Col 3:23), and respecting coworkers and customers. Also, you should be the same kind of person outside work as you are when you are working.

You can set a powerful example for your coworkers by how you treat others. An identifying characteristic of a follower of Christ should be love. Love makes a powerful statement that Christ is real and working in your life. You can demonstrate love through your words of concern and comfort and by listening to a person's issues and needs (listening is the language of love).

You can also take a stand for Christ through your speech. The Bible says much about the tongue and the words we use. Thankful words rather than "coarse and foolish talking or crude joking" indicate that you live a different kind of life than those around you (Eph 5:4). Gossip can derail your stand for Christ. Talking negatively about people when they are not around is easy, especially when someone is sharing juicy news that you are dying to know. Take a stand for Christ with your words and refuse to gossip.

A time may arise, however, when you have to refuse to do something that you know is wrong. If your supervisor has made such a request or demand, and you refuse, you will have a problem. In that situation, kindly and humbly, but firmly, explain your reasons for your choice and that you are willing to accept the consequences. Unfortunately, that may mean losing your job. Just remember that pleasing your heavenly Boss is much more important that pleasing your earthly one.

SNAPSHOT

LUKE 7:13–16

When the Lord saw her, He had compassion on her and said, "Don't cry." Then He came up and touched the open coffin, and the pallbearers stopped. And He said, "Young man, I tell you, get up!"

The dead man sat up and began to speak, and Jesus gave him to his mother. Then fear came over everyone, and they glorified God, saying, "A great prophet has risen among us," and "God has visited His people."

YOUR CHOICE

What can you do to be a positive example for Christ in your work (volunteer, part-time, or full-time)?

JULY 6

DAY 187

THE BIG PICTURE

MT 11:1–30

SNAPSHOT

MATTHEW 11:11–14

"I assure you: Among those born of women no one greater than John the Baptist has appeared, but the least in the kingdom of heaven is greater than he. From the days of John the Baptist until now, the kingdom of heaven has been suffering violence, and the violent have been seizing it by force. For all the prophets and the law prophesied until John; if you're willing to accept it, he is the Elijah who is to come."

JUST LIKE ME

JOHN THE BAPTIST: HIGHLY RECOMMENDED

Ever have someone write a recommendation for you? You wouldn't ask someone who didn't know you well to write it. Also, you'd want your recommendation to come from a person of integrity. For John the Baptist, no one had more integrity than Jesus, the Savior.

Jesus' spoken recommendation of John the Baptist came at a time when John was at a low point. Everyone faces discouragement from time to time, even fiery prophets. Like his predecessor, the Old Testament prophet Elijah, this second Elijah succumbed to it. Having been arrested by Herod the tetrarch, a discouraged John languished in prison.

Jesus answered John's doubts, expressed by John's followers, by an oral resume of John's work and His own. John was indeed the messenger promised in Malachi 4:5–6—the forerunner of the Messiah. John was one of the "old school" prophets who did the job he was given. Yet although John was a courageous and faithful man of God, he was not the most important person in the kingdom of God. As Jesus said, "Whoever welcomes this little child in My name welcomes Me. And whoever welcomes Me welcomes Him who sent Me. For whoever is least among you—this one is great" (Lk 9:48).

Jesus' recommendation showed John's integrity and lack of pretense. With John, what you saw was what you got; he had no hidden agendas or motives. Is that the case for you?

YOUR CHOICE

What qualities would someone address in a recommendation of you?

SNAPSHOT

LUKE 7:36–38

Then one of the Pharisees invited Him to eat with him. He entered the Pharisee's house and reclined at the table. And a woman in the town who was a sinner found out that Jesus was reclining at the table in the Pharisee's house. She brought an alabaster flask of fragrant oil and stood behind Him at His feet, weeping, and began to wash His feet with her tears. She wiped His feet with the hair of her head, kissing them and anointing them with the fragrant oil.

DEPOSIT

WORDS FROM GOD'S WORD TO STORE IN YOUR MIND AND HEART

"Therefore I tell you, her many sins have been forgiven; that's why she loved much. But the one who is forgiven little, loves little" (Lk 7:47).

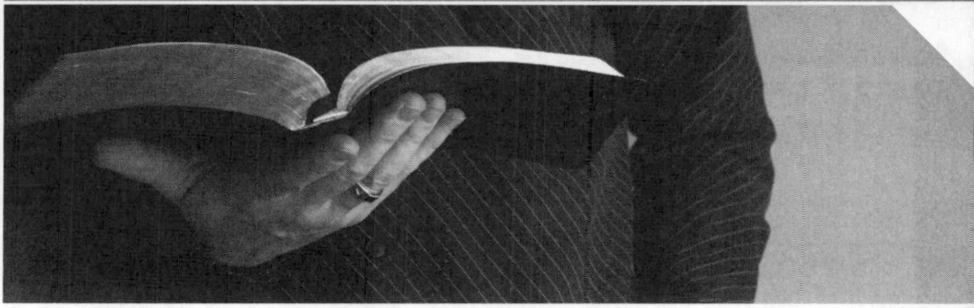

DAY 189

MT 12:22–50

SNAPSHOT

MATTHEW 12:38–42

Then some of the scribes and Pharisees said to Him, "Teacher, we want to see a sign from You."

But He answered them, "An evil and adulterous generation demands a sign, but no sign will be given to it except the sign of the prophet Jonah. For as Jonah was in the belly of the great fish three days and three nights, so the Son of Man will be in the heart of the earth three days and three nights. The men of Nineveh will stand up at the judgment with this generation and condemn it, because they repented at Jonah's proclamation; and look—something greater than Jonah is here! The queen of the south will rise up at the judgment with this generation and condemn it, because she came from the ends of the earth to hear the wisdom of Solomon; and look—something greater than Solomon is here!"

YOUR TURN

TROUBLES FOR JESUS

When are you tempted to have Jesus prove Himself to you?

THE BIG PICTURE

MK 4:1–29

JULY 9

DAY 190

SNAPSHOT

MARK 4:21–25

He also said to them, "Is a lamp brought in to be put under a basket or under a bed? Isn't it to be put on a lampstand? For nothing is concealed except to be revealed, and nothing hidden except to come to light. If anyone has ears to hear, he should listen!" Then He said to them, "Pay attention to what you hear. By the measure you use, it will be measured and added to you. For to the one who has, it will be given, and from the one who does not have, even what he has will be taken away."

YOUR CHOICE

What can you do to be a better listener to what God is telling you?

NO BRAINER

EARS THAT HEAR

Jesus would often use parables when He taught. A parable is a story that illustrates a truth. The story doesn't have to be about an actual person or event to be effective, but usually it features someone with whom the listeners could identify. So to people in Israel, Jesus spoke about plants, animals, household items, and relationships.

Sometimes Jesus would introduce His parables by saying "_____ is like_____," as in, "The kingdom of God is like this" (Mk 4:26). In Mark 4, we find parables about a sower and seeds, a lamp and a basket, seeds and the harvest, and a mustard seed. Then, after giving a parable, Jesus would often say something like, "Anyone who has ears to hear should listen!" (vv. 9 and 23).

Jesus spoke in parables so that those who were paying attention would understand what He was saying or would, at least, try to find out more. He knew that some people in the crowd were simply watching the show (spectators) and others were waiting for Him to slip up (enemies of the gospel). They wouldn't get it. Instead, they probably would mutter, "What's up with all the talk about seeds?" or something like that.

But the people who were listening—that is, they had their "ears" on—would hear that Jesus was talking about God's kingdom. Later, Jesus would explain the parable's meaning in even greater depth to His inner circle of followers, the disciples (v. 34).

Where would you be in the story? Do you think you would be listening intently, trying to understand Jesus' teachings? Really? Well then, how about now when you read the Bible, God's Word? Those who approach Scripture with the wrong attitude just won't get it.

So, if you have ears, listen!

JULY 10

DAY 191

THE BIG PICTURE

MT 13:24–43

SNAPSHOT

MATTHEW 13:37–40

He replied: "The One who sows the good seed is the Son of Man; the field is the world; and the good seed—these are the sons of the kingdom. The weeds are the sons of the evil one, and the enemy who sowed them is the Devil. The harvest is the end of the age, and the harvesters are angels. Therefore just as the weeds are gathered and burned in the fire, so it will be at the end of the age."

TOUGH CHOICE

CANOE

"Lucy!" I shouted, "we're going to get stuck in the . . ." *Brush! Snap! Thud!*

"Too late," said Lucy. "We're already stuck in the weeds." She looked back over her bulky life-jacket at me. Even from my end of the canoe I could see my best friend biting her lip, trying not to laugh.

After an eternity of pushing, paddling, and going in circles, we made it back into the middle of the lake. Mountains surrounded us on all sides, as we abandoned our paddles to the center of the boat and laid back, exhausted.

"I love coming to Colorado with your family. It's so pretty here." Lucy put her hands behind her head, staring up into the sky.

"Lucy . . ." I began, "Do you ever wonder how it all came to be?" Lucy and I shared just about everything with one another, but I had never really asked her about her faith. The overwhelming beauty of the lake and mountains was too awe-inspiring, though. I couldn't help but wonder what she believed about their Creator. *Plus, we're stuck in a canoe in the middle of the lake; she can't walk away.*

She sat up. "You mean, like, do I believe in God?" She paused for a moment, thoughtful. "Yeah, I believe in God," she said matter-of-factly.

I was surprised by her reaction. "Oh, well good." I hesitated. "What do you believe about Him?"

"Well, I don't know all that you do. You go to church every week. But I think God made all this," she motioned at the landscape. "And I think He knows who's going to heaven already, so I just figure I'll live my life and hope for the best!"

Her response caught me off guard. I had expected the "I believe in a higher being" answer. I fumbled for words. "Oh, well, I'm glad you believe in God. I didn't really know . . ."

Lucy stopped me short, "What do you believe about God? You're really into your faith, even though you get harassed about it sometimes. I don't get it."

I smiled. "I'm 'into' it because I believe that we can have a personal relationship with Christ. He's not this far-off, distant god. He came to earth to die for our sins. It doesn't matter how messed up we are. We can keep turning to Him because He is gracious. It's exciting, and I want to live my life for Him."

Lucy seemed thoughtful. "How do you 'live your life for Him'? Where do you start?"

I leaned back again. "Right here, I suppose. Enjoying God's creation, meditating on how powerful the Creator must be."

Lucy followed my lead, leaning back and taking in the surroundings.

"Then you start reading the Bible and join a church where you can fellowship with other Christians. . ." We continued talking about a personal relationship with Christ. Lucy didn't come away a born-again believer, but she had many questions answered and had much to ponder. Lucy also knew it wouldn't take getting stuck in a canoe to ask questions next time.

YOUR CHOICE **Will you be ready to share your faith with a friend when the opportunity arises?**

THE BIG PICTURE

MT 13:44–52

JULY 11

DAY 192

SNAPSHOT

MATTHEW 13:44–46

"The kingdom of heaven is like treasure, buried in a field, that a man found and reburied. Then in his joy he goes and sells everything he has and buys that field.

"Again, the kingdom of heaven is like a merchant in search of fine pearls. When he found one priceless pearl, he went and sold everything he had, and bought it."

ANCHOR POINT

PRICELESS!

The kingdom of heaven is pictured as life's greatest treasure. It is also pictured as an exquisite pearl, worth searching for and, when found, worth selling everything to possess.

Amazingly, this kingdom is free to all who believe—it costs no money. Yet it has a cost—Jesus' death on the cross. And being a member of the kingdom of heaven will involve great personal cost as well. Many have paid with their lives for it; some have been rejected by family and friends; others have sacrificed wealth and fame.

Believing that the kingdom of heaven is priceless will change how we live. If a person believes that something is important, he or she will sacrifice for it. Playing a sport, learning a musical instrument, and pursuing a career all come with price tags. How much more should we be willing to give up for the greatest treasure of all?

YOUR CHOICE

What has the kingdom of heaven cost you so far? Would you be willing to pay a much steeper cost, should God call you to it?

SNAPSHOT

LUKE 8:22–25

One day He and His disciples got into a boat, and He told them, "Let's cross over to the other side of the lake." So they set out, and as they were sailing He fell asleep. Then a fierce windstorm came down on the lake; they were being swamped and were in danger. They came and woke Him up, saying, "Master, Master, we're going to die!" Then He got up and rebuked the wind and the raging waves. So they ceased, and there was a calm. He said to them, "Where is your faith?"

They were fearful and amazed, asking one another, "Who can this be? He commands even the winds and the waves, and they obey Him!"

JUST LIKE ME

JESUS: A MAN IN CONTROL

Life seems out of control sometimes with weather-related disasters, school shootings, mental illnesses, and assorted issues. We look for leaders who seem to have their lives together and can help us weather the storms. But time after time we read about leaders who fail—many times in the area of control.

Jesus showed an amazing control through a series of needs. While His experienced-fishermen disciples were terrified by a sudden squall, Jesus showed control over the weather by calming it. He then exercised authority over the spirit realm by exorcising a legion of evil spirits out of a man. Two medical crises quickly followed: a dying girl and a hemorrhaging woman. One touch of His garment later, the woman was healed. And after His arrival at the home of the now dead girl, Jesus' control over life and death was proven.

What happens when your life gets out of control? Are you like the disciples—frightened and ready to push the panic button? Or are you like the hemorrhaging woman: desperate, but determined to find someone who can help? Sometimes the best thing we can do in an out-of-control situation is to admit that we're no longer in control. Thankfully, God is.

YOUR CHOICE

Which of these examples gives you greatest comfort? How will you react when life seems to be spinning out of control?

THE BIG PICTURE

MT 9:27–38

JULY 13

DAY 194

TOUGH QUESTION

I SEE SO MUCH NEWS ABOUT WORLD PROBLEMS THAT I FIND MYSELF BECOMING CALLOUSED AND JUST DON'T FEEL MUCH ANY MORE. HOW CAN I HAVE COMPASSION FOR THE "CROWDS," LIKE JESUS DID?

The fact that you are sensitive to this issue demonstrates that you aren't terribly "calloused." Otherwise, you wouldn't have even thought about it. The way to become more compassionate, however, begins by asking God to do this work in you. Only He can change hearts. Remember God's promise: "It is God who is working in you, [enabling you] both to will and to act for His good purpose" (Php 2:13). In other words, through the Holy Spirit living in you, God is changing your desires, and He is giving you the power to follow through, to do what He wants. And "He who started a good work in you will carry it on to completion until the day of Christ Jesus" (Php 1:6).

As God works in you, He may prompt you to serve the elderly, to volunteer at a homeless shelter, or to raise money for a family in need. Getting up close and personal with hurting people will help you understand people's real needs. It's hard to feel love from a distance or for nameless statistics. So be open to His leading and obedient in following through.

With news broadcasts regularly alerting us to international disasters, we can begin to almost become immune to them, or we can feel helpless as though we can do nothing to help. At that point, we need to ask God to help us see people as He sees them—His individual creations whom He loves and for whom Christ died. We need to remember that the "crowds" are comprised of individuals, with very personal stories.

SNAPSHOT

MATTHEW 9:35–38

Then Jesus went to all the towns and villages, teaching in their synagogues, preaching the good news of the kingdom, and healing every disease and every sickness. When He saw the crowds, He felt compassion for them, because they were weary and worn out, like sheep without a shepherd. Then He said to His disciples, "The harvest is abundant, but the workers are few. Therefore, pray to the Lord of the harvest to send out workers into His harvest."

YOUR CHOICE

To whom can you show compassion? For whose needs can you pray right now?

DAY 195

THE BIG PICTURE
MK 6:1–13

SNAPSHOT

MARK 6:7–11

He summoned the Twelve and began to send them out in pairs and gave them authority over unclean spirits. He instructed them to take nothing for the road except a walking stick: no bread, no traveling bag, no money in their belts. They were to wear sandals, but not put on an extra shirt. Then He said to them, "Whenever you enter a house, stay there until you leave that place. If any place does not welcome you and people refuse to listen to you, when you leave there, shake the dust off your feet as a testimony against them."

DEPOSIT

WORDS FROM GOD'S WORD TO STORE IN YOUR MIND AND HEART

"But the ones sown on good ground are those who hear the word, welcome it, and produce a crop: 30, 60, and 100 times [what was sown]" (Mk 4:20).

THE BIG PICTURE

MT 10:16–42

JULY 15

DAY 196

SNAPSHOT

MATTHEW 10:26–31

"Therefore, don't be afraid of them, since there is nothing covered that won't be uncovered, and nothing hidden that won't be made known. What I tell you in the dark, speak in the light. What you hear in a whisper, proclaim on the housetops. Don't fear those who kill the body but are not able to kill the soul; rather, fear Him who is able to destroy both soul and body in hell. Aren't two sparrows sold for a penny? Yet not one of them falls to the ground without your Father's consent. But even the hairs of your head have all been counted. Don't be afraid therefore; you are worth more than many sparrows."

YOUR TURN

PREPARED

In what ways do Jesus' words speak to the fears you have?

JULY 16

DAY 197

THE BIG PICTURE

MK 6:14–29

SNAPSHOT

MARK 6:17–20

For Herod himself had given orders to arrest John and to chain him in prison on account of Herodias, his brother Philip's wife, whom he had married. John had been telling Herod, "It is not lawful for you to have your brother's wife!" So Herodias held a grudge against him and wanted to kill him. But she could not, because Herod was in awe of John and was protecting him, knowing he was a righteous and holy man. When Herod heard him he would be very disturbed, yet would hear him gladly.

TOUGH CHOICE

ADVERSITY

Sitting opposite me, across the mahogany desk, the vice president of management poured over my resume. I skimmed the spines of advertising and marketing books that filled the shelves behind her, hoping she was impressed by my line-up of accomplishments.

"It states on your resume, Mr. Parker, that you've spent the last two summers working at a Christian camp . . ."

I sat up straight, prepared to answer the question: *How, exactly, does this apply to the advertising field?*

". . . It also says that you were involved in campus ministry groups, mission trips, and teaching Sunday school . . ."

"Yes, ma'am." *Answer to the question about an experience that impacted me. Biggest challenge.*

"Mr. Parker, this agency is very big and very diverse. We aren't the most prestigious agency in the nation because of our conservatism. We hire employees who are open-minded. I'm not sure your religion will agree with this. Clearly, it dominates your life." I shifted in my seat, unprepared for the question . . . statement about my faith. "Ms. Lopez, I can assure you that my faith will not hinder my ability to work hard and produce a standard of excellence." *There. Good answer.*

She looked down her nose at her folded hands, "Mr. Parker there is no doubt that you are a hard worker with talent. You wouldn't have gotten this far in the interview process if you weren't." She looked back up at me, annoyed, it seemed. "I'm asking how you're going to respond to working with people with other ideas and beliefs."

The initial shock of the question was quickly transitioning into defiance. Could you attack someone's faith in an interview? "Ma'am, I am a Christian, but this, in no way, impedes my ability to work with others who have different beliefs. On the contrary, my faith teaches us to show compassion and to avoid passing judgment. I am perfectly capable of and open to working with people with other beliefs—even contradicting my own. Now, I will not produce work that is morally objectionable, and I will not back down from opportunities to discuss my faith. But I am guaranteeing that I'll be a team player, who cooperates with and supports others."

The expression on my interviewer's face remained stoic, as I kept steady eye contact. *Good, Joey. Honest. Not afraid to confront a challenge.* A moment later, Ms. Lopez leaned forward and picked my resume up off her desk. She placed it back inside the folder, which held my untouched cover letter and letters of recommendation. "Thank you, Mr. Parker." She stood up and extended her hand.

"Oh, yes ma'am," I fumbled, caught off guard by the suddenness of her dismissal.

"Someone from human resources will be in touch." She shook my hand quickly and nodded, reassuming the seat at her desk.

Stunned, I turned toward the door. As my hand reached the handle, I turned around. "Thank you for your time, Ms. Lopez," and I left the room . . . and the job.

YOUR CHOICE **What might your stand for Christ, even where you respond sensitively and lovingly, cost you in the workplace? Is it worth that cost?**

THE BIG PICTURE

MT 14:13–36

JULY 17

DAY 198

SNAPSHOT

MATTHEW 14:25–31

Around three in the morning, He came toward them walking on the sea. When the disciples saw Him walking on the sea, they were terrified. "It's a ghost!" they said, and cried out in fear.

Immediately Jesus spoke to them. "Have courage! It is I. Don't be afraid."

"Lord, if it's You," Peter answered Him, "command me to come to You on the water."

"Come!" He said.

And climbing out of the boat, Peter started walking on the water and came toward Jesus. But when he saw the strength of the wind, he was afraid. And beginning to sink he cried out, "Lord, save me!"

Immediately Jesus reached out His hand, caught hold of him, and said to him, "You of little faith, why did you doubt?"

JUST LIKE ME

PETER: A SINKING FAITH

While watching the incredible grace of an athlete or a virtuoso performance by a musician, you may have thought, *I've got to try that!* While some feats seem beyond the realm of human possibility, some—even those that seem impossible—are just within our grasp, as Peter learned while watching Jesus.

All day long, Jesus performed amazing feats. He fed over five thousand people with five small loaves and two fish. And that evening He took a stroll on the water.

Not content to simply watch Jesus, the usually brash Peter put aside his fear and took a giant step of faith by stepping out of the boat and onto the water. The results were almost a textbook example of one of the challenges of the Christian life. As long as Peter looked to Jesus, he walked on the water's surface with no problem. But as soon as he took his eyes off Jesus and focused on the problem—the gale-force wind and the crashing waves—he freaked out and sank like a stone.

Like Peter, we can start off full of faith but wind up sinking when we focus on ourselves or our problems instead of on God. Without the buoyancy of belief in God's ability, problems tend to loom larger and God smaller. Peter's story reminds us not to simply have faith in our faith, but to focus on God.

YOUR CHOICE

What problems or issues cause you to doubt? In what situations do you feel God calling you to "walk on water"?

JULY 18

DAY 199

THE BIG PICTURE

JN 6:22–40

SNAPSHOT

JOHN 6:35–40

"I am the bread of life," Jesus told them. "No one who comes to Me will ever be hungry, and no one who believes in Me will ever be thirsty again. But as I told you, you've seen Me, and yet you do not believe. Everyone the Father gives Me will come to Me, and the one who comes to Me I will never cast out. For I have come down from heaven, not to do My will, but the will of Him who sent Me. This is the will of Him who sent Me: that I should lose none of those He has given Me but should raise them up on the last day. For this is the will of My Father: that everyone who sees the Son and believes in Him may have eternal life, and I will raise him up on the last day."

ANCHOR POINT

HEAVENLY BREAD

When asked to present a sign to prove He was from the Father, Jesus pointed to the fact that He was greater than all the signs that had been given so far in biblical history. The crowd asked about the manna provided to the people of Israel as they wandered in the desert. What could Jesus offer that could compare to that? As it turned out, quite a bit.

Instead of a transitory meal from the sky that would only last a day (manna would spoil if kept overnight), Jesus was offering a fulfilling bread—eternal life—that would last forever. And, Jesus promised not to lose anyone that the Father would give Him—all would be secure.

This means we can be confident that Christ will sustain us and care for us. As amazing as the miracle of the manna was in the desert, it pales in comparison to the bread we are offered. What an incredible thought, that Christ will take care of us in every way from now until eternity.

YOUR CHOICE

In what ways is Christ your Bread of Life?

THE BIG PICTURE
JN 6:41–71

JULY 19
DAY 200

SNAPSHOT

JOHN 6:60–66

Therefore, when many of His disciples heard this, they said, "This teaching is hard! Who can accept it?"

Jesus, knowing in Himself that His disciples were complaining about this, asked them, "Does this offend you? Then what if you were to observe the Son of Man ascending to where He was before? The Spirit is the One who gives life. The flesh doesn't help at all. The words that I have spoken to you are spirit and are life. But there are some among you who don't believe." (For Jesus knew from the beginning those who would not believe and the one who would betray Him.) He said, "This is why I told you that no one can come to Me unless it is granted to him by the Father."

From that moment many of His disciples turned back and no longer accompanied Him.

YOUR CHOICE

What will you say to your friends who say they don't want to follow Jesus any more?

NO BRAINER

DESERTED

This was a critical juncture in Jesus' ministry. He had spoken hard words about Himself and His mission and the text says, "From that moment many of His disciples turned back and no longer accompanied Him" (v. 66). So Jesus turned to the Twelve, His core followers, and asked if they would be leaving as well. Peter spoke up and answered: "Lord, who will we go to? You have the words of eternal life. We have come to believe and know that You are the Holy One of God!" (vv. 68-69)

Peter got it exactly right.

People may follow Christ, for a while, with a variety of motives. Some may join church for the business contacts. A politician may quote the Bible and act spiritual to get votes. A sales rep may mouth Christian clichés with a certain customer to make a sale. Some may attend religious events for the inspiring music, great drama, good-looking members of the opposite sex, or tasty refreshments. And many claim to be Christians simply because they were reared that way—it's a family thing. But if any of these folks hang around long enough and hear Jesus' claims and demands, they may just desert Him, too. Jesus' message can seem harsh, and His followers aren't promised fame, fortune, good health, and great times—the opposite, in fact.

So why do you follow Him?

Hear again Peter's response: You have the words of eternal life. . . . You are the Holy One of God!" In other words, "We're with You, Jesus, because there is no other. Only You can give eternal life."

It's all about truth. Because Jesus is truly God, He tells the truth and He delivers what He promises. How could we go anywhere else?

DAY 201

THE BIG PICTURE

MK 7:1–37

SNAPSHOT

MARK 7:17–23

When He went into the house away from the crowd, the disciples asked Him about the parable. And He said to them, "Are you also as lacking in understanding? Don't you realize that nothing going into a man from the outside can defile him? For it doesn't go into his heart but into the stomach and is eliminated." (As a result, He made all foods clean.) Then He said, "What comes out of a person—that defiles him. For from within, out of people's hearts, come evil thoughts, sexual immoralities, thefts, murders, adulteries, greed, evil actions, deceit, lewdness, stinginess, blasphemy, pride, and foolishness. All these evil things come from within and defile a person."

YOUR CHOICE

When are you most tempted toward lustful thoughts and actions? What can you do to avoid those situations?

TOUGH QUESTION

SEX IS A *BIG* DEAL WITH THE GROUP I'M IN—AT LEAST WE TALK ABOUT IT A LOT: JOKES, PORN, BRAGGING. AS A CHRISTIAN, I KNOW THAT'S NOT RIGHT. WHAT CAN I DO?

If you know that talking about sex flippantly and with no respect isn't right but are still tolerating people who do this, you need to find a new group of people to hang out with. As a Christian you cannot afford to be influenced by the world. If you are the only Christian in that group, you will discover that standing up for what is right all by yourself will be difficult.

The Bible is very clear about Christians discussing sex. Ephesians 5:3–4 states, "But sexual immorality and any impurity or greed should not even be heard of among you, as is proper for saints. And coarse and foolish talking or crude joking are not suitable, but rather giving thanks."

Because you know this behavior isn't right, you are responsible to set boundaries for yourself and not participate in these discussions with your friends. Participating is sin, even if your friends aren't Christians and don't care if you joke along with them. God cares, and your sin will separate you from him. Sex was designed by God to be something pure and set apart. Our culture has exploited it and made it nonchalant and not special.

When your friends strike up the next conversation about sex, kindly excuse yourself from their presence. This group of friends obviously is not encouraging you in your walk with Christ, and you need to risk your friendship with these people in order to protect yourself from sinful joking. If they ridicule you, reject you, and kick you out of their group, then you will avoid more bad conversations. If they keep you in their group, then perhaps your stand against not talking about sex in a crude way will influence your friends for Christ.

MT 15:32–16:12

SNAPSHOT

MATTHEW 16:8–12

Aware of this, Jesus said, "You of little faith! Why are you discussing among yourselves that you do not have bread? Don't you understand yet? Don't you remember the five loaves for the 5,000 and how many baskets you collected? Or the seven loaves for the 4,000 and how many large baskets you collected? Why is it you don't understand that when I told you, 'Beware of the yeast of the Pharisees and Sadducees,' it wasn't about bread?" Then they understood that He did not tell them to beware of the yeast in bread, but of the teaching of the Pharisees and Sadducees.

DEPOSIT

WORDS FROM GOD'S WORD TO STORE IN YOUR MIND AND HEART

"An evil and adulterous generation wants a sign, but no sign will be given to it except the sign of Jonah" (Mt 16:4a).

JULY 22

DAY 203

THE BIG PICTURE

MK 8:22–9:1

SNAPSHOT

MARK 8:27–29

Jesus went out with His disciples to the villages of Caesarea Philippi. And on the road He asked His disciples, "Who do people say that I am?"

They answered Him, "John the Baptist; others, Elijah; still others, one of the prophets."

"But you," He asked them again, "who do you say that I am?"

Peter answered Him, "You are the Messiah!"

YOUR TURN

PETER IDENTIFIES JESUS

In what specific ways have you come to understand Jesus better in the last few weeks?

THE BIG PICTURE

LK 9:28–45

JULY 23

DAY 204

SNAPSHOT

LUKE 9:28–32

About eight days after these words, He took along Peter, John, and James, and went up on the mountain to pray. As He was praying, the appearance of His face changed, and His clothes became dazzling white. Suddenly, two men were talking with Him—Moses and Elijah. They appeared in glory and were speaking of His death, which He was about to accomplish in Jerusalem.

Peter and those with him were in a deep sleep, and when they became fully awake, they saw His glory and the two men who were standing with Him.

ANCHOR POINT

JESUS IS TRANSFIGURED

Peter had witnessed an incredible sight. Not only was Christ physically changed—His face and His clothes—but suddenly two long-dead prophets had showed up and had begun talking to Him. On top of that, God had spoken from the clouds, saying, "This is My Son, the Chosen One; listen to Him!" Jesus was confirmed as the Son of God, the Messiah. After this experience, certainly Peter's faith would be unshakeable. Yet, not long afterward, we find Peter turning his back on Jesus and denying that he even knew Him.

How did Peter go from such an incredible confirmation of Jesus as the Christ to fleeing the scene in the garden and at the cross? Why didn't the events of the mountain top sustain him? What happened to his enthusiasm and excitement?

Mountain-top, emotional experiences often fade as time goes by. It could be a life-changing retreat, a perspective-changing mission trip, or a powerful sermon. Why does the effect of these events diminish?

Often, that happens because we fail to sustain the momentum. Thinking we've arrived, we lose sight of the reason for those experiences and their purpose—to draw us closer to Christ, the Son of God. Instead of rushing down the mountain and resuming life as usual, we need to keep our eyes on Him.

YOUR CHOICE

How do you respond to "mountain top" experiences? How can you keep them from being short-lived?

DAY 205

THE BIG PICTURE
MT 18:1–6

NO BRAINER

WHO'S THE GREATEST?

"We're number one! Were number one!" The familiar chant fills the gym as the home team cruises to another victory. Everyone wants to be on top, to be known as the best, the most outstanding, the most valuable, the greatest—it's human nature. So we have tournaments, culminating in events such as the Super Bowl and World Series, to determine sports championships and TV "reality" shows to determine the best singer, dancer, or whatever. In addition, news magazines tout the best hospitals, colleges, and high schools. And let's not forget all the awards shows.

We shouldn't be surprised at the disciples, then, for asking Jesus who would be the "greatest" in His kingdom. They must have hoped that they would meet the criteria—certainly, as Jesus' close associates they had the inside track to those positions.

But Jesus, as He often does, surprised them with a very counter-cultural answer: "Whoever humbles himself like this child—this one is the greatest in the kingdom of heaven. And whoever welcomes one child like this in My name welcomes Me."

In any culture, especially that one, a child was the polar opposite of "great," at the lowest social level, with no resources, worldly influence, or power. But in Jesus' kingdom, a childlike person would be in the top tier. So unlike those we idolize these days. Imagine, for a moment, what this new call to greatness might mean in your school or community. Jesus' choice might be a lunch lady, a career teacher, a shy freshman, or a garbage collector (people who humbly serve in His name) rather than the usual suspects—star athlete, elected official, local kid who made it big on Broadway, or young millionaire. And Jesus' opinion, His rating system, is the only one that counts.

So, who's the greatest in your pantheon of personalities? And an even more personal question: What ladder to "greatness" are you climbing? Keep it real; keep it humble; keep it Jesus.

SNAPSHOT

MATTHEW 18:1–5

At that time the disciples came to Jesus and said, "Who is greatest in the kingdom of heaven?"

Then He called a child to Him and had him stand among them. "I assure you," He said, "unless you are converted and become like children, you will never enter the kingdom of heaven. Therefore, whoever humbles himself like this child—this one is the greatest in the kingdom of heaven. And whoever welcomes one child like this in My name welcomes Me."

YOUR CHOICE

What can you do to put pride aside? What child can you welcome in Jesus' name?

MK 9:38–50

TOUGH QUESTION

MY FRIENDS USE LANGUAGE THAT I FEEL OFFENDS BOTH GOD AND ME. WHAT SHOULD I DO?

Using kind but firm words can combat foul language. Keeping a humble attitude validates what you are saying to your friends because getting mad and defensive can be just as bad and offensive to some as swearing.

When a friend uses bad language, pull that person aside and gently explain that you would like him or her to stop swearing. Don't embarrass your friend in front of the group. You can't control your friend, of course—he or she may ridicule you or, out of respect for you, agree to stop. Standing up for what you believe comes with a risk.

Your example, your request, and your explanation to the friend may intrigue him or her and elicit questions about your beliefs and about Christ. So be prepared with the gospel message and be ready to explain how your faith influences the way you live.

Your friend may be so offended by your request to stop swearing that he or she doesn't want to be your friend any more. If that's a real possibility, you may need to examine the types of people you are choosing to hang out with. The Bible has many references to the mouth being connected to the heart. Jesus said, "How can you speak good things when you are evil? For the mouth speaks from the overflow of the heart" (Mt 12:34). In other words, a person's words indicate what is in that person's heart. This doesn't mean that you should never spend any time with anyone who swears, but you need to understand the kind of person you're dealing with—the relationship between words and the heart.

SNAPSHOT

MARK 9:38–41

John said to Him, "Teacher, we saw someone driving out demons in Your name, and we tried to stop him because he wasn't following us."

"Don't stop him," said Jesus, "because there is no one who will perform a miracle in My name who can soon afterwards speak evil of Me. For whoever is not against us is for us. And whoever gives you a cup of water to drink because of My name, since you belong to the Messiah—I assure you: He will never lose his reward."

YOUR CHOICE

How does your conversation reflect on your relationship with God?

JULY 26

DAY 207

THE BIG PICTURE

MT 18:10–35

SNAPSHOT

MATTHEW 18:32–35

"Then, after he had summoned him, his master said to him, 'You wicked slave! I forgave you all that debt because you begged me. Shouldn't you also have had mercy on your fellow slave, as I had mercy on you?' And his master got angry and handed him over to the jailers until he could pay everything that was owed. So My heavenly Father will also do to you if each of you does not forgive his brother from his heart."

TOUGH CHOICE

FORGIVENESS

Knock! Knock! Knock! "Hannah, we need to talk." My dad stood on the other side of my bedroom door. I sat at my desk, trying to read . . . ignore him.

"Come on, Hannah. Stop giving me the cold shoulder."

I shoved my chair backward and opened the door, returning to my seat and book before he could make eye contact with me.

"Well, that's a step forward," he grumbled. "I came in here to apologize. The least you could do is close your book and look at me."

Tears burned in my eyes as I turned around. *Don't cry. Don't cry.* I hated feeling so angry. I felt like I was back in elementary school, unable to control my emotions.

"I came in here to apologize for losing my temper with you," he began, "I was wrong to do that, and I hope that you'll forgive me. It was just difficult to remain calm when I was driving somewhere unfamiliar and you and your mother were yelling at me from the back seat."

My breathing shortened. I turned away from him, toward my desk. "Hannah," his voice was stern, "do not turn your back on me. I just apologized."

"That wasn't an apology!" I yelled. "You never apologize!" I spun around to look at him, feeling uninhibited. I wanted him to know how he had hurt me. "Every time you apologize, you turn it back around on me. There's always a catch. 'You're sorry, *but* . . .' It was only because of something *I* did," I seethed.

"Hannah . . ."

"Just once I'd like to be right. You wrong; me right!" I stopped, shocked at my abrasiveness.

Silence. More silence. Finally my dad began to speak. "I am sorry, Hannah," he said quietly. "I didn't know you felt this way. My intent has always been to be a father who readily admitted his mistakes, but I see that I have failed." He turned to walk out of my room. "I hope you can forgive me."

The door closed behind him. I sat and stared at the closed door for a long time, numb. *What have I done? Why did I lose control? Why didn't I just forgive him?*

This last thought lingered, stung. *Because you* had *to be right. You* had *to make him suffer. You couldn't just forgive.*

I stood up, pacing across my room. "It's not that easy, God!" I said aloud. "It's not easy to forgive over and over again when it's unearned. I want him to know how he hurt me."

As always, my dad and I eventually made amends, but the lingering recollection of my anger was unnerving. For the first time in my life I was keenly aware of my inability to forgive. I wrestled with this realization, as I knew how the Lord had forgiven me seventy-times-seven times, even though I had wronged and would continue to wrong Him. Who are we to hold ourselves above Christ and deny forgiveness of others? We are to forgive as we have been forgiven.

YOUR CHOICE **Whom do you need to forgive? What relationship do you need to repair?**

SNAPSHOT

JOHN 7:16–18

Jesus answered them, "My teaching isn't Mine but is from the One who sent Me. If anyone wants to do His will, he will understand whether the teaching is from God or if I am speaking on My own. The one who speaks for himself seeks his own glory. But He who seeks the glory of the One who sent Him is true, and there is no unrighteousness in Him."

YOUR CHOICE

Lately, when have you been impatient with God? What should you be doing as you wait for His answers or actions?

NO BRAINER

TIMING IS EVERYTHING

In John 7 we overhear Jesus and the disciples discussing their itinerary—who will go where and when. A couple of times, both in this discussion and in the succeeding events, we find statements about the right timing: Jesus says, "My time has not yet arrived, but your time is always at hand" (v. 6); John comments, "His hour had not yet come" (v. 30).

That's a familiar theme throughout Jesus' ministry. He knew what He had to do, as He journeyed toward the cross. Jesus had been born at just the right time, and He would die at just the right time. Not a day, hour, minute, or second sooner or later. At this point in His ministry, Jesus must have been tempted to rush matters—but He didn't. And Jesus' followers were clueless about God's timetable, let alone His ultimate purpose in sending His Son. But Jesus knew, and He waited.

In so many areas, we hear that "timing is everything." It's true in cooking a meal, making a sale, buying and selling stocks, deepening a relationship, and telling a joke. And it's profoundly true in running a universe.

Often, as we wait for answers or guidance or solutions or healing, we want it *now*. But timing is everything, and God's timing is perfect. And remember, He sees the big picture; He knows the ultimate purpose; He knows the future; He's in control. So we can relax while we pray and obey—and wait for Him to act, in just the right time.

JULY 28

DAY 209

THE BIG PICTURE

JN 7:37–53

SNAPSHOT

JOHN 7:37–39

On the last and most important day of the festival, Jesus stood up and cried out, "If anyone is thirsty, he should come to Me and drink! The one who believes in Me, as the Scripture has said, will have streams of living water flow from deep within him." He said this about the Spirit, whom those who believed in Him were going to receive, for the Spirit had not yet been received, because Jesus had not yet been glorified.

DEPOSIT

WORDS FROM GOD'S WORD TO STORE IN YOUR MIND AND HEART

"The one who believes in Me, as the Scripture has said, will have streams of living water flow from deep within him" (Jn 7:38).

THE BIG PICTURE

JN 8:1–20

JULY 29

DAY 210

SNAPSHOT

JOHN 8:6b–11

Jesus stooped down and started writing on the ground with His finger. When they persisted in questioning Him, He stood up and said to them, "The one without sin among you should be the first to throw a stone at her."

Then He stooped down again and continued writing on the ground. When they heard this, they left one by one, starting with the older men. Only He was left, with the woman in the center. When Jesus stood up, He said to her, "Woman, where are they? Has no one condemned you?"

"No one, Lord," she answered.

"Neither do I condemn you," said Jesus. "Go, and from now on do not sin any more."

YOUR TURN

FORGIVENESS

Who is the last person you had to forgive?

THE BIG PICTURE
JN 8:21–59

NO BRAINER

GIVER OF FREEDOM

"You will know the truth, and the truth will set you free" (Jn 8:32). This, one of the most frequently quoted Bible passages, is etched in stone at the entrance to the CIA. The statement seems to affirm the justice system, democracy, freedom of the press, and other institutions and movements that emphasize "truth" or "freedom." But the "truth" referenced here is *Jesus* and *His words*, and "freedom" refers to being free from the bondage and penalty of sin.

Jesus told the Jews that *He* had set them free. At first His listeners didn't understand because they thought Jesus was talking about being out of jail or being able to do whatever they wanted—typical understandings of freedom. But the freedom experienced in Christ was (and is) much more profound and needed. And "if the Son sets you free, you really will be free" (v. 36).

Freedom is a felt need among young people, especially those who yearn to be released from the restrictions of their parents and others who restrain them. And when they get away from home, they often go wild. It's true, of course, that unless they break the law, they are free to "do what they want." But they really aren't free at all. Instead, without the previous restraints, they are simply doing what comes naturally, being pulled by the sinful nature. Sadly, many soon become trapped in this new, "free" lifestyle.

Don't mistake undisciplined self-indulgence for freedom. And know that the ultimate penalty for being a sinner and for sinning is eternal death (see Rm 6:23). But Jesus truly does bring freedom to those who trust in Him. He forgives us and frees us from that terrible penalty, and He gives us the ability to choose to do what is right.

So whether you're in high school or beyond, on a job, in the military, or enrolled in college, take your stand for truth and for true freedom—in Christ.

SNAPSHOT

JOHN 8:31–36

So Jesus said to the Jews who had believed Him, "If you continue in My word, you really are My disciples. You will know the truth, and the truth will set you free."

"We are descendants of Abraham," they answered Him, "and we have never been enslaved to anyone. How can You say, 'You will become free'?"

Jesus responded, "I assure you: Everyone who commits sin is a slave of sin. A slave does not remain in the household forever, but a son does remain forever. Therefore if the Son sets you free, you really will be free."

YOUR CHOICE

Have you exercised your freedom in Christ?

SNAPSHOT

LUKE 10:1–3

After this, the Lord appointed 70 others, and He sent them ahead of Him in pairs to every town and place where He Himself was about to go. He told them: "The harvest is abundant, but the workers are few. Therefore, pray to the Lord of the harvest to send out workers into His harvest. Now go; I'm sending you out like lambs among wolves."

TOUGH QUESTION

CHRISTIANS AT MY SCHOOL ARE OFTEN MOCKED AND RIDICULED. I'M AFRAID GOD WANTS ME TO SHARE MY FAITH WITH MY FRIENDS AT SCHOOL. WHAT SHOULD I DO?

You have no guarantees that you won't get labeled as weird or worse. In fact, Jesus warned His followers, "If the world hates you, understand that it hated Me before it hated you. If you were of the world, the world would love you as its own. However, because you are not of the world, but I have chosen you out of it, the world hates you" (Jn 15:18–19). Later, John the apostle reminded Jesus' followers, "Do not be surprised . . . if the world hates you" (1 Jn 3:13).

Taking a stand for Christ usually doesn't evoke a warm reception—at school, in the community, or on the job. In fact, the opposite is often the case. Your obedience to God's leading might take you where you aren't wanted, and you may be rejected and ridiculed. Yet you can be sure that God will give you what you need in those situations: "God will supply all your needs according to his riches in glory in Christ Jesus" (Php 4:19).

Unfortunately, some people take certain "stands" for strange causes or in weird and offensive ways. (Maybe those people really are "wackos.") But the Bible tells us to speak the truth in love (Eph 4:15) and to give answers about our faith "with gentleness and respect" (1 Pt 3:16). So *how* you take a stand and *how* you share your faith is extremely important.

When you are being slammed or slandered for following Christ, remember these words of Jesus: "Blessed are you when they insult you and persecute you and falsely say every kind of evil against you because of Me. Be glad and rejoice, because your reward is great in heaven. For that is how they persecuted the prophets who were before you" (Mt 5:11–12).

YOUR CHOICE

When have you been "persecuted" recently because of something you said or did in obedience to Christ? How did you respond?

AUGUSTUS
AOUT
AUGUST
AUGUST
AGOSTO
AGOSTO

THE BIG PICTURE

LK 10:25–42

AUGUST 1

DAY 213

SNAPSHOT

LUKE 10:38–42

While they were traveling, He entered a village, and a woman named Martha welcomed Him into her home. She had a sister named Mary, who also sat at the Lord's feet and was listening to what He said. But Martha was distracted by her many tasks, and she came up and asked, "Lord, don't You care that my sister has left me to serve alone? So tell her to give me a hand."

The Lord answered her, "Martha, Martha, you are worried and upset about many things, but one thing is necessary. Mary has made the right choice, and it will not be taken away from her."

JUST LIKE ME

MARY AND MARTHA: MAKING THE RIGHT CHOICE

No one expects siblings to be clones of one another. And Mary and Martha could not have been more different. Yet Martha often gets a bad rap because her service-oriented mind-set didn't get two thumbs up from Jesus, while her sister Mary's contemplative approach seemed to be what He preferred.

Martha's contribution to the evening seemed the logical choice. After all, Jesus was a guest in her home. Having a guest meant preparing food and all of the trappings that came with first-century hospitality—or so Martha believed. She didn't realize that Jesus wasn't after the logical choice, but the heart choice

Mary chose the latter by taking time to be with Jesus. Unlike Martha, who showed love by service, Mary showed love by listening. Since Jesus would remain on earth a short time, she knew that every minute in His presence was precious.

While both aspects of love—service and contemplation—are of value to God, certain times call for one or the other. Mary and Martha's experience with Jesus shows the value of seeking God's opinion about which approach is needed.

YOUR CHOICE

What is your favorite way to spend time with Jesus?

THE BIG PICTURE

LK 11:1–13

SNAPSHOT

LUKE 11:9–13

"So I say to you, keep asking, and it will be given to you. Keep searching, and you will find. Keep knocking, and the door will be opened to you. For everyone who asks receives, and the one who searches finds, and to the one who knocks, the door will be opened. What father among you, if his son asks for a fish, will give him a snake instead of a fish? Or if he asks for an egg, will give him a scorpion? If you then, who are evil, know how to give good gifts to your children, how much more will the heavenly Father give the Holy Spirit to those who ask Him?"

ANCHOR POINT

PRAYER

At the beginning of this chapter in Luke, we find one of the most well-known sections of Scripture: the Lord's Prayer. It is taught and recited all over the world. We would be hard pressed to find someone who has not heard it. But immediately following the Lord's Prayer, we find a statement by Jesus that seems to imply that God will give us whatever we want if we bother Him enough, if, like a whining child, we keep repeating our requests, over and over. If we stop reading there, however, we miss the point, which we see in the verses for today.

Jesus' words highlight three profound truths about prayer. First, we see that God *wants* us to come to Him with our needs—for daily sustenance, for forgiveness, and for guidance and protection. Second, God is always open and available to us—we can come to Him at any time, day or night and in any situation. Third, God will give us exactly what we need—He loves us that much.

Don't let anything keep you from your loving Father. Keep asking, searching, and knocking.

YOUR CHOICE

In what ways do your prayers match the Lord's Prayer? What keeps you from talking more with your heavenly Father? What can you do to keep asking, searching, and knocking?

LUKE 11:20–23

SNAPSHOT

"If I drive out demons by the finger of God, then the kingdom of God has come to you. When a strong man, fully armed, guards his estate, his possessions are secure. But when one stronger than he attacks and overpowers him, he takes from him all his weapons he trusted in, and divides up his plunder. Anyone who is not with Me is against Me, and anyone who does not gather with Me scatters."

AUGUST 3

DAY 215

THE BIG PICTURE

LK 11:14–32

TOUGH CHOICE

EATING DISORDER

"Dr. Grayson?"

A middle-aged man with dark hair and a five-o'clock shadow (from the previous day), looked up from his newspaper and black coffee.

"Ellie," he said, standing up to greet me, "great to see you, kiddo! Please, sit down."

I draped my coat over the back of the coffeehouse chair and sat down across from my psychiatrist. When I was between the ages of twelve and fifteen, I had visited him at his office once a week for an eating disorder and depression. Ten years later, thirty pounds healthier, and quite a bit happier, I would only meet with him once every year or two to catch up over a cup of coffee.

"You look great, Ellie, in every sense of the word!"

While fighting anorexia, I had become aware of the disease's extraordinarily low recovery rate. Week after week, I would see the same patients in the hospital's eating disorder ward. The majority of patients dealt with their eating disorder for a lifetime, to some extent or another. I was in the minority.

Dr. Grayson crossed his arms so that I could see the leather patches on his sport coat elbows. "Ellie," he said thoughtfully, "It's been a decade now. How did you do it? We continue to study this disease, down to the root of its roots, and we still aren't seeing progress in the recovery rates. You gained the weight, kept it on, avoided the relapse that so often blindsides patients, and beat the disorder. How did you do it?"

The question didn't surprise me. "Well, I suppose it came down to filling a void in my life with something other than achieving a 'perfect' image."

"So you substituted your desire for control—controlling your overall image—for something else," he summarized. "But how did you recognize that a void needed to be filled? Where did the desire to make the substitution originate?"

I shifted in my seat. This was the part of the question I didn't fully understand, myself. "I don't think I did recognize the void at first. I hadn't consciously thought that something was missing in my life. Healing had already begun when I considered this."

"Explain, doctor. What's your theory," he chuckled.

"Well, I believe that it all boils down to the void being the absence of Christ in a person's life. I believe that my struggle with anorexia was Satan's attack on me, and I caved in to it. I hated myself—God's perfect creation. I let the devil feed on me. By God's grace, loving relationships and friendships were placed in my life. Eventually I recognized this love as a reflection of Christ's, and I wanted more of it. I wanted Christ, Himself, back in my life. I couldn't hate myself and accept Christ's love at the same time, so I filled the void with Him and began living my life *for* Him."

"And there was no relapse because you had filled that void."

"Right. The eating disorder could no longer satisfy any need or fulfill me. Only Christ could." I watched Dr. Grayson's face, trying to interpret his facial expression.

"Ellie," he said after a moment, "I believe you're on to something. I do believe you're on to something, kiddo . . ."

YOUR CHOICE **How do you explain to a friend (or doctor) the transformation in your life?**

AUGUST 4

DAY 216

THE BIG PICTURE

LK 11:33–54

SNAPSHOT

LUKE 11:33–36

"No one lights a lamp and puts it in the cellar or under a basket, but on a lampstand, so that those who come in may see its light. Your eye is the lamp of the body. When your eye is good, your whole body is also full of light. But when it is bad, your body is also full of darkness. Take care then, that the light in you is not darkness. If therefore your whole body is full of light, with no part of it in darkness, the whole body will be full of light, as when a lamp shines its light on you."

DEPOSIT

WORDS FROM GOD'S WORD TO STORE IN YOUR MIND AND HEART

"No one lights a lamp and puts it in the cellar or under a basket, but on a lampstand, so that those who come in may see its light" (Lk 11:33).

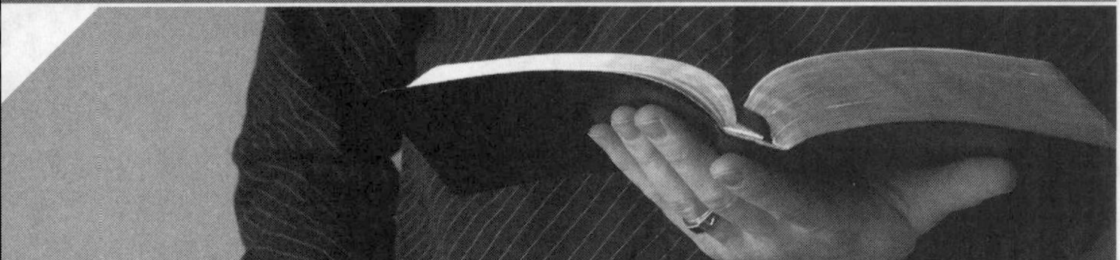

THE BIG PICTURE

LK 12:1–21

AUGUST 5

DAY 217

SNAPSHOT

LUKE 12:8–12

"And I say to you, anyone who acknowledges Me before men, the Son of Man will also acknowledge him before the angels of God, but whoever denies Me before men will be denied before the angels of God. Anyone who speaks a word against the Son of Man will be forgiven, but the one who blasphemes against the Holy Spirit will not be forgiven. Whenever they bring you before synagogues and rulers and authorities, don't worry about how you should defend yourselves or what you should say. For the Holy Spirit will teach you at that very hour what must be said."

YOUR TURN

ACKNOWLEDGING GOD

In what situations do you get too caught up in the goals of this world and forget about God and others?

DAY 218

SNAPSHOT

LUKE 12:27–31

"Consider how the wildflowers grow: they don't labor or spin thread. Yet I tell you, not even Solomon in all his splendor was adorned like one of these! If that's how God clothes the grass, which is in the field today and is thrown into the furnace tomorrow, how much more will He do for you—you of little faith? Don't keep striving for what you should eat and what you should drink, and don't be anxious. For the Gentile world eagerly seeks all these things, and your Father knows that you need them.

"But seek His kingdom, and these things will be provided for you."

YOUR CHOICE

What promises from God help you overcome your anxiety?

TOUGH QUESTION

I KNOW I'M NOT SUPPOSED TO BE ANXIOUS ABOUT ANYTHING, BUT I FIND MYSELF WORRYING ABOUT WHAT WILL HAPPEN AS A RESULT OF MY CHOICES. WHAT SHOULD I DO?

Anyone can be anxious and worry about things to come. Taking a stand for Christ can bring positive or negative results, and anticipating the negative reactions can bring so much anxiety and fear that you don't take the stand in the first place. It shouldn't be that way. Christ's followers must be bold, or the world will never know Him.

When Jesus was teaching the disciples about worry, He told them not to worry about anything—"your life, what you will eat; or about the body, what you will wear" (Lk 12:22). A bit later (v. 31), He encouraged them to "seek His kingdom, and these things will be provided for you." If we are seeking God's kingdom first and taking a stand for Him, then He will provide us with everything we need in the moment.

If your heart is in the right place, and you need wisdom or words while taking a stand, the Holy Spirit will bring them to your mind. If you need safety or protection, He will give it. Sometimes God provides in ways we don't expect, but He always comes through.

The fear you experience that leads to anxiety comes from a lack of faith. Truly believing not just *in* God, but believing *God* will change your life. You will be able to live with boldness and freedom. Believing God involves knowing His promises, and that comes from spending time in the Word. You can't take a stand for Christ based on emotion and the desire to be a hero. Taking an effective stand for Christ is deeply rooted in solid Bible-based faith.

LUKE 12:49–52

"I came to bring fire on the earth, and how I wish it were already set ablaze! But I have a baptism to be baptized with, and how it consumes Me until it is finished! Do you think that I came here to give peace to the earth? No, I tell you, but rather division! From now on, five in one household will be divided: three against two, and two against three."

SNAPSHOT

AUGUST 7

DAY 219

THE BIG PICTURE

LK 12:49–59

TOUGH CHOICE

JUDGMENT

Four thick strands of cheese extended in opposite directions as Loretta, Marty, Reed, and I pulled pieces of deep-dish pizza toward our plates.

"Oh, man, this looks good!" said Reed, reeling in his cheese.

"Yes it does," agreed Marty, lifting his slice of pizza to his mouth. "Cheers."

"Hold on. We forgot to pray," said Loretta, wiping her hands on her napkin and extending them to Reed and myself.

Reed and I followed her lead and bowed our heads. Marty groaned, but set down his pizza and joined in.

Loretta began, "Dear Lord, thank you for this food and the hands that prepared it. Bless it to our bodies, and thanks for letting the Dogs hammer the Bucks. Amen!"

"Amen!" We all resounded, digging into our food.

"So," I asked between bites, "how are we celebrating the victory after dinner?"

"Sigma's having an off-campus party at the Barn. The house band starts at midnight!," said Marty.

"I don't know," I said. "We've got church early tomorrow. That would make it a really late night."

"Hey, Marty, you ought to come with us tomorrow morning," said Loretta. We had invited Marty to church several times earlier that year, but he had never wanted to go.

Marty shifted in his seat. "Eh, I don't know."

"Come on, Marty, it might not be as painful as you think," said Reed, a sarcastic smile on his face.

"It's not church, itself, really," said Marty uncomfortably. "Don't take this personally, but I just find Christians to be judgmental, on the whole."

"Marty," asked Loretta, a bit stunned, "you don't find us judgmental, do you?"

"No, no," he fumbled. "You guys are the exception, and I appreciate that. It's just, well, the Christians in high school hounded me for not being into religion. They always wanted to argue and debate their points. They weren't interested in listening or even having a civil discussion. They just wanted to shove their beliefs down my throat."

His explanation discouraged me.

"Marty, I hope you know that when we invite you to church, it's not because we want to 'shove' our faith down your throat," said Reed, seriously.

"Our Christianity is the biggest part of our lives, and we want to share that with you," said Loretta.

Marty leaned back in his chair, smoothing the front of his sweatshirt. "I just don't know if I'm ready to go to church . . ."

"Would you ever be comfortable just talking to us about our faith?" I asked.

"Judgment-free," added Reed.

Marty tilted his head from side-to-side. "Actually, yeah. I would. That would be good . . ."

YOUR CHOICE **What negative ideas do your non-Christian friends have about Christians or Christianity? What can you do to change that image?**

THE BIG PICTURE

LK 13:1–21

NO BRAINER

VALUES AND PRIORITIES

Did you catch the interaction between Jesus and the leader of the synagogue in today's passage? What was *that* all about?

First, being the *leader* of the synagogue was a big deal in Jewish society. He would have been like the "president" or the administrative head of that place of worship. The man had a measure of power and prestige. And there was Jesus, encroaching on his territory and, supposedly, breaking one of his pet rules.

So the indignant leader, trying to assert himself and embarrass Jesus at the same time, accuses Him of breaking the Sabbath. But Jesus sees right through the man's hypocrisy and nails him and those like him. He reminds them of *their* Sabbath practices and points out how they were, in effect, putting a rule and animals before a hurting human being. Their values and priorities were twisted, wrong.

Actually, that happens a lot. We see it, sometimes, with a government or big business bureaucrat who insists on certain policies and procedures instead of common sense; or in a family where a parent chooses time at work over time with a child; or in church where we dare not make a change because "we've always done it that way." And we want to scream, "Don't you see what you're doing? You're blowing it big time!" People are more important than following a procedure or making a buck or preserving the past or some other sacred cow.

But before we get all worked up and self-righteous as we point out these flaws in others, we need to check our own values. We *say* God is first (Mt 6:33), but do our daily choices reflect that value? We *say* we love others, but are we acting in love toward them? If someone were to examine how we invest our time, money, and emotion, what would that person conclude is really important to us?

Jesus wants us to be like Him, not the hypocritical synagogue leader.

SNAPSHOT

LUKE 13:10–16

As He was teaching in one of the synagogues on the Sabbath, a woman was there who had been disabled by a spirit for over 18 years. She was bent over and could not straighten up at all. When Jesus saw her, He called out to her, "Woman, you are free of your disability." Then He laid His hands on her, and instantly she was restored and began to glorify God.

But the leader of the synagogue, indignant because Jesus had healed on the Sabbath, responded by telling the crowd, "There are six days when work should be done; therefore come on those days and be healed and not on the Sabbath day."

But the Lord answered him and said, "Hypocrites! Doesn't each one of you untie his ox or donkey from the feeding trough on the Sabbath and lead it to water? Satan has bound this woman, a daughter of Abraham, for 18 years—shouldn't she be untied from this bondage on the Sabbath day?"

YOUR CHOICE

What change do you need to make in your schedule or practices to better reflect Christ's values?

SNAPSHOT

JOHN 9:3–11

"Neither this man nor his parents sinned," Jesus answered. "This came about so that God's works might be displayed in him. We must do the works of Him who sent Me while it is day. Night is coming when no one can work. As long as I am in the world, I am the light of the world."

After He said these things He spit on the ground, made some mud from the saliva, and spread the mud on his eyes. "Go," He told him, "wash in the pool of Siloam" (which means "Sent"). So he left, washed, and came back seeing.

His neighbors and those who formerly had seen him as a beggar said, "Isn't this the man who sat begging?" Some said, "He's the one." "No," others were saying, "but he looks like him."

He kept saying, "I'm the one!"

Therefore they asked him, "Then how were your eyes opened?"

He answered, "The man called Jesus made mud, spread it on my eyes, and told me, 'Go to Siloam and wash.' So when I went and washed I received my sight."

JUST LIKE ME

BLIND MAN: SEEING IS BELIEVING

Those who can see can't imagine what being born blind is like. But a man encountered by Jesus and His disciples had an intimate knowledge of darkness—that is, until Jesus healed him through the judicious use of mud and a command to wash in the pool of Siloam.

This nameless man did not know Jesus' name or reputation. All he knew was that Jesus had healed him. Even the Pharisees' disdain couldn't dim the glow of this knowledge, which deepened after a second encounter with Jesus in the aftermath of his expulsion from the synagogue.

In a way, the blind man in this passage was like another blind man whom Jesus healed in stages at Bethsaida (Mk 8:22–26). Like the Bethsaida blind man, this man had trouble "seeing" Jesus at first as anything other than a prophet—a good man. But gradually he came to see the truth—that Jesus was, in fact, the promised Messiah. In this way, the man was healed of spiritual blindness as well. Ironically, the Pharisees remained in the dark, completely oblivious to their own spiritual blindness.

What "blind" spots have others made you aware of recently that have been preventing you from seeing Jesus clearly? The Pharisees chose to remain blind. You don't have to—you can see.

YOUR CHOICE

In what ways has God improved your "vision"? How has seeing the world from His perspective affected your choices?

AUGUST 10

DAY 222

THE BIG PICTURE

JN 10:1–18

SNAPSHOT

JOHN 10:1–5

"I assure you: Anyone who doesn't enter the sheep pen by the door but climbs in some other way, is a thief and a robber. The one who enters by the door is the shepherd of the sheep. The doorkeeper opens it for him, and the sheep hear his voice. He calls his own sheep by name and leads them out. When he has brought all his own outside, he goes ahead of them. The sheep follow him because they recognize his voice. They will never follow a stranger; instead they will run away from him, because they don't recognize the voice of strangers."

ANCHOR POINT

GOD'S GUIDANCE

Jesus compares Himself to a good shepherd, one who is willing to die for the sheep. While we may take comfort in knowing that our Shepherd watches over us and that He gave His life for us, we may feel a bit insulted to be called "sheep." Those dumb animals are exactly that—dumb. They can't figure out anything for themselves and follow in a herd, without question. Left alone in a field, a sheep would eat all of the grass in that field and then die of starvation if no one came to lead it to more food. And sheep are defenseless, easily picked off by wolves and other predators.

Not a pretty comparison; yet if we are honest, we fit that description—easily following the crowd, focused on our current needs and wants with little concern for the future, and vulnerable to attack from the enemy and false shepherds.

So how do we live as sheep following our Good Shepherd? Jesus says that His sheep know His voice. This means they spend time with Him and follow His lead. They may not know much, but they know that they need their Shepherd!

YOUR CHOICE

How well do you know the Good Shepherd? What can you do to stay close to Him and to better hear His voice?

THE BIG PICTURE

LK 13:22–35

AUGUST 11

DAY 223

SNAPSHOT

LUKE 13:23b–27

He said to them, "Make every effort to enter through the narrow door, because I tell you, many will try to enter and won't be able once the homeowner gets up and shuts the door. Then you will stand outside and knock on the door, saying, 'Lord, open up for us!' He will answer you, 'I don't know you or where you're from.' Then you will say, 'We ate and drank in Your presence, and You taught in our streets!' But He will say, 'I tell you, I don't know you or where you're from. Get away from Me, all you workers of unrighteousness!' "

DEPOSIT

WORDS FROM GOD'S WORD TO STORE IN YOUR MIND AND HEART

"Jerusalem, Jerusalem! The city who kills the prophets and stones those who are sent to her. How often I wanted to gather your children together, as a hen gathers her chicks under her wings, but you were not willing!" (Lk 13:34).

AUGUST 12

DAY 224

THE BIG PICTURE

LK 14:1–14

SNAPSHOT

LUKE 14:7–11

He told a parable to those who were invited, when He noticed how they would choose the best places for themselves: "When you are invited by someone to a wedding banquet, don't recline at the best place, because a more distinguished person than you may have been invited by your host. The one who invited both of you may come and say to you, 'Give your place to this man,' and then in humiliation, you will proceed to take the lowest place.

"But when you are invited, go and recline in the lowest place, so that when the one who invited you comes, he will say to you, 'Friend, move up higher.' You will then be honored in the presence of all the other guests. For everyone who exalts himself will be humbled, and the one who humbles himself will be exalted."

YOUR TURN

SEEKING HONOR

When would others say that you look out for yourself too much?

LUKE 14:25–27

Now great crowds were traveling with Him. So He turned and said to them: "If anyone comes to Me and does not hate his own father and mother, wife and children, brothers and sisters—yes, and even his own life—he cannot be My disciple. Whoever does not bear his own cross and come after Me cannot be My disciple."

SNAPSHOT

AUGUST 13

DAY 225

THE BIG PICTURE

LK 14:15–35

TOUGH CHOICE

INDIA

I felt my way across the dusty floorboards toward my desk next to the window. Only the stars were visible in the dark, warm night. I sat down, switched on my desk lamp, and opened the single desk drawer, retrieving an envelope. I removed the letter inside:

Hiya, Will! How goes life and the human rights work in South Asia? Hard to believe it's been almost a year now. Is the advocacy group making progress? I've been looking for more reports on the police brutality and illegal land seizures in your area and the surrounding villages, but the injustice is being kept pretty quiet, apparently . . .

. . . Love you and miss you dearly. Charlie.

I folded the pages and put them back inside the envelope. I had already read the letter from my best friend Charlotte several times since I had received it that morning. Her words were comforting and encouraging, yet they made me miss home terribly.

For the past year I had been in South Asia, working for a human rights group that represented thousands of clients who couldn't afford to file suits against slavery, illegal detention, police brutality, and illegal land seizure. I knew, through much prayer, that the Lord wanted me here, and I knew that I wanted to be doing this type of work. Still, there were many nights that I went to bed discouraged and wondering if I should have stayed in the states and gone to law school.

I pulled a piece of paper and a pen from the stack on my desk and repositioned the lamp so that the light fell onto my paper.

Hiya back, Charlie! Fantastic to receive your letter. Read it ten times, at least, today. The human rights work continues to move forward; though it is difficult to see true progress when the problems in this country are so vast and so deeply rooted. I must remind myself of this.

Yesterday I communicated with a woman who had been separated from her husband and two sons. Their small plot of land in one of the northern villages had been illegally seized about a year ago, and then her sons and husband were detained without cause. She came here, all alone, because she had heard about our group.

It's tough, though, Charlie. Encounters like these get me so fired up to change the world. But then you ask these people to open up and provide the necessary details to structure a case, and they clam up. They're petrified to provide information for fear that they will be severely punished if caught. They don't trust us! Please be praying that the Lord softens their hearts toward us and toward His Word. I really believe that if they understood and accepted the gospel, they'd be so much more willing to trust us and that the Lord would take care of them. These people want and need change and justice so badly. Just be praying that the Lord continues to use me, even if the results aren't apparent . . .

. . . Stop by the house and tell my folks hello. And Snoopy. Miss you like this desert misses rain, Charlie! And I promise to make it home for the holidays this year. Much love, Will.

YOUR CHOICE **What can you do to work for justice in the world?**

DAY 226

THE BIG PICTURE

LK 15:1–10

SNAPSHOT

LUKE 15:3–7

So He told them this parable: "What man among you, who has 100 sheep and loses one of them, does not leave the 99 in the open field and go after the lost one until he finds it? When he has found it, he joyfully puts it on his shoulders, and coming home, he calls his friends and neighbors together, saying to them, 'Rejoice with me, because I have found my lost sheep!' I tell you, in the same way, there will be more joy in heaven over one sinner who repents than over 99 righteous people who don't need repentance."

JUST LIKE ME

SINNERS AND PHARISEES: WHO IS LOST?

You can tell how people feel about you by the statements they make about you. If their talk is loaded with sarcasm, negativism, or cynicism, watch out! Jesus was often the brunt of those types of verbal jabs. His critics were usually Pharisees and scribes grumbling about His habit of associating with "sinners"—a group from which they obviously excluded themselves.

The so-called sinners—this category often included the much-reviled tax collectors—sought Jesus for a different reason. They were much like the lost sheep and lost coin of Jesus' parables. What's more, they knew they were lost and were grateful to be found.

The Pharisees, on the other hand, didn't know they were lost. After all, weren't they sons of Abraham who were keeping the law of Moses? Pleased by their *own* perceived righteousness, they couldn't see that the tax collectors and sinners they complained about were no longer lost per se. They had been found by the Savior who had welcomed them and would soon die for their sins. The Pharisees remained lost, far from the fold.

To which group do you belong—the sinners or the Pharisees? The statements you make about Jesus reveal to a waiting world what you really believe.

YOUR CHOICE

How do these stories help you understand God's love for you? How do they affect your attitude in relating to those who don't know Him?

THE BIG PICTURE

LK 15:11–32

AUGUST 15

DAY 227

SNAPSHOT

LUKE 15:20–24

"So he got up and went to his father. But while the son was still a long way off, his father saw him and was filled with compassion. He ran, threw his arms around his neck, and kissed him. The son said to him, 'Father, I have sinned against heaven and in your sight. I'm no longer worthy to be called your son.'

"But the father told his slaves, 'Quick! Bring out the best robe and put it on him; put a ring on his finger and sandals on his feet. Then bring the fattened calf and slaughter it, and let's celebrate with a feast, because this son of mine was dead and is alive again; he was lost and is found!' So they began to celebrate."

ANCHOR POINT

THE PRODIGAL

We know this parable well. The younger son takes his inheritance early, goes to the city, and squanders everything while the older brother stays behind, diligently working the family farm. When the prodigal, the destitute and desperate boy, returns, his father greets him with hugs and tears and throws a huge party in his honor. And, as siblings often do, the older, good brother is hurt and offended.

This familiar story paints a profound picture of the Father's grace and forgiveness, available through *His* Son, Jesus. "While the son was still a long way off, his father saw him and was filled with compassion. He ran, threw his arms around his neck, and kissed him" (Lk 15:20).

It is also a cautionary tale, however, to those of us who have not strayed but have remained faithful. We can easily resent those who return from a life of sin or who come to faith lately and receive all the celebration and honor.

Where are you in the story? Are you running toward the city? In the pig stye? On the way home? Or do you identify with the older brother? Wherever you are, remember that your Father waits with open arms, ready to embrace you, bring you home, and throw a party! Live in His love.

YOUR CHOICE

When have you felt like the prodigal? When have you felt like the older brother? How does knowing more about the Father's love for you affect your choices?

DAY 228

THE BIG PICTURE
LK 16:1–18

SNAPSHOT

LUKE 16:10–13

"Whoever is faithful in very little is also faithful in much, and whoever is unrighteous in very little is also unrighteous in much. So if you have not been faithful with the unrighteous money, who will trust you with what is genuine? And if you have not been faithful with what belongs to someone else, who will give you what is your own? No household slave can be the slave of two masters, since either he will hate one and love the other, or he will be devoted to one and despise the other. You can't be slaves to both God and money."

YOUR CHOICE

What will you do to make sure you are following Christ alone?

TOUGH QUESTION

SINCE JESUS IS RIGHT AND WE CAN'T SERVE MULTIPLE MASTERS, HOW DO WE MAKE SURE WE'RE NOT SERVING ANYONE OR ANYTHING ELSE?

Evaluating who we are actually serving can sometimes be tricky—we may think we are right on track in the Christian life when, in reality, some areas may be dedicated to serving other masters. Satan will try to pull us away from following Christ, distracting us with whatever he can—money, power, status, popularity.

Money can be a master. The drive to make more and more can be insatiable. Even if they don't realize it, many people believe money brings happiness, so they will dedicate themselves to making and keeping money. Relationships can be a master as well. Some want to be liked and accepted so badly that they will do anything to keep their friends, even if this means compromising their beliefs. Addiction can be a terrible master. Drugs, alcohol, food, pornography, and other addictions are destroying countless lives.

To determine who you are serving, take an honest inventory of your thoughts, words, and actions. What consumes your mind? The Bible says, "As he thinks within himself, so he is" (Pr 23:7). What do you talk about most? The Bible says, "If anyone thinks he is religious, without controlling his tongue but deceiving his heart, his religion is useless" (Jms 1:26). And have you checked out your checkbook? The Bible says, "For where your treasure is, there your heart will be also" (Mt 6:21). If your allegiance is to Christ alone, your actions will reflect the fruit of the Spirit: "love, joy, peace, patience, kindness, goodness, faith, gentleness, self-control" (Gl 5:22–23).

Asking a trusted friend can also help in this process. This person should be someone who knows you well and can give you helpful insight and counsel. The friend's words may be hard to hear, but receiving them without being defensive will help you become more like Christ, serving Him as your only Master.

LK 16:19–31

SNAPSHOT

LUKE 16:25–29

"'Son,' Abraham said, 'remember that during your life you received your good things, just as Lazarus received bad things, but now he is comforted here, while you are in agony. Besides all this, a great chasm has been fixed between us and you, so that those who want to pass over from here to you cannot; neither can those from there cross over to us.'

" 'Father,' he said, 'then I beg you to send him to my father's house—because I have five brothers—to warn them, so they won't also come to this place of torment.'

"But Abraham said, 'They have Moses and the prophets; they should listen to them.' "

YOUR CHOICE

Whose standards mean more to you—the world's or God's?

NO BRAINER

RICH MAN, POOR MAN

Recently we discussed values and priorities and the importance of keeping God first (see Day 220). We can easily get things out of order and focus on regulations and procedures instead of doing what God wants. Today's passage presents another example of this problem, only here the contrast is between rich and poor and between now and forever.

One man was rich by the world's standards and the other was dirt poor, a beggar, in fact. Not only did the first man have money, fine clothes, possessions, and the best food and drink, he also was self centered—he hardly noticed the poor beggar at his door. Yet when the rich man died, he discovered that he may have been wealthy in this world, but he was bankrupt in the next. His earthly comfort led only to torment. For the poor man, the scene had also changed, but for the better. His life after death included comfort and healing, with God. The contrast and the reversal of fortunes couldn't have been greater.

Elsewhere Jesus stated, "For whoever wants to save his life will lose it, but whoever loses his life because of Me and the gospel will save it. For what does it benefit a man to gain the whole world yet lose his life? What can a man give in exchange for his life?" (Mk 8:35–37). That seems so logical, yet people make that trade every day, exchanging success in this life for failure in the next. It's a bad deal, and it makes no sense.

When you gave your life to Christ, you passed from death to life—you became a child of God and, like the beggar, will one day live with Him. Keep that in mind when you see those who seem to have it all, when you feel so beggar-like, even leprous, compared to them. Remember that the next life is what *really* counts, and keep living for Him.

DAY 230

THE BIG PICTURE
JN 11:1–36

SNAPSHOT

JOHN 11:21–27

Then Martha said to Jesus, "Lord, if You had been here, my brother wouldn't have died. Yet even now I know that whatever You ask from God, God will give You."

"Your brother will rise again," Jesus told her.

Martha said, "I know that he will rise again in the resurrection at the last day."

Jesus said to her, "I am the resurrection and the life. The one who believes in Me, even if he dies, will live. Everyone who lives and believes in Me will never die—ever. Do you believe this?"

"Yes, Lord," she told Him, "I believe You are the Messiah, the Son of God, who was to come into the world."

DEPOSIT

WORDS FROM GOD'S WORD TO STORE IN YOUR MIND AND HEART

Jesus said to her, "I am the resurrection and the life. The one who believes in Me, even if he dies, will live. Everyone who lives and believes in Me will never die—ever. Do you believe this?" (Jn 11:25–26).

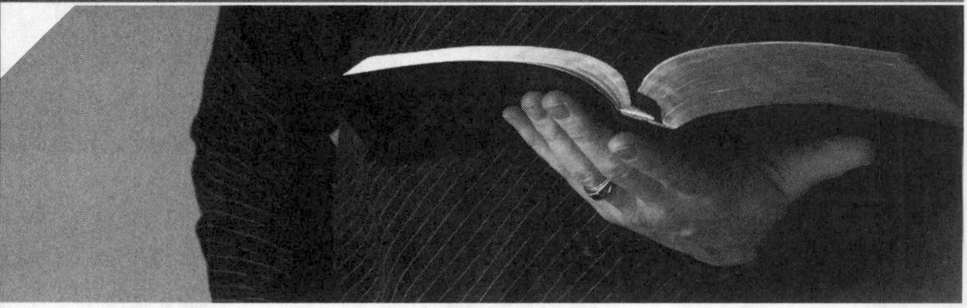

THE BIG PICTURE

JN 11:37–57

AUGUST 19

DAY 231

SNAPSHOT

JOHN 11:38–44

Then Jesus, angry in Himself again, came to the tomb. It was a cave, and a stone was lying against it. "Remove the stone," Jesus said. Martha, the dead man's sister, told Him, "Lord, he already stinks. It's been four days."

Jesus said to her, "Didn't I tell you that if you believed you would see the glory of God?"

So they removed the stone. Then Jesus raised His eyes and said, "Father, I thank You that You heard Me. I know that You always hear Me, but because of the crowd standing here I said this, so they may believe You sent Me." After He said this, He shouted with a loud voice, "Lazarus, come out!" The dead man came out bound hand and foot with linen strips and with his face wrapped in a cloth. Jesus said to them, "Loose him and let him go."

YOUR TURN

JESUS RAISES LAZARUS

How would you have felt watching Lazarus walk out of the tomb?

AUGUST 20

DAY 232

THE BIG PICTURE

LK 17:1–19

SNAPSHOT

LUKE 17:5–6

The apostles said to the Lord, "Increase our faith."

"If you have faith the size of a mustard seed," the Lord said, "you can say to this mulberry tree, 'Be uprooted and planted in the sea,' and it will obey you."

TOUGH CHOICE

THANKFUL INTERN

Autumn had settled over the Smoky Mountains, as deep shades of red, gold, and orange spread toward the horizon. It was full-fledged sweatshirt-and-jeans season. Marney, my best friend, and I were reclining in large, wooden rocking chairs on the front porch of the campgrounds' warming hut. For the past three years our campus ministry group, Insights, had come to this site for a weekend retreat.

Marney rocked back and forth in her chair, with her feet propped up on the railing. "Tyla, have you sent in your application for the journalist position in Atlanta?"

"Yep. Sent it in last Tuesday," I said, pulling my sleeves over my hands to warm them. "It's hard not to get my hopes up, but I really want this position. I haven't looked into much else yet because I love this position so much. I'd get to work on creative writing pieces and live in a fun city, and Jane is going to be in grad school there. We'd get to room together. I should probably start researching some fall-back plans, though."

A breeze swelled, rustling the trees that surrounded the warming hut. Falling leaves carried the smoky, autumn aroma as they floated across the porch.

"You'll get it," Marney said, looking over at me. "I read those pieces you were planning on submitting, and they were unbelievable! They'd be nuts not to take you."

I laughed, "Marney, you're a really good friend to me. I know I keep saying it, but, selfishly, I hope you take a job in Atlanta, too. Imagine how great it would be if you, Jane, and I could all share a place together!"

Marney looked out on the clearing in front of the porch. A few of the guys had started tossing a football around. "That would be so great," she said, thoughtfully.

"What are *you* thinking at this point?" I asked. "Have you found anything that peaks your interest?"

"Well, actually," she began, "I've been thinking about applying for the Insights internship. Being here this weekend has really reminded me of just how thankful I am for this ministry."

"Oh, Marney! You'd be perfect. You're such a good listener and encourager. Plus, it would be great practice for when you go back to seminary to get your counseling degree."

Marney tucked her legs into her seat and turned to face me. "I just really want to give back. This ministry has done so many great things for me and other students. I want to give of myself—my own time and energy and resources—to help reach even more students." She paused. "I guess my only hesitation is that it would mean not knowing where they would assign me. I could get placed on any campus in America. I could end up far away from you girls, Mason, my family . . ."

I watched her mull this thought over. "Do you feel like this is what God wants you to do?"

"Yeah, I really do think He does, Tyla. And I really want to do this, I think. It's the best way I know how to show my appreciation to the Lord and give back . . ."

YOUR CHOICE **Are you willing to go wherever God leads you?**

THE BIG PICTURE

LK 17:20–37

AUGUST 21

DAY 233

SNAPSHOT

LUKE 17:33–36

"Whoever tries to make his life secure will lose it, and whoever loses his life will preserve it. I tell you, on that night two will be in one bed: one will be taken and the other will be left. Two women will be grinding grain together: one will be taken and the other left. Two will be in a field: one will be taken, and the other will be left."

ANCHOR POINT

KINGDOM OF GOD

Jesus is the promised Messiah, the Christ, our King. When He came to earth the first time (the incarnation), He came as the Suffering Servant as prophesied in Isaiah 52 and 53, not as a conquering hero to vanquish evildoers, vindicate the righteous, and set up His kingdom on earth. Many, even most of Jesus' disciples, were expecting *that* type of king and kingdom. But Christ's kingdom is established first and foremost in the hearts of those who trust in Him.

But Christ will return. He will come again—this time as deliverer and judge. And in these verses from Luke 17 we hear Jesus describing that glorious event with the disciples. He doesn't give a time, a schedule, but He makes three important points: First, the world will get worse and life will get tough for believers; second, He will come suddenly, without warning, when people least expect it; third, believers need to be prepared.

We need to listen carefully to those points and heed Christ's warnings. He could return at any moment!

YOUR CHOICE

What signs do you see that seem to indicate Christ could return soon? What should you do to be ready?

AUGUST 22

DAY 234

THE BIG PICTURE

LK 18:1–14

SNAPSHOT

LUKE 18:9–14

He also told this parable to some who trusted in themselves that they were righteous and looked down on everyone else: "Two men went up to the temple complex to pray, one a Pharisee and the other a tax collector. The Pharisee took his stand and was praying like this: 'God, I thank You that I'm not like other people—greedy, unrighteous, adulterers, or even like this tax collector. I fast twice a week; I give a tenth of everything I get.'

"But the tax collector, standing far off, would not even raise his eyes to heaven but kept striking his chest and saying, 'God, turn Your wrath from me —a sinner!' I tell you, this one went down to his house justified rather than the other; because everyone who exalts himself will be humbled, but the one who humbles himself will be exalted."

YOUR CHOICE

About what issues do you need to continue to talk with God?

TOUGH QUESTION

I KEEP ASKING GOD FOR HELP WITH DIFFERENT STRUGGLES, BUT HE DOESN'T SEEM TO ANSWER. HOW DO I KEEP PRAYING WHEN GOD DOESN'T ANSWER THE WAY I EXPECT?

The Book of Psalms contains many of David's desperate cries to God. He expresses his feelings freely, and we learn from his outpouring of emotions that we can talk with God about anything. David also praises the Lord when "God has listened; He has paid attention to the sound of my prayer" (Ps 66:19).

Regardless of our circumstances or feelings, God always hears our prayers. We can be sure of that. He also answers. But just because we ask for something doesn't mean God is obligated to give us exactly what we want or expect. He's not a heavenly vending machine. And even if we don't feel Him near or hear Him, we should keep praying—He tells us to.

Philippians 4:6 says this about prayer: "Don't worry about anything, but in everything, through prayer and petition with thanksgiving, let your requests be made known to God." The next verse does not say that He will answer everything just as we ask. God's unspoken answer might be "no" or "not yet."

Even in those times of struggle, when God doesn't answer our prayers exactly as we want or expect, we need to keep praying and trusting. Sometimes our prayers are superficial; then the prayer-struggle can take us deeper, helping us be totally honest with God.

God refines us as we pray, changing our hearts and deepening our faith. We must believe that God hears us and will answer us. At times we might simply pray, "Lord, increase our faith" so that we can believe that His plan has a bigger purpose than we could ever imagine. Spiritual refinement might be part of His plan.

THE BIG PICTURE

MK 10:1–16

SNAPSHOT

MARK 10:7–9

"For this reason a man will leave

his father and mother

and be joined to his wife,

and the two will become one flesh.

"So they are no longer two, but one flesh. Therefore what God has joined together, man must not separate."

YOUR CHOICE

How will you make sure that your marriage will be for life?

NO BRAINER

GOD'S MARRIAGE PLAN

In their ongoing attempt to discredit Jesus, some Pharisees questioned Him about marriage and divorce. Jesus answered by asking *them* a question about what *they* thought the law permitted. Then He quoted Genesis 2:24, where God described His plan for putting a man and a woman together in the first place, and added, "What God has joined together, man must not separate" (Mk 10:9).

In Jesus' day, a man could divorce his wife without much trouble or complications. All he had to do was find an excuse and then write divorce papers, and the marriage would be over. (Wives didn't have much say in the matter.) Jesus was asserting that just because something was legal and accepted didn't make it right. And He was pointing the people to a much better way of dealing with this important relationship—God's way. Clearly, according to Jesus, God's plan is for each marriage to be between one man and one woman and to last a lifetime.

Things haven't changed much in two thousand years. These days, divorce is accepted as normal, and getting out of a marriage is fairly easy—even though studies continue to show the devastating effects on the children of those split families and on society. So what do you think Jesus would say today if asked? Clearly His answer would be the same: "Your laws regulate divorce and offer some protection to the weaker and wronged parties, but they don't make divorce right. God's plan is still best. Don't split what God has joined!"

That's why the wedding vows state, "For better or worse, for richer or poorer, in sickness and in health, as long as you both shall live." It's not multiple choice. It's all or nothing.

So as you consider marriage, remember Jesus' words and this ideal. Find someone who shares your commitment to Christ and to living His way, and walk that path together. Don't even *consider* divorce as an option. That will be counter-cultural, but it will be right.

THE BIG PICTURE

MK 10:17–31

SNAPSHOT

MARK 10:23–25

Jesus looked around and said to His disciples, "How hard it is for those who have wealth to enter the kingdom of God!" But the disciples were astonished at His words. Again Jesus said to them, "Children, how hard it is to enter the kingdom of God! It is easier for a camel to go through the eye of a needle than for a rich person to enter the kingdom of God."

JUST LIKE ME

THE RICH YOUNG RULER: YOUNG, RICH, AND EMPTY

Young and rich. This description fits a number of celebrities today. And often they are celebrities simply because they are "young and rich." Many believe that having wealth and youth is the answer to anything that ails you.

The young man who came to Jesus had a lifestyle that might have made him the envy of his crowd, the toast of the town. After all, he had everything! Yet this man knew something was missing.

Walk with him as he talks with Jesus about finding that missing piece—eternal life. Now walk away with him after he finds Jesus' advice—"sell all you have"—a little difficult to swallow. But Jesus knew something that this earnest young man didn't know: his wealth was a major stumbling block to his inheriting eternal life—the very item the young man had asked about.

Jesus never shied away from controversial statements—He wasn't afraid to take a stand. In His Sermon on the Mount, He declared, "If your right eye causes you to sin, gouge it out and throw it away" (Mt 5:29). In other words, get rid of whatever is keeping you from God!

The rich young ruler chose to hang on to his lifestyle instead of God. He went away in the same state as when he arrived: young and rich . . . but empty.

Sometimes we can think we have it all and really have nothing. The reverse is also the case. Sometimes we can think we have nothing whatsoever. But if we have Jesus, we have everything. Does that describe you?

YOUR CHOICE

What is the most difficult thing Jesus could ask you to give up in order to follow Him more closely?

THE BIG PICTURE

MT 20:1–19

AUGUST 25

DAY 237

SNAPSHOT

MATTHEW 20:9–15

"When those who were hired about five came, they each received one denarius. So when the first ones came, they assumed they would get more, but they also received a denarius each. When they received it, they began to complain to the landowner: 'These last men put in one hour, and you made them equal to us who bore the burden of the day and the burning heat!'

"He replied to one of them, 'Friend, I'm doing you no wrong. Didn't you agree with me on a denarius? Take what's yours and go. I want to give this last man the same as I gave you. Don't I have the right to do what I want with my business? Are you jealous because I'm generous?' "

DEPOSIT

WORDS FROM GOD'S WORD TO STORE IN YOUR MIND AND HEART

"So the last will be first, and the first last" (Mt 20:16).

DAY 238

SNAPSHOT

MARK 10:42–45

Jesus called them over and said to them, "You know that those who are regarded as rulers of the Gentiles dominate them, and their men of high positions exercise power over them. But it must not be like that among you. On the contrary, whoever wants to become great among you must be your servant, and whoever wants to be first among you must be a slave to all. For even the Son of Man did not come to be served, but to serve, and to give His life—a ransom for many."

YOUR TURN

SERVING OTHERS

In what ways are you learning to be a servant?

SNAPSHOT

LUKE 19:1–5

He entered Jericho and was passing through. There was a man named Zacchaeus who was a chief tax collector, and he was rich. He was trying to see who Jesus was, but he was not able because of the crowd, since he was a short man. So running ahead, he climbed up a sycamore tree to see Jesus, since He was about to pass that way. When Jesus came to the place, He looked up and said to him, "Zacchaeus, hurry and come down, because today I must stay at your house."

JUST LIKE ME

ZACCHAEUS: A LOST SON FOUND

"Zacchaeus was a wee little man" or so the kids' song goes. His small stature was a disadvantage for seeing over the heads of a crowd, but it proved to be what, eventually, brought him to Jesus. He had to climb a tree, and that's when Jesus saw him and called him out.

But what really gained Jesus' attention was the humility this "wee little man" showed after their interaction—even after some people in the crowd called him a "sinful man" (Lk 19:7). Zacchaeus had already begun to change in response to being in Jesus' presence. His public vow to pay back anyone he cheated was proof of that change.

Zacchaeus only sought a glimpse of Jesus and wound up with much more than that. Not only did he receive an amazing house guest, he also gained a Savior.

The complainers only saw a man they considered to be a loser—not worthy of Jesus' time and attention. But Jesus saw someone much more beloved—a lost sheep that had been found.

What we see as a disadvantage in our lives can actually be an advantage. That "thorn in the flesh" (2 Co 12:7)—the thing that may cause others to put us in the loser category—might be the very thing God uses to bring us to Himself.

YOUR CHOICE

What physical characteristic has most affected how you feel about yourself?

DAY 240

THE BIG PICTURE

JN 12:1–11

NO BRAINER

CHEAP TALK

We don't know much about Judas, really, except that he betrayed Jesus—turned Him in to the authorities—right after the Last Supper. We may wonder how Judas got to be a close follower of Jesus in the first place, since he was such a rat. He must have looked good or talked a good game. Whatever the case, the other disciples accepted him as one of their own. And they trusted him so much that they made him their treasurer—"He was in charge of the money-bag" (Jn 12:6).

Judas certainly knew what to say, to sound righteous, in this situation. When he saw the valuable oil being *wasted*, he protested by pointing out the plight of the poor. A much better use of that oil, he explained, would have been to sell it and use the money to relieve their suffering. But then John tells us, "[Judas] didn't say this because he cared about the poor but because he was a thief" (Jn 12:6).

Talk is cheap, and fooling people can be easy, especially if a person is somewhat articulate and can fake sincerity. Judas sure had the other disciples fooled!

But not Jesus. He saw into Judas's heart, and He knew exactly what was going on.

Now let's be honest here: Much too often *we* act like Judas, mouthing the right words about caring for others, sharing with the needy, standing for justice, reaching the lost, or supporting a worthy cause. But do we really mean them? Or do we have other motives?

Judas had God Himself right there in front of him, but Judas was so concerned for his own agenda and blinded by greed that he missed his Savior. No wonder he could betray Jesus big time eventually—he had been doing it in little ways all along.

We dare not make the same mistake.

SNAPSHOT

JOHN 12:1–3

Six days before the Passover, Jesus came to Bethany where Lazarus was, the one Jesus had raised from the dead. So they gave a dinner for Him there; Martha was serving them, and Lazarus was one of those reclining at the table with Him. Then Mary took a pound of fragrant oil—pure and expensive nard—anointed Jesus' feet, and wiped His feet with her hair. So the house was filled with the fragrance of the oil.

YOUR CHOICE

Do you really care about the causes you espouse? Do your actions match your words?

SNAPSHOT

MATTHEW 21:6–11

The disciples went and did just as Jesus directed them. They brought the donkey and the colt; then they laid their robes on them, and He sat on them. A very large crowd spread their robes on the road; others were cutting branches from the trees and spreading them on the road. Then the crowds who went ahead of Him and those who followed kept shouting:

Hosanna to the Son of David!

Blessed is He who comes

in the name of the Lord!

Hosanna in the highest heaven!

When He entered Jerusalem, the whole city was shaken, saying, "Who is this?" And the crowds kept saying, "This is the prophet Jesus from Nazareth in Galilee!"

ANCHOR POINT

JESUS RIDES INTO JERUSALEM

When Jesus rode into Jerusalem, He was swarmed by a great crowd lining the road, shouting praises, and laying down palm branches and their coats in a gesture of supplication before a king. They welcomed Jesus as their promised deliverer, expecting that He would soon overthrow their oppressors and set them free. A few days later, however, many of these same people would be shouting insults and clamoring for His execution. How quickly their attitude changed when they realized they wouldn't be getting what they wanted.

We're tempted to act the same way, at times. How do we feel, for example, when God doesn't answer our prayers the way we wanted? Or when we face hard times, suffering, or loss? Many people turn bitter and resentful, even those who may have been praising God in church a few weeks before.

This happens when we focus on ourselves. When we interpret God's Word through the filter of our personal needs, we won't hear His clear message of love and hope. Jesus never said He had come to defeat the Romans, for example, but the cheering crowd assumed He had.

And when we focus on *now*, we lose sight of God's long view and of eternity. We must remember that God works according to His timing, not ours. He will move when He is ready and not before.

Remember the people along the road to Jerusalem the next time you are frustrated or disappointed with God. If they had been right and had crowned Jesus as their earthly ruler, He wouldn't have died on the cross, in your place.

YOUR CHOICE

Have you been upset with God for an answer to prayer or perhaps the timing of His answer? How did you deal with that disappointment? How can you better handle it in the future?

AUGUST 30

DAY 242

THE BIG PICTURE

JN 12:20–36

SNAPSHOT

JOHN 12:23–26

Jesus replied to them, "The hour has come for the Son of Man to be glorified.

"I assure you: Unless a grain of wheat falls into the ground and dies, it remains by itself. But if it dies, it produces a large crop. The one who loves his life will lose it, and the one who hates his life in this world will keep it for eternal life. If anyone serves Me, he must follow Me. Where I am, there My servant also will be. If anyone serves Me, the Father will honor him."

TOUGH CHOICE

HATING LIFE

I sat next to my grandmother, holding her cold hand. Much of the past two days had been spent this way: sitting next to Mimi, holding her hand, waiting for her to sit up and say, "Come here, suga'! Give me a hug and then get yourself some fudge in the fridge. I've got about ten . . . no, twelve pounds in there."

But she never sat up or said anything. She lay paralyzed. The stroke had stolen her spirit. Only my grandmother's shell was covered by the thin hospital sheets, only her shell had plastic hospital bracelets dangling where her fancy-schmancy costume jewelry used to sparkle.

I could hear my mom and aunt in the restroom. My mom, the meek and shy sister while growing up, was comforting my weeping Aunt Rita, the vibrant and eccentric sister. Mimi had been not only Aunt Rita's mom, but her best friend.

"Mother! Mother! Please don't leave me. Do not leave me. Please, mother! Hang on. I know you're in there. Don't leave me! I'm not ready. You can't!"

Hold it together, Sophie. My throat burned and tears streamed down my clenched jaws, onto my grandmother's bed. *What do I do, God?* I stared at my grandmother, whose breathing was growing raspier. I stroked the top of her hand. *I love you, Mimi. I'm still here. I'm just going to keep holding your hand, okay?*

My aunt's sobs crumbled into shuddering, and I could hear my mother's voice. It was steady. "Rita . . . Rita, listen to me. You have to let mother go. She needs you to let her go. She won't quit fighting until she knows you'll be okay."

"But I'm not ready . . ."

"Rita, mother is in pain. She has suffered so much in this life. She had to be so strong and go through so much for us. But she loved Jesus and knew Him as her Savior. She will be in heaven—happy and healthy—when she leaves this earth. Let her go to heaven where Christ will welcome her in His arms!"

"I can't say good-bye."

"You don't have to! You can see mother again if you'll accept Christ as your Savior. This earth and life are temporary. Turn to the Lord, Rita, like mother did. She didn't love this earth; she hated it. She knew that a perfect eternity existed after this life because she believed that Jesus died for her sins so that she could live with Him forever. Let her go there!"

My Aunt Rita clung to my mom as they reentered the room. I laid my grandmother's hand gently down and moved toward the window so my aunt could sit next to Mimi's side. Weak and trembling, she sat down next to the hospital bed and took my grandmother's hand in her own. "Mother," she cried in a whisper, "Mother, I am going to be okay. You can go home now. You can go home . . ."

YOUR CHOICE **Who in your family needs to hear the Good News about Jesus?**

TOUGH QUESTION

THERE'S A GUY IN MY CLASS WHOSE DAD RECENTLY LEFT HIS FAMILY. I WANT TO SHARE CHRIST'S LOVE WITH HIM, BUT I'M AFRAID THAT HE'LL JUST TURN AGAINST ME AND BLAME GOD FOR HIS PROBLEMS. WHAT SHOULD I DO?

Being sensitive to the needs and hurts of other people shows that Christ's love and compassion live in you. Christ's love can't be hidden—it has to be shared—and sharing it is worth the risk of rejection. You could write a short note expressing how sorry you are, and that if he needs someone to listen, you would be more than willing. He may not take you up on it, but at least he will know that you care about him and his situation. Suffering *alone* can be the worst kind of suffering.

If he reacts negatively and blames God for his dad leaving, hear him out. It's all right to be mad at God—He can take it. So don't argue with the guy about his feelings or his emotional statements. Instead, continue to show him Christ's love. In fact, your compassion may eventually draw your classmate toward the Lord and into a personal relationship with Him.

Prayer is the best gift you can give this young man. You may even want to ask him how you can pray specifically for him and his family. Hopefully he will open up and share some of his needs. Don't be discouraged because you can't solve all of your classmate's problems. That's not your role or obligation. And be assured that God has a plan for you and your friend through these difficult circumstances.

SNAPSHOT

JOHN 12:44–50

Then Jesus cried out, "The one who believes in Me believes not in Me, but in Him who sent Me. And the one who sees Me sees Him who sent Me. I have come as a light into the world, so that everyone who believes in Me would not remain in darkness. If anyone hears My words and doesn't keep them, I do not judge him; for I did not come to judge the world but to save the world. The one who rejects Me and doesn't accept My sayings has this as his judge: the word I have spoken will judge him on the last day. For I have not spoken on My own, but the Father Himself who sent Me has given Me a command as to what I should say and what I should speak. I know that His command is eternal life. So the things that I speak, I speak just as the Father has told Me."

YOUR CHOICE

Who needs your prayers? Who needs your listening ear?

SEPTEMBER
SEPTEMBRE
SEPTEMBER
SEPTEMBER
SETTEMBRE
SETEMBRO
SEPTIEMBRE

MK 11:20–33

SNAPSHOT

MARK 11:22–26

Jesus replied to them, "Have faith in God. I assure you: If anyone says to this mountain, 'Be lifted up and thrown into the sea,' and does not doubt in his heart, but believes that what he says will happen, it will be done for him. Therefore, I tell you, all the things you pray and ask for—believe that you have received them, and you will have them. And whenever you stand praying, if you have anything against anyone, forgive him, so that your Father in heaven will also forgive you your wrongdoing. But if you don't forgive, neither will your Father in heaven forgive your wrongdoing."

DEPOSIT

WORDS FROM GOD'S WORD TO STORE IN YOUR MIND AND HEART

"And whenever you stand praying, if you have anything against anyone, forgive him, so that your Father in heaven will also forgive you your wrongdoing" (Mk 11:25).

THE BIG PICTURE
MT 21:28–46

SNAPSHOT

MATTHEW 21:28–32

"But what do you think? A man had two sons. He went to the first and said, 'My son, go, work in the vineyard today.'

"He answered, 'I don't want to!' Yet later he changed his mind and went.

"Then the man went to the other and said the same thing.

"'I will, sir,' he answered. But he didn't go.

"Which of the two did his father's will?"

"The first," they said.

Jesus said to them, "I assure you: Tax collectors and prostitutes are entering the kingdom of God before you! For John came to you in the way of righteousness, and you didn't believe him. Tax collectors and prostitutes did believe him, but you, when you saw it, didn't even change your minds then and believe him."

YOUR TURN

TWO SONS

Which son do you resemble most?

MATTHEW 22:11–14

SNAPSHOT

"But when the king came in to view the guests, he saw a man there who was not dressed for a wedding. So he said to him, 'Friend, how did you get in here without wedding clothes?' The man was speechless.

"Then the king told the attendants, 'Tie him up hand and foot, and throw him into the outer darkness, where there will be weeping and gnashing of teeth.'

"For many are invited, but few are chosen."

THE BIG PICTURE

MT 22:1–14

TOUGH CHOICE

FISHER OF MEN

"Brrr!" I splashed cold water on my face, attempting to coax my eyes open and force my nervous system out of sleep mode. "Why does school have to start so early? The birds aren't even up yet," I mumbled to my reflection in the mirror.

I had stayed up late the night before, studying for today's AP U.S. History exam. One late night might not have been such a big deal, but junior year had turned into two draining semesters, with minimal sleep. There just weren't enough hours in the day to accommodate Student Council meetings, classes, Yearbook, and track practices. Sleep was always the first thing to go; it didn't show up on my college applications or transcripts.

"Jefferson: wrote the Declaration of Independence, elected President in 1801, Louisiana Purchase in 1803, founded the University of Virginia in 1819, and died in 18 . . . 1826. Yes!" I recited facts to myself, as I brushed my teeth and threw my hair into a ponytail. "Hamilton: one of the founders of the Federalist Party. He was the first Secretary of the Treasury. He supported a strong central government and convinced Congress to adopt an elastic interpretation of the Constitution, start a national bank, allow national debt, and to use tariffs." I hurried down the stairs into the kitchen, pulling on my sweatshirt as I ran. "Oh, what was his role in the Quasi-War?"

I slid across the hardwood floor in my sock-feet toward the cupboard. *Cereal or waffles? No time for waffles. Cereal.* I grabbed a box of Honey-Oat-Somethings and sandwich ingredients for lunch.

"Hey, Mom! Do we have any of that bread from the bakery?" I shouted, as I walked around the corner.

"Well, good morning to you, too, Cindy," my mom said, jokingly. She and my younger sister Tabitha were sitting at the kitchen table.

"Sorry. Good morning, Mom. Do we still have any of that bread?" I asked, shaking flakes and clusters into my breakfast bowl.

"Look on the counter next to the oven."

"Thanks." I took a large bite of cereal, milk dripping from the bottom of my spoon, and walked to retrieve the bread. As I began building my sandwich, I could hear my mom reading to Tabitha: ". . . As Jesus walked beside the Sea of Galilee, He saw Simon and his brother Andrew casting a net into the lake, for they were fishermen. 'Come, follow me,' Jesus said, 'and I will make you fishers of men.' At once they left their nets and followed Him." My mom paused. "Tabby, how do you think this passage applies to your life as a sixth grader?"

"Well, I think it means I should be ready to obey God whenever He asks me to do something. Like . . ."

I watched and listened to my mom and little sister discuss different scenarios. *When was the last time I listened to God? When was the last time I made room in my schedule for Him . . . even for an afternoon? When was the last time I sat down and had a devotional, much less with my mom over breakfast? Has getting into a prestigious college become more important than Christ?*

YOUR CHOICE **How should you adjust your schedule to spend more quiet time with God?**

DAY 247

THE BIG PICTURE
LK 20:20–40

NO BRAINER

WHO'S IN CHARGE?

"God and country!" You may have heard that expression in a motto or in someone's description of his or her allegiance. Recently, newspapers, magazines, and the courts have been filled with debates over the connection of the two, as another phrase, "separation of church and state," is highlighted. And in election campaigns, candidates invoke God and quote Scripture. So how does that work, exactly—the interaction and relationship between God and country?

That question certainly was swirling in the first century, especially since Israel was ruled by a foreign invader. Not surprisingly, Jesus' enemies tried to trap Him into an answer that would anger the Romans. In essence they were asking, "Why should we give our occupiers, our Roman oppressors, money to help support their evil government? So should we pay taxes or not?" Jesus' profound response provides a guide for us, too. When Jesus said, "give back to Caesar the things that are Caesar's and to God the things that are God's," He was pointing out the true separation between "church and state." Jesus wasn't calling for rebellion against the government; in fact, the implication seems to be that His listeners should be law-abiding citizens. Instead, Jesus was raising the issue of *authority*. Who's in charge, anyway—God? Or country?

So what does that mean today? First, we must remember that our primary allegiance must be to God—we must obey Him, even when His commands go against the flow of popular opinion and practice. Second, while we should be law-abiding, tax-paying, and patriotic citizens, we must obey God even when His desires contradict what our government says. The apostles applied this a short time later. Commanded by the authorities not to preach the gospel, they replied, "We must obey God rather than men" (Ac 5:29).

If God has told you through His Word to act, to speak up, to take a stand, do it, even if it means breaking the law. "Give to God the things that are God's."

SNAPSHOT

LUKE 20:20–25

They watched closely and sent spies who pretended to be righteous, so they could catch Him in what He said, to hand Him over to the governor's rule and authority. They questioned Him, "Teacher, we know that You speak and teach correctly, and You don't show partiality, but teach truthfully the way of God. Is it lawful for us to pay taxes to Caesar or not?"

But detecting their craftiness, He said to them, "Show Me a denarius. Whose image and inscription does it have?"

"Caesar's," they said.

"Well then," He told them, "give back to Caesar the things that are Caesar's and to God the things that are God's."

YOUR CHOICE

What biblical mandates seem to be counter-cultural? If they were to become illegal, what would you do?

THE BIG PICTURE

MK 12:28–37

SEPTEMBER 5

DAY 248

SNAPSHOT

MARK 12:28–31

One of the scribes approached. When he heard them debating and saw that Jesus answered them well, he asked Him, "Which commandment is the most important of all?"

"This is the most important," Jesus answered:

"Listen, Israel! The Lord our God, the Lord is One. Love the Lord your God with all your heart, with all your soul, with all your mind, and with all your strength.

"The second is: Love your neighbor as yourself. There is no other commandment greater than these."

ANCHOR POINT

LOVE THE LORD

"Love the Lord your God with all your heart, with all your soul, with all your mind, and with all your strength. . . . Love your neighbor as yourself" (Mk 12:30–31). With these two simple sentences, Jesus summarized the law and encompassed the entirety of the life to which He was calling His followers. Incredibly, the scribe who had asked the question agreed and understood Jesus' words.

Those two simple sentences seem so basic, yet they can be difficult to live out. Loving God with heart (your allegiance), soul (your character), mind (your thoughts and beliefs), and strength (your actions) means centering our lives on Him. And we must commit to doing this every day; we can wake up one day and say, "OK, here I go; I'm right now loving God fully." Loving God this way involves focus and discipline—one day and one choice at a time.

Similarly, loving others as ourselves is not easy. We are good at loving ourselves but somewhat lacking when it comes to loving those around us. Loving others takes another choice—a commitment to reach out and engage them.

YOUR CHOICE

What steps can you take to love God more fully with more of yourself? How can you love those around you more and express that love in concrete ways?

DAY 249

THE BIG PICTURE

MT 23:1–39

SNAPSHOT

MATTHEW 23:8–12

"But as for you, do not be called 'Rabbi,' because you have one Teacher, and you are all brothers. Do not call anyone on earth your father, because you have one Father, who is in heaven. And do not be called masters either, because you have one Master, the Messiah. The greatest among you will be your servant. Whoever exalts himself will be humbled, and whoever humbles himself will be exalted."

YOUR CHOICE

At what times do you tend to be inconsistent in living for Christ? When have you sensed the Holy Spirit telling you the right choice to make?

TOUGH QUESTION

I HEAR JESUS' COMMAND TO TREAT OTHERS AS I DESIRE TO BE TREATED, BUT SOMETIMES I JUST GET SO FRUSTRATED WITH PEOPLE. WHAT CAN I DO ABOUT THIS INCONSISTENCY IN MY CHRISTIAN LIFE?

Demanding from others what we don't expect from ourselves comes easy—that's our *sinful* human nature. And when others see that sin, they call us hypocrites. That's one reason Jesus warned His followers, "Do not judge, so that you won't be judged. . . . Why do you look at the speck in your brother's eye but don't notice the log in your own eye?" (Mt 7:1–3). Jesus wants us to make sure that our judging words have first pierced our own hearts.

Making this change from focusing on our own problems instead of the shortcomings and sins of others isn't easy because, as already mentioned, sinning comes naturally to us—even after we have given our lives to Christ. In fact, Romans 7 records the great apostle Paul's struggle with doing what he knows he shouldn't and not doing what he knows he should. But he concludes with this amazing promise, "Who will rescue me from this body of death? I thank God through Jesus Christ our Lord!" (vv. 24–25).

Help is on the way! God will rescue us! This means that because we have the Holy Spirit living in us, we don't have to give up and give in. He gives us the power to do what is right. In other words, we *can* choose with God's help.

Dealing with "inconsistency in the Christian life" begins with recognizing this weakness and then talking to God about it and asking for His help in making you sensitive to your own sin and help in living His way.

You probably won't change instantly, but you'll recognize when you slip up. When that happens, see it as God's signal and go right back to Him. As you continue to yield to His control, He will continue to release the Holy Spirit's power in you. You can make the right choice.

THE BIG PICTURE

LK 21:1–24

SEPTEMBER 7

DAY 250

SNAPSHOT

LUKE 21:1–4

He looked up and saw the rich dropping their offerings into the temple treasury. He also saw a poor widow dropping in two tiny coins. "I tell you the truth," He said. "This poor widow has put in more than all of them. For all these people have put in gifts out of their surplus, but she out of her poverty has put in all she had to live on."

JUST LIKE ME

UNNAMED WIDOW: GIVING IT ALL AWAY

What's the most generous gift you've ever received? More than likely it cost more than two coins. In a chapter filled with calamity and terror (the predictions of the destruction of the temple and Jerusalem; the horror of the end times), the short account of the widow's offering is like a breath of fresh air. For the widow, the quality of her heart counted more in Jesus' opinion than the quantity of her gift. Instead of tithing 10 percent, she gave 100 percent. In a way the widow mirrored what Jesus was about to do: give everything—His life—away as an offering for sin.

Ironically, the very *permanent* things that many in Jerusalem took stock in—the temple and Jerusalem—would pass away. But the life of Jesus—a life that the teachers of Jerusalem didn't value—would never pass away.

Although we know nothing about the widow other than what she gave, her story stands as a testimony to her generosity as well as her faith. Her story shows what God values—gifts from the heart, boldly given without regret.

Perhaps you think you're as poor as the widow and don't have much to give. But the best gift you can give—and the only one God wants anyway—is yourself. Why not give it all away?

YOUR CHOICE

What will you give to God?

DAY 251

THE BIG PICTURE

LK 21:25–38

SNAPSHOT

LUKE 21:29–33

Then He told them a parable: "Look at the fig tree, and all the trees. As soon as they put out leaves you can see for yourselves and recognize that summer is already near. In the same way, when you see these things happening, recognize that the kingdom of God is near. I assure you: This generation will certainly not pass away until all things take place. Heaven and earth will pass away, but My words will never pass away."

DEPOSIT

WORDS FROM GOD'S WORD TO STORE IN YOUR MIND AND HEART.

"Heaven and earth will pass away, but My words will never pass away" (Lk 21:33).

SNAPSHOT

MATTHEW 25:1–13

"Then the kingdom of heaven will be like 10 virgins who took their lamps and went out to meet the groom. Five of them were foolish and five were sensible. When the foolish took their lamps, they didn't take oil with them. But the sensible ones took oil in their flasks with their lamps. Since the groom was delayed, they all became drowsy and fell asleep.

"In the middle of the night there was a shout: 'Here's the groom! Come out to meet him.'

"Then all those virgins got up and trimmed their lamps. But the foolish ones said to the sensible ones, 'Give us some of your oil, because our lamps are going out.'

"The sensible ones answered, 'No, there won't be enough for us and for you. Go instead to those who sell, and buy oil for yourselves.'

"When they had gone to buy some, the groom arrived. Then those who were ready went in with him to the wedding banquet, and the door was shut.

"Later the rest of the virgins also came and said, 'Master, master, open up for us!'

"But he replied, 'I assure you: I do not know you!'

"Therefore be alert, because you don't know either the day or the hour."

YOUR TURN

BE PREPARED

With which of the people in these two stories do you identify most?

SEPTEMBER 10

DAY 253

THE BIG PICTURE

MT 25:31–46

SNAPSHOT

MATTHEW 25:37–40

"Then the righteous will answer Him, 'Lord, when did we see You hungry and feed You, or thirsty and give You something to drink? When did we see You a stranger and take You in, or without clothes and clothe You? When did we see You sick, or in prison, and visit You?'

"And the King will answer them, 'I assure you: Whatever you did for one of the least of these brothers of Mine, you did for Me.' "

ANCHOR POINT

JUDGMENT

According to James, "faith without works is useless" (Jms 2:20). Today's passage speaks directly to this issue. At judgment day, Christ doesn't ask about church attendance, theological sophistication, Bible knowledge, or religious activities. And He doesn't mention church offices held or roles played. Instead, His pointed questions ask about acts of mercy—reaching out to others in His name, for His sake. Our faith is *real* if it affects how we live.

So the question is simply this: How would *you* answer Jesus? You say you follow Christ, that you love Him and that He has changed your life. Really? How would anybody know?

Feeding the hungry and doing other acts of mercy won't get you into heaven. Eternal life is a gift and can't be earned. But the person who focuses on self and ignores others, especially those with great needs, demonstrates a lack of faith and no relationship with God.

YOUR CHOICE

Who can you feed or clothe or visit or care for?

SNAPSHOT

LUKE 22:10–13

"Listen," He said to them, "when you've entered the city, a man carrying a water jug will meet you. Follow him into the house he enters. Tell the owner of the house, 'The Teacher asks you, "Where is the guest room where I can eat the Passover with My disciples?"' Then he will show you a large, furnished room upstairs. Make the preparations there."

So they went and found it just as He had told them, and they prepared the Passover.

YOUR CHOICE

Where do you need to obey God, without question?

NO BRAINER

DOING WHAT HE SAYS

The disciples had been around Jesus long enough (almost three years) to believe He knew what He was talking about. They wouldn't fully understand Jesus' identity, purpose, and message until after the resurrection, but at this point they were pretty sure that Jesus was the promised One. Remember, Peter had declared, "You are the Messiah, the Son of the living God!" (Mt 16:16).

So when Jesus told Peter and John what to do to make arrangements for celebrating the Passover, they did exactly what He told them. Jesus didn't share all the information. He didn't say that this Passover would be their last meal together before He would be arrested, tried, tortured, and killed like a criminal. Jesus also didn't tell them right then that Judas would betray Him, that Peter would deny Him, and that all of the Twelve would desert Him. He knew all that, of course—He knew the pain that was coming, that He would endure on their behalf . . . and ours.

Jesus simply told them what to do, and they did it—they obeyed.

We've learned to expect to know more of the story. When asked, or told, to do something by someone, we usually ask why and may wonder what will happen next. And sometimes we carry over those expectations to our relationship with God. We may think, for example, "I know You want me to take a stand against that, Lord, but what will it cost me?" or "I realize that You are telling me to talk to my friends about Christ, but how will they react? I'm afraid they will reject me."

Consider this: if we knew the future—if we knew exactly what was going to happen as a result of our actions, would we do what God asks us to? What if we learned that our obedience would lead to pain, to suffering?

May we be like Peter and John just before Passover and hear and obey the Master.

DAY 255

JN 13:1–20

SNAPSHOT

JOHN 13:2–5

Now by the time of supper, the Devil had already put it into the heart of Judas, Simon Iscariot's son, to betray Him. Jesus knew that the Father had given everything into His hands, that He had come from God, and that He was going back to God. So He got up from supper, laid aside His robe, took a towel, and tied it around Himself. Next, He poured water into a basin and began to wash His disciples' feet and to dry them with the towel tied around Him.

YOUR CHOICE

What teacher from your past needs to hear words of thanks from you?

TOUGH QUESTION

MY ENGLISH PROFESSOR IS CONSTANTLY GOING THE EXTRA MILE FOR US—HE ALWAYS COMES EARLY AND LEAVES LATE. HOW CAN I SHOW HIM MY APPRECIATION WITHOUT LOOKING LIKE I'M TRYING TO GET IN GOOD WITH HIM?

Worrying about what people will think if you show kindness to someone is not your problem. Unfortunately, some people may assume the worst and think you have ulterior motives for expressing your appreciation to your professor. If you know in your heart that your motives are pure, then don't worry about what other people think or say. Showing your appreciation for your teacher is a wonderful thing to do. Encouragement can keep people motivated. Good teachers hope to make a difference in their students' lives. Many work in obscurity for very little pay and receive no recognition or plaudits. So your positive gestures and comments will mean a lot. In Matthew 5 we hear Jesus talking about the reward for those who have pure motives, "Blessed are the pure in heart, because they will see God" (Mt 5:8). Awesome!

Here are a couple of guidelines. First, don't go over the top. A few words after class or a brief note will probably get your message across. Try to do this when other students aren't around, possibly as you leave class.

Second, don't do this very often. If you make this a daily practice, both your professor and your classmates will think you have ulterior motives.

Third, express your appreciation *after* the course has concluded, so your comments won't possibly affect your grade in any way. And teachers love receiving thank-you cards and letters from former students, even years after their graduation.

Finally, remember that the best way to show how much you appreciate your teacher is to be a conscientious student with a good attitude. Pray that your professor will see Christ in you. In fact, pray for all your teachers, that they will feel appreciated and encouraged and "called" to their profession.

SNAPSHOT

JOHN 13:36–38

"Lord," Simon Peter said to Him, "where are You going?"

Jesus answered, "Where I am going you cannot follow Me now, but you will follow later."

"Lord," Peter asked, "why can't I follow You now? I will lay down my life for You!"

Jesus replied, "Will you lay down your life for Me? I assure you: A rooster will not crow until you have denied Me three times."

JUST LIKE ME

JESUS: TAKING THE HIGH GROUND

Imagine knowing that two of your friends were going to badly hurt you. Welcome to Jesus' world. Hundreds of years before the birth of the Messiah, Isaiah called Jesus "a man of suffering" (Is 53:3)—an apt title for His life and purpose. Before being crucified, Jesus would face the double whammy of Judas's betrayal and a series of denials by a friend who was even closer—Peter.

The disciples' feet were barely dry from the foot-washing done by Jesus—a servant's task that He took as a symbol for His later work on the cross. As God, He couldn't help but speak truth. "One of you will betray Me" (Jn 13:21). "A rooster will not crow until you have denied Me three times" (Jn 13:38). But as a man, He chose not to retaliate or treat either man coldly. He knew that neither Judas's betrayal nor Peter's denial was really the launching pad toward His crucifixion. Jesus' own will and the Father's plan would lead Him there.

When we're hurt by others, it can be difficult to see beyond the hurt or grief. We can't imagine what plan God could have in the face of such pain. But Jesus' example and His words remind us that we can take the high ground: "Just as you want others to do for you, do the same for them" (Lk 6:31).

YOUR CHOICE

How have you responded in the past when someone hurt you?

SEPTEMBER 14

DAY 257

THE BIG PICTURE

JN 14:1–31

SNAPSHOT

JOHN 14:1–4

"Your heart must not be troubled. Believe in God; believe also in Me. In My Father's house are many dwelling places; if not, I would have told you. I am going away to prepare a place for you. If I go away and prepare a place for you, I will come back and receive you to Myself, so that where I am you may be also. You know the way where I am going."

TOUGH CHOICE

NAVY

I hummed to myself as I walked through my grandparents' foyer toward the sunlit kitchen where my grandmother was making ham sandwiches. Pictures of my family hung in frames down the entire length of the hall. A big, silver frame held a faded photograph of my great, great grandmother at the family farm. Next to that, a portrait of my aunt Sis as a teenager hung. I liked this picture because she and I looked an awful lot alike. There was a picture of my dad as a kid with his dog, Oscar; a picture of all the grandkids from the previous Christmas; a picture of an uncle's wedding. And toward the end of the wall, there was a picture of Poppop, my grandpa, in his naval uniform.

"He's quite handsome, isn't he?" said Mama from the kitchen island, watching me gaze at the picture.

"Very," I said, smiling. "Does he still have his uniform?" I climbed up into one of the tall chairs at the island and sat down.

Mama wiped her hands on a dishtowel and began spreading mustard on slices of bread. "I believe that your Poppop's uniform is in a trunk with my wedding dress down in the storage room. You know, he married me in that uniform."

I tried to envision my grandparents on their wedding day. They would have been just about my age. "Mama, was it hard for you to let Poppop go out to sea?"

"Yes." She placed the mustard to the side and began unwrapping a half-eaten block of Swiss cheese before looking up at me. "It was hard for everyone except your grandfather."

"How so?"

"Well, your great-uncles Ben and John had already served, and great-grandmother Maupin was not ready to let her baby boy go off to fight. She wanted him to go to medical school and become a doctor. Your great-grandfather wanted Poppop to take over the family farm. I wanted him to be happy, as long as it was in the country and on dry land," she said, grinning.

"So, why did Poppop decide to enlist if the whole family was against his joining?"

"Because your Poppop knew that the Lord was calling him there. One or two pieces of ham?"

"Two, please."

"Your Poppop loved the Lord deeply and desired His will. That's the main reason I married your grandfather. Poppop knew that he was being called to join the navy, and nothing was going to impede that calling—not even his family, which he respected and loved very dearly."

"Wasn't he even a little nervous about his decision?"

"Of course he was nervous, but not about the decision, itself. Poppop knew that the Holy Spirit would be with him as he went out to sea. That was far more comforting to him than denying the Lord's calling and staying back at home."

". . . at least that's what I wanted her to think," said Poppop as he strode into the kitchen. "Really I was just eager to live in a submarine and launch torpedoes. Quite the adrenaline rush!" He stole the piece of ham Mama had just cut, taking a bite. "Delicious!" He winked at me.

YOUR CHOICE **How can you determine God's call on your life? If you knew it, would you be willing to go where He wants and do what He desires?**

SNAPSHOT

JOHN 15:5–8

"I am the vine; you are the branches. The one who remains in Me and I in him produces much fruit, because you can do nothing without Me. If anyone does not remain in Me, he is thrown aside like a branch and he withers. They gather them, throw them into the fire, and they are burned. If you remain in Me and My words remain in you, ask whatever you want and it will be done for you. My Father is glorified by this: that you produce much fruit and prove to be My disciples."

DEPOSIT

WORDS FROM GOD'S WORD TO STORE IN YOUR MIND AND HEART

"Remain in Me, and I in you. Just as a branch is unable to produce fruit by itself unless it remains on the vine, so neither can you unless you remain in Me" (Jn 15:4).

DAY 259

THE BIG PICTURE

JN 15:17–16:4

SNAPSHOT

JOHN 15:18–21

"If the world hates you, understand that it hated Me before it hated you. If you were of the world, the world would love you as its own. However, because you are not of the world, but I have chosen you out of it, the world hates you. Remember the word I spoke to you: 'A slave is not greater than his master.' If they persecuted Me, they will also persecute you. If they kept My word, they will also keep yours. But they will do all these things to you on account of My name, because they don't know the One who sent Me."

YOUR TURN

SEEKING HONOR

What have you learned recently about loving others?

JN 16:5–33

SNAPSHOT

JOHN 16:5–11

"But now I am going away to Him who sent Me, and not one of you asks Me, 'Where are You going?' Yet, because I have spoken these things to you, sorrow has filled your heart. Nevertheless, I am telling you the truth. It is for your benefit that I go away, because if I don't go away the Counselor will not come to you. If I go, I will send Him to you. When He comes, He will convict the world about sin, righteousness, and judgment: about sin, because they do not believe in Me; about righteousness, because I am going to the Father and you will no longer see Me; and about judgment, because the ruler of this world has been judged."

YOUR CHOICE

What's your Bible study plan/method? How seriously do you take the timeless truths you discover in God's Word?

NO BRAINER

INSPIRED WRITING

The Bible is accurate and true, the inspired Word of God. We have several reasons for believing this, beginning with the fact that Jesus said, "Don't assume that I came to destroy the Law or the Prophets" (our Old Testament). "I did not come to destroy but to fulfill. For I assure you: Until heaven and earth pass away, not the smallest letter or one stroke of a letter will pass from the law until all things are accomplished" (Mt 5:17–18). He also said, "Heaven and earth will pass away, but My words will never pass away" (Mk 13:31). The case for divine inspiration also includes fulfilled prophecy, archaeological discoveries, Bible statements (see 2 Tm 3:16–17), and other proofs.

Today's passage presents another important piece of evidence. We hear Jesus telling His disciples about the person and work of the Holy Spirit. Jesus explains that this third member of the Trinity "will convict the world about sin, righteousness, and judgment" (v 8). Then Jesus uses the title "Spirit of truth" and makes a dramatic prediction. Speaking directly to the apostles, Jesus adds, "He will guide you into all the truth. . . . He will also declare to you what is to come" (Jn 16:13).

Jesus is saying, in effect, that after He leaves, the Holy Spirit will come and work in these disciples, giving them total and accurate recall of their time with Jesus and truth about the future as well. This is why the early church placed so much importance on knowing that the writers of the books they included in the New Testament had been *eyewitnesses*—apostles. Jesus had promised that the Holy Spirit would "guide them into all the truth."

So you can read your Bible with confidence, knowing that it is God-inspired and true. Scripture teaches you, rebukes you, trains you, and equips you to do good works, to make the right choices, and to take a stand for Him.

DAY 261

THE BIG PICTURE
JN 17:1–26

SNAPSHOT

JOHN 17:11

"I am no longer in the world,
but they are in the world,
and I am coming to You.
Holy Father,
protect them by Your name
that You have given Me,
so that they may be one as We are one."

ANCHOR POINT

FULLY ENGAGED

This passage is called Jesus' "high priestly prayer." Just before being arrested, tried, and crucified, He was spending time with the disciples. This is His prayer for them. He prayed that these men would be unified, protected, filled with joy, sanctified, and would be good examples to the watching world.

With all of these requests, however, came another. Jesus said, "I am not praying that You take them out of the world but that You protect them from the evil one" (v. 15). Considering all the hatred and abuse these followers of Christ would endure, we might imagine a desire to retreat—perhaps to a remote enclave—for mutual support and for protection. But that wasn't their Lord's desire for them. Jesus wanted the disciples to be fully engaged in the world, battling the enemy, leading men and women to Him, and transforming society, one life at a time.

Now look a bit later in the chapter. Verse 20 has Jesus praying, "I pray not only for these, but also for those who believe in Me through their message." *That's us!* When Jesus prayed for His followers, He had us in mind. This means that Christ wants His followers *today* to be unified, protected, filled with joy, sanctified, and good examples. He wants us to be *in the world* making a difference for Him.

What a challenge! What an opportunity!

YOUR CHOICE

When have you tended to retreat from the world? What can you do to be more fully engaged, for Christ?

MARK 14:32–36

Then they came to a place named Gethsemane, and He told His disciples, "Sit here while I pray." He took Peter, James, and John with Him, and He began to be deeply distressed and horrified. Then He said to them, "My soul is swallowed up in sorrow—to the point of death. Remain here and stay awake." Then He went a little farther, fell to the ground, and began to pray that if it were possible, the hour might pass from Him. And He said, "Abba, Father! All things are possible for You. Take this cup away from Me. Nevertheless, not what I will, but what You will."

SNAPSHOT

SEPTEMBER 19

DAY 262

THE BIG PICTURE

MK 14:27–52

TOUGH CHOICE

PRAYER

"Holly? Is that you?" My roommate's voice surprised me. A dim light in the corner of the family room provided just enough light for me to see Keegan curled up on the sofa.

"Keegan, what are you doing up so late?" I whispered. "It's almost 2 o'clock in the morning."

Keegan yawned and sat up, pulling a big blanket around her shoulders. "I wanted to see how everything went with Tyler tonight."

I walked into the room and sat down at the other end of the couch, kicking my shoes off under the coffee table. "Thanks, Keeg. You're wonderful."

She smiled, tossing part of the blanket in my direction. "Talk."

I pulled the blanket over my knees. "Well, we're still dating. We . . . I talked for a long time tonight. I told him that things are going to have to change; he has to be more open. I can't keep dating someone who's always distant." I stopped, waiting for Keegan to commend me on my abrasiveness. She had been urging me to confront Tyler on his commitment issues for nearly a year.

"How did Tyler respond?"

"'I just don't know what to say . . .'—that's all he really said."

Keegan let her head fall back. "Molly," she groaned, "you can't let him treat you like that. He just blows you off, over and over again. Why do you put up with it?"

"I know," I sighed. "It's just that, Tyler's had a rough year. I want to be there for him." I knew I had given Keegan the same reasoning before.

"Molly," she said, exasperated, "you're not responsible for taking care of him."

I sunk deeper into the couch. "Keeg, I've been praying that the Lord would save our relationship. I can't do it on my own, so I've surrendered it to Him."

Keegan stared at me. "Molly, I know how much Tyler means to you; it began as a great relationship. But I don't think that this relationship is healthy for either of you, and I don't think that you've truly given control to the Lord."

"What do you mean?"

"God allows us to go through challenging times and trials in order to grow us. But in order for His work to be fully experienced, we have to be willing for Him to take us in directions that push us out of our comfort zones and even scare us." She paused. "I think that your prayer needs to be for God's will; not that He'll salvage your relationship with Tyler."

My breathing was labored. I just wanted Tyler to be the same guy I had started dating two years ago. "I don't know if I'm ready to pray that," I whispered.

Keegan moved over next to me. "You don't have to *feel* ready. You just have to be willing to pray the prayer. Christ will take care of the rest. He will change your heart."

YOUR CHOICE **What area of life is a struggle for you to turn over to God? What holds you back?**

SNAPSHOT

JOHN 18:15–18

Meanwhile Simon Peter was following Jesus, as was another disciple. That disciple was an acquaintance of the high priest; so he went with Jesus into the high priest's courtyard. But Peter remained standing outside by the door. So the other disciple, the one known to the high priest, went out and spoke to the girl who was the doorkeeper and brought Peter in.

Then the slave girl who was the doorkeeper said to Peter, "You aren't one of this man's disciples too, are you?"

"I am not!" he said. Now the slaves and the temple police had made a charcoal fire, because it was cold. They were standing there warming themselves, and Peter was standing with them, warming himself.

JUST LIKE ME

JUDAS AND PETER: TWO DIRECTIONS TAKEN

Ever mess up so badly with a friend or a family member that you weren't sure your relationship would survive? Having betrayed their friend Jesus, Peter and Judas faced the aftermath of their wrong decisions and actions.

The road metaphor is very apt when it comes to facing consequences. We can choose to travel one direction or another. After betraying Jesus, Judas chose a direction that led to the literal dead end of suicide (see Mt 27:1–10.) Although Judas seemed to regret what he did, he couldn't believe that forgiveness could be extended for such an act.

After Peter "wept bitterly" (Mt 26:75), his brokenness drove him in another way—back to his old life of fishing. Little did he know that his ability to catch fish—a metaphor Jesus used long before when He said, "From now on you will be catching people" (Lk 5:10)—would come true once again after a later encounter with the risen Jesus. But for now, Peter clung to the only life he knew.

When we blow it, we have two choices: we can wallow in regret and other negative behaviors, or we can move on. Judas chose the dead end. Peter chose to move on and be faithful in the only way that he knew how. What direction will you choose?

YOUR CHOICE

When have you been tempted to deny Christ?

TOUGH QUESTION

I KNOW MY FRIEND CHEATED ON OUR TEST. I DON'T WANT TO BE A RAT, BUT WHAT SHE DID WAS WRONG. WHAT SHOULD I DO?

Cheating is wrong. You want to stand up for what is right, but you don't want to lose a friend in the process. Probably the best way to handle this is to privately and kindly inform your friend that you saw her cheating and that you both know that's wrong. Encourage your friend to turn herself in and to throw herself at the mercy of your teacher. You should let her know that you know—but don't push it further.

If your friend is a Christian, she has the same obligation as you to live under the authority of God's Word. So explain why cheating is wrong and the biblical principles that cheating violates (it is lying; it hurts everyone else in the class; it presents a bad example of how a Christian acts). Hopefully your friend will thank you for holding her accountable, but she may do the opposite and become angry and point out something you did wrong in the past. Sometime friendships are hurt by the truth. Keep in mind that your purpose should be to help your friend do what is right. So keep praying for her and for your relationship with her.

If your friend isn't a Christian, then although she doesn't feel the same as you about God's Word, she still probably knows that cheating is wrong. Certainly she knows the penalty for getting caught in the act. She may rationalize by saying that everyone cheats, that she *can't fail* this class, or that what she did doesn't hurt anyone. At that point, you can say you don't agree and explain that you believe you should live according to a higher standard—God's. Don't be condescending or "holier than thou." By loving your friend but being firm about not approving of her sin, you can demonstrate Christ's love to her.

SNAPSHOT

MATTHEW 26:59–64

The chief priests and the whole Sanhedrin were looking for false testimony against Jesus so they could put Him to death. But they could not find any, even though many false witnesses came forward. Finally, two who came forward stated, "This man said, 'I can demolish God's sanctuary and rebuild it in three days.' "

The high priest then stood up and said to Him, "Don't You have an answer to what these men are testifying against You?" But Jesus kept silent. Then the high priest said to Him, "By the living God I place You under oath: tell us if You are the Messiah, the Son of God!"

"You have said it," Jesus told him. "But I tell you, in the future you will see the Son of Man seated at the right hand of the Power and coming on the clouds of heaven."

YOUR CHOICE

What friend needs to hear from you a word of truth, spoken in love?

SEPTEMBER 22

DAY 265

THE BIG PICTURE

MT 27:1–13

SNAPSHOT

MATTHEW 27:3–5

Then Judas, His betrayer, seeing that He had been condemned, was full of remorse and returned the 30 pieces of silver to the chief priests and elders. "I have sinned by betraying innocent blood," he said.

"What's that to us?" they said. "See to it yourself!"

So he threw the silver into the sanctuary and departed. Then he went and hanged himself.

DEPOSIT

WORDS FROM GOD'S WORD TO STORE IN YOUR MIND AND HEART

And He said, "Abba, Father! All things are possible for You. Take this cup away from Me. Nevertheless, not what I will, but what You will" (Mk 14:36).

THE BIG PICTURE

LK 23:1–12

SEPTEMBER 23

DAY 266

SNAPSHOT

LUKE 23:6–12

When Pilate heard this, he asked if the man was a Galilean. Finding that He was under Herod's jurisdiction, he sent Him to Herod, who was also in Jerusalem during those days. Herod was very glad to see Jesus; for a long time he had wanted to see Him, because he had heard about Him and was hoping to see some miracle performed by Him. So he kept asking Him questions, but Jesus did not answer him. The chief priests and the scribes stood by, vehemently accusing Him. Then Herod, with his soldiers, treated Him with contempt, mocked Him, dressed Him in a brilliant robe, and sent Him back to Pilate. That very day Herod and Pilate became friends. Previously, they had been hostile toward each other.

YOUR TURN

JESUS RAISES LAZARUS

In what ways did your childhood and background prepare you to respond to Jesus?

DAY 267

SNAPSHOT

MARK 15:27–32

They crucified two criminals with Him, one on His right and one on His left. So the Scripture was fulfilled that says: And He was counted among outlaws. Those who passed by were yelling insults at Him, shaking their heads, and saying, "Ha! The One who would demolish the sanctuary and build it in three days, save Yourself by coming down from the cross!" In the same way, the chief priests with the scribes were mocking Him to one another and saying, "He saved others; He cannot save Himself! Let the Messiah, the King of Israel, come down now from the cross, so that we may see and believe." Even those who were crucified with Him were taunting Him.

YOUR CHOICE

When have you had to stand up for someone who was being put down?

TOUGH QUESTION

WHILE HANGING OUT, MY FRIENDS STARTED TALKING MEAN ABOUT A KID IN OUR CLASS. HOW CAN I TAKE A STAND AND HAVE THE COURAGE TO TELL THEM TO STOP?

People talk negatively about others for a variety of reasons: to enhance their position in a group, to lift themselves up by putting another person down, or to position himself or herself as the person with inside information (gossip). A number of biblical principles apply to this situation, with the most obvious being the Golden Rule: "Just as you want others to do for you, do the same for them" (Lk 6:31). The Bible also has much to say about showing others love and respect. And when it comes to gossip, the Bible is very clear about the harm it can cause: "A contrary man spreads conflict, and a gossip separates friends" (Pr 16:28).

Knowing what God thinks about this kind of talk, you can breathe new life into the situation. You can stick up for the person by not joining in and, thus, send a message by your silence. You can gently and kindly share that you think talking like that is wrong. You can encourage your friends to give your classmate the benefit of the doubt.

The courage to stick up for others also comes from knowing that all people are special and unique in the eyes of God. He created us, and Christ died for us.

In a perfect world, your friends would agree that their gossiping is wrong, and stop. The world is not perfect, however, and standing up for what is right will put your reputation and friendships at risk. The group may become angry with you for confronting them and might exclude you from the group and begin saying hurtful things about you. That's a chance you have to take if you choose to stand up for what is biblical and right. The Bible is very clear about obeying God and His commands. Though the way may be rough initially, following God's way is always the best path to follow.

THE BIG PICTURE

LK 23:32–49

SEPTEMBER 25

DAY 268

SNAPSHOT

LUKE 23:39–43

Then one of the criminals hanging there began to yell insults at Him: "Aren't You the Messiah? Save Yourself and us!"

But the other answered, rebuking him: "Don't you even fear God, since you are undergoing the same punishment? We are punished justly, because we're getting back what we deserve for the things we did, but this man has done nothing wrong." Then he said, "Jesus, remember me when You come into Your kingdom!"

And He said to him, "I assure you: Today you will be with Me in paradise."

ANCHOR POINT

KINGDOM OF GOD

A huge crowd had gathered that day. The people had come to see the death of a blaspheming insurrectionist. This enemy of the state was to die for claiming to be God, for attempting to subvert the religious and cultural order—a culture that had been attacked continually through the years.

But as this man hung condemned and dying, those who had just clamored for His death heard Him forgive them. They saw Him have compassion on a convicted criminal, even as He was being insulted by another. They experienced His last moments of life when He cried out to God, calling Him Father and placing Himself into His care. They heard the Roman guard call Him righteous. And if they stayed around, they saw Him pulled from the cross, dead, and carried away for burial.

As a follower of Christ, how does this passage affect you? When you read of how Christ suffered and died to pay the penalty for your sins, what is your response? Barabbas wasn't the only one set free that day.

YOUR CHOICE

Reread the account of Jesus' trial and death. And after each graphic description of His suffering, pray, "Thank You, Lord, for doing that for me."

SEPTEMBER 26

DAY 269

THE BIG PICTURE

MT 27:57–66

SNAPSHOT

MATTHEW 27:62–64

The next day, which followed the preparation day, the chief priests and the Pharisees gathered before Pilate and said, "Sir, we remember that while this deceiver was still alive, He said, 'After three days I will rise again.' Therefore give orders that the tomb be made secure until the third day. Otherwise, His disciples may come, steal Him, and tell the people, 'He has been raised from the dead.' Then the last deception will be worse than the first."

TOUGH CHOICE

ONLY ONE GOD

Cooper, Philip, and I settled down at the table with our steaming drinks. Cooper's face was still red from the blizzard outside. The chocolaty liquid scalded my tongue as I cautiously sipped, but I could at least feel the blood circulating in my body again.

"What are you guys working on tonight?" asked Philip, pulling a textbook on ancient ruins out of his backpack and placing it on the coffeehouse table.

"Wes and I need to plan our Bible study for Thursday," said Cooper.

"What is your devotional about?" asked Philip, genuinely curious.

"Well, Wes and I are going to be leading a discussion on why God is the one and only true God this week."

"Cooper and I basically just facilitate a small group discussion after the weekly Bible study we attend," I said.

Philip smiled to himself, taking a sip from his mug. "So what are you going to say in your discussion? Why do you think that your God is the one and only God?"

Cooper looked over at me. "Do you want to field this one?" Cooper knew as well as I did that Philip enjoyed playing the devil's advocate. He was well-read and could debate any topic.

"Sure thing, Coop," I said sarcastically. "The short answer to your question, Philip, is that God reveals Himself and His commandments through the Bible. No other god has provided such infallible evidence of its existence. God lays out exactly what is required of us in order to be reconciled with Him. We have to be perfect. Living a 'good life' won't cut it. Fortunately, Christ is also the only deity who came to earth as a man and died as atonement for our sins. If we accept Christ and believe that He paid the penalty for our sins, we can live eternally with Him."

Philip nodded his head purposefully. "Interesting . . ."

I waited for his rebuttal, but it didn't come. "So, what are your thoughts?" I asked, suspiciously.

"Honestly, I believe that Jesus existed. He was a good man who did great things. But I also believe that each of us defines our own truth and controls our own destiny. We should search for purpose and meaning in this life, and in doing so, we will become the best version of ourselves."

I listened closely. His intentions and desire to live a purposeful life were admirable, but his reliance upon himself for meaning was disheartening. "So you would rather be responsible for your own eternity than leaving it to God, who requires nothing more of you than to accept Christ as your Savior?" I asked.

"I just don't know that I could ever hand over control of my life to anyone other than myself," he confessed.

Cooper cleared his throat. "Philip, what would you think about coming to our discussion group this week? I think you might find it thought-provoking. And I think that you could stimulate some really meaningful discussion. What do you say?"

Philip chuckled. "Okay. I'll come. It will be . . . interesting."

YOUR CHOICE **How much about your faith do your non-Christian friends know? Given the opportunity, how would you explain the gospel to them?**

SNAPSHOT

JOHN 20:11–16

But Mary stood outside facing the tomb, crying. As she was crying, she stooped to look into the tomb. She saw two angels in white sitting there, one at the head and one at the feet, where Jesus' body had been lying. They said to her, "Woman, why are you crying?"

"Because they've taken away my Lord," she told them, "and I don't know where they've put Him." Having said this, she turned around and saw Jesus standing there, though she did not know it was Jesus.

"Woman," Jesus said to her, "why are you crying? Who is it you are looking for?"

Supposing He was the gardener, she replied, "Sir, if you've removed Him, tell me where you've put Him, and I will take Him away."

Jesus said, "Mary."

JUST LIKE ME

MARY MAGDALENE: NOW WHAT? NOW LIFE!

If you've suffered the loss of someone you love, you know how Mary probably felt when she woke up two days after Jesus' death and burial. The reality of Jesus' death was still painfully raw, and it colored her whole world a dismal gray. And to add insult to injury, Peter and John reported that Jesus' body was missing. Perhaps she thought, *Now what?*

But God had a "Now this!" to add to the *Now what?* of Mary's day. "Now this!" was a constant theme in Mary's life. According to Mark 16:9, Jesus had cast seven demons out of her, thus ushering in a new era of life. But first she had to pass through the fires of grief at the Savior's death.

Now Mary faced the risen Savior, whom she did not recognize. But this meeting with Jesus brought color to her gray-washed world and a new role—that of witness bearer to Jesus' disciples of His resurrection. God's "Now this!" pointed to the spiritual rebirth Mary could have as a result of Jesus' sacrificial death. God brought beauty out of ashes (see Is 61:3).

If you've wondered "Now what?" after distressing circumstances, consider the God who can bring good out of the worst disasters. He can take you through the other side of grief and beyond.

YOUR CHOICE

How has God helped you see a bad situation differently?

THE BIG PICTURE

MT 28:8–15

NO BRAINER

NO FEAR

In this passage, we find one of the most common phrases that Jesus used with His followers: "Do not be afraid."

At the beginning of His journey with the disciples, as Jesus was commissioning them to fish for people, He told them, "Don't be afraid" (Lk 5:10). He had the same encouragement when healing a little girl (Lk 8:50) and teaching about anxiety (Lk 12:7, 32). And at His triumphal entry into Jerusalem, Jesus quoted Zechariah 9:9, saying, "Fear no more, Daughter Zion; look! your King is coming, sitting on a donkey's colt" (Jn 12:15).

Here, then, at this most pivotal moment in history, Jesus, the risen Christ, meets the women at the open tomb and says again, "Do not be afraid." The phrase that directly follows is also significant: "Go and tell . . ."

What fears cause your heart to race, your palms to sweat, your throat to tighten, or your knees to quake? What anxious thoughts and nightmares cause you to toss and turn all night? What worries stop you from doing what you know you should, telling the truth, sharing the gospel, taking a stand?

Fear—gut-wrenching, debilitating—can turn the strong into cowards, and can move us in directions we'd rather not go.

So to us, Jesus says, "Don't be afraid."

» "Don't be afraid, for I have conquered death."

» "Don't be afraid, for I, your Lord, go before you."

» "Don't be afraid, for I am with you."

» "Now go and tell!"

SNAPSHOT

MATTHEW 28:8–10

So, departing quickly from the tomb with fear and great joy, they ran to tell His disciples the news. Just then Jesus met them and said, "Good morning!" They came up, took hold of His feet, and worshiped Him. Then Jesus told them, "Do not be afraid. Go and tell My brothers to leave for Galilee, and they will see Me there."

YOUR CHOICE

Release your fears to your Savior. Trust Him to be with you and to give you the strength and courage to do what He wants.

SNAPSHOT

LUKE 24:36–43

And as they were saying these things, He Himself stood among them. He said to them, "Peace to you!" But they were startled and terrified and thought they were seeing a ghost. "Why are you troubled?" He asked them. "And why do doubts arise in your hearts? Look at My hands and My feet, that it is I Myself! Touch Me and see, because a ghost does not have flesh and bones as you can see I have." Having said this, He showed them His hands and feet. But while they still could not believe because of their joy and were amazed, He asked them, "Do you have anything here to eat?" So they gave Him a piece of a broiled fish, and He took it and ate in their presence.

DEPOSIT

WORDS FROM GOD'S WORD TO STORE IN YOUR MIND AND HEART

Then He told them, "These are My words that I spoke to you while I was still with you—that everything written about Me in the Law of Moses, the Prophets, and the Psalms must be fulfilled." Then He opened their minds to understand the Scriptures (Lk 24:44–45).

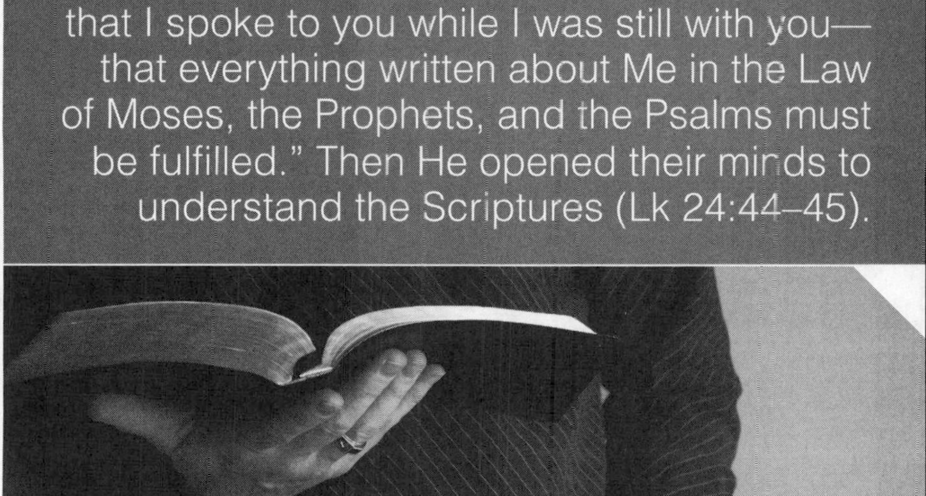

SNAPSHOT

JOHN 20:24–29

But one of the Twelve, Thomas (called "Twin"), was not with them when Jesus came. So the other disciples kept telling him, "We have seen the Lord!"

But he said to them, "If I don't see the mark of the nails in His hands, put my finger into the mark of the nails, and put my hand into His side, I will never believe!"

After eight days His disciples were indoors again, and Thomas was with them. Even though the doors were locked, Jesus came and stood among them. He said, "Peace to you!"

Then He said to Thomas, "Put your finger here and observe My hands. Reach out your hand and put it into My side. Don't be an unbeliever, but a believer."

Thomas responded to Him, "My Lord and my God!"

Jesus said, "Because you have seen Me, you have believed. Those who believe without seeing are blessed."

YOUR TURN

DOUBTS

How has Christ answered your doubts?

OCTOBER

OKTOBER
OCTOBRE
OKTOBER
OTTOBRE
OUTUBRO
OCTUBRE

THE BIG PICTURE

JN 21:15–25

OCTOBER 1

DAY 274

SNAPSHOT

JOHN 21:18–22

"I assure you: When you were young, you would tie your belt and walk wherever you wanted. But when you grow old, you will stretch out your hands and someone else will tie you and carry you where you don't want to go." He said this to signify by what kind of death he would glorify God. After saying this, He told him, "Follow Me!"

So Peter turned around and saw the disciple Jesus loved following them. That disciple was the one who had leaned back against Jesus at the supper and asked, "Lord, who is the one that's going to betray You?" When Peter saw him, he said to Jesus, "Lord—what about him?"

"If I want him to remain until I come," Jesus answered, "what is that to you? As for you, follow Me."

JUST LIKE ME

JOHN AND PETER: JUST DO YOUR PART

You've heard that the squeaky wheel gets the grease. In other words, the people who boast the most or complain the loudest are the ones who get the attention. For Jesus, the ones who blew it the most (for example, all of us) get His attention. And Peter had blown it by denying Jesus.

While eavesdropping on Jesus' conversation with Peter, John heard Peter ask about Jesus' plans for John. Jesus' exact reply might have been misconstrued, but His bottom line was not. Peter was to concern himself with his own tasks, rather than worry about Jesus' plans for someone else's life. Instead, both were to simply do the tasks God had called them to do.

Whether or not John ever compared himself with Peter is anybody's guess. Although John's mother had requested glory for him and his brother James (see Mt 20:21), John seemed content to refer to himself by the humble title of the "one Jesus loved" (Jn 13:23).

Rather than get into a discussion of glory or His plans for individual disciples, Jesus instead predicted that Peter and John would suffer for His sake (see Mt 20:23; Jn 21:18–19). Jesus' prediction took the focus off individual glory and returned the glory to God.

Sadly, in our concern for glory we sometimes compare ourselves with others. But Jesus' advice on this day in John's life deserves our undivided attention. Instead of worrying about how God plans to use others, we're to do what we know He wants us to do.

YOUR CHOICE

When are you most tempted to compare yourself with someone else?

DAY 275

THE BIG PICTURE

MT 28:16–20

NO BRAINER

THE GREAT COMMISSION

Heard (or thought) any comments like these?

"What's the big deal about missionaries, anyway? I mean God knows who's going to become a Christian—and He's all-powerful—He doesn't need us."

» "It seems so hopeless. Look at how many people around the world have never heard about Christ. We'll never reach them all."

» "I don't know enough, and I'm not a good speaker. God can't use me to spread His word."

» We could think of a million excuses for *not* sharing the gospel with others. Think of what the disciples could have thought: "No one will believe this crazy story"; "My family will disown me"; "I could get killed"; "How about using someone else!" But they didn't. Jesus gave them this final command that we call the Great Commission. He said "Go!" and they went . . . to all nations.

And if they hadn't gone, if they hadn't obeyed their Lord, you probably would still be lost, dead in your sins.

We don't know how it all works—the combination of God's sovereignty and our choices and efforts. We don't know who will respond—only God knows. We don't know what will cause some people to follow and others to reject—only the Spirit draws them.

But we do know that Jesus told us to pray for those who don't yet know Him, to support our brothers and sisters in the ministry, and to *go*.

Will we obey? Will we follow in the footsteps of those first-century martyrs and "make disciples of all nations"?

Oh, and by the way, Jesus promised, "I am with you always, to the end of the age" (Mt 28:20) and, "If God is for us, who is against us?" (Rm 8:31).

SNAPSHOT

MATTHEW 28:19–20

"Go, therefore, and make disciples of all nations, baptizing them in the name of the Father and of the Son and of the Holy Spirit, teaching them to observe everything I have commanded you. And remember, I am with you always, to the end of the age."

YOUR CHOICE

Where do you need to go to obey Christ? With whom do you need to share God's Good News?

LUKE 24:44–45

Then He told them, "These are My words that I spoke to you while I was still with you—that everything written about Me in the Law of Moses, the Prophets, and the Psalms must be fulfilled." Then He opened their minds to understand the Scriptures.

SNAPSHOT

OCTOBER 3

DAY 276

THE BIG PICTURE

LK 24:36–53

TOUGH CHOICE

DOUBT

It was a stormy night, magnified by cracks of lightning that illuminated my room. The ceiling fan spun overhead, as I laid in my bed watching its blades whip around.

Bam! Thunder rattled the windows.

". . . religion . . . the system of doctrines and promises which on the one hand explains to him the riddles of this world with enviable completeness, and, on the other, assures him that a careful Providence will watch over his life and will compensate him in a future existence for any frustrations he suffers here." Freud's explanation of religion from *Civilization and Its Discontents* ran through my head. The majority of the books we had read over the semester for my philosophy class had been thought-provoking but none of them had unnerved me to the point of keeping me awake at night. Until now.

Bam! Wild shadows burst across the walls in the flash of lightning. *What if everything I've believed about God really is just my feeble attempt to explain my purpose for being on this earth? What if it's all in my head?*

The branches outside my window scratched against the glass, as the sound of pelting raindrops surged with every gust of wind. *Stop playing mind games with yourself, Meredith.*

Bam! Bright light flooded the room.

"Faith . . . is the art of holding on to things your reason has once accepted, in spite of your changing moods . . . One must train the habit of Faith . . . We have to be continually reminded of what we believe . . . No belief will automatically remain alive in the mind. It must be fed." I recalled C. S. Lewis's words from *Mere Christianity*. I knew that Christianity required diving into the Word each day. *Faith is not a feeling, Meredith.*

"God, I don't like these feelings of doubt. It's unnerving. I know I believe, but sometimes the thought of You is just overwhelming. I can't get my mind around You and how You created everything. It's beyond my comprehension."

Bam! The whirring of my fan slowed and stopped. I rolled over, reaching for my lamp switch. *Twist, twist.* Nothing.

I slid out of bed, fumbling for my flashlight. "Here it is," I said aloud, flipping the switch on. The beam fell onto my Bible, which rested on the floor, next to my bedside table. I picked up the book and rolled back into bed, flipping to John 1.

"In the beginning was the Word, and the Word was with God, and the Word was God. He was with God in the beginning. All things were created through Him, and apart from Him not one thing was created that has been created. Life was in Him, and that life was the light of men. That light shines in darkness, yet the darkness did not overcome it . . ."

Bam! Bright light.

"Lord, overcome my doubts. I believe that all things were made at Your command. You were and are and will forever be. Help me to continue obeying and receiving You."

Bam!

"Amen."

YOUR CHOICE **What doubts about your faith have been gnawing at your mind? How are you dealing with them?**

THE BIG PICTURE
AC 1:1–11

SNAPSHOT

ACTS 1:4–8

While He was together with them, He commanded them not to leave Jerusalem, but to wait for the Father's promise. "This," He said, "is what you heard from Me; for John baptized with water, but you will be baptized with the Holy Spirit not many days from now."

So when they had come together, they asked Him, "Lord, at this time are You restoring the kingdom to Israel?"

He said to them, "It is not for you to know times or periods that the Father has set by His own authority. But you will receive power when the Holy Spirit has come upon you, and you will be My witnesses in Jerusalem, in all Judea and Samaria, and to the ends of the earth."

ANCHOR POINT

THE DEPARTURE OF JESUS

When Jesus left His disciples, He gave them a command, a promise, and an admonition. "Wait here," He commanded. "The Spirit is coming," He promised. "Don't worry about the future, do the work I have set before you," was the admonition. These three simple statements concluded years of teachings.

C. S. Lewis wrote that he had no use for simplicity, unless it was simplicity on the other side of complexity. The Christian life is full of complexities and often hard-to-understand truths, such as the Trinity, the truths in tension—free will and election, Jesus as the God-man, to name a few.

Yet on the other side of those complexities, we find simplicity. Wait, receive, do the work, and don't worry about the future—it all seems pretty straightforward and reassuring. If your brain hurts when studying theology, don't worry too much. At the end of the day we are called to receive the Spirit and then to be witnesses for Christ in our towns, the neighboring area and around the world. Take heart in the simplicity of Christ's last words.

YOUR CHOICE

How have you made your walk with Christ too complicated? Where have you added layers of complexity that are both unnecessary and, possibly, are holding you back from truly engaging the life to which you have been called?

TOUGH QUESTION

ALL OF MY CHRISTIAN FRIENDS ARE HAVING SEX. IF EVERYONE SAYS IT'S OKAY, HOW CAN I TAKE A STAND AND WAIT UNTIL MARRIAGE?

If an attitude, action, or activity is wrong, it's wrong, regardless of how many people do it or defend it. God doesn't make His rules according to the latest poll. He knows what is best for the world and best for us, and we need to line up with His standards.

Concerning sexual morality, the Bible is very clear that intimate sexual relations should be reserved for marriage, between one man and one woman. And the command against adultery is very clear. "Marriage must be respected by all, and the marriage bed kept undefiled, because God will judge immoral people and adulterers" (Heb 13:4). God designed sex for the marriage relationship.

Taking a stand, and waiting to have sex until marriage, is not easy. Temptations abound, and the sexual emphasis in entertainment, celebrated lifestyles, and pornography heighten lustful thoughts and feelings. Wanting to have sex can be so tempting when you are dating or are engaged to someone you love deeply. Refraining from it takes discipline, accountability, and the ability to say no. So you have to know, and really believe, that God's best is for sex within marriage. Being disciplined with someone you are dating or whom you love begins by creating parameters for your physical relationship. This may mean not spending time together after 10:00 P.M. or choosing to not spend time together, alone, after dark. Having a trusted friend or mentor hold you accountable will be a big help.

Just because you set up boundaries, however, doesn't mean that those boundaries will keep you from having sex before marriage. You and your boyfriend or girlfriend must be very intentional about enforcing them, both of you committed to experiencing God's best and living His way.

SNAPSHOT

ACTS 1:12–14

Then they returned to Jerusalem from the mount called Olive Grove, which is near Jerusalem—a Sabbath day's journey away. When they arrived, they went to the room upstairs where they were staying…

All these were continually united in prayer, along with the women, including Mary the mother of Jesus, and His brothers.

YOUR CHOICE

What boundaries do you need to set in your dating relationships?

DAY 279

THE BIG PICTURE
AC 2:1–13

SNAPSHOT

ACTS 2:1–4

When the day of Pentecost had arrived, they were all together in one place. Suddenly a sound like that of a violent rushing wind came from heaven, and it filled the whole house where they were staying. And tongues, like flames of fire that were divided, appeared to them and rested on each one of them. Then they were all filled with the Holy Spirit and began to speak in different languages, as the Spirit gave them ability for speech.

DEPOSIT

WORDS FROM GOD'S WORD TO STORE IN YOUR MIND AND HEART

"Go, therefore, and make disciples of all nations, baptizing them in the name of the Father and of the Son and of the Holy Spirit, teaching them to observe everything I have commanded you. And remember, I am with you always, to the end of the age" (Mt 28:19–20).

SNAPSHOT

ACTS 2:37–40

When they heard this, they were pierced to the heart and said to Peter and the rest of the apostles: "Brothers, what must we do?"

"Repent," Peter said to them, "and be baptized, each of you, in the name of Jesus the Messiah for the forgiveness of your sins, and you will receive the gift of the Holy Spirit. For the promise is for you and for your children, and for all who are far off, as many as the Lord our God will call." And with many other words he testified and strongly urged them, saying, "Be saved from this corrupt generation!"

YOUR TURN

AN AMAZING GIFT

How would you put this sermon into your own words?

DAY 281

THE BIG PICTURE
AC 2:41–3:10

NO BRAINER

TOGETHER

Today's highlighted passage begins, "Now all the believers were together . . . ." This is a simple but profound statement about the early church. Believers thought they needed to gather, so together they ate, helped those in need, and worshiped. In later passages, we read about the teaching that would take place as well. These get-togethers were marked by joy, and, the Bible says that people were coming to faith in Christ as a result of the believers' example and bold witness in the community: "And every day the Lord added to them those who were being saved."

So here's the question: How does that match with your church and your involvement? Unfortunately, believers, especially *young* people, seem to attend church out of obligation rather than desire. That's their habit, and they would feel guilty if they slept in. Or their parents insist that they hop in the car with the rest of the family and make the weekly trek. And studies show that increasingly youth "leave their faith" when they leave home.

Certainly, church services can seem out of touch or boring. But that's because they're comprised of sinners, just like you. No person is perfect; thus we won't find any perfect churches. The real problem is that we often focus on ourselves when we attend, complaining, in effect, that the church doesn't meet *our* needs. We go with the expectation of getting rather than giving. In contrast, the church described in Acts focused on everyone pitching in—helping one another and meeting others' needs.

Consider how your worship experience would change if you chose a different attitude—if you thought about what you could give, whose need you could meet, and how you could help and if you expected to meet God in that place, through the worship services, classes, and people.

Choose church.

SNAPSHOT

ACTS 2:44–47

Now all the believers were together and had everything in common. So they sold their possessions and property and distributed the proceeds to all, as anyone had a need. And every day they devoted themselves to meeting together in the temple complex, and broke bread from house to house. They ate their food with gladness and simplicity of heart, praising God and having favor with all the people. And every day the Lord added to them those who were being saved.

YOUR CHOICE

What can you offer other believers in your local church? How can you use your gifts to serve God and others there?

THE BIG PICTURE

AC 3:11–4:4

OCTOBER 9

DAY 282

SNAPSHOT

ACTS 3:19–21

Therefore repent and turn back, that your sins may be wiped out so that seasons of refreshing may come from the presence of the Lord, and He may send Jesus, who has been appointed Messiah for you. Heaven must welcome Him until the times of the restoration of all things, which God spoke about by the mouth of His holy prophets from the beginning.

ANCHOR POINT

SIN AND RESTORATION

Today's passage is from a sermon. Peter is speaking to a large crowd, many of whom had called for the death of Christ not too long before. Peter, the one who had denied Christ, boldly stands before them and preaches a message of repentance and forgiveness. Even those who had crucified Jesus could know Him.

You can do nothing that would place you outside the scope of God's forgiveness through Christ. Read that sentence again. Let it truly sink into your heart and mind. What an amazing truth! Nothing you do can remove you from that great gift, as long as you turn away from your sin and turn to Christ.

This doesn't mean we can do anything we want with no consequences. Sin still damages our relationship with God and others. But, praise God, the damage can be repaired. Relationships can be restored. A man who had abandoned and denied Christ preached this message to a crowd of people who had condemned and sent Him to His death, and over 5,000 people repented and believed. God's message and His Spirit have power. Let that power move in your life.

YOUR CHOICE

How can you more fully claim the wonderful forgiveness that is available to you through Christ?

OCTOBER 10

DAY 283

THE BIG PICTURE

AC 4:5–22

SNAPSHOT

ACTS 4:13–14

When they observed the boldness of Peter and John and realized that they were uneducated and untrained men, they were amazed and knew that they had been with Jesus. And since they saw the man who had been healed standing with them, they had nothing to say in response.

TOUGH CHOICE

CREATION

The clock above the door flashed 12:00 P.M. as the lunch bell rang.

"Kelsey, I'd like to talk to you, if you have a moment," said Mr. LaLonde, my Biology teacher, from his desk.

"Sure thing, Mr. LaLonde. What about?" I said, as my stomach grumbled.

"Kelsey, I'd like to discuss your unit paper on evolution." He flipped through the pages of my paper. Red, handwritten notes dotted the margins. *Not a good sign.*

"Kelsey, I know that you're a Christian and don't agree with evolution, but I'm concerned about some of the comments you made in your paper." I could feel my face growing hot. Mr. LaLonde settled his horn-rimmed glasses on the bridge of his nose. "In the unit evaluation section of the paper, you say: '. . . In my opinion, it is unfair to teach evolution in a course if other beliefs, such as Christianity, are not allocated equal time in the classroom . . .'"

He turned the page. "You go on to say that it was childish and insensitive of me to use comic strips in my lessons because they were degrading to Christians, making them look like buffoons." Mr. LaLonde took his glasses off and stared at me. "You called me *childish*?"

I fidgeted with the straps on my backpack. The assignment had been to write an overview of evolution, followed by an evaluation of how the unit had been taught. As a Christian, I had taken offense to some of the demeaning comments made about Christianity and the fact that the theory had been presented as truth. I couldn't *not* make comments in my paper. Still, I questioned whether I should have typed such bold statements.

"I'm sorry, Mr. LaLonde. I shouldn't have used that wording. It was disrespectful." I paused. "But I *am* serious about the statements I made."

"Pardon?" he asked, leaning back in his chair.

Come on, Kelsey. Stand up for what you believe is true. "Sir, I don't think that it is sensitive of you to use comic strips in class that belittle Christian views and intelligent design." I chose my words carefully. "It also seems that evolutionary theory shouldn't hold precedence over other theories by getting its own unit in class. There's a lot of scientific evidence supporting Creationism, too." I braced myself for his retort.

"Kelsey, perhaps using the comic strips was not tasteful. I will reconsider using them from now on. But as far as teaching evolution is concerned, it will continue to be part of the curriculum. There are scientific facts that have upheld and continue to uphold evolution. We don't have time to study every possible 'theory' out there, so we study the soundest one. Understand?"

"Sir," I began quietly, "I understand that a lot of people believe in evolution. But I still believe that intelligent design can be supported with scientific data and deserves to be taught, as well."

"Well, I suppose we'll just have to disagree on that point, Kelsey," he said, turning his attention back to a stack of papers needing grading. "And I would appreciate if from now on if you'd be a bit more respectful in your evaluation sections. Good day."

YOUR CHOICE **How can you make a responsible and respectful stand for your faith in a classroom setting?**

AC 4:23–37

SNAPSHOT

ACTS 4:32–37

Now the multitude of those who believed were of one heart and soul, and no one said that any of his possessions was his own, but instead they held everything in common. And with great power the apostles were giving testimony to the resurrection of the Lord Jesus, and great grace was on all of them. For there was not a needy person among them, because all those who owned lands or houses sold them, brought the proceeds of the things that were sold, and laid them at the apostles' feet. This was then distributed to each person as anyone had a need.

Joseph, a Levite and a Cypriot by birth, whom the apostles named Barnabas, which is translated Son of Encouragement, sold a field he owned, brought the money, and laid it at the apostles' feet.

JUST LIKE ME

BARNABAS: LIVING UP TO HIS NAME

Got a nickname? How closely does that nickname resemble your personality? Many try to escape from unwanted childhood nicknames, some of which stem from a deserved or undeserved reputation. But Joseph, a Levite from Cyprus, didn't have to escape his nickname. Being known as Barnabas, or the "Son of Encouragement," fully encapsulated his life of service.

Having encouraged the apostles by his generous offering, Barnabas later encouraged the newly converted Saul (Paul) despite the suspicions of the other believers in Jerusalem (Ac 9:27). His work of encouragement continued when he was sent by the church leaders in Jerusalem to Antioch to encourage Gentile believers in the newly formed church. Who better to send than "a good man, full of the Holy Spirit and of faith" (Ac 11:24)?

Barnabas's partnership with Paul began with teaching the believers in Antioch. Soon, he and Saul were the go-to guys to encourage believers during a famine (Ac 11:29–30; 12:25). And when the time came to send missionaries from Antioch, the Holy Spirit handpicked Barnabas to travel with Saul (Ac 13:2).

Barnabas honored God's name by being a credit to his own. Perhaps you don't have a name full of meaning like Barnabas. But you have the opportunity to be an encouragement to others and a credit to the name of God.

YOUR CHOICE

How can you be a "Barnabas" to someone this week?

DAY 285

SNAPSHOT

ACTS 5:12–16

Many signs and wonders were being done among the people through the hands of the apostles. By common consent they would all meet in Solomon's Colonnade. None of the rest dared to join them, but the people praised them highly. Believers were added to the Lord in increasing numbers—crowds of both men and women. As a result, they would carry the sick out into the streets and lay them on beds and pallets so that when Peter came by, at least his shadow might fall on some of them. In addition, a multitude came together from the towns surrounding Jerusalem, bringing sick people and those who were tormented by unclean spirits, and they were all healed.

YOUR CHOICE

In what ways have you experienced God's healing?

TOUGH QUESTION

I READ ABOUT ALL THE "SIGNS AND WONDERS" IN THE EARLY CHURCH. I WANT TO ENCOURAGE A HURTING FRIEND THAT GOD STILL HEALS, BUT I'M NOT SURE HE DOES. WHAT SHOULD I SAY?

Because we don't see blind people regain their sight and crippled people jump up and run, we may wonder if God still performs miracles. We know God has done this in the past, in Bible times. In fact, one of the signs of Jesus' divinity was the fact that He performed miracles. But did all that stop back in the first century?

The answer is, no—God *still* heals people. The Bible encourages Christians to pray for healing (Jms 5:13–18). God often answers those prayers through doctors and medicine. But often a recovery will baffle the medical community, and the only answer is "miracle."

God also heals mentally, socially, emotionally, and spiritually. After the creation, Adam and Eve knew no sickness, suffering, or death in the Garden of Eden. When they disobeyed God, sin entered the world, causing separation from God, and every person was born a sinner. Because our world is fallen, we experience sickness, accidents, terrorism, natural disasters, and many other terrible results of the Fall.

The world is not as God intended it to be, but some day it will be. One day He will restore creation in the new heaven and new earth. In the meantime, God wants to restore our relationship with Him—the ultimate healing. All who trust in Jesus can be spiritually healed.

God also heals people from sin done to them. Psalm 147:3 states, "He heals the brokenhearted and binds up their wounds."

So what do we say to someone who has pleaded with God to heal a loved one, and nothing has happened? First, trust God. He is good and is working for good even when things look bad and feel worse (Rm 8:28). Second, look beyond this life. Eternal life with God awaits all those who know the Son, and in heaven we will experience no more pain, suffering, or tears (Rv 21:4).

THE BIG PICTURE

AC 5:17–42

OCTOBER 13

DAY 286

SNAPSHOT

ACTS 5:29–32

But Peter and the apostles replied, "We must obey God rather than men. The God of our fathers raised up Jesus, whom you had murdered by hanging Him on a tree. God exalted this man to His right hand as ruler and Savior, to grant repentance to Israel, and forgiveness of sins. We are witnesses of these things, and so is the Holy Spirit whom God has given to those who obey Him."

DEPOSIT

WORDS FROM GOD'S WORD TO STORE IN YOUR MIND AND HEART

"There is salvation in no one else, for there is no other name under heaven given to people by which we must be saved" (Acts 4:12).

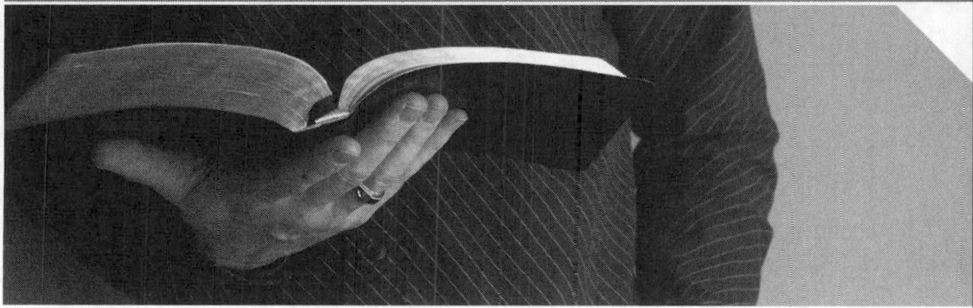

DAY 287

THE BIG PICTURE

AC 6:1–15

SNAPSHOT

ACTS 6:3–7

"Therefore, brothers, select from among you seven men of good reputation, full of the Spirit and wisdom, whom we can appoint to this duty. But we will devote ourselves to prayer and to the preaching ministry." The proposal pleased the whole company. So they chose Stephen, a man full of faith and the Holy Spirit, and Philip, Prochorus, Nicanor, Timon, Parmenas, and Nicolaus, a proselyte from Antioch. They had them stand before the apostles, who prayed and laid their hands on them.

So the preaching about God flourished, the number of the disciples in Jerusalem multiplied greatly, and a large group of priests became obedient to the faith.

YOUR TURN

SPECIAL SERVANT

What specific responsibilities do you have in your local church?

TOUGH QUESTION

HOW CAN I KNOW WHEN TO SPEAK UP AND WHEN TO KEEP QUIET? CAN'T I JUST TAKE A STAND THROUGH MY ACTIONS?

Noise and information assault us continually—iPods, radio, TV, Internet, text messages, calls—and we can feel overwhelmed. God says there is "a time to be silent and a time to speak" (Ec 3:7), so we need discernment to know when to speak and, perhaps add to the noise, and when to let our actions speak for themselves. Breaking through the clutter isn't easy.

Often our actions can speak louder than our words. First John 3:18 encourages, "Little children, we must not love in word or speech, but in deed and truth." And consistent actions over time will give us credibility with friends, family, and coworkers that will result in their trust. When we become known as trustworthy, people will seek us out for counsel and answers to their questions. Solid relationships earn us the right to be heard and that's the ideal time to speak.

One of the problems with speaking *first* is that we lay ourselves open to the charge of hypocrisy. A young man came home from an amazing camp experience and announced to his friends and family that he had "become a Christian" and that they needed to as well. His parents responded defensively with "What do you think we are?" His friends' responses said, in effect, "You're not so good . . . " and then began to point out his flaws. The young man needed to first *live out* his faith. Then, when his parents and friends saw the change and asked what happened, he could humbly share the gospel.

Words are important, however. Eventually we will have the opportunity to speak up, to take our stand, to explain what we believe. When the Holy Spirit prompts us to do so, we need to obey. If we have built a relational and example "bridge," we need to cross it.

SNAPSHOT

ACTS 7:1–5

"Is this true?" the high priest asked.

"Brothers and fathers," he said, "listen: The God of glory appeared to our father Abraham when he was in Mesopotamia, before he settled in Haran, and said to him: Get out of your country and away from your relatives, and come to the land that I will show you.

"Then he came out of the land of the Chaldeans and settled in Haran. And from there, after his father died, God had him move to this land in which you now live. He didn't give him an inheritance in it, not even a foot of ground, but He promised to give it to him as a possession, and to his descendants after him, even though he was childless."

YOUR CHOICE

What kind of example are you setting for those who know you best? What do they know about God and your values by how you act?

DAY 289

SNAPSHOT

ACTS 7:54–60

When they heard these things, they were enraged in their hearts and gnashed their teeth at him. But Stephen, filled by the Holy Spirit, gazed into heaven. He saw God's glory, with Jesus standing at the right hand of God, and he said, "Look! I see the heavens opened and the Son of Man standing at the right hand of God!"

Then they screamed at the top of their voices, stopped their ears, and rushed together against him. They threw him out of the city and began to stone him. And the witnesses laid their robes at the feet of a young man named Saul. They were stoning Stephen as he called out: "Lord Jesus, receive my spirit!" Then he knelt down and cried out with a loud voice, "Lord, do not charge them with this sin!" And saying this, he fell asleep.

JUST LIKE ME

STEPHEN: THE RISK OF TRUTH TELLING

At the end of the year retrospectives dominate the newsstands and news broadcasts. These "looks back" shine the light of truth on a year, a decade, or a lifetime. Through these accounts, we can see how far we've come and how far we need to go. But as was proved through Stephen's experience, some retrospectives go unheeded.

Stephen rose into prominence as a result of the controversy over the Greek-speaking widows who missed out on food distribution. Although he was known for being a man of good repute "full of faith and the Holy Spirit" (Ac 6:5), Stephen was accused of blasphemy by men who were jealous of his eloquence.

Like Jesus, Stephen was a purveyor of truth, and he took a stand for truth when giving his defense. His retrospective began with the lives of the patriarchs—Abraham, Isaac, Jacob, and Jacob's sons—and included a side trip through the life and ministry of Moses. But the laser of truth was too much for Stephen's listeners. Instead of heeding the lesson of history, they decided to kill the messenger.

Truth can anger or soothe. But once truth is internalized, it does not leave a person unchanged. The men who sought Stephen's death thought they could do away with the mirror he held up to their lives. But the image of truth remained.

We can try to ignore truth, harden ourselves against it, or allow it to soften us and chip away at our pride. Only then can we be useful.

YOUR CHOICE:

How do you react to truth?
What might it cost you to take a stand for truth?

ACTS 8:9–13

SNAPSHOT

OCTOBER 17

DAY 290

THE BIG PICTURE

AC 8:1–25

A man named Simon had previously practiced sorcery in that city and astounded the Samaritan people, while claiming to be somebody great. They all paid attention to him, from the least of them to the greatest, and they said, "This man is called the Great Power of God!" They were attentive to him because he had astounded them with his sorceries for a long time. But when they believed Philip, as he proclaimed the good news about the kingdom of God and the name of Jesus Christ, both men and women were baptized. Then even Simon himself believed. And after he was baptized, he went around constantly with Philip and was astounded as he observed the signs and great miracles that were being performed.

TOUGH CHOICE

MEDICAL SCHOOL

Jill and I wove our way through the rows of wooden graduation chairs, which had been set up on the main quad for the big event.

"Gingie, I am so lost," said Jill, in stride next to me. "I've kind of been second-guessing my med school decision the last couple days."

I looked sideways at her. "Like, which schools you applied to?" Jill had spent the entirety of our junior year studying for the MCATs and preparing her med school applications. She had always known that she wanted to be a doctor.

"No." She hesitated. "Gingie, I don't know if I'm supposed to go to med school."

I stopped in my tracks. "Are you crazy, Jill? Of course you are. You've worked harder than anyone else I know. Med schools are going to be tripping over one another to get their hands on you."

Jill sat down in one of the chairs. I sat down next to her. A large oak tree cast a pleasant bit of shade around us. "Thanks, Gingie. That means a lot."

"Where's this doubt coming from?" I asked. "You still want to be a doctor, don't you?"

"Yes, I think so." She rested her elbows on her knees and let her face fall into her hands. "But I also know that I want to be a wife and a mom. What if I can't do both? What if I get part way through school and have to quit?"

"Jill," I interjected, "you can't make decisions and live based on 'what-ifs'! You'll drive yourself mad."

"I hate this, Gingie." Jill sat back up in her chair. "I've always been in control of my life and pursuits. I've known what I wanted and gone after it. Why would God suddenly leave me stranded at this crossroads?"

"You're not stranded, Jill," I said quietly. "The Lord's still standing right beside you. Maybe this is His way of recapturing your attention. No matter how sure you are of your future, you still need to depend on Christ."

Jill slouched in her chair, looking up at the oak branches. "I just don't want to make the wrong decision and fail."

"You won't, Jill. If you trust the Lord, He will open the right doors at the right time. If that means getting two years into med school and realizing that it's not going to work out, trust that there's a reason for it. We only fail when we convince ourselves that we can do a better job at controlling our lives than God."

Jill looked at me sheepishly. "I know you're right; it's just so hard to let go of that control at times. Makes me feel crazy."

"Yes," I laughed, "you are crazy. But not because you desire control—because you are voluntarily signing up for eight more years of school!"

YOUR CHOICE **How do you determine what God wants for your future? What role does the counsel of trusted friends play in the process?**

DAY 291

THE BIG PICTURE
AC 8:26–40

SNAPSHOT

ACTS 8:36–40

As they were traveling down the road, they came to some water. The eunuch said, "Look, there's water! What would keep me from being baptized?" And Philip said, "If you believe with all your heart you may." And he replied, "I believe that Jesus Christ is the Son of God." Then he ordered the chariot to stop, and both Philip and the eunuch went down into the water, and he baptized him. When they came up out of the water, the Spirit of the Lord carried Philip away, and the eunuch did not see him any longer. But he went on his way rejoicing. Philip appeared in Azotus, and passing through, he was evangelizing all the towns until he came to Caesarea.

ANCHOR POINT

UNEXPECTED APPOINTMENT

Philip was able to connect with the Ethiopian official and explain the gospel of Christ to him because he was listening to the voice of God and he knew the Word of God. Twice in this passage, we read that Philip heard and responded to direction from God. First, an angel told him to "get up and go south" (Ac 8:26). Then, the Holy Spirit directed him to run and catch up with a chariot. What is interesting here is that these were not overly spiritual commands. Philip wasn't told to hold a massive demonstration, speak to thousands, or claim a city for God. "Go south and jump on that chariot" are fairly common statements. Yet Philip's obedience helped spread the gospel to another part of the world.

Are you listening for God's voice? He may be asking you to do something relatively small and simple, such as to sit next to a certain classmate, befriend the new kid, or help a neighbor. Are you ready for the seemingly small assignments?

After taking those small steps, Philip took the next ones and clearly shared about Christ. God knows where His path will lead. We just need to walk, one step at a time.

YOUR CHOICE

How can you practice listening for God to direct your path? What more can you do to prepare yourself to present the gospel to others?

SNAPSHOT

ACTS 9:1–4

Meanwhile Saul, still breathing threats and murder against the disciples of the Lord, went to the high priest and requested letters from him to the synagogues in Damascus, so that if he found any who belonged to the Way, either men or women, he might bring them as prisoners to Jerusalem. As he traveled and was nearing Damascus, a light from heaven suddenly flashed around him. Falling to the ground, he heard a voice saying to him, "Saul, Saul, why are you persecuting Me?"

YOUR CHOICE

Who have you written off as a lost cause? What "enemies" do you need to add to your prayer list?

NO BRAINER

WHAT A CHANGE!

If you were a follower of Christ, a member of what this passage refers to as "the Way," you tried to avoid Saul. He was obsessed with hunting down believers and bringing them back to Jerusalem to be tried as heretics. Saul was a devout and highly trained Jew who thought Christians believed and taught a false religion and that they must be stopped. Yet suddenly we read about him "proclaiming Jesus in the synagogues: 'He is the Son of God'" (Ac 9:20). And eventually Saul (the apostle Paul) became the greatest Christian missionary, church planter, and teacher/preacher of all time and, incidentally, the writer of thirteen of our New Testament books.

How could someone change directions so dramatically? Because of God—Saul met Christ in person, on the road to Damascus.

That's not how it always happens. In fact, the conversion experience for the vast majority of believers is much less dramatic—no blinding lights or voices from heaven. But the result is the same: God begins transforming the person through the Holy Spirit. As Paul described, "Therefore if anyone is in Christ, there is a new creation; old things have passed away, and look, new things have come" (2 Co 5:17).

The important point is not *how* God transformed Saul but that He bothered at all. And it highlights this important truth: No one is beyond God's reach.

It's easy to dismiss someone as hopeless, especially those who mock our Lord and persecute us for believing in Him. We learn from Saul's example that that's a mistake. And, let's be honest, at times we don't want them to discover the truth. Like Jonah, we like the idea of them being judged for their sins. But Jesus says, "Love your enemies and pray for those who persecute you" (Mt 5:44).

So don't give up on that "enemy." He or she just might be the next "Saul."

OCTOBER 20

DAY 293

THE BIG PICTURE

AC 9:20–31

SNAPSHOT

ACTS 9:26–30

When he arrived in Jerusalem, he tried to associate with the disciples, but they were all afraid of him, since they did not believe he was a disciple. Barnabas, however, took him and brought him to the apostles and explained to them how, on the road, Saul had seen the Lord, and that He had talked to him, and how in Damascus he had spoken boldly in the name of Jesus. Saul was coming and going with them in Jerusalem, speaking boldly in the name of the Lord. He conversed and debated with the Hellenistic Jews, but they attempted to kill him. When the brothers found out, they took him down to Caesarea and sent him off to Tarsus.

DEPOSIT

WORDS FROM GOD'S WORD TO STORE IN YOUR MIND AND HEART

But the Lord said to him, "Go! For this man is My chosen instrument to carry My name before Gentiles, kings, and the sons of Israel. I will certainly show him how much he must suffer for My name!" (Acts 9:15–16).

AC 9:32–42

DAY 294

SNAPSHOT

ACTS 9:32–35

As Peter was traveling from place to place, he also came down to the saints who lived in Lydda. There he found a man named Aeneas, who was paralyzed and had been bedridden for eight years. Peter said to him, "Aeneas, Jesus Christ heals you. Get up and make your own bed," and immediately he got up. So all who lived in Lydda and Sharon saw him and turned to the Lord.

YOUR TURN

MEETING NEEDS

This past week, what special ability did you use to meet someone's need?

THE BIG PICTURE
AC 10:1–23

SNAPSHOT

ACTS 10:1–8

There was a man in Caesarea named Cornelius, a centurion of what was called the Italian Regiment. He was a devout man and feared God along with his whole household. He did many charitable deeds for the Jewish people and always prayed to God. At about three in the afternoon he distinctly saw in a vision an angel of God who came in and said to him, "Cornelius!"

Looking intently at him, he became afraid and said, "What is it, Lord?"

And he told him, "Your prayers and your acts of charity have come up as a memorial offering before God. Now send men to Joppa and call for Simon, who is also named Peter. He is lodging with Simon, a tanner, whose house is by the sea."

When the angel who spoke to him had gone, he called two of his household slaves and a devout soldier, who was one of those who attended him. After explaining everything to them, he sent them to Joppa.

JUST LIKE ME

CORNELIUS: GOOD, BUT NOT GOOD ENOUGH

Ever been the best at something? We often walk the tightrope between being humble and avoiding false modesty. What helps is to have someone speak truth into our lives to help us gain perspective.

Cornelius, a first-century Roman centurion, could have coasted through life on his unimpeachable reputation among his own people and the people of Israel. After all, a Roman legionnaire rose to the rank of centurion by having great connections and by simply being the best of the best. But having added "God-fearer" to his résumé, Cornelius left himself open to God's critique.

Although God was pleased by Cornelius's humility and generosity, even a good man like him was not good enough to save himself. Only Jesus was good enough to secure salvation at the cost of *His* life. Cornelius needed the new life offered through the Holy Spirit. After a sermon delivered by a once-reluctant Peter, Cornelius found himself on the receiving end of grace.

Even the wisest person knows that he or she still has much to learn. Cornelius eagerly accepted the eternal life he was not good enough to earn. Are you open to that possibility?

YOUR CHOICE

What has God been teaching you lately?

SNAPSHOT

ACTS 10:44–48

While Peter was still speaking these words, the Holy Spirit came down on all those who heard the message. The circumcised believers who had come with Peter were astounded, because the gift of the Holy Spirit had been poured out on the Gentiles also. For they heard them speaking in other languages and declaring the greatness of God.

Then Peter responded, "Can anyone withhold water and prevent these from being baptized, who have received the Holy Spirit just as we have?" And he commanded them to be baptized in the name of Jesus Christ. Then they asked him to stay for a few days.

YOUR CHOICE

What kinds of people would you least like to talk to about Christ? Why? What can you do to remove that barrier?

NO BRAINER

ALL IN THE FAMILY

Peter was kosher; that is, he was Jewish through and through, as were all the apostles and other church leaders. And though the Jewish community, especially the religious leaders, rejected Jesus as the Messiah and repudiated the growing group of Christ followers, the early church was essentially a Jewish movement—as though a "No Gentiles Allowed" sign had been posted.

But through a dramatic dream and God's prodding and leading, Peter overcame his prejudice and ventured into foreign territory. There, in a Gentile home, he declared, "In truth, I understand that God doesn't show favoritism, but in every nation the person who fears Him and does righteousness is acceptable to Him" (Ac 10:34–35). Then, immediately, we see Cornelius, a Roman army officer no less, confessing Jesus as Lord and receiving the Holy Spirit.

The news of Gentiles confessing Jesus and receiving the Spirit was difficult for the early church to accept, as we see in Acts 11 and beyond. But eventually they relented and commissioned courageous missionaries like Barnabas, Silas, and Paul to take the gospel beyond Jerusalem, making disciples of "all nations" (Mt 28:19).

What keeps the church from taking the Good News to certain types of people today? What keeps you? Or we could ask what kind of people would *not* feel welcomed in your church or Christian group.

A wide variety of barriers divide us from others: race, economic status, clique or social group, language or accent, moral reputation, politics, geography. It take courage to walk across the cafeteria and sit with "those kids," to befriend the outcast, to visit the junkie, or to invite "them" to your party.

May we learn, with Peter, that "God doesn't show favoritism," and break down those barriers for Christ. After all, they're family!

SNAPSHOT

ACTS 11:15–18

"As I began to speak, the Holy Spirit came down on them, just as on us at the beginning. Then I remembered the word of the Lord, how He said, 'John baptized with water, but you will be baptized with the Holy Spirit.' Therefore, if God gave them the same gift that He also gave to us when we believed on the Lord Jesus Christ, how could I possibly hinder God?"

When they heard this they became silent. Then they glorified God, saying, "So God has granted repentance resulting in life to even the Gentiles!"

YOUR CHOICE

For what causes would you consider making a public protest?

TOUGH QUESTION

I REALLY FEEL STRONGLY ABOUT A CERTAIN SOCIAL ISSUE AND THINK I SHOULD JOIN A PUBLIC PROTEST, BUT I'M AFRAID. WHAT SHOULD I DO?

Joining a public protest is a difficult decision to make because it puts the person out there, in view, and on record as standing against something. So fear is a natural response.

Before making a decision, examine the reasons for your fear. Do you fear being seen by your friends? Are you afraid of being punished or beat up? Taking a public stand for social issues may come with a price, sometimes a steep one. Some people have lost friends; others have lost jobs; in some countries, people have been physically harmed. Not only is your fear natural, it's not wrong. We always need to count the cost of our actions.

Next, search Scripture regarding the issue in question to make sure that what you are standing for is biblically based. Choose your battles carefully. Your friends may want to march on the administration to protest cafeteria food, for example, but that's not nearly as important as marching against racism, abortion, or genocide. If you join every protest, you won't be taken seriously.

Protesting in a biblical way is also important. A great irony is seeing the rage-contorted face of someone protesting for peace, or people marching for the environment and leaving litter in their wake. And make sure that the protest will be peaceful, not violent.

Another consideration is whether your involvement will help bring people to Christ. If this protest will offend and turn people off, not only to the issue, but also to Christ, you probably shouldn't participate.

On the other hand, at times you will be called to take a stand for Christ. And if taking that stand means protesting publicly, then do it. Ask God to give you courage and strength and to use you to make a difference for His kingdom.

ACTS 11:27–30

SNAPSHOT

In those days some prophets came down from Jerusalem to Antioch. Then one of them, named Agabus, stood up and predicted by the Spirit that there would be a severe famine throughout the Roman world. This took place during the time of Claudius. So each of the disciples, according to his ability, determined to send relief to the brothers who lived in Judea. This they did, sending it to the elders by means of Barnabas and Saul.

OCTOBER 25

DAY 298

THE BIG PICTURE

AC 11:19–30

TOUGH CHOICE

ETHIOPIA

"Tall Rob!" A dark-skinned, Ethiopian boy bounded into the small room, where I was lacing up my tennis shoes. "Come wit' me," he said, eagerly grabbing my hand. "Come wit' me to de river bank!"

I laughed, hurrying out of the room and into the hot, Ethiopian morning behind Steven. Down by the river bank, where the children at St. Luke's orphanage enjoyed playing in the cool water and shade, a small group had congregated around what appeared to be a collection of brush and branches.

"Tall Rob," said Eda, as she scrambled up a rock and leaped onto my back, "we found de branches for de foosball."

I stared at the brush pile, heaped inside the circle of bare feet. Sure enough, they had collected the long, thin branches we still needed for the poles of our foosball table. "Good job! These are perfect. How long did it take you to collect all these?"

The smiles on their faces broadened, as they clapped their hands in satisfaction. "Not so long," said Steven. "Now we are ready to build de table? Yes?"

None of the children at the orphanage had ever heard of foosball before our mission team had arrived at the orphanage eight months earlier. After I showed them a picture of my college buddies and me playing, however, they had been curious and excited to learn this game for themselves.

"I think . . ." I said slowly, "that we are ready to begin!"

Over the next week, I awoke each morning to: "Tall Rob, it's time to get up and work on de table!" Our little group measured, cut, and nailed together the pieces of mismatched wood; and by the end of the week, our creation actually resembled a foosball table.

"Tall Rob," said Steven, who was perched atop a rock and diligently focusing upon the little, whittled man he was painting green, "dis is you." He held up the figure. "See?"

I stared at the miniature man. He looked just like all the other green and yellow men that the kids had been painting. "Steven, he kind of looks like all the other figures," I chuckled.

"No, Tall Rob. Look close!" He held his hand close to my nose and pointed at the figure's face. "See? He has a big smile like you. And you know why he is smiling?"

"Because he's really good-looking like me?" I laughed.

"No! Because he loves Jesus like you. Jesus makes him happy like He makes you happy."

I took the green foosball player in my hand. The paint was still wet. "It's perfect, Steven," I said quietly. And it was. As we assembled the twenty-six little foosball players onto the table that afternoon, I recognized how true Steven's words were. I was happy. And I was happy because of Jesus. Living in a poverty-stricken country on the opposite side of the world from my home was not always easy. But watching the elation on the faces of these young Ethiopian orphans as they played their first, simple foosball game was true joy. *Thank you, God, for letting these children know joy.*

YOUR CHOICE **How do you think God might use you to make a difference in the world?**

THE BIG PICTURE
AC 12:1–25

SNAPSHOT

ACTS 12:6–8

On the night before Herod was to bring him out for execution, Peter was sleeping between two soldiers, bound with two chains, while the sentries in front of the door guarded the prison. Suddenly an angel of the Lord appeared, and a light shone in the cell. Striking Peter on the side, he woke him up and said, "Quick, get up!" Then the chains fell off his wrists. "Get dressed," the angel told him, "and put on your sandals." And he did so. "Wrap your cloak around you," he told him, "and follow me."

ANCHOR POINT

A GREAT ESCAPE

In this passage we see an interesting dichotomy. Peter, freed from prison by an angel in the middle of the night, is led by that angel past guards and right out the gates of the city, which open by themselves! An angelic rescue mission—all because people prayed, and God answered by sending His messenger.

Right after this incredible story, we read about haughty, arrogant Herod (Ac 12:20–24). Setting himself up as a god, he pays the price for his pride. God again sends a messenger, though this time it is a messenger of death. The angel simply strikes Herod and he dies, infected with worms. This is an interesting corollary to the first story and a stark contrast. One man was a prisoner facing possible execution; the other man was a rich and powerful ruler. God rescues one and kills the other.

Obviously God has great power, both to rescue and to punish. "The fear of the LORD is the beginning of wisdom" (Ps. 111:10) because when we begin to understand God, we realize that He is not a little, feel-good god who we can keep on hand to help us out from time to time. He is the God of the universe, and He will not be trifled with.

We serve an all-powerful, sovereign God. And He chooses to use us to do His work. Awesome!

YOUR CHOICE

What has caused you to stand in awe of God? In what ways does His might give you courage and hope?

AC 13:1–12

OCTOBER 27

DAY 300

SNAPSHOT

ACTS 13:1–3

In the local church at Antioch there were prophets and teachers: Barnabas, Simeon who was called Niger, Lucius the Cyrenian, Manaen, a close friend of Herod the tetrarch, and Saul.

As they were ministering to the Lord and fasting, the Holy Spirit said, "Set apart for Me Barnabas and Saul for the work that I have called them to." Then, after they had fasted, prayed, and laid hands on them, they sent them off.

DEPOSIT

WORDS FROM GOD'S WORD TO STORE IN YOUR MIND AND HEART

Then he [Barnabas] went to Tarsus to search for Saul, and when he found him he brought him to Antioch. For a whole year they met with the church and taught large numbers, and the disciples were first called Christians in Antioch (Acts 11:25–26).

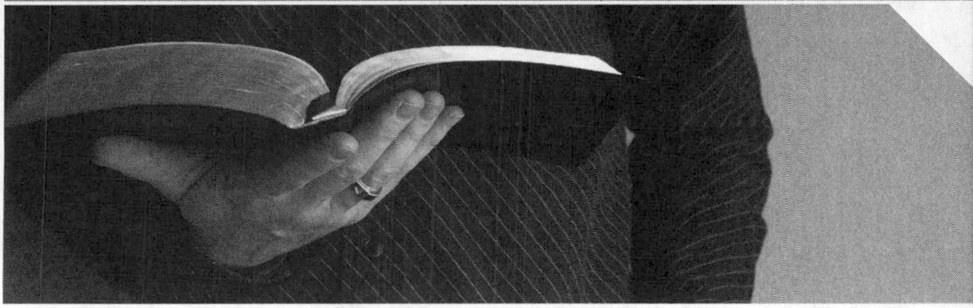

DAY 301

AC 14:1–28

SNAPSHOT

ACTS 14:19–22

Then some Jews came from Antioch and Iconium, and when they had won over the crowds and stoned Paul, they dragged him out of the city, thinking he was dead. After the disciples surrounded him, he got up and went into the town. The next day he left with Barnabas for Derbe.

After they had evangelized that town and made many disciples, they returned to Lystra, to Iconium, and to Antioch, strengthening the hearts of the disciples by encouraging them to continue in the faith, and by telling them, "It is necessary to pass through many troubles on our way into the kingdom of God."

YOUR TURN

RESPONSE AND REACTION

How does the gospel act like Good News in your life?

AC 15:1–21

TOUGH QUESTION

OBVIOUSLY LEADERS LIKE PAUL AND PETER IN THE EARLY CHURCH WORKED HARD AT BREAKING DOWN BARRIERS BETWEEN PEOPLE. WHY DO RACE, NATIONALITY, STATUS, AND OTHER FACTORS DIVIDE CHRISTIANS TODAY? WHAT CAN I DO ABOUT IT?

Until we are in heaven with Jesus, strife and division between groups of people will exist. That's because we humans are finite and sinful. We don't see people the way God sees them. Humans classify and rank people, but "the LORD sees the heart" (1 Sm 16:7). This problem isn't limited to nonbelievers; Christians have this tendency as well—it comes with our sinful nature. In fact, that's one of the topics addressed by James (Jms 2:1–9). So we should ask God to help us see people as He sees them.

Remembering that God is the judge, not us, can also help prevent us from creating and maintaining barriers. Paul wrote to the Christians in Rome on this topic: "Therefore, anyone of you who judges is without excuse. For when you judge another, you condemn yourself, since you, the judge, do the same things. We know that God's judgment on those who do such things is based on the truth" (Rm 2:1–2). Our place isn't to judge others but to love them and point them to Christ through our "speech, in conduct, in love, in faith, in purity" (1 Tm 4:12).

As we grow in our relationship with God, the Holy Spirit will make us sensitive to sin in our lives. So we shouldn't be surprised if we become increasingly aware of incidents of discrimination and frustrated with this problem. We can stand against this sin by refusing to discriminate and to break down those prejudicial barriers when we find them. This may involve walking across the cafeteria and sitting with an outcast student, making friends with someone of another race or nationality, going to a social event in that "wrong" side of town, or something similar. We should ask God for direction in breaking down those walls.

SNAPSHOT

ACTS 15:7–11

After there had been much debate, Peter stood up and said to them: 'Brothers, you are aware that in the early days God made a choice among you, that by my mouth the Gentiles would hear the gospel message and believe. And God, who knows the heart, testified to them by giving the Holy Spirit, just as He also did to us. He made no distinction between us and them, cleansing their hearts by faith. Why, then, are you now testing God by putting on the disciples' necks a yoke that neither our forefathers nor we have been able to bear? On the contrary, we believe we are saved through the grace of the Lord Jesus, in the same way they are."

YOUR CHOICE

What artificial barriers do you see in your social circles? How about at church? What can you do to break down those walls?

DAY 303

AC 15:22–41

SNAPSHOT

ACTS 15:36–41

After some time had passed, Paul said to Barnabas, "Let's go back and visit the brothers in every town where we have preached the message of the Lord, and see how they're doing." Barnabas wanted to take along John Mark. But Paul did not think it appropriate to take along this man who had deserted them in Pamphylia and had not gone on with them to the work. There was such a sharp disagreement that they parted company, and Barnabas took Mark with him and sailed off to Cyprus. Then Paul chose Silas and departed, after being commended to the grace of the Lord by the brothers. He traveled through Syria and Cilicia, strengthening the churches.

ANCHOR POINT

RELATIONALLY CHALLENGED

Paul was right—John Mark (also known as Mark, the writer of the Gospel that bears his name) had left them in Pamphylia. He had quit the work and had simply walked away. Mark had broken their trust, so Paul did not want to include him on this trip.

Barnabas was correct—John Mark was a young man and deserved to get a second chance. He needed the opportunity to prove himself and restore the trust he had broken.

Have you ever found yourself in such a disagreement? On one hand, you have the right to be upset and hold your position. You can see, however, that the other side also has merit. How do you respond, typically, in such a situation? Can you rise above your personal feelings and try to see all sides?

Relationships come with conflicts, and determining who is correct is not always clear. The challenge is to be able to deal constructively with the issue and to be able to move on in forgiveness when it is over. That's what happened with Paul, Barnabas, and Mark. The mission continued with Barnabas taking Mark under his wing. And during Paul's last days, in a Roman prison, he wrote to Timothy, "Bring Mark with you, for he is useful to me in the ministry" (2 Tm 4:11).

YOUR CHOICE

How do you deal with conflict with a fellow Christian? What can you do to resolve the conflict and keep focused on the mission?

THE BIG PICTURE

AC 16:1–15

OCTOBER 31

DAY 304

SNAPSHOT

ACTS 16:13–15

On the Sabbath day we went outside the city gate by the river, where we thought there was a place of prayer. We sat down and spoke to the women gathered there. A woman named Lydia, a dealer in purple cloth from the city of Thyatira, who worshiped God, was listening. The Lord opened her heart to pay attention to what was spoken by Paul. After she and her household were baptized, she urged us, "If you consider me a believer in the Lord, come and stay at my house." And she persuaded us.

JUST LIKE ME

PAUL AND SILAS: PICKING PRAISE OVER POUTING

When we perform a good deed, we hope that good comes from it. After all, we reap what we sow, right? But sometimes bad things happen to good people, as the lives of missionaries like Paul and Silas show.

Having cast a spirit out of a fortune-telling slave girl, Paul and Silas were rewarded by a severe beating and imprisonment. They were doing God's work and were almost killed for their efforts. The immediate lack of profit greatly offended the owners of the slave girl. While such a trial would have caused many of us to complain, Paul and Silas chose to praise instead of pout. In this way, they showed their submission to God's sovereignty. Their praise reaped a harvest of freedom: physical freedom for themselves through supernatural means and spiritual freedom for the jailer.

Jesus promised His followers that "you will have suffering in this world" (Jn 16:33). Yet how many times do we rage when persecution happens as a result of our faithfulness to God? But Paul reminds us that "all things work together for the good of those who love God: those who are called according to His purpose" (Rm 8:28). We can choose to either trust God through a trial or allow the trial to bury us in bitterness.

YOUR CHOICE

How has God used a trial to draw you closer to Him?

NOVEMBER
NOVEMBRE
NOVEMBER
NOVEMBER
NOVEMBRE
NOVEMBRO
NOVEMBRE

AC 16:16–40

SNAPSHOT

ACTS 16:25–31

About midnight Paul and Silas were praying and singing hymns to God, and the prisoners were listening to them. Suddenly there was such a violent earthquake that the foundations of the jail were shaken, and immediately all the doors were opened, and everyone's chains came loose. When the jailer woke up and saw the doors of the prison open, he drew his sword and was going to kill himself, since he thought the prisoners had escaped.

But Paul called out in a loud voice, "Don't harm yourself, because all of us are here!"

Then the jailer called for lights, rushed in, and fell down trembling before Paul and Silas. Then he escorted them out and said, "Sirs, what must I do to be saved?"

So they said, "Believe on the Lord Jesus, and you will be saved—you and your household."

YOUR CHOICE

What do your fellow "prisoners" and your "jailer" know about your relationship with God through your attitudes and other choices?

NO BRAINER

ADVENTURES IN JAIL

Talk about "courageous choices." This chapter in Acts gives us a bunch. We find Paul and Silas (Luke, too) choosing to follow God's leading and taking the gospel to Asia and Europe. We see them choosing to share the message of Christ with everyone and anyone—Jews, Gentiles, men, women, slaves, free, prisoners, guards—all who would listen. Out of compassion, they chose to challenge a local "businessman" and nearly paid for it with their lives at the hands of an angry mob. And, after being arrested, severely beaten, and thrown in jail, they chose to pray and sing in their cells. Finally, they chose *not* to escape when they had the chance.

Because of their courage and their God-honoring choices, Paul and Silas saw God work powerfully through their actions and words.

We probably will never be arrested, beaten, and jailed for being a follower of Christ. But suppose we were, could we—falsely imprisoned, deprived of freedom, and hurting in every muscle and bone—choose to praise God? Most of us would complain about the injustice, wonder why God could allow such suffering, and wallow in self-pity. And in the process, we would miss the opportunity to see God work through us in changing a life, a family, and a community.

So, how are you being falsely accused—perhaps through ridicule or gossip? What form of persecution are you experiencing? When do you feel trapped, imprisoned (on the job, in school, with a circle of friends)? Ask God to give you the courage and power to choose prayer, to choose praise, and to choose joy, giving glory to Him in your trials.

NOVEMBER 2

DAY 306

THE BIG PICTURE

AC 17:1–15

SNAPSHOT

ACTS 17:10–12

As soon as it was night, the brothers sent Paul and Silas off to Beroea. On arrival, they went into the synagogue of the Jews. The people here were more open-minded than those in Thessalonica, since they welcomed the message with eagerness and examined the Scriptures daily to see if these things were so. Consequently, many of them believed, including a number of the prominent Greek women as well as men.

TOUGH CHOICE

FCA

"Thanks for coming out tonight, fellas. Good luck in the game on Saturday." Reverend Carmichael, a former defensive end, stood at the front of the crowded room in the FCA house. He was well-liked and respected by practically every coach and student athlete at the school for his dedication and encouragement to the teams. As such, the majority of the college football team had gathered for his weekly team Bible study.

Reverend Carmichael walked over in my direction as I stood up from my folding chair. "Hey, Reverend. Great talk tonight," I said, shaking his hand.

"Thanks, Logan. Hey, I wanted to ask: Would you and a couple buddies be interested in helping serve food at the FCA fund-raising dinner next week?"

"Sure thing, Reverend. Get me the details, and I'll round up a few guys to come help out."

"Thanks, Logan. Really appreciate it. You have a good night."

"You too." I nodded and bent over to collect my Bible and notes.

"Man, you got suckered into that one." Roger, who had been standing next to me, laughed.

"What are you talking about," I asked, incredulously. "I don't mind helping out."

Roger, whose neck was barely visible between his shoulders and head, folded his arms and tilted his head. "Right. You just didn't want to hurt Reverend Carmichael's feelings. Face it, dude, you just can't say no."

"You know, Roger," I said, "helping people . . . it's not as painful as you might think."

Roger shook his head. "I like Reverend Carmichael, but why should we have to volunteer, do charity events, and serve dinner at fund-raisers?" He rested his hand on my shoulder. "Face it. You're a sucker."

I looked down at his hand. "Roger, do you ever listen to a word that Reverend Carmichael has to say when he's preaching from the Bible?" I asked.

He stepped back. "Of course . . . sort of—if it's interesting."

I stared at him blankly, "If you don't pay attention, why do you come?"

"Coach likes us to come and I can support Reverend Carmichael. Plus, I figure it will make God happy if I show up."

I pulled my Bible out from under my arm. "Roger," I began, thumbing the pages, "I come to Bible study and enjoy helping Reverend Carmichael because of this book. The Bible is God's Word to us. It's truth; it tells of Christ's love for us and how to best live our lives. I study the Bible because I love the Lord and want to live to glorify Him."

Roger stared at the book in my hands, without speaking. He laughed tentatively. "Okay, I follow you. I'll do some reading this week and pay closer attention to the Reverend." He paused, raising his eyebrows and pointing at me, "But don't think this means that you're going to talk me into serving mashed potatoes at that fund-raiser next week."

YOUR CHOICE **How would you respond to someone challenging your motives for going to church and for reading the Bible?**

AC 17:16–34

SNAPSHOT

ACTS 17:16–21

While Paul was waiting for them in Athens, his spirit was troubled within him when he saw that the city was full of idols. So he reasoned in the synagogue with the Jews and with those who worshiped God, and in the marketplace every day with those who happened to be there. Then also, some of the Epicurean and Stoic philosophers argued with him. Some said, "What is this pseudo-intellectual trying to say?"

Others replied, "He seems to be a preacher of foreign deities"—because he was telling the good news about Jesus and the resurrection.

They took him and brought him to the Areopagus, and said, "May we learn about this new teaching you're speaking of? For what you say sounds strange to us, and we want to know what these ideas mean." Now all the Athenians and the foreigners residing there spent their time on nothing else but telling or hearing something new.

DEPOSIT

WORDS FROM GOD'S WORD TO STORE IN YOUR MIND AND HEART

"For as I was passing through and observing the objects of your worship, I even found an altar on which was inscribed: TO AN UNKNOWN GOD. Therefore, what you worship in ignorance, this I proclaim to you" (Ac 17:23).

DAY 308

THE BIG PICTURE

AC 19:1–20

SNAPSHOT

ACTS 19:8–10

Then he entered the synagogue and spoke boldly over a period of three months, engaging in discussion and trying to persuade them about the things related to the kingdom of God. But when some became hardened and would not believe, slandering the Way in front of the crowd, he withdrew from them and met separately with the disciples, conducting discussions every day in the lecture hall of Tyrannus. And this went on for two years, so that all the inhabitants of the province of Asia, both Jews and Greeks, heard the word of the Lord.

YOUR TURN

DISCOURAGEMENT

In what situations are you most likely to become discouraged?

SNAPSHOT

ACTS 19:23–27

During that time there was a major disturbance about the Way. For a person named Demetrius, a silversmith who made silver shrines of Artemis, provided a great deal of business for the craftsmen. When he had assembled them, as well as the workers engaged in this type of business, he said: "Men, you know that our prosperity is derived from this business. You both see and hear that not only in Ephesus, but in almost the whole province of Asia, this man Paul has persuaded and misled a considerable number of people by saying that gods made by hand are not gods! So not only do we run a risk that our business may be discredited, but also that the temple of the great goddess Artemis may be despised and her magnificence come to the verge of ruin—the very one whom the whole province of Asia and the world adore."

YOUR CHOICE

In your future career, when do you think telling the truth might be bad for business? How will you respond when faced with that dilemma?

NO BRAINER

BAD FOR BUSINESS

Imagine a town whose local economy centered on a certain agricultural product. Extracts were used in a wide variety of goods, from pharmaceuticals to fast food because of the amazing testimonials of manufacturers, marketers, and customers. Some citizens grew the grain; others processed it; a company or two shipped it worldwide.

But one day a scientist declared on all the news outlets that the claims were bogus and the grain and its extracts, worthless. The town wouldn't react very positively and would work hard at refuting the scientist's report. Sometimes the truth is bad for business.

That's what Paul discovered in Ephesus. There much of the local commerce centered on the worship of Artemis because that city had a huge temple of the goddess. When Paul began to preach, he gained a small audience and was tolerated by the rest of the Ephesians. But over the months, as his message spread and more people believed and began to follow Christ, business leaders became alarmed—especially "Demetrius, a silversmith who made silver shrines of Artemis" (Ac 19:24). Demetrius claimed, rightly, that Paul was portraying Artemis as a phony god, a worthless idol. This enraged the Artemis merchants. The truth was bad for business.

Today many businesses are patently unchristian (for example, pornography, prostitution, abortion, and organized crime). Other workplaces present unique challenges for followers of Christ. We may be asked to promote something that we know is a lie, to sell a product that we know is worthless, or to engage in shady business practices. At those times and in those places we want to tell the truth, to take a stand. But we know that the truth, God's Truth, will be bad for business, and the consequences for those who tell the truth can be painful—ostracism, unemployment, or worse.

Sometimes, however, that's the choice we must make. We know, however, that God has put us there for a reason and that we must obey Him.

SNAPSHOT

ACTS 20:7–12

On the first day of the week, we assembled to break bread. Paul spoke to them, and since he was about to depart the next day, he extended his message until midnight. There were many lamps in the room upstairs where we were assembled, and a young man named Eutychus was sitting on a window sill and sank into a deep sleep as Paul kept on speaking. When he was overcome by sleep he fell down from the third story, and was picked up dead. But Paul went down, threw himself on him, embraced him, and said, "Don't be alarmed, for his life is in him!" After going upstairs, breaking the bread, and eating, he conversed a considerable time until dawn. Then he left. They brought the boy home alive and were greatly comforted.

JUST LIKE ME

EUTYCHUS: WAKING THE DEAD

Ever fall asleep during a sermon? While nodding off in church does not usually lead to death, it did for Eutychus. His story isn't exactly a cautionary tale; yet it has overtones of such.

All we know about Eutychus is that he was a young man who fell out of a third-story window after falling asleep during a long sermon preached by Paul. But tragedy was forestalled when Paul brought Eutychus back to life through the power of the Holy Spirit. This miracle undoubtedly had a huge impact on those present.

While we might not be able to relate to Eutychus's exact experience, we can relate to "sleeping" through some aspects of our lives as Christians. This happens whenever we attend church or read the Bible out of obligation instead of being fully engaged with worship. We rack up another notch on our Bible-reading chart or feel we've done our duty for the week by attending church. Yet our hearts and minds remain disengaged from God. Sometimes, it takes a fall or something else drastic to wake us up to the reality of God's presence.

Awake? Asleep? Only you and God know for sure.

YOUR CHOICE

What helps you to be fully engaged in worship?

TOUGH QUESTION

WHAT'S WRONG WITH DOING SOMETHING IF NO ONE WILL GET HURT AND NO ONE WILL EVER KNOW?

A sin is an action or thought that violates God's standard or command. We can also sin by *not doing* something that we should. And here's an important point to remember: A sin is a sin, no matter who else is affected or knows about it.

Suppose, for example, that while driving home at night, you blow through a stop sign. No one is around—no other drivers and no police. So, as far as you know, no one was hurt and no one, besides yourself, knows. Did you break the law? Yes. Although you didn't get caught, you still violated the rules of the road.

But here's the most important truth: God knows. And He's the only One who truly matters, anyway.

Integrity means living right when people are not looking. It's one thing to do what is right (and to avoid wrong) when people are watching; it's something else altogether, to live according to God's standards when no one sees you. That's when your true character comes out. Proverbs 10:9 speaks to walking with integrity: "The one who lives with integrity lives securely, but whoever perverts his ways will be found out." Living a secure life is a rich benefit of living with integrity, even when no one is looking or no one will ever find out.

A person trying to get away with sin, under the excuse that no one will ever know, is not living for God. When you live for God, you live with the knowledge that He sees your actions, thoughts, and motivations and you strive to live according to His commands.

SNAPSHOT

ACTS 20:17–24

Now from Miletus, he sent to Ephesus and called for the elders of the church. And when they came to him, he said to them: "You know, from the first day I set foot in Asia, how I was with you the whole time—serving the Lord with all humility, with tears, and with the trials that came to me through the plots of the Jews—and that I did not shrink back from proclaiming to you anything that was profitable, or from teaching it to you in public and from house to house. I testified to both Jews and Greeks about repentance toward God and faith in our Lord Jesus.

"And now I am on my way to Jerusalem, bound in my spirit, not knowing what I will encounter there, except that in town after town the Holy Spirit testifies to me that chains and afflictions are waiting for me. But I count my life of no value to myself, so that I may finish my course and the ministry I received from the Lord Jesus, to testify to the gospel of God's grace.'

YOUR CHOICE

When are you tempted to do something you know is wrong because 'no one will ever know"?

DAY 312

THE BIG PICTURE
AC 21:1–17

SNAPSHOT

ACTS 21:12–14

When we heard this, both we and the local people begged him not to go up to Jerusalem.

Then Paul replied, "What are you doing, weeping and breaking my heart? For I am ready not only to be bound, but also to die in Jerusalem for the name of the Lord Jesus."

Since he would not be persuaded, we stopped talking and simply said, "The Lord's will be done!"

TOUGH CHOICE

LONDON

The engine of the 747 roared in my ear, as I looked out over the plane's wing and down upon the shrinking houses and cars. *Back to school.*

I wrestled my backpack out from under the seat in front of me and pulled out a thick folder. A large graphic of students standing in front of Buckingham Palace covered the front, with "You could study *about* London . . . or you could study *abroad* in London" typed across the top. I opened the folder carefully. From the left-hand pocket, I removed a completed application form.

"So, you're applying to study abroad, I take it?" The elderly gentleman in the seat next to me smiled and pointed at the open folder.

"Oh, well . . . maybe," I stammered, not expecting a conversation.

"It is amazing, the opportunities that are available today," he chuckled to himself.

I managed a weak smile. He sounded like my parents. *This is the chance of a lifetime, Frank. What would we have given to spend three months studying and traveling in Europe? You'll create great networks, and it will be invaluable on your resume. Think about it!* I had thought about it—long and hard. I'd prayed about it—long and hard.

"When would you go overseas?" the gentleman inquired.

"*If* I go, it would be this summer."

"If you don't mind my asking, why the 'if'?"

I shifted in my narrow seat, readjusting the flimsy pillow behind my back. "I don't mind. I've also been offered a leadership position at a Christian sports camp this summer. I was a camper there for years, and I've been a counselor there for the past two summers. Studying in London would be a fantastic experience, but now . . ."

"Now you aren't so sure." He finished my thought.

I sighed, leaning my head back. "Everyone I know thinks I should go to London. That I'll never have another opportunity like this."

"But you want to go to camp?"

I smiled. It was nice to have someone understand my thought process. "Yes. I feel like the Lord wants me back at camp. That's where my heart is. Taking this leadership position would be great training for a future in a ministry position, which is what I see myself ultimately doing some day." I paused. "It would just be nice to have someone else supporting me, affirming my decision."

The man stared past me out the window, rubbing his chin. "Son, I believe you do have someone affirming your decision: God, Himself." He turned his gaze back to me. "Only you can be sure of where the Lord is guiding you. Pay attention to your heart's desire. It is one of the ways the Lord communicates with us."

YOUR CHOICE **Where do you believe God wants you to minister for Him? What's holding you back?**

SNAPSHOT

ACTS 21:30–36

The whole city was stirred up, and the people rushed together. They seized Paul, dragged him out of the temple complex, and at once the gates were shut. As they were trying to kill him, word went up to the commander of the regiment that all Jerusalem was in chaos. Taking along soldiers and centurions, he immediately ran down to them. Seeing the commander and the soldiers, they stopped beating Paul. Then the commander came up, took him into custody, and ordered him to be bound with two chains. He asked who he was and what he had done. Some in the mob were shouting one thing and some another. Since he was not able to get reliable information because of the uproar, he ordered him to be taken into the barracks. When Paul got to the steps, he had to be carried by the soldiers because of the mob's violence, for the mass of people were following and yelling, "Kill him!"

ANCHOR POINT

POPULARITY

Paul was catching flak from all sides. Jewish believers accused him of abandoning the law of Moses by teaching new non-Jewish followers of Christ that they didn't need to follow the laws and traditions. The Jews, of course, saw him as a complete heretic for following Jesus, and they were outraged at his association with non-Jews whom they considered unclean. Today's passage has them dragging Paul from the temple and accusing him of defiling the holy place.

Paul was committed to Christ and His truth—following it and teaching it. This made Paul an agent of change. But most people don't like change, even if it is based on truth. Change makes them feel insecure, uncomfortable; they'd rather keep things as they are, as they have always been. So the people described in today's passage attacked the change agent rather than realign their lives to the truth.

Christ is all about change—transformation. He changes people from the inside out and, through them, transforms families, neighborhoods, communities, and nations. That's why the traditionalists, the establishment, often feel threatened by Him and by His messengers. And by rejecting change, they reject the truth.

Your commitment to Christ may threaten others because of the changes to the status quo they see in you. And, frankly, your faith will move you to take stands that will limit your popularity. You may find yourself outside the mainstream. Are you prepared for that?

YOUR CHOICE

Who has been threatened by the Holy Spirit-empowered changes in your life? What changes do you see Christ making in your values, attitudes, and actions?

DAY 314

AC 21:37–22:29

SNAPSHOT

ACTS 22:22–25

They listened to him up to this word. Then they raised their voices, shouting, "Wipe this person off the earth—it's a disgrace for him to live!"

As they were yelling and flinging aside their robes and throwing dust into the air, the commander ordered him to be brought into the barracks, directing that he be examined with the scourge, so he could discover the reason they were shouting against him like this. As they stretched him out for the lash, Paul said to the centurion standing by, "Is it legal for you to scourge a man who is a Roman citizen and is uncondemned?"

DEPOSIT

WORDS FROM GOD'S WORD TO STORE IN YOUR MIND AND HEART

"But I count my life of no value to myself, so that I may finish my course and the ministry I received from the Lord Jesus, to testify to the gospel of God's grace" (Ac 20:24).

SNAPSHOT

ACTS 23:4–10

And those standing nearby said, "Do you dare revile God's high priest?"

"I did not know, brothers," Paul said, "that it was the high priest. For it is written, You must not speak evil of a ruler of your people." When Paul realized that one part of them were Sadducees and the other part were Pharisees, he cried out in the Sanhedrin, "Brothers, I am a Pharisee, a son of Pharisees! I am being judged because of the hope of the resurrection of the dead!" When he said this, a dispute broke out between the Pharisees and the Sadducees, and the assembly was divided. For the Sadducees say there is no resurrection, and no angel or spirit, but the Pharisees affirm them all.

The shouting grew loud, and some of the scribes of the Pharisees' party got up and argued vehemently: "We find nothing evil in this man. What if a spirit or an angel has spoken to him?" When the dispute became violent, the commander feared that Paul might be torn apart by them and ordered the troops to go down, rescue him from them, and bring him into the barracks.

YOUR TURN

A PLAN TO KILL

How well do you know your rights and fulfill your responsibilities as a citizen of your country?

DAY 316

AC 23:23–24:27

SNAPSHOT

ACTS 23:23–30

He summoned two of his centurions and said, "Get 200 soldiers ready with 70 cavalry and 200 spearmen to go to Caesarea at nine tonight. Also provide mounts so they can put Paul on them and bring him safely to Felix the governor."

He wrote a letter of this kind:

"Claudius Lysias,

To the most excellent governor Felix:

Greetings.

When this man had been seized by the Jews and was about to be killed by them, I arrived with my troops and rescued him because I learned that he is a Roman citizen. Wanting to know the charge for which they were accusing him, I brought him down before their Sanhedrin. I found out that the accusations were about disputed matters in their law, and that there was no charge that merited death or chains. When I was informed that there was a plot against the man, I sent him to you right away. I also ordered his accusers to state their case against him in your presence."

JUST LIKE ME

CLAUDIUS LYSIAS: AT A PIVOTAL POINT

A pivot is a shaft that supports something that turns. But a pivot is also a person around whom others turn. Paul proved to be the pivot in the life of one Roman commander—Claudius Lysias.

We first meet Claudius Lysias in Acts 21:31–40 in the midst of quelling a mob that was threatening Paul's life. Claudius was a man of authority and ambition. After hearing about a plot to murder Paul, Claudius tried to make himself look good to Felix, the governor appointed by Rome, by explaining how he had rescued Paul, a citizen of Rome. But little did Claudius know that his plan to send Paul safely to Felix in Caesarea was all part of God's plan.

Proverbs 21:1 describes God's sovereignty over events: "A king's heart is a water channel in the Lord's hand: He directs it wherever He chooses." God puts the right people in position to carry out His will. In the case of Claudius, God used Paul as the pivot to point Claudius to the truth about Jesus, and He used Claudius to preserve Paul's life.

Are you at a pivotal moment? You could either be a cog in the wheel like Claudius or, like Paul, a pivot whom God uses for His glory.

YOUR CHOICE

How has God used you in someone else's life?

ACTS 25:17–21

SNAPSHOT

DAY 317

THE BIG PICTURE

AC 25:1–27

"Therefore, when they had assembled here, I did not delay. The next day I sat at the judge's bench and ordered the man to be brought in. Concerning him, the accusers stood up and brought no charge of the sort I was expecting. Instead they had some disagreements with him about their own religion and about a certain Jesus, a dead man whom Paul claimed to be alive. Since I was at a loss in a dispute over such things, I asked him if he wished to go to Jerusalem and be tried there concerning these matters. But when Paul appealed to be held for trial by the Emperor, I ordered him to be kept in custody until I could send him to Caesar."

TOUGH CHOICE

CHEYENNE

McCormick account . . . finished. Garrison account . . . still needs work. I sat in my cubicle, sifting through a stack of accounting spreadsheets. I rubbed my eyes, which stung from staring at numbers all morning. My ears rang from the buzzing florescent lights overhead.

"Hey, Reese!" Cheyenne knocked on my cubicle wall, peeking her head around the corner. "You up for lunch?" Cheyenne was one of my few friends in the office. She was fun, pretty, always in a good mood, and had a good sense of humor. I wished I could be more like her.

I stood up from my chair and grabbed my purse. "Yes, please!"

Cheyenne and I sat at a picnic table in the park, eating our BBQ sandwiches from Bo Dean's. It was refreshing to be outside.

"It's hard to top good BBQ on a beautiful day," said Cheyenne, waving to a group of passersby. "We should get a group from the office to come out here for dinner next week!"

I laughed between bites, shaking my head. "Cheyenne, I have never met anyone like you. I bet you've never experienced a dull day in your life."

"Well, I just figure God's given me one life to live and purpose to fulfill—to enjoy and glorify Him! How could there be a dull day knowing that? You know?"

I pushed my coleslaw around my plate with my plastic fork. "Actually," I said hesitantly, "I don't know. I believe that there's a God, but I don't understand why that makes you so joyful. There's just something different about you . . . intriguing."

Cheyenne looked at me intently. "Reese, my joy comes from a personal relationship with Christ. It's a state of being."

I pulled my hair behind my shoulders as a breeze picked up. "How do you get to that state of being, though?"

"First," said Cheyenne, pulling a book out of her bag, "you start reading about God's promises to us in the Bible." She set the Bible on the table between us. "The Bible explains how Jesus came to this earth and died on the cross for our sins. He did this so that our sins would be accounted for. If we believe that Christ paid for our sins, we can have a personal relationship with Him and live eternally in Heaven."

I opened the Bible carefully. "So by studying the Bible, I can have the same kind of joy?"

Cheyenne grinned. "That's just the beginning, Reese. As you come to know God's Word, you'll come to know Him. And it's this relationship that will fill you with contentment and purpose. It can't be helped."

I smoothed the pages of the Bible as the wind rippled through them. "Cheyenne, would you teach me how to study the Bible?"

"Of course, Reese! It would bring me great joy!"

YOUR CHOICE **With whom do you think you could begin to share your faith today?**

DAY 318

THE BIG PICTURE

AC 26:1–32

SNAPSHOT

ACTS 26:1–7

Agrippa said to Paul, "It is permitted for you to speak for yourself."

Then Paul stretched out his hand and began his defense: "I consider myself fortunate, King Agrippa, that today I am going to make a defense before you about everything I am accused of by the Jews, especially since you are an expert in all the Jewish customs and controversies. Therefore I beg you to listen to me patiently.

"All the Jews know my way of life from my youth, which was spent from the beginning among my own nation and in Jerusalem. They had previously known me for quite some time, if they were willing to testify, that according to the strictest party of our religion I lived as a Pharisee. And now I stand on trial for the hope of the promise made by God to our fathers, the promise our 12 tribes hope to attain as they earnestly serve Him night and day. Because of this hope I am being accused by the Jews, O king!"

JUST LIKE ME

PAUL: MAKING HIS CASE

According to our legal system, an accused person is innocent until proven guilty. In Paul's case, however, he was considered guilty by his own people and then had to prove himself innocent before Festus, the Roman governor, and King Agrippa.

Paul's life perfectly embodied Jesus' warning to His disciples: "You will even be brought before governors and kings because of Me, to bear witness to them and to the nations. . . . You will be given what to say at that hour, because you are not speaking, but the Spirit of your Father is speaking through you" (Mt 10:18,20). In his defense against the vague charges brought against him, Paul relied on the Holy Spirit and the truth about Jesus as Messiah instead of histrionics. He knew that the real defendant in this situation was Jesus.

How do you react when someone willfully misunderstands you or demands that you justify your faith in a God that we can't see? Like Paul, you can choose to stand on truth, the Word of God, and rely on the Holy Spirit. Truth needs no embellishment.

YOUR CHOICE

How do you usually respond when you have to defend yourself?

TOUGH QUESTION

WHEN I READ THIS STORY, I'M AMAZED AT HOW PAUL COULD BE SO CALM IN SUCH A VIOLENT STORM. HOW CAN I TRUST GOD MORE AND BE COURAGEOUS IN *MY* STORMS?

Life can seem out of control at times. Huge waves—failed relationship, debt, unemployment, severe illness, natural disaster, or death of a loved one—can threaten to overwhelm us emotionally and spiritually. We may be convinced intellectually that God is in control, but somehow we need to get that message to our emotions and our actions. That's where faith comes in.

In many ways, faith is like a muscle. Athletes know that a successful performance greatly depends on conditioning and preparation. We can see a direct parallel in the faith arena. Those who have exercised their faith-muscle—they have trusted God each day in small and medium-size situations—are better prepared to trust Him in crucial confrontations and conflicts.

Faith begins by believing the facts about God as revealed in His Word. That's why regular Bible reading is so important. We read about His attributes and character, and we see Him in action. But worship and prayer can take faith further, for that's where we grow the *relationship* with God—our trust level increases because we know that God wants the best for us.

Then we get into the habit of yielding to Him—turning over every aspect of our lives: relationships, decisions, values . . . everything. Those are daily choices that help us become accustomed to submitting to God's leadership.

As you consider Paul, remember that this storm hit after years of living by faith. He was ready. James challenges us: "Consider it a great joy, my brothers, whenever you experience various trials, knowing that the testing of your faith produces endurance. But endurance must do its complete work, so that you may be mature and complete, lacking nothing" (Jms 1:2–4).

Trusting God in our daily trials tests us and prepares us to trust Him in the storms.

SNAPSHOT

ACTS 27:20–25

For many days neither sun nor stars appeared, and the severe storm kept raging; finally all hope that we would be saved was disappearing. Since many were going without food, Paul stood up among them and said, "You men should have followed my advice not to sail from Crete and sustain this damage and loss. Now I urge you to take courage, because there will be no loss of any of your lives, but only of the ship. For this night an angel of the God I belong to and serve stood by me, saying, 'Don't be afraid, Paul. You must stand before Caesar. And, look! God has graciously given you all those who are sailing with you.' Therefore, take courage, men, because I believe God that it will be just the way it was told to me."

YOUR CHOICE

What do you need to yield to Christ's control? What can you do to build your faith-muscle?

DAY 320

AC 27:27–44

SNAPSHOT

ACTS 27:39–44

When daylight came, they did not recognize the land, but sighted a bay with a beach. They planned to run the ship ashore if they could. After casting off the anchors, they left them in the sea, at the same time loosening the ropes that held the rudders. Then they hoisted the foresail to the wind and headed for the beach. But they struck a sandbar and ran the ship aground. The bow jammed fast and remained immovable, but the stern began to break up with the pounding of the waves.

The soldiers' plan was to kill the prisoners so that no one could swim off and escape. But the centurion kept them from carrying out their plan because he wanted to save Paul, so he ordered those who could swim to jump overboard first and get to land. The rest were to follow, some on planks and some on debris from the ship. In this way, all got safely to land.

ANCHOR POINT

STORMS

The storm had been raging for fourteen days—two terrible weeks of nonstop wind and rain, tossed about on the rough seas, holding on for dear life, with little to eat. Tough sailors feared the worst; a few tried to run away in a skiff. On a flimsy ship in the middle of the ocean was not the best place to be. Yet Paul remained confident that though the ship would be lost, all on board would be saved. An angel had revealed that truth to him.

One of the great gifts that God gives us is the ability to experience peace in the midst of turmoil. Through the ministry of the Holy Spirit, we can be assured that regardless of our circumstances, God is with us—He never leaves. We know that He is sovereign and in control. We also remember past events—in Scripture, through the witness of others, and in our own experience—where God has brought His people through the storms.

We need merely to cling to Him; He will carry us through.

YOUR CHOICE

What's the worst "storm" you've experienced? How did God bring you through that frightful experience?

SNAPSHOT

ACTS 28:1–6

Safely ashore, we then learned that the island was called Malta. The local people showed us extraordinary kindness, for they lit a fire and took us all in, since rain was falling and it was cold. As Paul gathered a bundle of brushwood and put it on the fire, a viper came out because of the heat and fastened itself to his hand. When the local people saw the creature hanging from his hand, they said to one another, "This man is probably a murderer, and though he has escaped the sea, Justice does not allow him to live!" However, he shook the creature off into the fire and suffered no harm. They expected that he would swell up or suddenly drop dead. But after they waited a long time and saw nothing unusual happen to him, they changed their minds and said he was a god.

DEPOSIT

WORDS FROM GOD'S WORD TO STORE IN YOUR MIND AND HEART

"Therefore, let it be known to you that this saving work of God has been sent to the Gentiles; they will listen!" (Ac 28:28).

DAY 322

THE BIG PICTURE

AC 28:15–31

SNAPSHOT

ACTS 28:17–22

After three days he called together the leaders of the Jews. And when they had gathered he said to them: "Brothers, although I have done nothing against our people or the customs of our forefathers, I was delivered as a prisoner from Jerusalem into the hands of the Romans who, after examining me, wanted to release me, since I had not committed a capital offense. Because the Jews objected, I was compelled to appeal to Caesar; it was not as though I had any accusation against my nation. So, for this reason I've asked to see you and speak to you. In fact, it is for the hope of Israel that I'm wearing this chain."

And they said to him, "We haven't received any letters about you from Judea; none of the brothers has come and reported or spoken anything evil about you. But we consider it suitable to hear from you what you think. For concerning this sect, we are aware that it is spoken against everywhere."

YOUR TURN

PAUL IN ROME

What would you most like to be doing when your time on this earth is over?

THE BIG PICTURE

RM 5:1–11

NOVEMBER 19

DAY 323

SNAPSHOT

ROMANS 5:1–5

Therefore, since we have been declared righteous by faith, we have peace with God through our Lord Jesus Christ. Also through Him, we have obtained access by faith into this grace in which we stand, and we rejoice in the hope of the glory of God. And not only that, but we also rejoice in our afflictions, because we know that affliction produces endurance, endurance produces proven character, and proven character produces hope. This hope does not disappoint, because God's love has been poured out in our hearts through the Holy Spirit who was given to us.

ANCHOR POINT

FAITH BRINGS JOY

This passage reminds us how incredibly fortunate we are to have Christ as our Savior and God as our Father. We have been declared righteous; we have peace, we live in grace; we can know hope and joy.

We rejoice, even when being harassed or persecuted or suffering in other ways because we know that God is working in us, making us more like Christ (see Rm 8:28–29). And God reassures us of His love and purpose through the Holy Spirit.

We should read this passage over and over, especially when undergoing trials. Christ has done so much for us, and God has given so much to us! Then, secure in our relationship with God and filled with His joy and hope, His love should overflow to everyone we meet. Just as this was God's gift to us, let it be our gift to others.

YOUR CHOICE

Do you truly believe everything in this passage? Have you experienced it? If so, how can you share it with others? If not, how can you begin to grab hold of these great promises?

DAY 324

THE BIG PICTURE

RM 8:1–17

NO BRAINER

TRULY FREE

Imagine standing before a judge. The evidence clearly points to your indisputable guilt. And the penalty is death. Standing there with no defense and no escape, you know you're doomed. Suddenly the judge brings his gavel crashing down, and declares, "Not guilty!" Not accused, not charged, not condemned—you're free.

That's the message of Romans 8.

This amazing chapter begins with the declaration that those who trust in Christ are totally free from sin and its penalty and ends with the stirring promise that we can never be lost to God's love. And in the middle of the chapter we read about God working all things together for our good (v. 28) and that we have been chosen, called, and justified (vv. 29–30).

The reason for all this? "God is for us," answers Paul, so no one can stand against us" (see v. 31). Did you get that? God is *for* us—on our side, working for us, defending us, protecting us, and, most important of all, redeeming us (see v. 32).

These truths should bolster your self-esteem, encourage you, embolden you, and give you hope. When you feel abandoned by those you thought were friends, because you stood up for Christ, God hasn't left you. When rumors are spread and you are falsely accused, God knows the truth. When you know the sting of disappointment, rejection, or defeat, God is working behind the scenes and turning "bad" into good. And when gnawing guilt engulfs and condemns you, God forgives and forgets.

You are free—totally, eternally free.

Pay no attention to voices that say otherwise, reminding you of sins of the past, playing on insecurities of the present, or dredging up fears for the future. Listen only to God's clear affirmation: "Therefore, no condemnation now exists for those in Christ Jesus" (v. 1). And live free.

SNAPSHOT

ROMANS 8:1–5

Therefore, no condemnation now exists for those in Christ Jesus, because the Spirit's law of life in Christ Jesus has set you free from the law of sin and of death. What the law could not do since it was limited by the flesh, God did. He condemned sin in the flesh by sending His own Son in flesh like ours under sin's domain, and as a sin offering, in order that the law's requirement would be accomplished in us who do not walk according to the flesh but according to the Spirit. For those whose lives are according to the flesh think about the things of the flesh, but those whose lives are according to the Spirit, about the things of the Spirit.

YOUR CHOICE

When have you felt "condemned"? How does your freedom in Christ affect how you feel? How you live?

RM 8:18–39

DAY 325

TOUGH QUESTION

NOTHING CAN SEPARATE US FROM GOD AND HIS LOVE, BUT AT TIMES I FEEL VERY DISTANT FROM HIM. WHY DOES THIS HAPPEN?

Absolutely right—nothing can separate us from God's love. That's the powerful and profound message of today's passage. We can't do anything to remove us from the reach of His forgiveness or love. God never changes, and we don't fall in or out of favor with Him, as often happens with people. But *we* change. We block our communication with Him with our sins. That's why confession is so important—admitting our wrongs and thanking Him for His mercy and grace. Someone has said, "If you don't feel as close to God as you once did, guess who moved!" The answer? Not God. So keep short accounts with Him; stay close.

Just as in any relationship, spending time together brings us closer. We become close friends with someone by spending time with that person, talking, listening, and asking questions. (Note: We can talk to God about anything: feelings, doubts, questions, fears, and hurts—past, present, and future.) We listen to God by reading His Word and spending time in silence and solitude. We talk to Him through prayer. He's always there, waiting for us to come to Him for a good conversation. With busy schedules and a world of distractions, we can easily forget those appointments with God, but nothing could be more important.

SNAPSHOT

ROMANS 8:38–39

For I am persuaded that neither death nor life,

nor angels nor rulers,

nor things present, nor things to come, nor powers,

nor height, nor depth, nor any other created thing

will have the power to separate us

from the love of God that is in Christ Jesus our Lord!

YOUR CHOICE

How does the assurance of God's love and presence encourage and motivate you? What can you do to improve your relationship with Him?

NOVEMBER 22

DAY 326

THE BIG PICTURE

RM 12:1–21

SNAPSHOT

ROMANS 12:1–2 Therefore, brothers, by the mercies of God, I urge you to present your bodies as a living sacrifice, holy and pleasing to God; this is your spiritual worship. Do not be conformed to this age, but be transformed by the renewing of your mind, so that you may discern what is the good, pleasing, and perfect will of God.

TOUGH CHOICE

SACRIFICE

Professor Abernathy, examined my transcript and resume, peering through his bifocals. He nodded and commented to himself, looking up only after he had finished reading. "Excellent, Peter. Now, do you have any specific post-graduate plans in mind? You are certainly in fine form to consider, say, law school." His eyebrows peaked at the suggestion, landing somewhere near mid-forehead.

I scooted forward in my chair. "Actually, my plan is to pursue a master's degree in education."

"Your M.Ed.?" He inquired.

"Yes, sir. I want to be a high school history teacher and a coach."

Mr. Abernathy chuckled. "Son, why ever would you want to teach teenagers with an education like yours? You've laid the foundation for great success. Now honestly, what do you say to law school applications?"

"No disrespect, professor, but my definition of success isn't measured in dollars and titles. I believe that God designed me to be a teacher. Success, for me, is developing and using my gifts to serve others."

Five years later . . .

"Good to see you, Pete!" Wyatt, one of my college buddies shook my hand, as I sat down in the swanky chophouse booth. "Thanks for joining me."

"Wouldn't miss it, Wyatt. How's life as a lawyer these days?"

He leaned back in his seat, straightening his silk tie. "Hard to top, that's for sure. Kim and I just moved into a condo on the coast. Spectacular view of the harbor . . ." he trailed off. "But listen, Chuck and I were talking over lunch the other day—he and his wife are also living in the city—and we're thinking about going in together to get a Hatteras. We could take her out on the weekends, do some fishing, travel up to the Cape. What do you think?"

I shook my head and laughed. "Wyatt, that would be incredible. Just like college when we'd take your dad's boat out for the weekend. You and Chuck ought to do it."

"Hold on, now, Pete. We want you to buy in. We need our third shipman!"

I nodded, staring out over the tables occupied by men and women in tailored business suits—quite a different scene than my students, sitting at their desks.

"Son, why ever would you want to teach teenagers with an education like yours?" Professor Abernathy's words surfaced in my mind. *What if I had gone to law school? I had been a better student than Wyatt and Chuck. I could be living on the coast in a fancy condo.* "Wyatt, I really appreciate you thinking of me, but I'm afraid I'm going to have to pass."

"Are you sure, Pete?"

"Wyatt, I'll definitely take you up on a ride some time, but there's no way I can afford a Hatteras on a teacher's salary."

There was an awkward silence that followed. "Do you really like teaching?"

"Yeah, I do, Wyatt. It's fulfilling. I'm where the Lord wants me. There's nothing I'd rather be doing."

YOUR CHOICE **What factors enter in to your consideration of a career? Where does God come in to the equation?**

SNAPSHOT

1 CORINTHIANS 13:4–8a

Love is patient; love is kind. Love does not envy;
is not boastful; is not conceited;
does not act improperly; is not selfish;
is not provoked; does not keep a record of wrongs;
finds no joy in unrighteousness, but rejoices in the truth;
bears all things, believes all things,
hopes all things, endures all things.
Love never ends.

ANCHOR POINT

REAL LOVE

In just about every Christian wedding, someone reads verses from this passage—1 Corinthians 13, the love chapter. But this is not a light, romantic poem, like something we might find on a greeting card. It goes right to the heart of true love.

We see that love is selfless, focusing on the other person. Too often, what passes for love these days is the opposite—one person falls "in love" with another for what he or she can *get*.

We also see that true love involves choice. Listen to these words: Love "bears all things, believes all things, hopes all things, endures all things." When we love someone, we believe the best about that person and act in his or her best interests.

During His last few hours with the disciples, Jesus told them to love one another (Jn 15:9–17). Love should mark every follower of Christ. All of our actions should be ruled by love. How often has the church acted in truth but not in love? How often have we? Relationships can be shattered when our actions are motivated by self-interest or pride. Our greatest achievements are tainted when they are mere monuments to ego.

You can be known for many things in this life. Choose love.

YOUR CHOICE

What relationship needs a dose of real love?
What can you do to love others more?

DAY 328

THE BIG PICTURE

1 CO 15:1–20

SNAPSHOT

1 CORINTHIANS 15:8–11

Last of all, as to one abnormally born, He also appeared to me.

For I am the least of the apostles, unworthy to be called an apostle, because I persecuted the church of God. But by God's grace I am what I am, and His grace toward me was not ineffective. However, I worked more than any of them, yet not I, but God's grace that was with me. Therefore, whether it is I or they, so we preach and so you have believed.

DEPOSIT

WORDS FROM GOD'S WORD TO STORE IN YOUR MIND AND HEART

For if the dead are not raised, Christ has not been raised. And if Christ has not been raised, your faith is worthless; you are still in your sins (1 Co 15:16–17).

THE BIG PICTURE

1 CO 15:42–58

NOVEMBER 25

DAY 329

SNAPSHOT

1 CORINTHIANS 15:50–53

Brothers, I tell you this: flesh and blood cannot inherit the kingdom of God, and corruption cannot inherit incorruption. Listen! I am telling you a mystery:

We will not all fall asleep, but we will all be changed,
in a moment, in the twinkling of an eye, at the last trumpet.
For the trumpet will sound,
and the dead will be raised incorruptible, and we will be changed.
Because this corruptible must be clothed with incorruptibility,
and this mortal must be clothed with immortality.

YOUR TURN

DESTINY!

How much are you looking forward to all Christ has planned for you?

NOVEMBER 26

DAY 330

THE BIG PICTURE

2 CO 4:1–18

SNAPSHOT

2 CORINTHIANS 4:16–18

Therefore we do not give up; even though our outer person is being destroyed, our inner person is being renewed day by day. For our momentary light affliction is producing for us an absolutely incomparable eternal weight of glory. So we do not focus on what is seen, but on what is unseen; for what is seen is temporary, but what is unseen is eternal.

ANCHOR POINT

EYE ON ETERNITY

Paul declares that what is in us is greater than we are—the power of God. So we need not worry about our current troubles or future hardships. Although our "clay jars" (2 Co 4:7) may be broken beyond repair, what is on the inside can never be destroyed. We are made for eternity.

We are dying and growing to life at the same time. This physical being is wearing out, but the renewed soul that we have been given is growing closer to God and stronger each day as we walk in the Spirit. What a wonderful hope we have! Even as we feel the effects of age and bear the loss of loved ones, we know that the promise of eternity lives within all who believe. We know that this will endure everything and one day will reunite us with the risen Christ. Paul concludes, "So we do not focus on what is seen, but on what is unseen; for what is seen is temporary, but what is unseen is eternal."

YOUR CHOICE

Where's your focus? How does knowing that you were designed for eternity affect how you live?

GALATIANS 5:22–25

SNAPSHOT

But the fruit of the Spirit is love, joy, peace, patience, kindness, goodness, faith, gentleness, self-control. Against such things there is no law. Now those who belong to Christ Jesus have crucified the flesh with its passions and desires. If we live by the Spirit, we must also follow the Spirit.

NOVEMBER 27

DAY 331

THE BIG PICTURE

GL 5:1–26

TOUGH CHOICE

CASEY

Leigh tapped on my door with her toe, pushing it open with her shoulder. A large basket of laundry occupied her hands. "Hey, Izzie. I took your clothes out of the dryer. I hope that's okay; I didn't want to interrupt your studying."

"Yeah, that's fine. Just set my stuff wherever." I glanced up from my textbook, motioning Leigh toward my dresser. "It would be nice if you wouldn't always decide to do laundry on the same day as me, though," I mumbled under my breath.

Leigh set the basket down and turned toward me. "What?"

"Nothing . . . I just wish I could do my laundry without being hurried along for once."

"Oh. Sorry . . ." Leigh started to leave my room, but stopped before reaching the door. "Is there something bothering you, Izzie?"

I looked up at my roommate, whose face was marked with concern. A sinking feeling flooded my gut. "Sorry, Leigh. That was rude of me. I'm just frustrated with some stuff."

"What's frustrating you?" Leigh walked back into the room, sitting down on the end of my bed.

I closed my book, balancing it on the arm rest of my chair. "Casey," I said, scowling.

Casey and I had become friends in middle school, but our friendship had soured over time due to a long series of hurtful situations. I had decided to attend college far from home to get a fresh start, but Casey had followed me here, too. I couldn't escape.

"What happened?" Leigh asked, aware of my rocky history with Casey.

"I just got a long e-mail from her, letting me know I'm a terrible friend. She's mad that I haven't been spending time with her since she came back from her semester abroad."

Leigh rolled her eyes. "Are you kidding? That girl creates more drama . . ."

"I know! Leigh, her semester abroad was the best semester of my life! I finally got to be my own person and do my own thing. Then she sends this e-mail! I don't want to mend ties. I don't want to be friends!" Anger boiled inside my veins.

"Izzie, I'm so sorry. This is not fair to you. Casey shouldn't have sent that e-mail." Leigh propped her elbows up on her knees, resting her chin on her clasped hands. "But, I do think you need to let go of your anger," she added cautiously.

"How can I? This has been going on for so long. She continues to hurt me, and I'm tired of letting her walk all over me. I don't want to let go of my anger."

"I know it's not easy, Izzie, but it is possible to have a change of heart with prayer, even if you aren't ready to let go of the hurt."

I leaned my head back on the chair. "It's just so hard to forgive an . . . enemy."

"Izzie, we're commanded in the Bible to not only forgive our enemies, but to love them! Christ's love for us is a perfect example. We wrong Him day after day, and He still loves us. You can't beat your feelings toward Casey on your own, but if you turn this over the Lord, He will help you succeed in your attempt to honor His command."

YOUR CHOICE **Who do you need to forgive?**

DAY 332

THE BIG PICTURE

EPH 1:3–23

SNAPSHOT

EPHESIANS 1:15–19

This is why, since I heard about your faith in the Lord Jesus and your love for all the saints, I never stop giving thanks for you as I remember you in my prayers. I pray that the God of our Lord Jesus Christ, the glorious Father, would give you a spirit of wisdom and revelation in the knowledge of Him. I pray that the eyes of your heart may be enlightened so you may know what is the hope of His calling, what are the glorious riches of His inheritance among the saints, and what is the immeasurable greatness of His power to us who believe, according to the working of His vast strength.

JUST LIKE ME

THE BELIEVERS IN EPHESUS: RECIPIENTS OF GRACE

Ever wish you had a wealthy relative who left you a ton of money? While most are still on the wishing end of that, the experience of the believers in Ephesus reminds us of an inheritance in which we can share—true wealth beyond our wildest dreams. And it's all due to grace.

Having spent years in Ephesus among the believers, Paul knew of the temptations in that city, especially those connected to the temple of the goddess Artemis. The Ephesian society was culturally rich but morally bankrupt. In that society, following Christ meant choosing a different, often difficult, way of life. So Paul encouraged and challenged his readers by detailing an inheritance to which they, as believers, were privy. In this "will," God was the active party, giving believers redemption and forgiveness (1:7). God also chose to lavish "all wisdom and understanding" (1:8) on His children. Best of all, Paul reminded the Ephesian believers, they had the Holy Spirit as their guarantee (1:14) and they had "every spiritual blessing in the heavens" (1:3).

On those days when we place ourselves in the "have-not" category and find ourselves envying those who seem to have everything, consider Paul's words to the Ephesians. In Christ, you have everything.

YOUR CHOICE

Which item on Paul's list in Ephesians gives you the most joy? Why?

SNAPSHOT

EPHESIANS 2:19–22

So then you are no longer foreigners and strangers, but fellow citizens with the saints, and members of God's household, built on the foundation of the apostles and prophets, with Christ Jesus Himself as the cornerstone. The whole building is being fitted together in Him and is growing into a holy sanctuary in the Lord, in whom you also are being built together for God's dwelling in the Spirit.

YOUR CHOICE

How can you use your gifts to serve God and other believers?

NO BRAINER

FITTING IN

The Bible uses several metaphors to describe how believers relate to one another. We are "sheep," a "family," and a "body," for example. Here Paul pictures us as a building, with each Christian as a stone or building block.

Paul says that the foundation for this building has been laid in the past—the apostles and prophets—and that Christ is the cornerstone (v. 20). And here's the kicker—Paul adds, "The whole building is being fitted together in Him and is growing into a holy sanctuary in the Lord, in whom you also are being built together for God's dwelling in the Spirit" (vv. 21–22).

Notice that every believer has a place (the "whole building"). Every believer has a purpose. Paul doesn't say that all the stones are the same but that God is fitting them together. Elsewhere (using the body metaphor) Paul highlights the individual uniqueness of each believer (see Rm 12:4–8; 1 Co 12:12–31; and Eph 4:11–13, just a couple of chapters from today's passage). Each follower of Christ—each member of the body, each building block—has specific gifts and abilities. Some of these gifts are more obvious and public than others, but all are important. Returning to the building analogy, the blocks will have different shapes and different uses. But—here's the crucial point—all are necessary.

In God's building, all the stones fit. Isn't that great!

Remember when your physical changes were dramatic, and you felt awkward, clumsy, and ugly? Or remember when you wanted to be in a certain group at school but were never invited? Or how about those days (years?) when you wondered about the *real* you—your true identity? In those painful and doubt-filled moments, you may have wondered if you'd ever fit in, anywhere.

You do. God has uniquely gifted you, and He has a place for you and your gifts in His building.

DAY 334

THE BIG PICTURE
EPH 4:1–16

SNAPSHOT

EPHESIANS 4:1–6

I, therefore, the prisoner in the Lord, urge you to walk worthy of the calling you have received, with all humility and gentleness, with patience, accepting one another in love, diligently keeping the unity of the Spirit with the peace that binds us. There is one body and one Spirit, just as you were called to one hope at your calling; one Lord, one faith, one baptism, one God and Father of all, who is above all and through all and in all.

YOUR CHOICE

Think of two or three irritating or obnoxious people in your circle of friends and acquaintances. What can you do in the next few days to demonstrate love for them?

TOUGH QUESTION

ACCORDING TO THE BIBLE, CHRISTIANS ARE SUPPOSED TO LOVE ONE ANOTHER. BUT SOME CHRISTIANS ARE SO IRRITATING. HOW CAN I GET PAST THE FACT THAT I DON'T LIKE THEM, MUCH LESS "LOVE" THEM?

Difficult relationships are part of life, and some people irritate us more than others. No one's perfect (even you); we all have rough edges, blind spots, weaknesses, and annoying habits. After all, we're sinners. And these issues are most obvious in people with whom we spend lots of time: siblings, parents, teammates, and so forth. Because the church is the "family of God" and the "body of Christ," fellow believers will worship, learn, and work together. And, at times, we will get on one another's nerves.

Jesus told His disciples to love each other—that's how the world would know they were His followers (Jn 13:34–35; 15:12–17). This command can be confusing because we usually associate love with strong, positive feelings toward another person. But when Jesus made that statement, He wasn't expecting the disciples to feel good about one another all the time; He wanted them to *act* in love toward one another. True love begins with a choice to act in another person's best interests. Love means being unselfish and serving.

A great way to start loving someone is to get to know the person and his or her personal struggles. We will be more empathetic and compassionate for people we know. Even with the most obnoxious people who rebuff every attempt at relationship, we can pray for them—for their relationship with the Lord and with their family.

Loving difficult people is not easy, but it is vital for the body of Christ. First John 4:20 states, "If anyone says, 'I love God,' yet hates his brother, he is a liar. For the person who does not love his brother whom he has seen cannot love God whom he has not seen." If we don't love the people around us, we don't love God!

DECEMBER
DECEMBRE
DEZEMBER
DECEMBER
DICEMBRE
DEZEMBRO
DICIEMBRE

SNAPSHOT

EPHESIANS 6:10–13

Finally, be strengthened by the Lord and by His vast strength. Put on the full armor of God so that you can stand against the tactics of the Devil. For our battle is not against flesh and blood, but against the rulers, against the authorities, against the world powers of this darkness, against the spiritual forces of evil in the heavens. This is why you must take up the full armor of God, so that you may be able to resist in the evil day, and having prepared everything, to take your stand.

DEPOSIT

WORDS FROM GOD'S WORD TO STORE IN YOUR MIND AND HEART

This is why you must take up the full armor of God, so that you may be able to resist in the evil day, and having prepared everything, to take your stand (Eph 6:13).

THE BIG PICTURE
PHP 2:1–18

SNAPSHOT

PHILIPPIANS 2:1–4

If then there is any encouragement in Christ, if any consolation of love, if any fellowship with the Spirit, if any affection and mercy, fulfill my joy by thinking the same way, having the same love, sharing the same feelings, focusing on one goal. Do nothing out of rivalry or conceit, but in humility consider others as more important than yourselves. Everyone should look out not only for his own interests, but also for the interests of others.

YOUR TURN

THE MIND OF JESUS

In what ways would having Christ's attitude make you face this day differently?

THE BIG PICTURE

PHP 4:1–23

DECEMBER 3

DAY 337

SNAPSHOT

PHILIPPIANS 4:1–7

So then, in this way, my dearly loved brothers, my joy and crown, stand firm in the Lord, dear friends. I urge Euodia and I urge Syntyche to agree in the Lord. Yes, I also ask you, true partner, to help these women who have contended for the gospel at my side, along with Clement and the rest of my co-workers whose names are in the book of life. Rejoice in the Lord always. I will say it again: Rejoice! Let your graciousness be known to everyone. The Lord is near. Don't worry about anything, but in everything, through prayer and petition with thanksgiving, let your requests be made known to God. And the peace of God, which surpasses every thought, will guard your hearts and your minds in Christ Jesus.

JUST LIKE ME

EUODIA AND SYNTYCHE: CHRISTIAN CAT-FIGHT

Is there anyone who lives under the belief that Christians never disagree? Sadly, the fact that Christians can and do disagree has been numbered among the excuses some people give for rejecting Christ.

A disagreement usually won't make the church bulletin. But in the New Testament, an argument made the headlines—the one between Euodia and Syntyche in the church at Philippi. How sad to be forever noted in the New Testament for a disagreement! Yet Paul's inclusion of the issue is a reminder of how the body works together. Just as a pain in a physical body affects the whole body, a conflict between two members of a church body affects others in that body.

Paul also used a good strategy to encourage a resolution. Step 1 was to avoid championing one person over another. Step 2 was to ask the women to resolve the issue themselves. Step 3 was to end the explanation of the issue on a positive note by reminding those reading the letter of the women's previous faithfulness.

We might think that our minor or major conflicts are strictly our business. Sometimes we're too close to a situation to see a solution. Like Euodia and Syntyche, we might need the fresh perspective of a third party.

YOUR CHOICE

With whom do you currently have a conflict or disagreement? What can you do to resolve the issue?

DAY 338

THE BIG PICTURE

COL 2:1–15

NO BRAINER

ERASED

"I forgive you." That straightforward statement sounds good but can be taken several ways, depending on voice inflection, body language, and context. Suppose a person had let out a big sigh and then had said something like, "All right . . ." (dramatic pause) "I forgive you. There, I said it!" I doubt we would feel forgiven.

Then we have the situation where a person has sincerely expressed the desire to forgive. We believe our friend and walk away feeling free. But later this person reminds us of the offense, and we learn that "forgiving" and "forgetting" are quite different.

If we have experienced scenarios like those, we may be skeptical when we hear statements about God's forgiveness. Today's passage, for example, states: "He made you alive with Him and forgave us all our trespasses" (Col 2:13). We know God is truthful and has actually forgiven us, but we may think that He could bring up our sins again at any time, perhaps at the judgment.

But here's the truth to hang your life on: When God forgives, He totally wipes out the sin and its penalty. The price has been paid—with Christ our sins were nailed to the cross. They have been totally erased (v. 14).

"But," you may respond," if that's true, why do I still feel guilty about what I've done? Why does God keep reminding me?"

That's not God, it's our enemy. Even if Satan uses others to condemn us, he's behind it. That's why Paul writes, "Be careful that no one takes you captive through philosophy and empty deceit based on human tradition, based on the elemental forces of the world, and not based on Christ" (Col 2:8).

When you trusted Christ as Savior, God forgave you of your sins—past, present, and future. And you are forgiven—totally, forever free from their penalty and power. Don't let anyone convince you otherwise.

SNAPSHOT

COLOSSIANS 2:12–15

Having been buried with Him in baptism, you were also raised with Him through faith in the working of God, who raised Him from the dead. And when you were dead in trespasses and in the uncircumcision of your flesh, He made you alive with Him and forgave us all our trespasses. He erased the certificate of debt, with its obligations, that was against us and opposed to us, and has taken it out of the way by nailing it to the cross. He disarmed the rulers and authorities and disgraced them publicly; He triumphed over them by Him.

YOUR CHOICE

Why do you find it difficult to forgive yourself? When are you most vulnerable to condemning yourself for what God has forgiven?

SNAPSHOT

COLOSSIANS 3:12–17

Therefore, God's chosen ones, holy and loved, put on heartfelt compassion, kindness, humility, gentleness, and patience, accepting one another and forgiving one another if anyone has a complaint against another. Just as the Lord has forgiven you, so also you must forgive. Above all, put on love—the perfect bond of unity. And let the peace of the Messiah, to which you were also called in one body, control your hearts. Be thankful. Let the message about the Messiah dwell richly among you, teaching and admonishing one another in all wisdom, and singing psalms, hymns, and spiritual songs, with gratitude in your hearts to God. And whatever you do, in word or in deed, do everything in the name of the Lord Jesus, giving thanks to God the Father through Him.

ANCHOR POINT

CHRISTIAN RELATIONSHIPS

In this passage, Paul states how believers should relate to one another. Does his description sound like your church, your Christian community? He lists compassion, kindness, humility, gentleness, patience, acceptance, forgiveness, love, unity, peace, and thanksgiving, along with wise teaching and exhortation, all done with the goal of glorifying God. Imagine what life would be like if you and your fellow Christians lived that way—what a powerful testimony! What a world-changing force!

If your Christian church or group doesn't measure up, remember that change begins with you. You can't force others to live that way, but *you* can, regardless of what anyone else may do. It's your choice. And here's a guarantee that it will happen: "Whatever you do, in word or in deed, do everything in the name of the Lord Jesus, giving thanks to God the Father through Him."

YOUR CHOICE

Using the descriptive words and phrases in today's passage as a check list, how do you measure up? Where can you begin to do "everything in the name of the Lord Jesus, giving thanks"?

DAY 340

SNAPSHOT

1 THESSALONIANS 1:2–6

We always thank God for all of you, remembering you constantly in our prayers. We recall, in the presence of our God and Father, your work of faith, labor of love, and endurance of hope in our Lord Jesus Christ, knowing your election, brothers loved by God. For our gospel did not come to you in word only, but also in power, in the Holy Spirit, and with much assurance. You know what kind of men we were among you for your benefit, and you became imitators of us and of the Lord when, in spite of severe persecution, you welcomed the message with the joy from the Holy Spirit.

YOUR CHOICE

About what "stumbles" do you need to talk to God? What needs to change in your spiritual training routine?

TOUGH QUESTION

I'VE BEEN TRYING TO MAKE THE RIGHT CHOICES AND TO BE A GOOD BELIEVER, BUT I KEEP STUMBLING, AND EVEN FALLING. WHAT DOES GOD THINK ABOUT THAT, AND WHAT CAN I DO TO CHANGE?

When we become followers of Christ, God doesn't make us instantly perfect and remove all our temptations, problems, struggles, and stumbles. We're still human, and we're still sinners who live in a sinful world. But God does give us amazing resources and promises:

- He is making all things new for us, beginning with a new perspective on life (2 Co 5:17).
- The Holy Spirit takes up residence in us, and begins His work in us, forming us more like Christ (Jn 14:16,23–26; 15:26; Rm 8:26–29).
- Through the Holy Spirit, God is helping us want to obey Him and then helping us do what He wants (Php 2:12–13).

Perhaps the most amazing attribute of God is His grace. Grace means showing favor on someone who doesn't deserve it. And the Bible makes it very clear that *no one* deserves God's favor. "But God proves His own love for us in that while we were still sinners Christ died for us!" (Rm 5:8). Thus God forgives all those who trust in Christ as Savior. No matter how badly we stumble and fall, He will forgive us if we confess our sins to Him (1 Jn 1:9).

We shouldn't stop there, however, but be growing in our faith and our relationship with the Father. This involves spiritual training: studying Scripture, praying, spending time alone with God, worshiping, and learning under godly teachers and mentors.

Think of the Christian life as a climb up a mountain. Although the going can be tough at times, and we may encounter switchbacks and obstacles, we steadily move higher, toward our goal.

Keep climbing. And remember, God is with you on the journey, guiding, protecting, giving strength, and picking you up when you fall.

1 THESSALONIANS 4:1–2 SNAPSHOT

Finally then, brothers, we ask and encourage you in the Lord Jesus, that as you have received from us how you must walk and please God—as you are doing —do so even more. For you know what commands we gave you through the Lord Jesus.

THE BIG PICTURE

1 TH 4:1–18

TOUGH CHOICE

CLAIRIE

I slung my bag and coat on the kitchen table. The commute from the college campus in the city to my home in the suburbs had tripled in time due to a winter storm that had dumped eight inches of snow since lunchtime. I dropped into our reading chair in the family room, propping my feet up on the ottoman. *Yes, relaxation.*

"Hello, my name is Clairie." A small hand extended toward me from around the side of the chair.

I jumped, startled by the sudden appearance of a young girl with long dark hair, standing in our family room. "Um, hi?" I hesitantly took her hand and shook it.

"Oh, Rosie, I see you've met Clairie." My mom walked down the stairs, fumbling with a pair of earrings. "I meant to tell you on the phone yesterday, but Clairie will be staying with us for the weekend," she said cheerfully.

I picked my feet up as Clairie made herself comfortable on the ottoman. "My little brother is in the hospital because he has a rare heart condition. My mom is staying with him since he may not live much longer." There was little expression on the girl's face as she provided the reason for her presence in our family room.

"Oh, I'm sorry about your brother . . ." I mumbled, bewildered by the blunt explanation.

"I'm picking up your father, and we're going to a meeting at church, but there's soup on the stove for you and Clairie," my mom said as she pulled on her coat and hurried out the back door. "We should be back around ten o'clock." She waved, and the door closed behind her.

I turned back around. Clairie was still sitting at my feet, staring at me. "So," I started, looking around at all the other empty chairs in the room, "do you want dinner?"

"It's okay if you want to ask me about my brother," she stated. "I'm used to talking about his illness."

I stood up, clearing my throat. "Clairie, how about we get some dinner." I started toward the kitchen, needing a little space.

"My brother's pretty much been in the hospital ever since he was four. He's ten now." Clairie followed me into the kitchen and was now standing at my elbow as I ladled soup into a bowl. "It's hard knowing that my brother's going to die. Sometimes I cry a lot. But I know that he's going to heaven, and he's helped encourage a lot of other sick kids in the hospital. We even started a charity website together to help raise money for kids with heart conditions."

Her composure rattled me. "Clairie . . . I'm so . . . um, here's some soup."

We ate dinner together that night. I listened to Clairie talk about her brother and his terminal heart condition. I didn't ask many questions; I just listened. Her encounter with death at such a young age saddened me, but her perspective on eternal life moved me.

"Everybody will die some day, and it's never easy to say good-bye. But I don't want to be sad about my brother for the rest of my life. I want to be excited that I get to see him again some day. And when I do, it won't be in his hospital bed."

YOUR CHOICE **How would you react to the news about a severe illness for someone you love?**

DAY 342

2 TH 1:1–12

SNAPSHOT

2 THESSALONIANS 1:3–7a

We must always thank God for you, brothers, which is fitting, since your faith is flourishing, and the love of every one of you for one another is increasing. Therefore we ourselves boast about you among God's churches—about your endurance and faith in all the persecutions and afflictions you endure. It is a clear evidence of God's righteous judgment that you will be counted worthy of God's kingdom, for which you also are suffering, since it is righteous for God to repay with affliction those who afflict you, and to reward with rest you who are afflicted, along with us.

DEPOSIT

WORDS FROM GOD'S WORD TO STORE IN YOUR MIND AND HEART

And in view of this, we always pray for you that our God will consider you worthy of His calling, and will, by His power, fulfill every desire for goodness and the work of faith, so that the name of our Lord Jesus will be glorified by you, and you by Him, according to the grace of our God and the Lord Jesus Christ (2 Th 1:11–12).

THE BIG PICTURE

2 TH 3:1–18

DECEMBER 9

DAY 343

SNAPSHOT

2 THESSALONIANS 3:6–9

Now we command you, brothers, in the name of our Lord Jesus Christ, to keep away from every brother who walks irresponsibly and not according to the tradition received from us. For you yourselves know how you must imitate us: we were not irresponsible among you; we did not eat anyone's bread free of charge; instead, we labored and toiled, working night and day, so that we would not be a burden to any of you. It is not that we don't have the right to support, but we did it to make ourselves an example to you so that you would imitate us.

YOUR TURN

FINAL REQUESTS

How aware and involved are you in the worldwide spread of the gospel?

SNAPSHOT

1 TIMOTHY 4:11–16

Command and teach these things. No one should despise your youth; instead, you should be an example to the believers in speech, in conduct, in love, in faith, in purity. Until I come, give your attention to public reading, exhortation, and teaching. Do not neglect the gift that is in you; it was given to you through prophecy, with the laying on of hands by the council of elders. Practice these things; be committed to them, so that your progress may be evident to all. Be conscientious about yourself and your teaching; persevere in these things, for by doing this you will save both yourself and your hearers.

ANCHOR POINT

ALWAYS GOING FORWARD

Timothy was a young man with big responsibilities. As the pastor of the church at Ephesus, he held the position of spiritual leader for many who were older than he, with much more life experience. So Paul encouraged his protégé to "command" and "teach," and to not let anyone look down on him simply because he was young. But then Paul added this important instruction: "be an example to the believers in speech, in conduct, in love, in faith, in purity." And Paul reminded Timothy to use his spiritual gifts in the church, with courage and confidence.

What is your leadership arena? As a young person, you may find yourself leading those who are older or who have been Christians longer. A situation like that can feel intimidating. "What can I say to them?" you might think. Or, "Why should they follow me?" That's when you should remember who called you and put you in that position and the gifts He has given you to do His work. Then you can lead with confidence.

YOUR CHOICE

In what situations do you feel intimidated by the group or the task at hand? What can you do to confidently do God's work where He has placed you?

SNAPSHOT

1 TIMOTHY 6:11–15a

Now you, man of God, run from these things; but pursue righteousness, godliness, faith, love, endurance, and gentleness.

Fight the good fight for the faith;
take hold of eternal life,
to which you were called
and have made a good confession
before many witnesses.

In the presence of God, who gives life to all, and before Christ Jesus, who gave a good confession before Pontius Pilate, I charge you to keep the commandment without spot or blame until the appearing of our Lord Jesus Christ, which God will bring about in His own time.

NO BRAINER

RUN AND FIGHT

Timothy was a young man when Paul, his mentor, wrote this letter to him. He was also the pastor of the church at Ephesus. Paul wanted his protégé to understand what was important in life and ministry. He knew that God's values often conflict directly with the world's; thus conscientious followers of Christ will often find themselves having to make some difficult choices.

Paul highlights the prevalence of false doctrine and human greed and the terrible destinations for following those paths (1 Tm 6:3–5,9–10). And he urges Timothy to "run" from them—to put as much distance as possible between him and that way of thinking and that way of life. But it's not enough to run away from something wrong; Paul also points out that we need to run toward what is right—God-honoring goals. So he challenges Timothy to "pursue righteousness, godliness, faith, love, endurance, and gentleness" (v. 11). Then Paul changes the metaphor and tells Timothy to "fight the good fight for the faith" (v. 12).

Things haven't changed much since Paul wrote those words about two thousand years ago. We still face cults, pop theology, and other false teachings. And society's highest values still center on money and status, leaving God out of the picture. Thus, Paul's, and God's, message for us is clear—we must *actively* ("run") and *aggressively* ("fight") stand for and live the truth.

Sometimes the temptations will be blatant, easy to identify, making the choice clear. Often, however, they will be subtle—media messages, entertainment choices, enticing job offers, patterns of speech, relationship compromises, and so forth. Whatever the situation, we must run from the temptation and toward righteousness, and we must fight for the faith, to make a difference for Christ in this world and to be ready for His return.

YOUR CHOICE

From what temptations do you need to "run"? Where do you need to "fight the good fight"?

SNAPSHOT

2 TIMOTHY 1:3–7

I thank God, whom I serve with a clear conscience as my forefathers did, when I constantly remember you in my prayers night and day. Remembering your tears, I long to see you so that I may be filled with joy, clearly recalling your sincere faith that first lived in your grandmother Lois, then in your mother Eunice, and that I am convinced is in you also.

Therefore, I remind you to keep ablaze the gift of God that is in you through the laying on of my hands. For God has not given us a spirit of fearfulness, but one of power, love, and sound judgment.

JUST LIKE ME

TIMOTHY: CHOOSING THE RIGHT EXAMPLE

You've probably heard people complain about being MKs or PKs (missionary or preacher's kids)—the pressure of trying to live up to high expectations in attitudes, speech, and actions. In trying to carve their own identity, some go in a direction opposite to that of a parent's lifestyle, especially if a parent's actions seem hypocritical.

Not Timothy. He was content to follow the examples of his mother Eunice and his grandmother Lois, a fact for which Paul commended Timothy. He had a choice: to follow his unbelieving father's example or his mother's. The apostle Paul helped him choose the latter.

Timothy might have been a teen when Paul first met him in Lystra (Ac 16:1). Since Paul later called Timothy "my true child in the faith" (1 Tm 1:2), Paul probably had led Timothy to Christ. Timothy so impressed the other believers and Paul that Paul determined to include Timothy in his missionary entourage. Paul later mentored Timothy as a young pastor in Ephesus.

Timothy's life shows the value of having good examples to follow. But like Timothy, we also have choices. We can either go with the examples of those whose lives seem glamorous and fulfilling, but are ultimately spiritually empty, or we can go the harder path—the path of examples like Paul, Lois, and Eunice.

YOUR CHOICE

Who influences you in your faith?
Whose example are you trying to follow?

2 TIMOTHY 3:10–12 But you have followed my teaching, conduct, purpose, faith, patience, love, and endurance, along with the persecutions and sufferings that came to me in Antioch, Iconium, and Lystra. What persecutions I endured! Yet the Lord rescued me from them all. In fact, all those who want to live a godly life in Christ Jesus will be persecuted.

SNAPSHOT

DECEMBER 13

DAY 347

THE BIG PICTURE

2 TM 3:1–17

TOUGH CHOICE

ETERNAL CONSEQUENCES

"Welcome back to KCB Sports Talk. Ladies and gentlemen, today we have left-handed pitcher Adam Brooks on the show with us. He is a native of our very own Kansas City, and he was just drafted by the Seattle Mariners. Adam, welcome to the show."

The radio host, Jake Jacobs, nodded at me from behind his microphone. I took this as my cue. "Thanks, Jake. Good to be here."

"So tell us, what is it like playing for a professional ball club?"

I leaned into the microphone, holding its base. "Oh, well, it's good so far. We're barely out of spring training, so everything still feels pretty new."

"What is the training regimen like for you fellas? Anything like college?"

I laughed off a few nerves. "They work us pretty hard, but most of the guys are used to pushing it. The drills are similar, but everything's taken up a notch when you're surrounded by the best of the best."

"Speaking of being one of the best, you made quite a name for yourself as a high school All-Star and college All-American. How do you foresee your success as a major league pitcher?"

I felt my face grow warm. "Well, obviously I'm hoping to do well," I said, clearing my throat. "My plan is just to train hard and smart and to always give my best effort."

Jake Jacobs slapped the desk with the palm of his hand. "Ha! Adam, come on man. 'Well' is not in your vocabulary. You've been nothing short of a phenomenon since you were playing little league. Take a little bit of credit. People—a certain GM comes to mind—are expecting some great things out of you!"

I stared down at my microphone. *Who's listening on the other end of this?* I could picture people driving home from work with their radios turned to the station, my friends and family tuned in at home, my old coaches listening at their desks. "I appreciate the vote of confidence, Jake. God willing, the Mariners will have a great upcoming year. The franchise definitely has a talented roster."

"Which, as I'm sure the greater audience and all of Seattle would agree, is commandeered by you! Am I right?" Jake Jacobs leaned back in his chair, with a smirk on his face and his arms extended. It was as though he expected an answer to burst through the microphone.

"Jake," I interjected, "I am fortunate to be part of a fantastic baseball team. The Lord blessed me with the ability to throw a ball, and I won't pretend for a minute that I had anything to do with that gift. Now, I work hard and try my best to be a good steward of that gift, but it's not to bring glory to myself. I give my best effort as a way of glorifying and worshiping the Lord."

Jake Jacobs rolled his chair close to the desk, crossing his arms on its surface. "Adam, as long as you're bringing home victories, I believe fans are going to be happy."

"Teams rise and fall, Jake. Players, even legendary, eventually grow old. The consequences of living a life for Christ are far more important . . . and eternal . . . than a pennant."

YOUR CHOICE **What opportunities is God giving you to take a public stand for Him and His values?**

DAY 348

TI 3:1–11

SNAPSHOT

TITUS 3:4–7

But when the goodness and love for man appeared from God our Savior,

He saved us—

not by works of righteousness that we had done, but according to His mercy, through the washing of regeneration and renewal by the Holy Spirit.

This Spirit He poured out on us abundantly through Jesus Christ our Savior, so that having been justified by His grace, we may become heirs with the hope of eternal life.

YOUR CHOICE

When have you been reminded lately about past sins? How can you remember that you are forgiven? How should being totally forgiven affect the way you live?

TOUGH QUESTION

BEFORE I BECAME A CHRISTIAN, I WAS PRETTY MESSED UP. NOW I'M TRYING TO FOLLOW CHRIST AND MAKE THE RIGHT CHOICES, BUT I KEEP HAVING MENTAL AND EMOTIONAL FLASHBACKS, AND A LITTLE VOICE SEEMS TO BE SAYING I'M NOT GOOD ENOUGH FOR GOD. HOW CAN I FIND HEALING FOR MY PAST?

Whoever is in Christ is "a new creation; old things have passed away, and look, new things have come!" (2 Co 5:17). All of our sins have been forgiven, the slate wiped clean. God has declared, "For as high as the heavens are above the earth, so great is His faithful love toward those who fear Him. As far as the east is from the west, so far has He removed our transgressions from us" (Ps 103:11–12).This means the past is over and gone and should be forgotten. God's not going to bring it up again, so we shouldn't either.

We can hear that truth and believe it, but sometimes letting go emotionally can be tough. At those times we have to remind ourselves that if we have dealt with the sin, we have been forgiven, so those guilt feelings aren't valid. The reminders of our past sins do not come from God. Satan is an expert at whispering those lies. He wants us to believe that we aren't good enough and always will be failures.

Part of Satan's message is true: that is, we *aren't* good enough on our own. But our relationship with God doesn't depend on how good *we* are because no one can ever be good enough: "The Lord looks down from heaven on the human race to see if there is one who is wise, one who seeks God. All have turned away; all alike have become corrupt. There is no one who does good, not even one" (Ps 14:2–3). Instead, we are right with God because of Christ's righteousness—we are only good in Him. Check out Romans 5:6–11.

So when you hear those devilish lies, tell Satan to take a hike. God loves you. Jesus gave His life for you. God forgives you. You are good!

THE BIG PICTURE

HEB 4:1–16

DECEMBER 15

DAY 349

SNAPSHOT

HEBREWS 4:12–13

For the word of God is living and effective and sharper than any two-edged sword, penetrating as far as to divide soul, spirit, joints, and marrow; it is a judge of the ideas and thoughts of the heart. No creature is hidden from Him, but all things are naked and exposed to the eyes of Him to whom we must give an account.

DEPOSIT

WORDS FROM GOD'S WORD TO STORE IN YOUR MIND AND HEART

Therefore since we have a great high priest who has passed through the heavens—Jesus the Son of God—let us hold fast to the confession. For we do not have a high priest who is unable to sympathize with our weaknesses, but One who has been tested in every way as we are, yet without sin. Therefore let us approach the throne of grace with boldness, so that we may receive mercy and find grace to help us at the proper time (Heb 4:14–16).

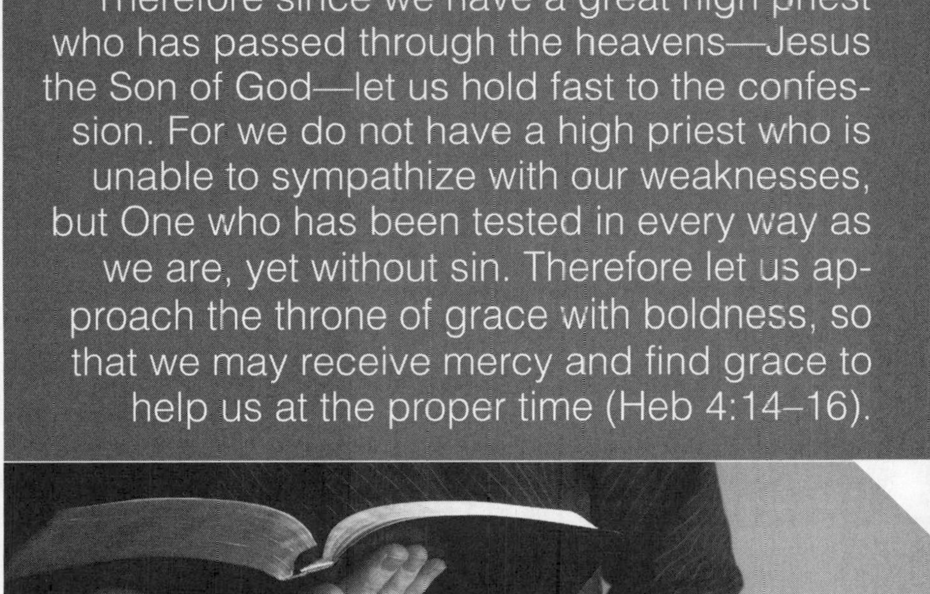

DECEMBER 16

DAY 350

THE BIG PICTURE

HEB 11:1–40

SNAPSHOT

HEBREWS 11:37–40

They were stoned, they were sawed in two, they died by the sword, they wandered about in sheepskins, in goatskins, destitute, afflicted, and mistreated. The world was not worthy of them. They wandered in deserts, mountains, caves, and holes in the ground.

All these were approved through their faith, but they did not receive what was promised, since God had provided something better for us, so that they would not be made perfect without us.

YOUR TURN

A REVIEW OF FAITH

How deep is your commitment to Christ?

HEB 12:1–13

SNAPSHOT

HEBREWS 12:1–2

Therefore since we also have such a large cloud of witnesses surrounding us, let us lay aside every weight and the sin that so easily ensnares us, and run with endurance the race that lies before us, keeping our eyes on Jesus, the source and perfecter of our faith, who for the joy that lay before Him endured a cross and despised the shame, and has sat down at the right hand of God's throne.

ANCHOR POINT

RUN THE RACE

Life is often said to be a "race," as in today's passage. And many helpful lessons can be learned from that analogy. When we make this comparison, however, we should realize that the life journey is much more like a marathon than a sprint. That's what the writer implies with the statement, "run with endurance." Each person's race is unique—in length and course. Yet we have much in common. For example, every marathon runner realizes that in order to finish well, he or she must prepare well, run smart, and certainly not carry any unnecessary weight or other potential encumbrances.

In the Christian race, sins, even the "little" ones, can trip us up, and other issues can weigh us down. But God needs runners who understand the goal and are keeping their eyes focused there and putting all their energies into running the course successfully (see Php 3:12–14). The writer also notes that other runners who have gone before are cheering us on. We compete with an amazing heritage of courageous followers of Christ.

So keep running, with your eyes on the prize.

YOUR CHOICE

How are you preparing for your life race?
What "weights" do you need to shed?
What can you do to encourage other runners?

SNAPSHOT

JAMES 1:2–4

Consider it a great joy, my brothers, whenever you experience various trials, knowing that the testing of your faith produces endurance. But endurance must do its complete work, so that you may be mature and complete, lacking nothing.

YOUR CHOICE

How have you grown in your faith because of adversity? What do you think God is teaching you through your setbacks?

TOUGH QUESTION

I FIND IT EASY TO LIVE FOR CHRIST, TO MAKE THE RIGHT CHOICES, WHEN EVERYTHING IS GOING WELL. BUT HOW SHOULD I RESPOND TO A MAJOR SETBACK?

Let's face it, life is filled with major setbacks—even when we're not being verbally or physically abused because of our stand for Christ. That's what comes with living in an imperfect world with imperfect people. A romance will crumble, a close friend will move away, a big test (or class) will be failed, accident or illness will cripple, a job will be lost, a loved one will die. Despite all this, we can have hope because we know the truth.

We know that God is good and that His timing and reasoning are perfect. Often the circumstances of life don't make sense. We think a situation should have turned out differently or we should have been spared the pain and heartbreak. But Jeremiah 29:11 tells us, "For I know the plans I have for you"—this is the LORD's declaration——"plans for your welfare, not for disaster, to give you future and a hope." God can be trusted, and He knows what He is allowing and what He is doing.

We know, too, that nothing that happens can separate us from God. Listen to these amazing words: "For I am persuaded that neither death nor life, nor angels nor rulers, nor things present, nor things to come, nor powers, nor height, nor depth, nor any other created thing will have the power to separate us from the love of God that is in Christ Jesus our Lord!" (Rm 8:38–39). Check out that list—it covers everything. And Paul, who wrote those inspired words, had been through much more hardship, pain, and suffering than we will ever face.

We also know that life does not end when we die. In fact, that's when true living begins.

Don't let setbacks set you back. Look up; look ahead; look beyond—look to Christ.

JAMES 2:1–4

My brothers, hold your faith in our glorious Lord Jesus Christ without showing favoritism. For suppose a man comes into your meeting wearing a gold ring, dressed in fine clothes, and a poor man dressed in dirty clothes also comes in. If you look with favor on the man wearing the fine clothes so that you say, "Sit here in a good place," and yet you say to the poor man, "Stand over there," or, "Sit here on the floor by my footstool," haven't you discriminated among yourselves and become judges with evil thoughts?

SNAPSHOT

DECEMBER 19

DAY 353

THE BIG PICTURE

JMS 2:1–13

TOUGH CHOICE

ALISON

"Alison, there isn't room in this boat. You'll have to get in the other one." Pamela, one of the well-liked and popular campers in our cabin, pointed at a boat down the pier.

Alison shoved her glasses up the bridge of her nose and squinted in the direction Pamela had pointed. With one leg already in the boat, she threw her towel back on the dock. "Fine," she muttered. "Make me walk all the way down there. Jerks."

Nobody in the cabin wanted anything to do with Alison. She was different: she suffered multiple learning disabilities, had difficulty managing her anger, and was often downright mean. Even the counselors tried their best to avoid her.

I watched Alison stomp down the pier, where the girls in that boat were just as hesitant to invite her in.

I grabbed a wake board from the dock shed and began lowering it into the boat, where Pamela and a few of my other favorite campers guided it onto the floor. "All right, girls! This is going to be great!" I started to climb in, but Lorna, one of the camp directors, stopped me.

"Micah! Would you mind riding in boat one? The girls want to go tubing, and they need an even number in the boat so they can partner up."

Please, no! This is the fun boat with the fun campers. I'm the fun counselor who's supposed to hang out with the fun campers. "Sure, Lorna. No problem," I lied, lunging back onto the dock. I turned and mouthed, "Sorry," to the frowning girls.

As I neared the first boat, I could hear Alison in a huff. "Come on! The counselors say we have to pair up, so somebody had better be my partner!" None of the other girls would even make eye contact with Alison.

Why me, God?

Out on the lake, I hoisted myself up on the tube (and drug Alison up out of the water). I watched the wake boarders speed across the other side of the lake. I looked back down at Alison. She was sprawled across the tube, clutching the handles tightly.

"Ready. Give the thumbs up," she ordered. I took my position on the tube and gave the driver the go-ahead signal. The rope between the boat and the tube grew taut, and we jerked forward. "Woohoo!" cheered Alison. Her eyes were wide, and a grin had replaced her normal, sour expression. "This is going to be awesome!" She smiled up at me.

We whipped over the lake, as water sprayed up in our faces. Alison's cheers, I'm sure, couldn't be heard by anyone in the boat. But I could hear and see her joy. For just a few minutes, she was free from the ostracism and exclusion that stained her life.

Lord, forgive me for my attitude toward Alison. She is Your child. Teach me to let go of popularity and image. Teach me to treat others the way in which I so desperately wanted and still want to be treated—with value.

YOUR CHOICE **When did you choose to befriend an unpopular and annoying person? How might God work through you in a situation like that?**

DAY 354

THE BIG PICTURE

JMS 3:1–12

NO BRAINER

WORDS AS WEAPONS

Just about everyone struggles with the mouth, the tongue—his or her words. We blurt without thinking, make hurtful comments to those we love, twist or hide the truth in conversations, make prideful boasts, curse, gossip, insult, blab. . . . Often we wish we could retract our words or just keep our mouth shut. So James's comments about the tongue hits home. We know "the tongue is a fire" (3:6), and that "out of the same mouth come blessing and cursing" (3:10), and we agree that "these things should not be this way" (3:10).

But we also know that words can praise God, heal a relationship, affirm a friend, explain fears, hopes, and faith, express gratitude, declare allegiance, offer support. Words are powerful and must be used with care. Even a person whose love language is *not* words appreciates positive ones. Mark Twain said that he could live for two months on one good compliment.

Today's passage from James states that a person's speech affects his or her actions. That person's words also provide a good measure of his or her true character—Jesus said that "the mouth speaks from the overflow of the heart" (Mt 12:34). This means that our friends, teachers, associates, employers, neighbors—just about everyone—can tell what we're like by what we say. Scary thought, right?

Clearly, then, the best place to begin getting serious about living for Christ is by controlling what we say. But we can only do this through His power working in us by the Holy Spirit. Controlling the tongue begins by acknowledging our weakness and relying on God for strength. So we should ask God to help us think before speaking, refrain from put-downs and sarcasm, remove certain words from our vocabulary, refuse to spread rumors, and look for opportunities to lift up rather than tear down.

When people see *that change*, they will truly be amazed and know that we can "do all things through Him who strengthens us" (Php 4:13).

SNAPSHOT

JAMES 3:3–6

Now when we put bits into the mouths of horses to make them obey us, we also guide the whole animal. And consider ships: though very large and driven by fierce winds, they are guided by a very small rudder wherever the will of the pilot directs. So too, though the tongue is a small part of the body, it boasts great things. Consider how large a forest a small fire ignites. And the tongue is a fire. The tongue, a world of unrighteousness, is placed among the parts of our bodies; it pollutes the whole body, sets the course of life on fire, and is set on fire by hell.

YOUR CHOICE

Today, where can you build up instead of tear down with your words? Who can you encourage, affirm, and bless?

THE BIG PICTURE

1 PT 2:1–25

DECEMBER 21

DAY 355

SNAPSHOT

1 PETER 2:1–5

So rid yourselves of all wickedness, all deceit, hypocrisy, envy, and all slander. Like newborn infants, desire the unadulterated spiritual milk, so that you may grow by it in your salvation, since you have tasted that the Lord is good. Coming to Him, a living stone—rejected by men but chosen and valuable to God—you yourselves, as living stones, are being built into a spiritual house for a holy priesthood to offer spiritual sacrifices acceptable to God through Jesus Christ.

JUST LIKE ME

YOU: THE LIVING STONES CHALLENGE

Pop quiz! Can you think of any phrase that chills the blood quicker—especially if you're not prepared? But the whole point of a pop quiz is to assess how much you know. If you have been paying attention in class and have studied all along, you should pass with flying colors.

Now that *this* study is nearing its end, it's time for a pop quiz to see how far you've really come. In his first letter, the apostle Peter wrote, "You yourselves, as living stones, are being built into a spiritual house for a holy priesthood to offer spiritual sacrifices acceptable to God through Jesus Christ" (1 Pt 2:5). Have you taken on these characteristics during the fifty weeks of this study? How have you taken advantage of the many opportunities for self-examination and change?

If you've ever trained for a marathon, triathlon, or some other sporting challenge, you know the value of discipline. You need to stick with the regimen and not give up when the going gets tough. That's also the challenge of being a living stone. Are you willing to tough it out?

YOUR CHOICE

What challenge to your faith have you experienced recently?

DAY 356

1 PT 3:1–22

SNAPSHOT

1 PETER 3:13–17

And who will harm you if you are passionate for what is good? But even if you should suffer for righteousness, you are blessed. Do not fear what they fear or be disturbed, but set apart the Messiah as Lord in your hearts, and always be ready to give a defense to anyone who asks you for a reason for the hope that is in you. However, do this with gentleness and respect, keeping your conscience clear, so that when you are accused, those who denounce your Christian life will be put to shame. For it is better to suffer for doing good, if that should be God's will, than for doing evil.

DEPOSIT

WORDS FROM GOD'S WORD TO STORE IN YOUR MIND AND HEART

But set apart the Messiah as Lord in your hearts, and always be ready to give a defense to anyone who asks you for a reason for the hope that is in you (1 Pt 3:15).

SNAPSHOT

2 PETER 1:3–7

For His divine power has given us everything required for life and godliness, through the knowledge of Him who called us by His own glory and goodness. By these He has given us very great and precious promises, so that through them you may share in the divine nature, escaping the corruption that is in the world because of evil desires. For this very reason, make every effort to supplement your faith with goodness, goodness with knowledge, knowledge with self-control, self-control with endurance, endurance with godliness, godliness with brotherly affection, and brotherly affection with love.

YOUR TURN

KNOWING GOD

How would you answer someone who asked you what it means to know God?

DECEMBER 24

DAY 358

THE BIG PICTURE

1 JN 1:1–10

SNAPSHOT

1 JOHN 1:5–7

Now this is the message we have heard from Him and declare to you: God is light, and there is absolutely no darkness in Him. If we say, "We have fellowship with Him," and walk in darkness, we are lying and are not practicing the truth. But if we walk in the light as He Himself is in the light, we have fellowship with one another, and the blood of Jesus His Son cleanses us from all sin.

TOUGH CHOICE

CONFESSION

Jack West, our retreat speaker, stood on the auditorium stage with his arms outstretched and earnestness in his eyes. "Guys and gals, you and I deserve an eternity in Hell. We are stinkin' sinful. And when we are covered in sin, the Lord can have nothing to do with us."

"I've heard this same message at other conferences," whispered Connor, my boyfriend, who was sitting next to me. "They dwell on how sinful we all are, but we always get our sins cleared in the end."

"At least the speaker's using props this time," I whispered with a smile.

Jack moved toward the front of the stage, where a large cross lay. He kneeled down and picked up an object off the ground, as necks around me strained forward.

"In my hands, I'm holding a mallet and a railroad stake." He raised the objects above his head. The stake was at least a foot long. "Jesus was crucified, but not using the little nails and hammer that your daddy uses to hang picture frames. These paint a more accurate picture."

I stared at the railroad stake. I had never given much thought to the actual nails used to crucify Jesus before.

"Folks, every time we sin—disrespect our parents, cuss on the athletic field—we crucify Christ." I sat on the edge of my seat as he positioned the stake on the arm of the cross and raised the mallet. "For gossiping about my classmate," he whispered. And with a mighty swing, Jack swung the mallet down upon the stake and let out a horrible scream.

"For looking at pornography." Again he screamed as the mallet drilled the stake further into the wood.

"For being jealous of my best friend." *Scream.* The hairs on my arms stood on end.

Jack stood up from his kneeling position and stared out over the audience, still holding the mallet. "Who wants to take a turn? It's fun." He extended the handle toward the rows of seats. "Getting drunk won't *hurt* anyone. Cheating on exams won't *hurt* anyone." He looked down, shaking his head. "Whoever tells you that is feeding you a load of lies. What do you need to confess today? What sins are you trying to hide, and by doing so, nailing Christ to the cross day after day?"

I glanced at Connor, but dropped my stare to the palms of my hands. *Oh, Jesus! Forgive me. I didn't think.* Tears welled up in my eyes. *All those late nights with Connor . . . we pushed the boundaries. I gave in to temptation to feel close to him. I didn't think it was hurting anyone, but it was hurting You.*

"Guys and gals, God loves each of you so much that He was willing to send His very own Son to pay for your sins." He held up a stake and the mallet. "Don't forget the price He paid for us. Confess your sins. Make yourself right with God. He knows that we will mess up because we are sinners. But He wants us to run to Him when we falter. Run to Him."

YOUR CHOICE **What sins came to mind when you read the story? What will you do about them?**

SNAPSHOT

1 JOHN 3:16–22

This is how we have come to know love: He laid down His life for us. We should also lay down our lives for our brothers. If anyone has this world's goods and sees his brother in need but shuts off his compassion from him—how can God's love reside in him?

Little children, we must not love in word or speech, but in deed and truth; that is how we will know we are of the truth, and will convince our hearts in His presence, because if our hearts condemn us, God is greater than our hearts and knows all things.

Dear friends, if our hearts do not condemn us we have confidence before God, and can receive whatever we ask from Him because we keep His commands and do what is pleasing in His sight.

ANCHOR POINT

GOD IS LOVE

Many New Testament passages talk about love. But today's passage puts a bit of an edge on the discussion. John states rather bluntly that those who ignore a brother in need aren't true believers—they don't have God's love in them. His point is simply this: "We must not love in word or speech, but in deed and truth" (v. 18). Talk is cheap, so statements about love can roll off our tongues quite easily. But the true test of our love is how we act, what we *do*, not just what we say.

Loving others is a mandate. In fact, John says, if we do not love, that's a sign that we are not God's to begin with. There's no debate: If we want to follow Christ, we must love one another.

How do we know what love is? We have a great example—Christ gave Himself for us. We must love the same way, giving ourselves for others, perhaps even laying down our lives for them. True love begins with a choice to act.

YOUR CHOICE

How can you put love into action?
What needy brother or sister can you serve?

DAY 360

1 JN 5:1–21

SNAPSHOT

1 JOHN 5:9–12

If we accept the testimony of men, God's testimony is greater, because it is God's testimony that He has given about His Son. (The one who believes in the Son of God has the testimony in himself. The one who does not believe God has made Him a liar, because he has not believed in the testimony that God has given about His Son.) And this is the testimony: God has given us eternal life, and this life is in His Son.

The one who has the Son has life. The one who doesn't have the Son of God does not have life.

YOUR CHOICE

What do your non-Christian friends understand about your faith by watching how you live?
What opportunities has God given you lately to tell others how to know Him?

TOUGH QUESTION

WHEN I THINK ABOUT THE PEOPLE I LOVE, I REMEMBER THAT IF THEY DON'T HAVE CHRIST, THEY DON'T HAVE LIFE. WHAT CAN I BE DOING ABOUT THAT?

We can get so caught up in our busy schedules, responsibilities, and activities that we forget that people are utterly lost without Christ and that we have been given the responsibility of spreading the Good News. No one else. Us. God's people. Remember the Great Commission? "Go, therefore, and make disciples of all nations, baptizing them in the name of the Father and of the Son and of the Holy Spirit, teaching them to observe everything I have commanded you" (Mt 28:19–20).

Effective sharing of our faith begins with prayer, asking God to provide opportunities and praying for our relatives, friends, neighbors, coworkers, and others who don't know Christ. Next, we need to consider the message that our values, attitudes, and actions portrays. Do we truly reflect Christ?

When we get the chance to speak up, when the prayed-for opportunity arises, we need to ask God to give us the words to say. Because we have asked God to lead us to people with whom we can share the Good News, we need to expect that He will. This involves being "ready to give a defense to anyone who asks you for a reason for the hope that is in you" (we should prepare). Then Peter adds, "do this with gentleness and respect" (1 Pt 3:15–16).

When explaining the gospel, share from your heart openly and honestly about what God has done in your life, how He has changed you, and how He wants your friend to be in relationship with Him. God changes people's hearts, not you. And remember that God loves them more than you.

Do you dare to share?

2 JN 4–6; 3 JN 3–5; JD 17–25

DAY 361

SNAPSHOT

JUDE 20–25

But you, dear friends, building yourselves up in your most holy faith and praying in the Holy Spirit, keep yourselves in the love of God, expecting the mercy of our Lord Jesus Christ for eternal life. Have mercy on some who doubt; save others by snatching them from the fire; on others have mercy in fear, hating even the garment defiled by the flesh. Now to Him who is able to protect you from stumbling and to make you stand in the presence of His glory, blameless and with great joy, to the only God our Savior, through Jesus Christ our Lord, be glory, majesty, power, and authority before all time, now, and forever. Amen.

YOUR CHOICE

How are you doing at living out love, truth, and mercy?

NO BRAINER

CONTENDING

In these three short books, appearing right near the end of the Bible, the writers—the apostle John and Jude (Jesus' brother)—give their final words to believers. These men wanted those left behind, especially the next generation, to remember the truly important matters.

John challenges them to "walk in love" (2 Jn 6) and to "walk in truth" (3 Jn 4). Jude points out that the church was being infiltrated by those who would turn people away from Christ, so he urges his readers to "contend for the faith that was delivered to the saints once for all" (v. 3) and to "have mercy" (v. 22).

Today, more than ever it seems, Jude's description of devious, ungodly false believers rings true. And his admonition to "contend for the faith" has never been more urgent. Followers of Christ need to stand for the faith.

What should that look like? Thus far in this book we've seen many ways to make a difference for Christ and have highlighted dozens of courageous choices. Today's passages provide a profound summary.

"Walk in love" means choosing a humble and selfless, serving attitude, preferring others over ourselves and reaching out to those in need. Jesus gave Himself for us; we emulate Him by giving ourselves to others.

"Walk in truth" implies that truth does, in fact, exist. We believe that Jesus is the Truth (Jn 14:6) and that the Bible, God's Word, is truth. So we refuse to compromise the non-negotiables of our faith and boldly refute the lies of our culture and of false teachers.

Having "mercy" is where we reflect God's love, knowing that He withholds the punishment we deserve (mercy) and gives us what we don't deserve (grace). We extend mercy to others by not being judgmental and condescending and, instead, pointing them to the cross.

And did you catch this amazing promise? Jude says that God will "protect you from stumbling and to make you stand in the presence of His glory, blameless and with great joy."

DAY 362

THE BIG PICTURE

RV 1:1–20

SNAPSHOT

REVELATION 1:12–16

I turned to see the voice that was speaking to me. When I turned I saw seven gold lampstands, and among the lampstands was One like the Son of Man, dressed in a long robe, and with a gold sash wrapped around His chest. His head and hair were white like wool—white as snow, His eyes like a fiery flame, His feet like fine bronze fired in a furnace, and His voice like the sound of cascading waters. In His right hand He had seven stars; from His mouth came a sharp two-edged sword; and His face was shining like the sun at midday.

JUST LIKE ME

JESUS: JUST LIKE HIM

Many budding artists of all disciplines (painting; writing; sculpture; singing) find the finished work of old masters inspiring but daunting. They can't help comparing their still-in-training talent to that of a person in full command of his or her considerable ability.

The "finished work" of the glorified Jesus—"eyes like a fiery flame" and "His face . . . shining like the sun at midday" (Rv 1:14,16)—literally knocked the apostle John over. This was no "flower child" Jesus but one whose glory and authority rendered a viewer speechless and terrified. Yet Jesus was also flesh and blood like John—like you.

This glimpse of Jesus in full King array represents our future glory. It is the by-product of being "called . . . to His eternal glory" (1 Pt 5:10) and God's persistence in crafting us to be like His Son (Php 1:6). But God requires our cooperation even as He shapes us. Unlike the clay that has no say over how it is shaped, the sculptor God allows His clay—us—to take part in the process of becoming just like Jesus.

Some day we truly will be just like Christ; all it takes is being faithful. But even in that, God offers grace: "Now to Him who is able to protect you from stumbling and to make you stand in the presence of His glory, blameless and with great joy" (Jd 24).

YOUR CHOICE

What characteristics of Jesus do you sense God working on in your life?

SNAPSHOT

REVELATION 21:1–2

Then I saw a new heaven and a new earth, for the first heaven and the first earth had passed away, and the sea existed no longer. I also saw the Holy City, new Jerusalem, coming down out of heaven from God, prepared like a bride adorned for her husband.

DEPOSIT

WORDS FROM GOD'S WORD TO STORE IN YOUR MIND AND HEART

And He said to me, "It is done! I am the Alpha and the Omega, the Beginning and the End. I will give to the thirsty from the spring of living water as a gift. The victor will inherit these things, and I will be his God, and he will be My son" (Rv 21:6–7).

SNAPSHOT

REVELATION 22:1–5

Then he showed me the river of living water, sparkling like crystal, flowing from the throne of God and of the Lamb down the middle of the broad street of the city. On both sides of the river was the tree of life bearing 12 kinds of fruit, producing its fruit every month. The leaves of the tree are for healing the nations, and there will no longer be any curse. The throne of God and of the Lamb will be in the city, and His servants will serve Him. They will see His face, and His name will be on their foreheads. Night will no longer exist, and people will not need lamplight or sunlight, because the Lord God will give them light. And they will reign forever and ever.

YOUR TURN

LIFE IN THE NEW CITY

When was the last time you were excited about heaven?

RV 22:12–21

SNAPSHOT

REVELATION 22:12–13

"Look! I am coming quickly, and My reward is with Me to repay each person according to what he has done. I am the Alpha and the Omega, the First and the Last, the Beginning and the End."

YOUR CHOICE

Who can you tell about how God's story turns out? What's holding you back from sharing that great news?

NO BRAINER

VICTORY!

You probably have read a mystery novel and have become so attached to certain characters that you wondered if they would survive in the story. If so, you may have flipped to the back of the book and looked for their names, just to make sure. You didn't want to read too much and give away the plot—that would spoil the experience. You just wanted to be reassured that, eventually, everything would work out for the heroes. Then you could return to where you left off, much more relaxed.

That's pretty much what you've just done with the Bible. You've read Revelation, at the back of the Bible and the end of the story, and you've discovered an important truth: We win! At the end of the battle, at the end of time, when the dust has settled, God and His people stand victorious, triumphant.

Right now, in the present, at today's point in life, your story can feel much different. In fact, hearing news reports of school shootings, terrorist attacks, abuse, crime, fractured families, and broken lives, you may think we're losing or have already lost the battle. So it's good to flip to the last page of God's Book to read how everything will turn out.

Consider what the apostle John was going through. He had witnessed Jesus arrested, tortured, and crucified. And, after the resurrection, he had seen Jesus leave the earth. Knowing the truth, John had courageously stood for Christ in a pagan society, and he had seen the Romans brutally try to suppress this new religion, murdering most of his closest friends and banishing him to an island. So imagine John's joy when, in his inspired vision, he saw what we just read! No wonder he could exclaim, "Amen! Come, Lord Jesus!" (v. 20).

If you get discouraged; if you begin to wonder if taking your stand for Christ is worth the cost; if you teeter on the brink of losing hope—remember the end of the story. God wins!

TOPICAL INDEX

FEATURE INDEX

ANCHOR POINT

JUST LIKE ME

Day 304: *Paul and Silas: Picking Praise over Pouting*
Day 310: *Eutychus: Waking the Dead*
Day 316: *Claudius Lysias: At a Pivotal Point*
Day 318: *Paul: Making His Case*
Day 332: *The Believers in Ephesus: Recipients of Grace*
Day 337: *Euodia and Syntyche: Christian Cat-Fight*
Day 346: *Timothy: Choosing the Right Example*
Day 355: *You: The Living Stones Challenge*
Day 362: *Jesus: Just Like Him*

NO BRAINER

Day 5: *The First Deadline*
Day 8: *Who Wants to Be Bigger Than God?*
Day 18: *God's Role in Helping Us Stand*
Day 26: *What's Better Than Getting Even?*
Day 33: *God's Burning Bush*
Day 39: *Pay Attention*
Day 45: *God's Holiness*
Day 50: *Due Diligence*
Day 57: *Finishing Well*
Day 65: *Hope to History*
Day 74: *Right Friends and Lasting Relationships*
Day 82: *Lost Donkeys*
Day 85: *Appearances*
Day 92: *Occult Practices*
Day 101: *Good Decisions*
Day 107: *Wise Counsel*
Day 114: *God's Decision*
Day 121: *Reading God's Word*
Day 129: *When Bad Things Happen*
Day 134: *A Sheep's Song*
Day 145: *The Book Burning*
Day 149: *A King's Dream*
Day 158: *Ready to Serve*
Day 162: *Jesus' First Trip to Church*
Day 171: *Pointing to Jesus*
Day 178: *Righteous Rules*
Day 184: *A Critical Eye*
Day 190: *Ears That Hear*
Day 200: *Deserted*
Day 205: *Who's the Greatest?*
Day 208: *Timing Is Everything*
Day 211: *Giver of Freedom*
Day 220: *Values and Priorities*
Day 229: *Rich Man, Poor Man*
Day 235: *God's Marriage Plan*
Day 240: *Cheap Talk*
Day 247: *Who's in Charge?*
Day 254: *Doing What He Says*
Day 260: *Inspired Writing*
Day 271: *No Fear*
Day 275: *The Great Commission*

Day 281: *Together*
Day 292: *What a Change!*
Day 296: *All in the Family*
Day 305: *Adventures in Jail*
Day 309: *Bad for Business*
Day 324: *Truly Free*
Day 333: *Fitting In*
Day 338: *Erased*
Day 345: *Run and Fight*
Day 354: *Words as Weapons*
Day 361: *Contending*
Day 365: *Victory!*

TOUGH CHOICE

Day 4: *Drinking*
Day 10: *Strangers*
Day 22: *Volleyball*
Day 32: *Running from God*
Day 36: *Rejection*
Day 43: *No Complaints*
Day 51: *Peer Pressure*
Day 60: *Guidance*
Day 72: *Popular*
Day 79: *Missionary*
Day 81: *Sisters*
Day 86: *Evolution*
Day 94: *Mocking*
Day 99: *Leaving the Party*
Day 108: *Obedience*
Day 116: *Hero*
Day 122: *For Granted*
Day 131: *Mountain Top*
Day 138: *Creativity*
Day 142: *Despite Myself*
Day 148: *Faithfulness*
Day 157: *Forest Fire*
Day 164: *Excitement*
Day 169: *Surprises*
Day 179: *Salt and Light*
Day 183: *Money*
Day 191: *Canoe*
Day 197: *Adversity*
Day 207: *Forgiveness*
Day 215: *Eating Disorder*
Day 219: *Judgment*
Day 225: *India*
Day 232: *Thankful Intern*
Day 242: *Hating Life*
Day 246: *Fisher of Men*
Day 257: *Navy*
Day 262: *Prayer*
Day 269: *Only One God*
Day 276: *Doubt*
Day 283: *Creation*

TOUGH QUESTION

Day 264: *I know my friend cheated on our test. I don't want to be a rat, but what she did was wrong. What should I do?*

Day 267: *While hanging out, my friends started talking mean about a kid in our class. How can I take a stand and have the courage to tell them to stop?*

Day 278: *All of my Christian friends are having sex. If everyone says it's okay, how can I take a stand and wait until marriage?*

Day 285: *I want to encourage a hurting friend that God still heals, but I'm not sure He does. What should I say?*

Day 288: *Can't I just take a stand through my actions?*

Day 297: *I really feel strongly about a certain social issue and think I should join a public protest, but I'm afraid. What should I do?*

Day 302: *Why do race, nationality, status, and other factors divide Christians today? What can I do about it?*

Day 311: *What's wrong with doing something if no one will get hurt and no one will ever know?*

Day 319: *How can I trust God more and be courageous in my storms?*

Day 325: *Nothing can separate us from God and His love, but at times I feel very distant from Him. Why does this happen?*

Day 334: *Christians are supposed to love one another, but some are so irritating. How can I get past the fact that I don't like them?*

Day 340: *I keep stumbling and even falling in my choices. What does God think about that, and what can I do to change?*

Day 348: *How can I find healing for my past?*

Day 352: *I find it easy to live for Christ, to make the right choices, when everything is going well. But how should I respond to a major setback?*

Day 360: *When I think about the people I love, I remember that if they don't have Christ, they don't have life. What can I be doing about that?*